Pamela; or Virtue Rewarded. In a Series of
Familiar Letters From a Beautiful Young
Damsel to her Parents and Afterwards, in her
Exalted Condition, Between her, and Persons
of Figure and Quality, The Fourth Edition,
Corrected. Vol.III of 4

## GEORGE R.

GEORGE the Second, by the Grace of GOD, King of *Great* *Britain*, *France*, and *Ireland*, Defender of the Faith, &c. To all to whom these Presents shall come, Greeting. Whereas our trusty and well beloved *Charles Rivington, Samuel Richardson*, and *John Osborn*, of our City of *London*, Stationers, have by their Petition humbly represented unto Us, That they have at great Expence and Labour prepared for the Press a Work, intituled, PAMELA Or, VIRTUE REWARDED In a Series of Familiar Letters from a beautiful young Damsel to her Parents And afterwards, in her exalted Condition, between Her and Persons of Figure and Quality, upon the most Important and Entertaining Subjects, in Genteel Life Publish'd in order to cultivate the Principles of Virtue and Religion in the Minds of the Youth of Both Sexes. In Four Volumes, the Property whereof is wholly vested in the said Petitioners, and which Work they, with the utmost Submission, apprehend may be of great Service to the Publick; and being desirous of reaping the Fruits of their great Expence and Labour, and of enjoying the full Profit and Benefit that may arise from Printing and Vending the same, the said Petitioners have prayed Us to grant them our Royal Privilege and Licence, for the sole Printing, Publishing, and Vending the said Work, in as ample Manner and Form as has been done in Cases of the like Nature We, being willing to give Encouragement to so useful an Undertaking, are graciously pleased to condescend to their Request; and do, by these Presents, so far as may be agreeable to the Statute in that Case made and provided, grant unto them the said *Charles Rivington, Samuel Richardson*, and *John Osborn*, their Executors, Administrators, and Assigns, Our Licence, for the sole Printing, Publishing, and Vending the said Work, for the Term of Fourteen Years, to be computed from the Date hereof, strictly forbidding all Our Subjects within Our Kingdoms and Dominions to reprint or abridge the same, either in the like, or in any other Volume or Volumes whatsoever, or to import, buy, vend, utter, or distribute any Copies thereof reprinted beyond the Seas, during the aforesaid Term of Fourteen Years, without the Consent or Approbation of the said *Charles Rivington, Samuel Richardson*, and *John Osborn*, their Heirs, Executors, or Assigns, under their Hands and Seals first had and obtained, as they will answer the Contrary at their Peril Whereof the Commissioners and other Officers of our Customs, the Master, Wardens, and Company of Stationers, are to take Notice, that due Obedience may be rendered to our Pleasure herein declared Given at our Court at *St. James's*, the Thirteenth Day of *January* 1741-2. in the Fifteenth Year of our Reign.

By His MAJESTY's Command,

HARRINGTON.

# PAMELA;

OR,

## VIRTUE Rewarded.

### In a SERIES of
# FAMILIAR LETTERS

From a Beautiful

## Young DAMSEL to her PARENTS:

And afterwards,

## In her EXALTED CONDITION,
### BETWEEN
HER, and Persons of *Figure* and *Quality*,
#### UPON THE MOST
Important and Entertaining Subjects,
### In GENTEEL LIFE.

---

Publish'd in order to cultivate the Principles of
VIRTUE and RELIGION in the Minds of
the YOUTH of BOTH SEXES.

---

The FOURTH EDITION, *Corrected.*

---

## VOL. IV.

---

## LONDON:

Printed for S. RICHARDSON:
And Sold by J. OSBORN, in *Pater-noster Row*, And
J. RIVINGTON, in *St Paul's Church Yard.*

MDCC.XLII.

# PAMELA:

## OR,

### VIRTUE Rewarded.

*In a Series of* FAMILIAR LETTERS.

## VOL. IV.

## LETTER I.

*My dear Father and Mother,*

KNOW you will be pleased to hear, that we arrived safely in Town last Night We found a stately, well-furnish'd, and convenient House; and I had my Closet, or Library, and my Withdrawing-room, all in complete Order, which Mr. B gave me Possession of, in a manner the most obliging that can be imagined

I am in a new World, as I may say, and see such vast Piles of Building every-where, and such a Concourse of People, and hear such a Rattling of Coaches in the Day, that I hardly know what to make of it, as yet. Then the nightly Watch, going their hourly Rounds, difturbed me laft Night. But I fhall foon be us'd to that, and fleep the founder perhaps, for the Security it affures to us

Mr *B.* is impatient to fhew me what is curious in and about this vaft City, and to hear, as he is pleafed to fay, my Obfervations upon what I fhall fee, and he has carried me thro' feveral of the fine Streets this Day, in his Chariot · But, at prefent, I have too con'ufed a Notion of Things, to give any Account of them Nor fhall I trouble you with Defcriptions of that kind, for you being within a Day's Journey of *London*, I hope for the Pleafure of feeing you oftener, than I could expect before, and fhall therefore leave thefe Matters to your own Obfervations, and what you'll hear from others

I am impatient for the Arrival of my dear Mifs *Darnford*; whofe Company and Converfation will reconcile me, in a great meafure, to this new World

Our Family, at prefent, are Mr. *Colbrand*, Mr. *Jonathan*, and Six Men-fervants, including the Coachman The four Maids are alfo with us.

But my good Mrs *Jervis* was indifpofed, fo came not up with us, but we expect her, and Mr *Longman*, in a Day or two · For Mr *B* has given her to my Wifhes, and *Arthur* the Gardener, and his Wife, with *Benjamin*, are to keep Houfe in the Country And as Mr *Longman*'s Bufinefs will require him to be up and down frequently, Mrs *Jervis*'s Care will be the better difpens'd with there; and I long to fee the dear good Woman, and fhall be more in my Element, when I do.

Then I have, befides, my penitent *Polly Barlow*: But the poor Girl has never held up her Head fince that deplorable inftance of her Weaknefs, which I mentioned to you and to Mifs *Darnford*, yet am I as

kind

kind to her, as if nothing had happen'd I wish, however, some good Husband would offer for her.

Mr *Adams*, our worthy Chaplain, is, at present, with Mr *Williams* He purposes to give us his Company here till *Christmas*, when, probably, Matters will be so adjusted, as that he may take Possession of his Living Mean time, that we may not let fall a good Custom, when perhaps we shall have most Occasion for it, I make Mr *Jonathan*, who is reverend by his Years, and silver Hairs, supply his Place, appointing him the Prayers he is to read

God preserve you both in Health, and continue to me, I beseech you, your Prayers and Blessings, concludes me

*Your ever-dutiful Daughter,*

P B.

---

## LETTER II.

### From *Mrs.* B. *to Lady* DAVERS.

*My dearest Lady,*

I Must beg Pardon, for having been in this great Town, more than a Week, and not having found an Opportunity to tender my Devoirs to your Ladyship. You know, dear Madam, what Hurries and Fatigues must attend such a Journey, to one in my way, and in an intire new Settlement, in which an hundred things must be done, and attended to, with a Preference to other Occasions, however delightful Yet, I must own, we found a stately, a wellorder'd, and a convenient House : But although it is not far from the Fields, and has an airy Opening to its back Part, and its Front to a Square, as it is called, yet I am not reconcil'd to it, so intirely as to the beloved Mansion we left.

My.

My dear Mr. *B* has been, and is, busily imploy'd in ordering some few Alterations, to make Things still more commodious He has furnish'd me out a little pretty Library, and has allotted me very convenient Apartments besides. And the Furniture of every Place is rich, as befits the Mind and Fortune of the generous Owner. But I shall not offer at Particulars, because we hope to have the Honour of a Visit from my good Lord, and your Ladyship, before the Winter Weather sets in, to make the Roads too dirty and deep, but it is proper to mention, that the House is so large, that we can make a great Number of Beds, the more conveniently to receive the Honours your Ladyship, and my Lord, and Mr. *B*'s other Friends will do us.

I have not yet been at any of the publick Diversions. Mr. *B*. has carry'd me, by gentle Turns, out of his Workmens way, Ten Miles round this overgrown Capital, and through the principal of its numerous Streets. The Villages, that lie spangled about this vast Circumference, as well on the other Side the noble *Thames*, (which I had before a Notion of, from Sir *John Denham's* celebrated *Cooper's Hill*) as on the *Middlesex* Side, are beautiful, both by Buildings and Situation, beyond what I had imagined, and several of them seem larger than many of our Country Towns of Note. But it would be impertinent to trouble your Ladyship with these Matters, who are no Stranger to what is worthy of Notice in *London* But I was surpris'd, when Mr *B*. observed to me, that this whole County, and the Two Cities of *London* and *Westminster*, are represented by no more than Eight Members of Parliament, when so many Borough Towns in *England* are inferior to the meanest Villages about *London*.

I am in daily Expectation of the Arrival of Miss *Darnford*, and then I shall wish (accompanied by a young Lady of so polite a Taste) to see a good Play.

Mr.

Mr *B* has already fhewn me the Opera-houfe, and the Two Play-houfes, tho' filent, as I may fay , that, as he was pleafed to obferve, they fhould not be new to me, and that the Sight might not take off my Attention to the Performance, when I went to the Play · So that I can conceive a tolerable Notion of every thing, from the Difpofition of the Seats, the Boxes, the Galleries, the Pit, the Mufick, the Scenes, and the Stage , and fo fhall have no Occafion to gaze about me like a Country Novice, whereby I might attract a Notice, that I fhould not wifh, either for my own Credit, or your dear Brother's Honour.

I have had a Pleafure, which I had not in *Bedfordfhire* , and that is, that on *Sunday* I was at Church, without gaping Crouds to attend us, and Bleffings too loud for my Wifhes Yet, I was more gazed at, (and fo was Mr. *B* ) then I expected, confidering there were fo many well-drefs'd Gentry, and fome Nobility there , and *they* ftar'd as much as any body ; but will not do fo, I hope, when we ceafe to be a Novelty.

We have already had feveral Vifitors to welcome Mr *B*. to Town, and to congratulate him on his Marriage,——but fome, no doubt, to fee, and to find Fault with, his Ruftick ; for it is impoffible, you know, Madam, that a Gentleman fo diftinguifh'd by his Merit and Fortune, fhould have taken a Step of fuch Confequence to bimfelf and Family, and not be known by every body fo to have done

Sir *Thomas Atkyns* is in Town, and has taken Apartments in the new-built ftately Pile of Edifices, called *Hanover-fquare* ; and he brought with him a younger Brother of Mr. *Arthur's*, who, it feems, is a Merchant.

Lord *F* has been to pay his Refpects to Mr. *B*. likewife, whofe School-fellow he was at *Eaton*, the little time Mr *B* was there. His Lordfhip promifes, that his Lady fhall make me a Vifit, and ac-

company

company me to the Opera, as soon as we are fully settled.

A Gentleman of the *Temple*, Mr *Turner* by Name, and Mr *Fanshaw*, of *Grey's-Inn*, both Lawyers, and of Mr *B*'s former Acquaintance, very sprightly and modish Gentlemen, have also welcom'd us to Town, and made Mr *B* abundance of gay Compliments on my account, to my Face, all in the common frothy Run.

They may be polite Gentlemen; but I can't say, I over-much like them. There is something so forward, so opinionated, so seemingly insensible of Rebuke, either from *within* or *without*, and yet not promising to avoid deserving one occasionally, that I could as *lieve* wish Mr *B* and they would not renew their former Acquaintance.

I am very bold, your Ladyship will say —— But you command me to write freely. Yet I would not be thought to be uneasy, with regard to your dear Brother's Morals, from these Gentlemen; for, Oh, Madam, I am a blessed Creature, and am hourly happier and happier in the Confidence I have as to that Particular. But I imagine they will force themselves upon him, more than he himself may wish, or would permit, were the Acquaintance now to begin, for they are not of his Turn of Mind, as it seems to me; being, by a Sentence or two that dropt from them, very free, and very frothy, in their Conversation, and by their laughing at what they say themselves, taking that for Wit, which will not stand the Test, if I may be allow'd to say so.

But they have heard, no doubt, what a Person Mr *B*'s Goodness to me, has lifted into Notice, and they think themselves warranted to say any thing before his Country Girl.

He was pleased to ask me, when they were gone, How I liked his two Lawyers? And said, they were Persons of Family and Fortune.

I am

I am glad of it, Sir, faid I; for their own fakes

Then you don't approve of them, *Pamela* ?——

They are *your* Friends, Sir ; and I cannot have any Diflike to them.

They fay good Things *fometimes,* returned he

I don't doubt it, Sir. But you fay good Things *always.*

'Tis happy for me, my Dear, you think fo. But tell me, What think you of 'em ?

I fhall be better able, Sir, to anfwer your Que-ftion, if I fee them a fecond time.

But we form Notions of Perfons, at firft Sight, fometimes, my Dear, and you are feldom miftaken in yours

I only think, Sir, That they have neither of them any Diffidence But their Profeffion, perhaps, may fet them above that.

They don't *practife,* my Dear; their Fortunes in-able them to live without it ; and they are too ftudious of their Pleafures, to give themfelves any Trouble they are not oblig'd to take.

They feem to me, Sir, to be *qualified* for Pra-ctice : They would make great Figures at the Bar, I fanfy.

Why fo ?

Only, becaufe they feem prepared to think *well* of what they fhall fay *themfelves* , and *lightly* of what *other People* fay, or may think of *them*

That indeed, my Dear, is the neceffary Qualifica-tion of a publick Speaker, be he Lawyer, or what he will The Man who cannot doubt *himfelf,* and can think meanly of his *Auditors,* never fails to fpeak with *Self-applaufe* at leaft

But you'll pardon me, good Sir, for fpeaking my Mind fo freely, and fo early, of thefe *your Friends*

I never, my Love, afk you a Queftion, I wifh you not to anfwer; and always expect your Anfwer fhould be without Referve, for many times I may afk your

Opinion, as a Corrective or a Confirmation of my own Judgment

How kind, how indulgent was this, my good Lady? But you know, how generously your dear Brother treats me, on all Occasions, and this makes me so bold as I often am.

It may be necessary, my dear Lady, to give you an Account of our Visitors, in order to make the future Parts of my Writing the more intelligible; because what I may have to write, may turn sometimes upon the Company we see: For which Reason, I shall also just mention Sir *George Stuart*, a *Scotish* Gentleman, with whom Mr *B.* came acquainted in his Travels, who seems to be a polite, and (Mr *B.* says, is) a learned Man, and a Virtuoso. He, and a Nephew of his, of the same Name, a bashful Gentleman, and who, for that Reason, I imagine, has a Merit that lies deeper than a first Observation can reach, are just gone from us, and were received with so much Civility by Mr. *B.* as intitles them to my respectful Regard

Thus, Madam, do I run on, in a manner, without Materials, and only to shew you the Pleasure I take in obeying you. I hope my good Lord *Davers* enjoys his Health, and continues me in his Favour, which I value extremely, as well as your Ladyship's. Mr *H* I hope, likewise enjoys his Health But let me not forget my particular and thankful Respects to the Countess, for her Ladyship's Favour and Goodness to me, which I shall ever place next, in my grateful Esteem, to the Honours I have received from your Ladyship on so many Occasions, and which bind me to be, with the greatest Respect, my dear Lady,

*Your faithful and obliged Servant,*

P B.

LET-

# LETTER III.

*My dear Father and Mother,*

I Write to you both, at this time, for your Advice in a particular Difpute, which is the only one I have had, or I hope ever fhall have, with my dear Benefactor; and as he is pleafed to infift upon his Way, and it is a Point of Confcience with me, I I muft refolve to be determin'd by your joint Advice, for, if my Father and Mother, and Husband, are of one Opinion, I muft, I think, yield up my own

This is the Subject.---I think a Mother ought, if fhe can, to be the Nurfe to her own Children.

Mr *B* fays, He will not permit it

It is the firft *will not* I have heard from him, or given Occafion for: And I tell him, That as it is a Point of Confcience witu me, I hope he will indulge me But the dear Gentleman has an odd way of arguing, that fometimes puzzles me. He pretends to anfwer me from Scripture, but I have fome Doubts of *his* Expofition, and he gives me Leave to write to you, tho' yet he won't promife to be determin'd by your Opinions, if they are not the fame with his own, and I fay to him, Is this fair, my deareft Mr. *B* ? Is it ?

He has got the Dean's Opinion with him, for our Debate began before we came to Town • But then he would not let me ftate the Cafe, but did it himfelf, and yet 'tis but an half Opinion, as I may fay, neither For it is, That if the Husband is fet upon it, it is a Wife's Duty to obey.

But I can't fee how that is, for if it be the *natural* Duty of a Mother, it is a *Divine* Duty, and how can a Husband have Power to difcharge a Divine Duty ?---- As great as a Wife's Obligation is to.

B 5 obey

obey her Husband, which is, I own, one Indifpenfable of the Marriage Contract, it ought not to interfere with what one takes to be a fuperior Duty.
And muft not one be one's own Judge of Actions,
by which we muft ftand or fall ?

I'll tell you my Plea ·

I fay, That where a Mother is unhealthy, fubject to
communicative Diftempers, as fcrophulous, or fcor-
butick, or confumptive Diforders, which have infected
the Blood or Lungs; or where they have not Plenty
of Nourifhment for the Child, as, I have heard, is
the Cafe of fome, that in thefe Cafes, a Difpenfation lies of courfe

But where there is good Health, free Spirits, and
plentiful Nourifhment; I think it an indifpenfable Duty

For this was the Cuftom, of old, of all the good
Wives we read of in Scripture

Then the Nourifhment of the Mother muft be
moft natural to the Child

Then a Nurfe may have a bad Husband, may
have Diftempers, may have private Vices, as
to Liquors, &c may be carelefs, and a Self-
lover, while a Mother prefers the Health of
her Child to her own private Satisfactions, or
Appetites

A Nurfe may be of a fordid Nature; and when I
have heard Mr B fo fatirical on Lords and
Gentlemen in Coach-boxes, why may not Charity make one think, that the Lady of the Family was innocent of fordid and unpardonable
Crimes, imputed by fevere Judges, and that
the Child, when grown up, owes its Tafte to
the Coach-box, to its Nurfe's being the Coachman's Wife, or the Wife of one of like Degree,
who may not have a Mind or Qualities above
that Degree? For, as the Blood and Spirits are
augmented, with the Child's Growth, by the
Food

Food it takes in, a fordid Nature may as well be communicated from a found Woman, as bad Health by an unfound, as I fhould imagine.

Then the Child, by the Defignation of Nature, generally brings its Nourifhment into the World with it. And Art muft be ufed, as I prefume, to dry up the Fountains of fuch its Nourifhment And is not this quite unnatural? And is not what is unnatural, finful ?

Then I have lately read, my Circumftances having made me curious on this Subject, That a new-born Child has, in its little Bowels, a pitchy Subftance, that wants to be purged off, and when it is not, occafions thofe Gripings and Convulfions which deftroy fo many miferable Infants, even (as one finds by the Weekly Bills here in Town) more than half of thofe who die in Infancy · Whereas Nature has defign'd, it feems, a Cure for this, in the purgative Quality, and fine thin Bluenefs given to the firft Milk, which in three Weeks or a Month, or may be lefs, carries off that pitchy Subftance, and gives Freedom and Eafe to the Bowel of Babies; which Quality not being in ftaler Milk, the poor Child often falls a Sacrifice to this Negligence or Inattention, and the Mother's Pains and Hazards are all caft away, and her Griefs, at lofing the dear Infant, are much greater than her Joys, at its Birth, when all the Danger was over

Then, dear Sir, faid I, there is another Point, refpecting the Health of our Sex ---- Great Hurts to one's Conftitution may arife from too frequently being in this Way, and, for my own Part, you have made me fo happy, that I cannot help being *covetous* of Life, if I may fo fay ---But the Sin, dear Sir, the Sin of committing that Task to others, which is fo

B 6 right

right to be perform'd by one's felf, if one has
Health and Strength to perform it, is the chief
thing with me, and, you know, Sir, that even
a Husband's Will is not fufficient to excufe one
from a natural or divine Obligation.

Thefe were my Pleas, among others · And this is
his Anfwer; for he was fo good as to give it me in
Writing

'As to what you allege, my Dear, of old Cu-
' ftoms, Times and Fafhions are much changed
' If you tell me of *Sarah's*, or *Rachel's*, or *Rebekah's*,
' or *Leah's*, nurfing their own Children, I can an-
' fwer, That the one drew Water at a Well, for her
' Father's Flocks; another kneaded Cakes, and baked
' them on the Hearth, for her Guefts, another per-
' fonally drefs'd favoury Meat, for her Husband;
' and all of them performed the common Offices
' of the Houfhold · And when our modern Ladies
' are willing to follow fuch Examples in *every thing*,
' their Plea ought to be allow'd in this.

'As to the matter of fordid Natures----We read,
' that there were among *Jacob's* twelve Sons, bad
' as well as good Natures, tho' born of, and nurfed
' by, the fame Mothers, *Reuben* particularly com-
' mitted an unpardonable Crime You are too well
' read in Scripture-hiftory, to need being told what
' it was. Two others were Murderers, treacherous
' Murderers, in cold Blood; and how did all their
' Hearts burn with fordid and unbrotherly Envy
' againft their Father's favourite Son ?

'Then it requires but the more Care in finding
' out a wholfome Woman, who has an honeft and
' good-natur'd Husband · And, let me tell you,
' *Pamela*, that the beft Natures, and the beft Con-
' ftitutions, (tho' your Cafe is an Exception) are not
' always to be met with in High-life, and the lefs, per-
' haps, becaufe they don't exercife themfelves, as the
'                                                    ' patri-

'patriarchal Nurfes you hinted at, ufed to do. In-
'deed I have feen Spirits, in fome of the High-born
'of your Sex, that one would not wifh to be pro-
'pagated ; but, contrarily, (if there be fo much in
'the Nature of the Nourifhment) I fhould think it
'matter of Prudence, that the Child fhould have
'any other Nurfe than its Mother

'As to the Nurfe's private Vices, with regard to
'Liquors, Diftempers, &c. this will be anfwer'd,
'by what I have hinted, of the greater Care to be
'taken in the Choice of the Nurfe  And I am fo
'well pleafed with your Apprehenfions of this Na-
'ture, that it is a moral Security to me, that you
'will make a proper Choice ; and I fhall be intirely
'eafy, in committing this Province to fo prudent
'and difcreet a Wife

'I allow, that there is a great deal in what you
'fay, as to the pitchy Subftance in new-born Chil-
'dren, and I think it very proper, that the Child
'fhould have the firft Milk  But cannot fuch a
'Nurfe be found, as may anfwer this Intention? --
'If fhe cannot, I will, provided you deal by me
'with your ufual Sincerity, and not make Scruples
'againft a Recommendation, on purpofe to carry
'your own Point, permit you to be your own Nurfe
'for one Month, or fo, if, by the Opinion of proper
'Judges, it be found neceffary  But then, as i know
'the pretty wire-drawing ways of your Sex, you muft
'not fo much as afk to go farther ; for I fhall not
'care to have my Reft difturbed ; and it may not
'be quite fo well, perhaps, to lay us under the Ne-
'ceffity of feparate Beds

'Befides, my Fondnefs for your perfonal Graces,
'and the laudable, and, I will fay, honeft Pleafure,
'I take in that eafy, genteel Form, which every
'body admires in you, at firft Sight, oblige me to
'declare, that I can by no means confent to facri-
'fice thefe to the Carelefsnefs into which I have
'feen

‘ feen very nice Ladies fink, when they became
‘ Nurfes  Moreover, my chief Delight in you is
‘ for the Beauties of your Mind, and, unequall’d as
‘ they are, in my Opinion, you have ftill a Genius
‘ capable of great Improvement; and I fhan’t care,
‘ when I want to hear my *Pamela* read her *French*
‘ and *Latin* Leffons, which I take fo much Delight
‘ to teach her, (and to endeavour to improve my-
‘ felf from her Virtue and Piety, at the fame time)
‘ to feek my Beloved in the Nurfery, or to permit
‘ her to be ingrofs’d by thofe Baby Offices, which
‘ wil better befit weaker Minds

‘ No, my Dear, you muft allow me to look
‘ upon you as my Scholar, in one Senfe ; as my
‘ Companion, in another, and as my Inftructrefs,
‘ in a third  You know I am not govern’d by the
‘ worft Motives  I am half overcome by your
‘ Virtue, and you muft take care, that you leave
‘ not your Work half-done  But I cannot help
‘ looking upon the Nurfe’s Office, as an Office be-
‘ neath my *Pamela*  Let it have your Infpection,
‘ your Direction, and your fole Attention, if you
‘ pleafe, when I am abroad  But when I am at
‘ home, even a Son and Heir, fo jealous am I of
‘ your Affections, fhall not be my Rival in them
‘ Nor will I have my Reft broken in upon, by your
‘ Servants bringing to you, as you once propos’d,
‘ your dear Li tle one, at Times, perhaps, as unfuit-
‘ able to my Repofe, and your own, as to the Child’s
‘ Neceffities, for I have no Notion of ftifling even
‘ a Cry, by cramming its little Stomach, when that
‘ very Cry fhall, perhaps, be neceffary for Exercife
‘ to its Lungs, and to open its little Organs

‘ You have been often fomewhat uneafy, when I
‘ have talked, for Argument’s fake, in favour of
‘ Polygamy  But when you mention the Defigna-
‘ tions of Nature, and form from thence your
‘ Notions of Duty on this Subject, what will you
‘ fay,

‘ fay, if I could, from your very Arguments of this
‘ kind, plead for that Practice, and bring all your
‘ good patriarchal Folks on my Side, on whom you
‘ lay fuch Strefs, in one Inftance?----For Example,
‘ my Dear · Suppofe I put you in mind, that while
‘ *Rachel* was giving her Little-one all her Attention,
‘ as a good Nurfe, the worthy Patriarch had feveral
‘ other Wives----Don’t be fhock’d, my deareft
‘ Love----The Laws of one’s own Country, are a
‘ fufficient Objection to me againft Polygamy, at
‘ leaft, I will not think of any more Wives, till you
‘ convince me, by your Adherence to the Example
‘ given you by the Patriarch Wives, that I ought to
‘ follow thofe of the Patriarch Husbands’

So here is that nafty Word *Polygamy* again ! Mr *B.*
knows, I had rather he fhould mention any thing
than that---But be fo good as to mind his next Argument  He is pleafed to entertain very high Notions (tho’ he puts them not in Practice ; and, indeed,
I think it my Duty to avoid giving him Occafion
for it) of the Prerogative of a Husband.  Upon my
Word, he fometimes, for Argument’s fake, makes a
body. think a Wife fhould not have the leaft Will
of her own.  He fets up a difpenfing Power, in
fhort, altho’ he knows, that that Doctrine once coft
a Prince his Crown.  And thus, proceeding with his
Anfwer to my Plea, he argues ·

‘ The chief Thing, that fticks with you, my dear
‘ *Pamela*, is, that you think it unnatural in a Mother
‘ not to be a Nurfe to her own Child, if fhe can ;
‘ and what is unnatural, you fay, is a Sin  Now,
‘ my Dear, altho’ your *Practice* be fo unexception-
‘ able, you feem not to have a right Notion of the
‘ Obedience which a Wife naturally *owes*, as well
‘ as voluntarily *vows*, to a Husband’s Will---
‘ In all *lawful* Things, you’ll fay---But fuppofe,
‘ my Dear, you were to make a folemn Vow, either
‘ as a fingle Woman, or as a Wife, to do any thing
                                                  ‘ that

‘ that you had a natural Power to do. No doubt you
‘ would think yourself under an Obligation to per-
‘ form it, let the Confequence be what it would.
‘ But to fhew *you*, who are fo learned in the old
‘ Law, of how little Force even the *Vows* of your
‘ Sex are, and how much you are under the Con-
‘ troul of ours, read the following Verfes in *Numbers*
‘ xxx *If a* MAN *vow a Vow unto the Lord, or*
‘ *fwear an Oath to bind his Soul with a Bond, he*
‘ *fhall not break his Word , he fhall do according to*
‘ *all that proceedeth out of his Mouth* The Reafon
‘ of this is, he is fole and independent, and Mafter
‘ of his own Will and Actions —But what follows ?
‘ *If a* WOMAN *alfo vow a Vow unto the Lord, and*
‘ *bind herfelf by a Bond, being in her Father's Houfe,*
‘ *in her Youth ; and her Father hear her Vow, and*
‘ *her Bond, wherewith fhe hath bound her Soul, and*
‘ *her Father fhall hold his Peace at her Then all*
‘ *her Vows fhall ftand, and every Bond, wherewith*
‘ *fhe hath bound her Soul, fhall ftand. But if her*
‘ *Father d'fallow her in the Day that he heareth,*
‘ *not any of her Vows, or of her Bonds, wherewith*
‘ *fhe hath bound her Soul, fhall ftand: And the Lord*
‘ *fhall forgive her, becaufe her Father d'fallowed her.*
‘ The very fame Thing is, with equal Strength,
‘ expreffed in the Verfes immediately following, in
‘ relation to a HUSBAND's allowing or difallowing
‘ his WIFE's Vows, nor is it diftinguifh'd at all,
‘ whether the Vow be juft or unjuft And it is
‘ worthy of Obfervation too, that the Laws of
‘ *England*, in Confideration of the Obedience a
‘ Wife owes to a Husband, will acquit a WOMAN
‘ of certain Crimes, for which they will punifh a
‘ MAN with Death
‘ What I have mentioned, therefore, fhews how
‘ much the *Daughter* is under the abfolute Controul
‘ of her *Father*, and the *Wife* of her *Husband* So
‘ that, you fee, my Dear, even in fuch a ftrong
‘ Point

' Point as a *folemn Vow to the Lord*, the Wife may
' be abfolv'd by the Husband, from the Perform-
' ance of it.

' And by the way, this is no bad Piece of inform-
' ation to young Ladies, who are urged by their
' defigning Lovers to enter into Vows and Contracts
' in their Favour: Not one of which, you fee, is of
' Force, unlefs the Father, and, by the fame Rule,
' thofe who have Authority over her, and ftand in
' the Father's Place, approve and confirm it.

' If this therefore be the Cafe in fo folemn a Point,
' furely, a Husband may take upon himfelf to dif-
' penfe with fuch a fuppofed Obligation, as that
' which you feem fo loth to give up, even although
' you had made a Vow, that you would nurfe your
' own Child —And the rather, if the Principle a
' Husband acts upon, is laudable, a Defire to con-
' tinue his affectionate and faithful Regards to his
' Wife, to preferve in her, as long as may be pre-
' ferved, thofe Graces, and thofe Delicacies of Per-
' fon, which he admires in her, and which it is im-
' poffible a thorough Nurfe fhould keep up, and as,
' moreover, in your Cafe, her Time may be im-
' ploy'd to fo much greater Improvement to her own
' Mind, and her Husband's Morals, while he can
' look upon her in a Light above that of an infipid
' prattling Nurfe, who muft become a Fool and a
' Baby herfelf, before fhe can be complete in the
' Character, into which you, my Dear, want to
' dwindle.

' Some Gentlemen may be fond of having their
' Ladies undertake this Province, and very good
' Reafons may be affigned for fuch their Fondnefs;
' but it fuits not me at all. And yet no Man
' would be thought to have a greater Affection for
' Children than myfelf, or be more defirous to do
' them Juftice; for I think every one fhould look
' forward to Pofterity with a Preference: But if my
' *Pamela*

' *Pamela* can be *better* imploy'd : If the Office can
' be equally well perform'd  If your Direction and
' Superintendence will be sufficient, and if I cannot
' look upon you in that way with equal Delight, as
' if it was otherwise, I insist upon it, my *Pamela*,
' that you acquiesce with my *Dispensation*, and don't
' think to let me lose my beloved Wife, and have
' an indelicate Nurse put upon me instead of her

 ' As to that Hint, the nearest to me of all, of
' Dangers to your Constitution, there is as much
' Reason to hope it may *not* be so, as to fear that
' it *may*  For Children sometimes bring Health with
' them as well as Infirmity, and it is not a little
' likely, that the *Nurse's* Office may affect the Health
' of a dear Lady, who has no very robust Consti-
' tution, and thinks it so much her Duty to attend
' it, that she will abridge herself of half the Pleasures
' of Life, and on that Account confine herself with-
' in Doors, or, in the other Case, must take with
' her, her Infant and her Nursery-maid, where-ever
' she goes ; and I shall either have very fine Com-
' pany, (shall I not ?) or be obliged to deny myself
' yours.

 ' Then, as I propose to give you a Smattering of
' the *French* and *Italian*, I know not but I may take
' you with me on a little Tour into *France* and *Italy*,
' at least to *Bath*, to *Tunbridge*, to *Oxford*, to *York*,
' and the principal Places of *England*. Wherefore,
' as I love to look upon you as the Companion of
' my Pleasures, I advise you, my dearest Love, not
' to weaken, or, to speak in a Phrase proper to the
' present Subject, *wean* me from that Love *to* you,
' and Admiration *of* you, which hitherto has been
' rather increasing than otherwise, as your Merit, and
' Regard for me, have increased '

 These, my dear Parents, are charming Allure-
ments, almost irresistible Temptations! And that
makes me mistrust myself the more, and be the more

diffident

diffident—For we are but too apt to be perſuaded into any thing, when the Motives are ſo tempting as theſe laſt.---- But do you take it *indeed*, that a Husband has ſuch a vaſt Preı ogative? Can it be, now under the *Goſpel*, that this ſetting themſelves, as it were, in God's Place, and *diſpenſing* with our Wills, as pleaſes theirs, is ſtill in Force?----Yet it is ſaid, that our Saviour came not to *break the Law, but to fulfil it*

I take it for granted, that many Ladies will not chuſe to diſpute this Point ſo earneſtly as I have done, for we have had ſeveral little Debates about it, and it is the only Point I have ever yet debated with him But one would not be altogether implicit neither. It is no Compliment to him to be quite paſſive, and to have no Will at all of one's own : Yet would I not diſpute one Point, but in Suppoſi-tion of a ſuperior Obligation : And this, he ſays, he can *diſpenſe* with :----But, alas! my dear Mr. *B.* was never yet thought ſo intirely fit to fill up the Cha-racter of a Caſuiſtical Divine, as that one may abſo-lutely rely upon his Deciſions in theſe ſerious Points. And you know we muſt all ſtand or fall by our own Judgments.

Upon Condition, therefore, that he requires not to ſee this my Letter, nor your Anſwer to it, unleſs I pleaſe, I write for your Advice, for you both have always made a Conſcience of your Duties, and taught me to do ſo too, or perhaps I had not been what I am, and I know, moreover, that nobody is more converſant with the Scriptures than you are, and, ſome how or other, he has got the Dean againſt me, and I care not to be ſo free with the worthy Miniſter of our Pariſh here, and ſtill leſs with the younger Clergymen I am acquainted with

But this I ſee plainly enough, that he will have his own Way; and if I cannot get over my Scruples, what ſhall I do? For if I think it a *Sin* to ſubmit

to

to the Difpenfation he infifts upon as in his Power to grant, and yet *do* fubmit to it, what will become of my Peace of Mind? For it is not in our Power to believe as one will. Then weak Minds will have their Doubts, and the Law allows a Toleration for fcrupulous and tender Confciences : But my beloved Husband, my Lawgiver, and my Prince, I doubt, will allow none to poor me!

As to the Liberty he gives me for a Month, I fhould be loth to take it, for one does not know the Inconveniences that may attend a Change of Nourifhment, or if I did, I fhould rather----But I know not what I would fay; for I am but a young Creature to be in this Way, and very unequal to it in every refpect! So I commit myfelf to God's Direction, and your Advice, as becomes

*Your ever-dutiful Daughter*, P B.

## LETTER IV.

*My deareft Child,*

YOUR Mother and I have as well confidered the Cafe you put, as we are able ; and we think your own Reafons very good , and it is pity, a thoufand Pities, your honoured Husband will not allow them, as you, my Dear, make it fuch a Point with you    Very few Ladies would give their Spoufes, we believe, the Trouble of this Debate , and few Gentlemen are fo very nice as yours in this refpect; for I (but what fignifies what fuch a mean Soul as I think, compar'd to fo learned and brave a Gentleman ; yet I) always thought your dear Mother, and fhe has been a pretty Woman too in her Time, never look'd fo lovely, as when I faw the dear Creature, like the *Pelican* in the Wildernefs, feeding her young ones from her kind Breaft :----And had I had
ever

ever fo noble an Eftate, I am fure I fhould have had the fame Thoughts

But fince the good 'Squire cannot take this Pleafure, fince he fo much values your Perfon; fince he gives you Warning, that it may eftrange his Affections; fince he is impatient of Denial, and thinks fo highly of his Prerogative; fince he may, if difobliged, refume fome bad Habits, and fo you may have all your Prayers and Hopes in his perfect Reformation fruftrated, and find your own Power to do Good more narrow'd, as I may fay; we think, befides the Obedience you have vowed to him, and is the Duty of every good Wife, you ought to give up the Point, and acquiefce; for this feemeth to us, to be the leffer Evil, and God Almighty, if it fhould be your Duty, will not be lefs merciful than Men, who, as his Honour fays, by the Laws of the Realm, excufe a Wife when fhe is faulty by the Command of the Husband, and we hope, the Fault he is pleafed to make you commit, (if a Fault, for he really gives very praife-worthy Motives for his Difpenfation) will not be laid at his own Door  So e'en refolve my deareft Child, to fubmit to it, and with Chearfulnefs too.

God fend you an happy Hour! But who knows, when the Time comes, whether it may not be proper to difpenfe with this Duty, as you deem it, on other Accounts? for every young Perfon is not inabled to perform it. So, to fhew his Honour, that you will chearfully acquiefce, your dear Mother advifes, that you would look out for a wholfome, good-humour'd, honeft Body, as near your Complexion, and Temper, and Conftitution, as may be, and it may not be the worfe, fhe thinks, if fhe is Twenty, or One or Two-and-twenty; for fhe will have more Strength and Perfection, as one may fay, than even you can have at your tender Age  And, above all, for the wife Reafon you give from your

Reading,

Reading, that she may be brought to-bed much about your Time, if it be possible ---We will look out, if you please, about us for such an one  And as Mr. *B.* is not averse to have the dear Child in the House with you, you will have as much Delight, and the dear Baby may fare as well, under your prudent and careful Eye, as if you were to be obliged in the Way you would chuse

So, God direct you, my dearest Child, in all your Ways, and make you acquiesce in this Point with Chearfulnefs, (altho', as you say, one cannot believe as one pleases, for we verily are of Opinion you safely may, as Matters stand) and continue to you, and your beloved and honoured Husband, Health, and all manner of Happiness, are the Prayers of

*Your most affectionate Father and Mother,*

J and E ANDREWS.

I have privately shew'd our worthy Minister your Letter · You know, my Dear, he is a learned and judicious Gentleman: And he is of our Opinion, that it is best for you, on all Accounts, to acquiesce  Besides, it may disoblige the 'Squire, and it will signify nothing, after all, for he will have his Way, that's sure enough.

## LETTER V.

I Thank you, my dearest Parents, for your kind Letter; it was given to Mr. *B* and he brought it to me himself, and was angry with me · Indeed he was, as you shall hear ·

'Tis from the good Couple, my Dear, I see  I hope they are of my Opinion. But whether they be or not----But I will leave you; and do you, *Pamela*, step down to my Closet when you have perus'd it

He was pleased to withdraw; and I read it, and sat down, and consider'd it well, but, as you know I made it always my Maxim to do what I could not avoid to do, with as good a Grace as possible, I waited on the dear Gentleman.

Well, *Pamela*, said he, a little seriously, what say the worthy Pair?

O Sir! they declare for you. They say, it is best for me to yield up this Point

They are certainly in the right ---But were you not a dear little perverse Slut, to give me all this Trouble about your saucy Scruples?

Nay, Sir, don't call them so, said I; little thinking he was displeased with me.---I still am somewhat wavering, tho' they advise me to acquiesce: And, as it is your Will, and you have determined how it shall be, it is my Duty to yield up the Point.

But do you yield it up cheartully, my Dear?

I do, Sir, and will never more dispute it, let what will happen ----And I beg Pardon for having so often enter'd into this Subject with you ----But you know, Sir, if a Body's Weakness of Mind gives one Scruples, one should not yield implicitly, till they are satisfy'd, for that would look as if one gave you not the Obedience of a free Mind

You are very obliging, *just now*, my Dear: But I can tell you, you had made me half serious, yet I would not shew it, in Compliment to your present Condition; for I did not expect, that you would have thought *any* Appeal necessary, tho' to your Father and Mother, in a Point that I was determin'd upon, as you must see, every time we talk'd of it

This struck me all in a Heap I look'd down to the Ground, having no Courage to look up to his

Face,

Face, for fear I fhould behold his Afpect as morti-
fying to me as his Words  But he took both my
Hands, and drew me kindly to him, and faluted
me---Excufe me, my deareft Love , I am not
angry with you ----Speak to me, my Dear-----
Why drops this precious Pearl? and kifs'd my Cheek.
---Speak to me, *Pamela!*---

I will, Sir---I will---as foon as I can----for this
being my firft Check, fo ferioufly given, my Heart
was full.  But as I knew he would be angry, and
think me obftinate, if I did not fpeak; I faid, full
of Concern----I wifh, Sir---I wifh---you had been
pleafed to fpare me longer, a little longer, for the
fame kind, very kind, Confideration.

But is it not better, my Dear, to tell you I *was*
a little out of Humour with you, than that I *am?*---
But you had been very earneft with me on this
Point more than once, and you put me upon a hated,
becaufe ungenerous, Neceffity of pleading my Prerogative, as I call it  And yet this would not do, but
you would appeal againft me in the Point I was determin'd upon, for Reafons altogether in your Favour; and if this was not like my *Pamela*, excufe
me, my deareft Love, that I could not help being
a little unlike myfelf

Ah! thought I, this is not fo very unlike your dear
Self, if I were to give the leaft Shadow of an Occafion, for it is of a Piece with your Leffons formerly *

I am fure, faid I, I was not in the leaft aware,
that I had offended ---But I was too little circumfpect.  I had been ufed to your Goodnefs for fo long
a Time, that I expected it, it feems, and thought I
was fure of your favourable Conftruction

Why fo you may be my Dear, in every thing
*almoft*.  But I don't love to fpeak † twice my Mind

---

* *See* Vol II. *p.* 311, *&c.*    † Ibid. *p* 317.

on the fame Subject, you know I don't; and you have really difputed this Point with me Five or Six times: Infomuch, that I wonder'd what was come to my Deareft.

I thought, Sir, you would have diftinguifh'd between a Command where my *Confcience* was concerned, and a *common* Point. You know, Sir, I never had any Will but yours in *common* Points. ---But indeed you make me fearful, becaufe my Task is render'd too difficult for my own weak Judgment. But then, Sir---- But I fhall offend again---

And then what? Say all you would fay, *Pamela.* ---And then what?

Why, Sir, if I muft fpeak---You threaten me fo at every Turn with that cruel Word *Polygamy,* that it fhews me, it is too much in your Mind--- ButI fhall make you angry again.

Was not the Patriarch Husbands Practice, *Pamela,* a fit Thing to be oppos'd to that of the Patriarch Wives? But do you fay, I *threaten* you with that Word? Take care, my Love. You have been a *faultlefs Angel* hitherto. Don't let me find you ready to make fuch harfh Conftructions as a *mere Woman* is accuftom'd to make, when fhe is difpos'd to be captious; altho' a better Conftruction lies before her.

I was filent, but by my Tears.

Now I doubt, *Pamela,* your Spirit is high. You won't fpeak, becaufe you are out of Humour at what I fay I will have no fullen Referves, my Deareft. What means that heaving Sob? I know, my dear Love, that this is a Time with your Sex, when, fadden'd with your Apprehenfions, and indulg'd becaufe of them, by the fond Husband, it is needful, for both their fakes, to watch over the Changes of their Temper. For Ladies in your Way, are often like incroaching Subjects: They are apt to ex-end what they call their Privileges, on the Indulgence shewed them; and the Husband never again recovers the Afcendant he had before.

You know thefe Things better than I, Mr *B*. But I had no Intention to invade your Province, or to go out of my own. Yet I thought I had a Right to a little Free-will, a very little, efpecially on fome greater Occafions.

Why fo you have, my Dear. But you muft not plead one Text of Scripture in Behalt of your own Will; and refufe to another its due Weight, when it makes for mine.

Well, Sir, I muft needs fay, I have one Advantage above others of my Sex. For if Wives in my Circumftances are apt to grow upon Indulgence, I am very happy, that your kind and watchful Care will hinder me from failing into that Error.

He gave me a gentle Tap on the Neck Let me beat my beloved Sawcebox, faid he: Is it thus you railly my watchful Care over you for your own Good? But tell me truly, *Pamela*, are you not a little fullen? Look up to me, my Dear---Are you not?

I believe I am, but 'tis but a very little, Sir---It will foon go off---Pleafe to let me withdraw, that I may take myfelf to Task about it,---for at prefent, I know not what to do, becaufe I did not expect the Difpleafure I have incurr'd

Is it not the fame Thing, reply'd he, if this our firft Quarrel end here, without your withdrawing? ---I forgive you heartily, my *Pamela*; and give me one Kifs, and I will think of your faucy Appeal againft me no more

I will comply with your Condition, Sir; but I have a great Mind to be faucy. I wifh you would let me for this once

What would you fay, my Deareft? Be faucy then, as you call it, as faucy as you can

Why

Why then, I *am* a little fullen at prefent, that I am .---- And I am not fully convinc'd, whether it muft be I that forgive you, or you me ---For indeed, till I can recollect, I cannot think my Fault fo great in this Point, that was a Point of Confcience to me, as (pardon me, Sir) to ftand in need of your Forgivenefs

Well then, my Deareft, faid he, we will forgive one another; but take this with you, That it is my Love to you, that makes me more delicate than otherwife I fhould be; and you have inur'd me fo much to a faultlefs Conduct, that I can hardly bear with natural Infirmities from you.---But, giving me another Tap, Get you gone, I leave you to your Recollection; and let me know what Fruits it produces; for I muft not be put off with a Half-compliance; I muft have your whole Will with me, if poffible

So I went up, and recollecting every thing, *fatis-fic'd to my Sex*, as Mr. *B* calls it, when he talks of a Wife's Reluctance to give up a favourite Point, for I fhed a good many Tears, becaufe my Heart was fet upon it, and this Patriarchal Retort hung heavy upon my Mind

And fo, my dear Father and Mother, Twenty charming Ideas and Pleafures, which I had formed to myfelf, had I obtained this Permiffion, are vanifhed from me, and my Meafures are quite broken But after my Heart was relieved by my Eye, I was lighter and eafier And the Refult is, we have heard of a good fort of Body, that is to be my poor *Baby's Mother*, when it comes, and fo your kindly-offer'd Inquiries are needlefs, I believe

I can't tell but this fort of Rebuff might be a little neceffary, after all, for I had forgotten, thro' Mr. *B's* paft Indulgence for fo long a Time, his Injunctions and Leffons, and this awfully-inforced Remembrance fhews me, that the Rules he formerly

pre-

prescribed, were not Words of Course, but that he intended to keep me up to the Letter of them ---- So I must be a little more circumspect, I find that, than of late I thought I had Occasion to be

But he is the best and tenderest of Husbands, for all this, and yet I was forced to accept of *his* Forgiveness, and he did not think himself obliged to me for *mine*; and has carry'd his Point all to nothing, as the Racing Gentlemen say. But I can see one Thing, nevertheless, on this Occasion, that the Words *Command* and *Obey* are not quite blotted out of his Vocabulary, as he said they should be *

But, truly, I did not imagine before, that the Husband had so very extensive a Prerogative neither. ----Nor do I believe, that many Ladies would sit down so satisfy'd with it, as I am forced to do.---- Yet he vows, that it must have been so, had he marry'd a *Princess*,----and that it is not because of the former Inequality of Condition between us.

I can't tell what to say to that: But I fansy there would then have been some *princely* Struggles between them ---It may be, if he could not have conquer'd, he would not have liv'd with her; or, perhaps, would have run into his wicked Polygamy Notions.

Mr. *B.* to my *further* great Comfort, has just been telling me, how little a Wife of his must expect from her Tears; and has most nicely been distinguishing between Tears of *Sullenness*, and Tears of *Penitence* · The one, he declares, shall always meet with his Indulgence and Kindness, and never pass unrewarded · But the other, being the last Resources of the Sex, after they are disarmed of all others, and by which they too often, as he says, carry all their Purposes, he will never suffer to have any Force at all upon him.

* *See* Vol. II p 317.

Very

Very heroick, truly!---One ftands a poor Chance in a Conteft with fuch a Husband ---It muft be all pure unmixed Obedience and Submiffion. And I find, half the Tears a poor Wife might fhed in matrimonial Bickerings, (fo frequent with fome, even of thofe not unhappily married, as the World thinks) would be of no Effect, were all Men of his Mind

'Tis well for our Sex in general, that there are not many Gentlemen who diftinguifh thus nicely. For, I doubt, there are but very few fo well intitled to their Ladies Obfervances as Mr *B* is to mine; and who would act fo generoufly and fo tenderly by a Wife as he does, in every material Inftance on which the Happinefs of Life depends.

But we are quite reconciled; altho', as I faid, upon his own Terms. And fo I can ftill ftyle myfelf,

*My dear honoured Parents,*

*Your* happy, *as well as dutiful Daughter,*

P. B.

---

## LETTER VI.

### From Lady DAVERS *to Mrs.* B.

*My dear* PAMELA,

I HAVE fent you a Prefent, the completeft I could procure, of every thing that may fuit your approaching happy Circumftance; as I hope it will be to you, and to us all · But it is with a Hope annex'd, That altho' both Sexes are thought of in it, yet that you will not put us off with a Girl: No, Child, we will not permit, may we have our Wills, that you fhall *think* of giving us a Girl, till you have prefented us with half a dozen fine Boys. For our

Line

Line is gone so low, that we expect that human
Security from you in your first Seven Years, or we
shall be disappointed, I can tell you that

And now, *Pamela*, I will give you their Names, if
my Brother and you approve of them. Your First
shall be BILLY, my Lord *Davers*, and the Earl of
C------, shall be Godfathers; and it must be doubly
God-mother'd too, or I am afraid the Countess and
I shall fall out about it. Your Second, shall be
DAVERS, before remember that--- Your Third shall
be CHARLEY, your Fourth, JEMMY, your Fifth,
HARRY, your Sixth---DUDLEY, if you will---and
your Girl, if you had not rather call it PAMELA,
shall be BARBARA---The rest you must name as you
please ---And so, my Dear, I wish all Seven happily
over with you.

I am glad you got safe to Town, and long to hear
of Miss *Darnford's* Arrival, because I know you'll
be out of your Bias in your new Settlement till then
She is a fine Lady, and writes the most to my Taste
of any one of her Sex, that I know, next to you.
I wish she'd be so kind as to correspond with me But
before don't omit to give me the Sequel of her Sister's
and *Murray's* Affair, and what you think will please me
in relation to her You do well to save yourself the
Trouble of describing the Town and the publick
Places We are no Strangers to them, and they are
too much our Table-talk, when any Country Lady
has, for the first time, been carried to Town, and
return'd Besides, what *London* affords, is nothing
that deserves Mention, compar'd to what we have
seen at *Paris*, and at *Versailles*, and other of the
*French* Palaces. You exactly, therefore, hit our Tastes,
and answer our Expectations, when you give us, in
your peculiar manner, Sentiments on what we may
call the *Soul of Things*, and such Characters as you
draw with a Pencil borrow'd from the Hand of Nature, intermingled with those fine Lights and Shades,

of

of Reflections and Observations, that make your Pictures glow, and instruct as well as delight

There, *Pamela,* is Encouragement for you to proceed in obliging us. We are all of one Mind in this respect; and more than ever, since we have seen your Actions so well answer to your Writings; and that Theory and Practice, with regard to every Excellence that can adorn a Lady, is the same thing with you

We are pleased with your Lawyers Characters. There are Life and Nature in them; but never avoid giving all the Characters that occur to you, for that seems to be one of your Talents; and in the ugliest you can draw, there will be Matter of Instruction; especially as you seem naturally to fall upon such as are so general, that no one who converses, but must see in them the Picture of one or other he is acquainted with.

By this Time, perhaps, Miss *Darnford* will be with you—Our Respects to her, if so.—And you will have been at some of the Theatrical Entertainments: So will not want Subjects to oblige us —'Twas a good Thought of your dear Man's, to carry you to see the several Houses, and to make you a Judge, by that Means, of the Disposition and Fashion of every thing in them. Tell him, I love him better and better. I am proud of my Brother, and do nothing but talk of what a charming Husband he makes. But then, he gives an Example to all who know him, and his uncontroulable Temper, (which makes against many of us) that it is possible for a good Wife to make even a bad Man a worthy Husband and this affords an Instruction, which may stand all our Sex in good stead —But then they must have been cautious first, that they have chosen a Man of natural good Sense, and good Manners, and not a brutal or abandon'd Debauchee.

But

But hark ye-me, my fweet Girl, what have I done to you, that you won't write yourfelf *Sifter* to me? I could find in my Heart to be angry with you on this Account. Before my laft Vifit, indeed, I was fcrupulous to fubfcribe myfelf fo to *you* But fince I have feen myfelf fo much furpafs'd in all manner of Excellence, that I would take Pleafure in the Name; you affume a Pride in your Turn, and think it an undervaluing of yourfelf, I fuppofe, to call *me* fo — Ay, that's the Thing, I doubt — Altho', I can tell you, I have endeavour'd, by feveral Regulations fince my Return, (and the Countefs, too, keeps your Example in diftant View, as well as I) to be more worthy of the Appellation If, therefore, you would avoid the Reproaches of fecret Pride, under the Shadow of fo remarkable an Humility, for the future never omit fubfcribing, as I do, with great Pleafure,

*Your truly affectionate Sifter, and Friend,*

B DAVERS.

I always take it for granted, that my worthy Brother fends his Refpects to us; as you muft, that Lord *Davers*, the good Countefs, and *Jackey*, (who, as well as his Uncle, talks of nothing elfe but you) fend theirs; and fo unneceffary Compliment will be always excluded our Correfpondence.

---

## LETTER VII.

### *In Anfwer to the preceding.*

HOW you overwhelm me with your Goodnefs, my deareft Lady, in every Word of your laft welcome Letter, is beyond my Power to exprefs! How nobly has your Ladyfhip contrived, in your ever-

to-

to-be-valu'd Prefent, to encourage a doubting and apprehenfive Mind! And how does it contribute to my Joy and my Glory, that I am deemed by the noble Sifter of my Beft-beloved, not wholly unworthy of being the humble Means to continue, and, perhaps, to perpetuate, a Family fo antient and fo honourable!

This, Madam, when I contemplate, and look upon what I was---What can I fay!---How fhall I exprefs the Senfe of the Honour done me!--- And when, skipping over for a few Moments, the other engageing Particulars in your Ladyfhip's Letter, I come to the laft charming Paragraph, I am doubly affected to fee myfelf feemingly upbraided, but fo politely embolden'd to affume an Appellation, that otherwife I hardly dared to affume

I---*humble I*--- who never had a Sifter before, ---To find one now in *Lady* DAVERS! O Madam, You, and *only* You, can teach me Words fit to exprefs the Joy and the Gratitude that fill my delighted Heart!----But thus much I am taught, and thus much I can fay, tho' at a Lofs for other Words, that there is fomething more than the Low-born can imagine in Birth and Education. This is fo evident in your Ladyfhip's Actions, Words, and Manner, that it ftrikes one with a becoming Reverence; and we look up with Awe to a Condition we emulate in vain, when raifed by partial Favour, like what I have found, and are confounded, when we fee Grandeur of Soul join'd with Grandeur of Birth and Condition, and a noble Lady acting thus nobly, as Lady *Davers* acts

My beft Wifhes, and a Thoufand Bleffings, attend your Ladyfhip in all you undertake! And I am perfuaded the latter will, and a Peace and Satisfaction of Mind incomparably to be preferr'd to whatever elfe this World can afford, in the new Regulations, which you, and my dear Lady Countefs, have fet on Foot in your Families. And when I can have the

Happi-

Happineſs to know what they are, I ſhall, I am confident, greatly improve my own Methods by them

Were we to live for ever in this Life, we might be careleſs and indifferent about theſe Matters, but when ſuch an Uncertainty as to the Time, and ſuch a Certainty as to the Event, is before us, a prudent Mind will be always preparing, till prepared, and what can be a better Preparative, than charitable Actions to our Fellow-creatures in the Eye of that Majeſty, which wants nothing of us himſelf, but to do juſt and merciful Things to one another?

Pardon me, my deareſt Lady, for this my free Style Methinks I am out of myſelf, I know not how to deſcend all at once from the Height to which you have raiſed me And you muſt forgive the Reflections to which you yourſelf, and your own noble Actions, have given Birth

Here, having taken Reſpite a little, I find I naturally enough ſink into *Body* again —And will not your Ladyſhip confine your Expectations from me within narrower Limits?— I hope you will — For, O my excellent Lady, I cannot, even with my Wiſhes, ſo ſwiftly follow your Expectations, if ſuch as they are! But, however, leaving Futurity to HIM, who only governs Futurity, and who conducts us all, and our Affairs, as ſhall beſt anſwer his own Divine Purpoſes, I will proceed, as well as I can, to obey your Ladyſhip in thoſe Articles, which are, at preſent, more within my own Power

My dear Miſs *Darnford*, then, let me acquaint your Ladyſhip, arrived here on *Thurſday* laſt She had given us Notice, by a Line, of the Day ſhe ſet out, and Sir *Simon* and Lady *Darnford* ſaw her Ten Miles on the Way to the Stage-coach in Sir *Simon*'s Coach, Mr *Murray* attending her on Horſeback. They parted with her, as was eaſy to gueſs from her Merit, with great Tenderneſs, and we

are

are to look upon the Vifit, (as we do) as a high
Favour from her Papa and Mamma, who, however,
charge her not to exceed a Month in and out, which
I regret much   Mr B kindly propofed to me, as
Mifs came in the Stage-coach, attended with one
Maid-fervant, to meet her part of the Way in his
Coach and Six, if, as he was pleafed to fay, it would
not be too fatiguing to me, and we would go fo
early, as to dine at *St Albans.* I gladly confented,
and we got thither about One o'Clock, attended by
Mr *Colbrand, Abraham,* and *John,* and while
Dinner was preparing, he was pleafed to fhew me
the great Church there, and the curious Vault of
the Good Duke of *Gloucefter,* and alfo the Monument
of the great Lord Chancellor *Bacon* in St. *Michael's*
Church; all which, no doubt, your Ladyfhip has feen

There happen'd to be Six Paffengers in the Stage-
coach, including Mifs and her Maid, and Mifs was
exceedingly glad to be relieved from them, tho' the
Weather was cold enough, Two of the Paffengers
being not very agreeable Company, one a rough
military Man, the other a pofitive humourfome old
Gentlewoman, and the other Two, not fuch as fhe
had Reafon to be loth to part with, Two Sifters, who
jangled now-and-then, faid Mifs, as much as *my* Sifter,
and my Sifter's *Sifter*

Your Ladyfhip will judge how joyful this Meeting was to Mifs and to me   Mr B was no lefs
delighted, and faid, He was infinitely obliged to
Sir *Simon* for this precious Truft

Mifs faid, I come with double Pleafure to fee the
greateft Curiofity in *England,* a Husband and a
Wife, who have not, in fo many Months, that you
have been marry'd, if I may believe Report, and
your Letters, Mrs B once repented.

You are fevere, Mifs, reply'd Mr. B. upon People
in the marry'd State: I hope there are many fuch
Inftances.

C 6

Thefe

There might, return'd she, if there were more such Husbands as Mr *B* makes —— Oh! you are a charming Man '---I hated you once, and I thought you very wicked, but I revere you now.

If you will *revere* any body, my dear Miss, said he, let it be this good Girl, for it is all owing to her Conduct and Discretion, that I make a tolerable Husband. Were there more such Wives, I am persuaded, there would be more such Husbands, than there are.

You see, my dear Miss, said I, what it is to be wedded to a generous Gentleman. Mr *B* by his noble Treatment of me, creates a Merit in me, and disclaims the natural Effects of his own Goodness

Well, you're a charming Couple--- Person and Mind, I know not any Equal either of you have —But, Mr. *B* I will not compliment You too highly. I may make *you* proud, for Men are saucy Creatures, but I cannot make your *Lady* so · And in this Doubt of the one, and Confidence in the other, I must join with you, that *her* Merit is the greatest---- Since, excuse me, bold Gentleman, as I know you have been! her Example has reform'd her Rake, and you have only confirm'd in her the Virtues you found ready formed to your Hand

That Distinction, said Mr. *B* is worthy of Miss *Darsford's* Judgment

My dearest Miss, my dearest Mr *B* said I, takeing each by the Hand, how can you go on thus! ---As I look upon every kind thing, Two such dear Friends say of me, as Incentives for me, to endeavour to deserve it, you must not task me too high, for then, instead of encouraging, you'll make me despair

Mr *B* clasped us both in his Arms, and saluted each---And called us his Two Nonpareils

He led us into the Coach, placing Miss and me on the Front-feat, and himself on the other, with Miss's Maid-servant, a genteel, prudent young Body, 

whom

whom her Lady would fain have left in the Stage
Coach, to avoid the Honour of fitting with Mr. *B.*
And in a free, eafy, joyful Manner, not in the leaft
tir'd or fatigu'd, did we reach the Town and Mr *B.'s*
Houfe; with which, and its Furniture, and the Apart-
ments allotted for her, Mifs is highly pleafed

But the dear Lady put me into fome little Con-
fufion, when fhe faw me firft; taking Notice of my
Improvements, as fhe called them, before Mr *B*
I look'd at him, and look'd at her---Dear Mifs!
faid I, with a blufhing Cheek, and down-caft Eye.
He fmiled at Mifs, and faid, Would *you*, my good
Mifs, look fo filly, after fuch a Length of Time, with
a Husband you had no Occafion to be afham'd of?

No, indeed, Sir, not I, I'll affure you; nor will
I forgive thofe Maiden Airs in a Wife fo happy as
you are

I faid nothing. But I wifh'd myfelf, in Mind and
Behaviour, to be juft what Mifs *Darnford* is.

But, my dear Lady, Mifs *Darnford* has had thofe
early Advantages from Converfation, which I had
not; and fo I muft never expect to know how to
deport myfelf with that modeft Freedom and Eafe,
which I know I want, and fhall always want, altho'
fome of my partial Favourers think I do not For,
I am every Day more and more fenfible of the
great Difference there is between being us'd to the
politeft Converfation as an Inferior, and being born
to bear a Part in it · In the one, all is fet, ftiff, aukward, and the Perfon juft fuch an Ape of Imitation
as poor I In the other, all is natural Eafe and Sweetnefs—like Mifs *Darnford*

Knowing this, I don't indeed aim at what I am
fenfible I cannot attain, and fo, I hope, am lefs
expofed to Cenfure, than I fhould be, if I did For,
I have heard Mr *B.* obferve with regard to Gentlemen who build fine Houfes, and make fine Gardens,
and open fine Profpects, that Art fhould never take
place

place of, but be subfervient to Nature; and a Gentleman, if he is confin'd to a Situation, had better conform his Defigns to that, than to do as at *Chatfworth* was done, that is to fay, level a Mountain at a monftrous Expence; which, had it been fuffer'd to remain, in fo wild and romantick a Scene as *Chatfworth* affords, might have been made one of the greateft Beauties of the Place

So I, Madam, think I had better endeavour to make the beft of thofe natural Defects I cannot mafter, than by affuming Airs and Dignities in Appearance, to which I was not born, act neither Part tolerably By this means, inftead of being thought neither Gentlewoman nor Ruftick, as Sir *Jacob* hinted, (*Linfey-wolfey*, I think, was his Term too) I may be look'd upon as an Original in my Way, and all Originals pafs Mufter well enough, you know, Madam, even with Judges

Now I am upon this Subject, I can form to myfelf, if your Ladyfhip will excufe me, Two fuch polite Genrlemen, as my Lawyers, mentioned in my former, who, with a true *London* Magnanimity and Penetration, (For, Madam, I fanfy your *London* Criticks will be the fevereft upon the Country Girl) will put on mighty fignificant Looks, forgetting, it may be, that they have any Faults themfelves, and apprehending that they have nothing to do, but to fit in Judgment upon others, one of them expreffing himfelf after this manner· "Why, truly, *Jack*, "the Girl is well enough— *confidering*— I can't "fay"—(then a Pinch of Snuff, perhaps, adds Importance to his Air) "but a Man might love her for "a Month or two" (Thefe Sparks talk'd in this manner of other Ladies before me)—— "She be- "haves better than I expected from her— *con- "fidering*"—again will follow—"So I think," cries the other; and toffes his Tye behind him, with an Air partly of Contempt, and partly of Rakery. ---As

" —As you say, *Jemmy*, I expected to find an auk-
" ward Country Girl, but she tops her Part, I'll
" assure ye!—Nay, for that matter, behaves very
" tolerably for *what she was*—And is right, not to
" seem desirous to drown the Remembrance of her
" Original in her Elevation—And, I can't but say"
(for something like it they did say) " is mighty
" pretty, and passably genteel." And thus, with their
poor Praise of Mr *B*'s Girl, they think they have
made a fine Compliment to his Judgment.

But for *his* sake, (for as to my own, I am not
solicitous about *such* Gentlemens good Opinions) I
owe them a Spite; and believe, I shall find an Opportunity to come out of their Debt For I have the
Vanity to think, now your Ladyship has made me
proud by your kind Encouragements and Approbation, that the Country Girl will make 'em look about
them, with all their *genteel Contempts*, which they
miscal *Praise*

But how I run on! Your Ladyship expects that
I should write as freely to you, as I used to do to
my Parents. I have the Merit of obeying you, that
I have, but, I doubt, too much to the Exercise of
your Patience

This (like all mine) is a long Letter; and I will
only add to it Miss *Darnford*'s humble Respects and
Thanks for your Ladyship's kind Mention of her,
which she receives as no small Honour

And now, Madam, with a greater Pleasure than I
can express, will I make use of the Liberty your
Ladyship so kindly allows me to take, of subscribing
myself, with that profound Respect which becomes
me,

*Your Ladyship's most obliged Sister and Servant,*

P. B.

Mr *Adams*, Mr. *Longman*, and Mrs. *Jervis*,
are just arrived, and our Houshold is now
complete
LET-

## LETTER VIII.

### From Lady DAVERS to Mrs. B.

*My dear* PAMELA,

AFTER I have thank'd you for your laſt agree-able Letter, which has added the Earl, and Lord *John*, and Lady *Jenny*, to the Number of your Admirers, (you know Lady *Betty*, their Siſter, was ſo before) I ſhall tell you, that I now write, at all their Requeſts, as well as at thoſe of my Lord *Davers*, the Counteſs you ſo dearly love, and Lady *Betty*, for your Deciſion of an odd Diſpute, that, on reading your Letter, and talking of your domeſtick Excellencies, happened among us.

Lady *Betty* would have it, That notwithſtanding any Aukwardneſs which you attribute to yourſelf, ſhe cannot but decide, by all ſhe has ſeen of your Writings, and has heard us ſay, that yours is the perfecteſt Character ſhe ever heard or read of, in the Sex

The Counteſs ſaid, That you wrong yourſelf, in ſuppoſing, that you are not every thing that is polite and genteel, as well in your Behaviour, as in your Perſon, and that ſhe knows not any Lady in *England*, who better becomes her Station than you do

Why then, ſaid Lady *Jenny*, Mrs. *B* muſt be quite perfect, that's certain  So ſaid her Brother, Lord *John*  So ſaid the Earl, their Father. So ſaid they all  And Lord *Davers* confirm'd, that you were  And *Jackey ſwore* to it.

Yet, as we are ſure, there cannot be ſuch a Character, in this Life, as has not one Fault, altho' we could not tell where to fix it, the Counteſs made a whimſical Motion ----Lady *Davers*, ſaid ſhe, pray do you write to Mrs *B* and acquaint her with our Subject, and as it is impoſſible, that one who can act as ſhe does,

does, fhould not know herfelf better than any body elfe can do, defire her to acquaint us with fome of thofe fecret Foibles, that leave room for her to be ftill more perfect

A good Thought! faid I  A good Thought! faid they all.----And this is the prefent Occafion of my writing, and pray fee, that you accufe yourfelf of no more than you know yourfelf guilty  For Over-modefty borders nearly on Pride, and too liberal Self-accufations are generally but fo many Traps for Acquittal with Applaufe; fo that (whatever other Ladies might) you will not be forgiven, if you deal with us in a way fo poorly artful· Let your Faults therefore, be fuch, as you think we can fubfcribe to, from what we have *feen* of *you*, and what we have *read* of *yours*, and you muft try to extenuate them too, as you give them, left we fhould think you above that Nature, which, in the *beft* Cafes, is your un-doubted Talent.

I congratulate you and Mifs *Darnford*, on her Arrival. She is a chaiming young Lady, but tell her, that we fhall not allow her to take you at your Word, and to think, that fhe excels you in any one thing· Only, indeed, we think you nicer in fome Points, than you need to be, as to your prefent agree-able Circumftance.  And yet, let me tell you, that the eafy and unaffected conjugal Purity, in Word and Behaviour, between your good Man and you, is worthy of Imitation, and what the Countefs and I have with Pleafure contemplated fince we left you, an hundred times, and admire in you both  And 'tis good Policy too, Child, as well as high Decorum, for it is what will make you ever new and refpectful to one another

But *You* have the Honour of it all, whofe fweet, natural, and eafy Modefty, in Perfon, Behaviour, and Converfation, forbid Indecency, even in Thought, much more in Word, to approach you, infomuch
that

that no Rakes can be Rakes in your Prefence, and yet they hardly know to what they owe their Reftraint

However, as People who fee you at this time, will take it for granted, that You and Mr *B.* have been very intimate together, I fhould think you need not be afham'd of your Appearance, becaufe, as he rightly obferves, you have no Reafon to be afham'd of your Hufband

Excufe my Pleafantry, my Dear And anfwer our Demand upon you, as foon as you can, which will oblige us all; particularly

*Your affectionate Sifter*,

B DAVERS.

## LETTER IX.

*My deareft Lady*,

WHAT a Task have you impofed upon me! And, according to the Terms you annex to it, how fhall I acquit myfelf of it, without incurring the Cenfure of Affectation, if I freely accufe myfelf as I may deferve, or of Vanity, if I do not? Indeed, Madam, I have a great many Failings; and you don't know the Pain it cofts me to keep them under, not fo much for fear the World fhould fee them, for, I blefs GOD, I can hope they are not capital, as for fear they fhould become capital, if I were to let them grow upon me

And this, furely, I need not have told your Ladyfhip, and my Lady Countefs, who have read my Papers, and feen my Behaviour in the kind Vifit you made to your dear Brother, and had from *both* but too much Reafon to cenfure me, did not your generous and partial Favour make you overlook my greater Failings, and pafs under a kinder Name many of my lefer.

lesser· For, surely, my good Ladies, you must both of you have observed, in what you have read and seen, that I am naturally of a spiteful, saucy Temper; and, with all my appearing Meekness and Humility, can resent, and sting too, when I think myself provok'd

I have also discover'd in myself, on many Occasions, (of some of which I will by-and-by remind your Ladyship) a Malignancy of Heart, that, it is true, lasts but a little while----nor had it need--·--but for which I have often called myself to Account---- to very little Purpose, hitherto

And, indeed, Madam, (now for a little Extenuation, as you expect from me) I have some Difficulty, whether I ought to take much Pains to subdue myself in some Instances, in the Station to which I am raised, that otherwise it would have become me to attempt to do: For it is no easy Task, for a Person in my Circumstances, to distinguish between the *ought* and the *ought not* ; to be humble without Meanness, and decent without Arrogance And let me add, That if all Persons thought as justly as I flatter myself I do, of the Inconveniencies, as well as Conveniencies, which attend their being rais'd to a Condition above them, they would not imagine all the World was their own, when they came to be distinguish'd as I have been · For, what with the Contempts of superior Relations on one side, (which all such must undergo at first) the Envy of the World, and low Reflections arising from that Envy, on the other, from which no one must hope to be totally exempted, and the Aukwardness, besides, with which they support their elevated Condition, if they have Sense to judge of their own Imperfections ; and if the Gentleman be not such an one as mine--- (and where will such another be found ?) --- On all these Accounts, I say, they will be made sensible,

That,

That, whatever they might once think, Happiness and an high Estate are Two very different Things

But I shall be too grave, when your Ladyship, and all my kind and noble Friends, expect, perhaps, I should give the uncommon Subject a pleasanter Air. Yet what must that Mind be, that is not serious, when it is oblig'd to recollect, and give Account of, its Defects?

But I must not *only* accuse myself, it seems: I must give *Proofs*, such as your Ladyship can subscribe to, of my Imperfections. There is so much *real Kindness* in this *seeming Hardship*, that I will obey you, Madam, and produce Proofs in a Moment, which cannot be controverted

Let me then, in the first Place, as to the Self-accusation of *Spitefulness*, refer your Ladyship, and those of my noble Friends who have read my Papers, to the Character I gave in them of poor Mrs *Jewkes* *, also to honest Mr. *Colbrand*'s Character, as I gave it, when I suspected he was to be imploy'd for the worst Purposes †, both of which, tho' not untrue in the main, are so drawn, as to shew a very spiteful Nature in the Characterizer.

And as to my *Sauciness*, those Papers will give an hundred Instances against me----as well to your dear Brother, as to others----Indeed, to extenuate, as you command me, as I go along, these were mostly when I was apprehensive for my Honour, that they were.

And then, my dear Lady, I have a little Tincture of *Jealousy*, which sometimes has made me more uneasy than I ought to be, as the Papers you have not seen, would have demonstrated, particularly in Miss *Godfrey*'s Case §, and in my Conversation with your Ladyships, in which I have frequently betray'd my Apprehensions of what might happen when we

---

* *See* Vol I. *p.* 146          † Ibid. *p.* 220.
§ *See* Vol. II. *p.* 325, *&c.*

came

came to *London* : Yet, to extenuate again, I have examin'd myself very ſtrictly on this Head ; and I really think, that I can aſcribe a great Part of this Jealouſy to laudable Motives ; no leſs than to the Concern I have for your dear Brother's future Happineſs, in the Hope, that I may be an humble Means in the Hands of Providence, to induce him to abhor thoſe Crimes of which young Gentlemen too often are guilty, and to bring him over to the Practice of thoſe Virtues, in which he will for ever have Cauſe to rejoice ---- Yet, my Lady, ſome other Parts of the Charge muſt ſtand againſt me ; for, as, to be ſure, I love his Perſon, as well as his Mind, I have Pride in my Jealouſy, that would not permit me, I verily think, to ſupport myſelf as I ought, under the Trial of a Competition, in this tender, very tender Point.

And this obliges me to own, that I have a little Spark---not a little one, perhaps----of *ſecret Pride* and *Vanity*, that will ariſe, now-and-then, on the Honours done me , but which I keep under as much as I can · And to this Pride, let me tell your Ladyſhip, I know no one contributes, or can contribute, more largely than yourſelf.

So you ſee, my dear Lady, what a naughty Heart I have, and how far I am from being a faultleſs Creature----I hope I ſhall be better and better, however, as I live longer, and have more Grace, and more Wit For here, to recapitulate my Faults, is, in the firſt Place, *Vindictiveneſs*, I will not call it downright Revenge, that I will not----For, as the Poet ſays,

> *Revenge is but a Frailty, incident*
> *To craz'd and ſickly Minds ; the poor Content*
> *Of little Souls, unable to ſurmount*
> *An Injury, too weak to bear Affront*

And I would not be thought to have a *little* Mind, becauſe I know I would not do a *little Thing*. *Vindictiveneſs,*

*dictiveness*, then, let it stand, tho' that's a harsh Word to accuse one's self of----*Spitefulness*----*Jealousy*----*Secret Pride*---*Vanity*---which I cannot, for my Life, keep totally under----O dear Madam, are not here Faults enow, without naming any more?----And, how much Room do all these leave for Amendment, and greater Perfection?

Had your Ladyship, and my Lady Countess, favour'd us longer, in your late kind Visit, it had been impossible but I must have so improv'd, by your charming Conversations, and by that natural Ease and Dignity which accompany every thing your Ladyships do and say, as to have got over such of these Foibles as are not rooted in Nature: Till in time I had been able to do more than emulate those Perfections, which, at present, I can only at an awful Distance revere; as becomes,

*My dear Ladies,*

*Your most humble Admirer, and obliged Servant,*

P B.

---

## LETTER X.

### *From Miss* Darnford, *to her Father and Mother.*

*My ever-honoured Papa and Mamma,*

I Arrived safely in *London* on *Thursday*, after a tolerable Journey, considering *Deb* and I made Six in the Coach, (Two having been taken up on the Way, after you left me) and none of the Six highly agreeable Mr. *B* and his Lady, who looks very stately upon us, (from the Circumstance of *Person*, rather than of *Mind*, however) were so good as to meet me at *St Albans*, in their Coach and Six. They have a fine House here, richly furnish'd in every

every Part, and have allotted me the beft Apartment in it

We are happy beyond Expreffion : Mr. B. is a charming Husband , fo eafy, fo pleas'd with, and fo tender of his Lady ; and fhe fo much All that we faw her in the Country, as to Humility and Affability, and improv'd in every thing elfe, which we hardly thought poffible fhe could be----that I never knew fo happy a Matrimony ----All that *Prerogative Saucinefs,* which we apprehended would fo eminently difplay itfelf in his Behaviour to his Lady, had fhe been ever fo diftinguifh'd by Birth and Fortune, is vanifh'd, and no Traces of it left. I did not think it was in the Power of an Angel, if our Sex could have produc'd one, to have made fo tender and fo fond a Husband of Mr. B as he makes. And fhould I have the Senfe to follow Mrs B 's Example, if ever I marry, I fhould not defpair of making myfelf happy, let it be to whom it would, provided he was not a Brute, nor fordid in his Temper , which two Characters are too obvious to be conceal'd, if Perfons take due Care, and make proper Inquiries, and if they are not led by blind Paffion May Mr. *Murray,* and Mifs *Nancy,* make juft fuch a happy Pair !

You commanded me, my honour'd Mamma, to write to you an Account of every thing that pleas'd me--I faid I would . But what a Task fhould I then have '—I did not think I had undertaken to write Volumes ---You muft therefore allow me to be more brief than I had intended

In the firft Place, It would take up five or fix long Letters to do Juftice to the Oeconomy obferved in this happy Family. You know, that Mrs. B has not changed one of the Servants of the Family, and only added her *Polly* to the Number. This is an unexampled thing, efpecially as they were all her *Fellow-fervants,* as we may fay · But fince they have the Senfe to admire fo good an Example, and are

proud

proud to follow it, each to his and her Power, I think it one of her peculiar Felicities to have continued them, and to chuse to reform such as were exceptionable, rather than dismiss them

Their Mouths, *Deb* tells me, are continually full of their Lady's Praises, and Prayers, and Blessings, utter'd with such Delight and Fervour for the happy Pair, that it makes her Eyes, she says, ready to run over to hear them

Moreover, I think it an extraordinary Piece of Policy (whether design'd or not) to keep them, as they were honest and worthy Folks; for had she turn'd them all off, what had she done but made as many Enemies as she had discarded Servants, and as many more, as those had Friends and Acquaintance? And we all know, how much the Reputation of Families lies at the Mercy of Servants; and 'tis easy to guess to what Cause each would have imputed his or her Dismission. And so she has escaped, as she ought to escape, the Censure of Pride; and has made every one, instead of reproaching her with her Descent, find those Graces in her, which turn that very Disadvantage to her Glory.

She is exceeding affable to every one of them; always speaks to them with a Smile, but yet has such a Dignity in her Manner, that it secures her their Respect and Reverence; and they are ready to fly at a Look, and seem proud to have any Commands of hers to execute: Insomuch that the Words, *My Lady commands so or so,* from one Servant to another, are sure to meet with an indisputable Obedience, be the Duty requir'd what it will.

If any of them are the least indisposed, her Care and Tenderness for them engage the Veneration and Gratitude of all the rest, who see in that Instance, how kindly they will be treated, should they ail any thing themselves And in all this, I must needs say, she is very happy in Mrs *Jervis*, who is an excellent

I

lent Second to her admirable Lady, and is treated
by her with as much Respect and Affection, as if
she was her Mother.

You may remember, Madam, that in the Account
she gave us of her *benevolent Round,* as Lady *Davers*
calls it, she says, That as she was going to *London,*
she should leave Directions with Mrs *Jervis* about
some of her *Clients,* as I find she calls her Poor, to
avoid a Word, which her Delicacy accounts harsh
with regard to them, and ostentatious with respect
to herself. I ask'd her, How (since, contrary to her
then Expectation, Mrs. *Jervis* was permitted to be
in Town with her) she had provided to answer her
Intention as to those her Clients, whom she had
referr'd to the Care of that good Woman?

She said, That Mr *Barlow* her Apothecary was a
very worthy Man, and she had given him a plenary
Power in that Particular, and likewise desired him to
recommend any new and worthy Case to her, that
no deserving Person among the destitute sick Poor,
might be unreliev'd by reason of her Absence.

And here in *London* she has applied herself to Dr.
—— (her Parish-minister, a fine Preacher, and sound
Divine, who promises on all Opportunities to pay his
Respects to Mr *B*) to recommend to her any poor
Housekeepers, who will be glad to accept of some
private Benefactions, and yet, having lived credita-
bly, till reduced by Misfortunes, are ashamed to apply for publick Relief. And she has several of these
already on her *benevolent List,* to some of whom
she sends Coals now at the Entrance on the wintry
Season, to some a Piece of *Irish* or *Scotish* Linen,
or so many Yards of *Norwich* Stuff, for Gowns and
Coats for the Girls, or *Yorkshire* Cloth for the Boys;
and Money to some, of whose Prudence she is most
assur'd in laying it out in the way they best can
judge of. And she has moreover *mortify'd,* as the
*Scots* call it, 150 *l.* as a Fund for Loans, without

Intereſt, of 5, 10, or 15, but not exceeding 20 *l.*
to anſwer ſome preſent Exigence in ſome honeſt
Families, who find the beſt Security they can, to
repay it in a given Time, and this Fund ſhe purpoſes, as ſhe grows richer, ſhe ſays, to increaſe, and
prides herſelf every now-and-then, for having ſav'd
ſo much Money already, and eſtimates pleaſantly her
Worth by this Sum, ſaying ſometimes, Who would
ever have thought I ſhould have been worth 150 *l.*
ſo ſoon? I ſhall be a rich Body in time. But in all
theſe things ſhe injoins Secrecy, which the Donor
has promis'd.

She told the Doctor, what Mr *Adams's* Office
is in her Family, and hop'd, ſhe ſaid, he would
give her his Sanction to it, aſſuring him, That ſhe
thought it her Duty to ask it, as ſhe was one of his
Flock, and he, on that account, her principal Shep-
herd, which made a ſpiritual Relation between them,
the Requiſites of which, on her Part, were not to
be diſpenſed with. You may be ſure, the good Gentleman very chearfully and applaudingly gave her his
Conſent, and when ſhe told him, how well Mr.
*Adams* was provided for, and that ſhe ſhould apply
to him to ſupply her with a Town-Chaplain, when
ſhe was depriv'd of him, he wiſh'd, that the other
Duties of his Function (for he has a large Pariſh)
would permit him to be the happy Perſon himſelf,
ſaying, That till ſhe was ſupply'd to her Mind, either
he or his Curate would take care, that ſo laudable
a Method ſhould be kept up.

You will do me the Juſtice, Madam, to believe,
that I very chearfully join in my dear Friend's *Sunday* Duties, and I am not a little edify'd with the good
Example, and with the Harmony and Good-will that
this excellent Method contributes to keep up in the
Family.

I muſt own, I never ſaw ſuch a Family of Love
in my Life. For here, under the Eye of the beſt
and

and moft refpected of Miftreffes, they twice every *Sunday* fee one another all together, (as they ufed to do in the Country) fuperior as well as inferior Servants , and *Deb.* tells me, after Mrs *B* and I are withdrawn, there are fuch friendly Salutations among them, that fhe never heard the like.----Your Servant, good Mafter *Longman*, Your Servant, Mafter *Colbrand,* cries one and another : How do you. *John* ? I'm glad to fee you, *Abraham* !---All bleffedly met once more ! cries *Jonathan* the venerable Butler, with his filver Hairs, as Mrs. *B* always diftinguifhes him . Good Madam *Jervis,* cries another, you look purely this bleffed Day, thank GOD !----And they return to their feveral Vocations, fo light, fo eafy, fo pleas'd, fo even-temper'd in their Minds, as their chearful Countenances, as well as Expreffions, teftify, that it is a Heaven of a Houfe . And being wound up thus conftantly once a Week, like a good Eighr-day Clock, no Piece of Machinery that ever was made, is fo regular and uniform, as this Family is.

What an Example does this dear Lady fet to all who fee her, to all who know her, and to all who hear of her ! and how happy are they who have the Grace to follow it !---What a publick Bleffing would fuch a Mind as hers be, could it be vefted with the Robes of Royalty, and adorn the Sovereign Dignity ! But what are the Princes of the Earth, look at them in every Nation, and what have they been for Ages paft, compar'd to this Lady ? who acts from the Impulfes of her own Heart, unaided, in moft Cafes, by any human Example. In fhort, when I contemplate her innumerable Excellencies, and that Sweetnefs of Temper, and univerfal Benevolence, which fhine in every thing fhe fays and does, I cannot fometimes help looking upon her in the Light of an Angel, dropp'd down from Heaven, and receiv'd into Bodily Organs, to live among Men and Women, in

order

order to fhew what the firft of the Species was defigned to be

This reminds me of what my honoured Papa faid
once at our own Houfe to Mr. *B* \* That there was
but one fuch Angel defcended from Heaven in a
thoufand Years, and he had her

And yet, here is the Admiration, That one fees
all thefe Duties performed in fuch an eafy and pleafant manner, as any body may perform them, for
they interfere not with any Parts of the Family Management, take up no Time from the neceffary Imployments, but rather aid and infpirit every one in
the Difcharge of all their domeftick Services, and,
moreover, keep their Minds in a State of Prepara
tion for the more folemn Duties of the Day, and
all without the leaft Intermixture of Affectation, Enthufiafm, or Oftentation. O my dear Papa and
Mamma, permit me but to tarry here till I am perfect in all thefe good Leffons, and how happy fhall
I be!

I am mindful, my dear Mamma, of yours and
our good Neighbours Requefts to Mrs *B* to oblige
you with the Converfations fhe mentioned, the one
with the young Ladies related to Mrs *Towers* and
Mrs. *Arthur*, the other with Mr *B* on her Father
and Mother, a Subject, which always, however
humble, raifes her Pen, and of Confequence our
Expectations; and I will prevail upon her to let me
tranfcribe them for your Entertainment  She writes
down every thing that paffes, which fhe thinks may
one Day be of Ufe to Mifs *Goodwin*, and to her own
Children, if fhe fhall live to have any, and to fee
them grown up   What a charming Mamma, as
well as Wife and Miftrefs, will this dear Lady make!

As to the Town, and the Diverfions of it, I fhall
not trouble you with any Accounts of them, becaufe

\* *See* Vol. II *p.* 266.

you know the one, and from the Time we paſſed here laſt Winter, as well as your former thorough Knowlege of both, you will want no Information about the other , for, generally ſpeaking, all who reſide conſtantly in *London,* allow, that there is little other Difference in the Diverſions of one Winter and another, than ſuch as are in Cloaths, a few Variations of the Faſhions only, which are moſtly owing to the ingenious Contrivances of Perſons who are to get their Bread by diverſifying them.

Mrs *B* has undertaken to give Lady *Davers* an Account of Matters as they paſs, and her Sentiments on what ſhe ſees  There muſt be ſomething new in her Obſervations, becauſe ſhe is a Stranger to theſe Diverſions, and unbiaſſed intirely by Favour or Prejudice, and ſo will not play the partial Critick, but give to a Beauty its due Praiſe, and to a Fault its due Cenſure, according to that Truth and Nature which are the unerring Guides of her Actions, as well as Sentiments  Theſe I will procure for you, as ſhe gives me Leave to tranſcribe what ſhe writes, and you'll be ſo good as to return them when peruſ'd, becauſe I will lend them, as I uſed to do her Letters, to her good Parents, and ſo I ſhall give her a Pleaſure at the ſame time, in the accommodating them with the Knowlege of all that paſſes, which ſhe makes it a Point of Duty to do, becauſe they take Delight in her Writings

My Papa's Obſervation, that a Woman never takes a Journey that ſhe don't forget ſomething, is juſtify'd by me ; for with all my Care, I have forgot my Diamond Buckle, which Miſs *Nancy* will find in the inner Till of my Bureau, wrapt up in Cotton, and I beg it may be ſent me, by the firſt Opportunity.  With my humble Duty to you both, my dear indulgent Papa and Mamma, Thanks for the Favour I now rejoice in, and affectionate Reſpects to Miſs

*Nancy,*

*Nancy*, (I wish she would love me as well as I love her) and Service to Mr *Murray*, and all our good Neighbours, conclude me,

*Your dutiful and highly favour'd Daughter,*

M DARNFORD

Mr B and Mrs. B desire their Compliments of Congratulation to Mr. and Mrs *Peters*, on the happy Marriage of their worthy Niece, which they knew nothing of till I told them of it Also to your honoured Selves they desire their kind Respects and Thanks for the Loan of your worthless Daughter

I experience every Hour some new Token of their Politeness and Affection, and I make no Scruple to think I am with just such a Brother, and such a Sister, as any happy Creature may rejoice in, and be proud of---Mr B I cannot but repeat, is a charming Husband, and a most polite Gentleman. His Lady is always accusing herself to me of Aukwardness and Insufficiency, but not a Soul who sees her, can find it out She is all genteel Ease, and the Admiration of every one who beholds her.---Only I tell her, with such Happiness in Possession, she is a little of the gravest sometimes

---

[The Letter which contains the Account of the Conversation, requested by Miss *Darnford*, Letter XL. Vol III and mentioned by Miss in the preceding Letter, will be found the last Letter but one of this Volume For Miss *Darnford*, having mislaid the first Copy of it, requested another, two or three Years after this, when married herself, for the sake of two young Ladies in her Neighbourhood, whose inconsiderate Rashness

Rafhnefs had given great Affliction to their honourable Parents  And Mrs B with a View to their
particular Cafe, having made divers Additions and
Improvements to it, it will come in more'properly,
as we conceive, in the Courfe of thefe Letters, at
or near the Time when thofe Improvements were
made to it ]

## LETTER XI.

### *From Mrs.* B. *to Lady* DAVERS.

*My good Lady,*

YOU command me to acquaint you with the
Pioceedings between Mr. *Murray* and Mifs
*Nanny Darnford* · And Mifs *Polly* makes it very eafy
for me to obey you, in this Particular, and in very
few Words, for fhe fays, every thing was adjufted
before fhe came away, and the Ceremony, fhe believes, may be performed by this Time  She rejoices
that fhe was out of the way of it  For fhe fays, Love
is fo aukward a Thing to Mr *Murray*, and Good-
humour fo uncommon an one to Mifs *Nancy*, that
fhe hopes fhe fhall never fee fuch another Courtfhip.

Mr B teizes Mifs, that fhe is a little piqu'd, (and
that fhe fhew'd it by a fatirical Fling or two in a
former Letter to me) that her humble Servant took
her at her Word  And yet he acknowleges, that he
believes fhe defpifes him ; and indeed Mr *Murray*
has fhewn, that he deferves to be defpifed by her.

She fays, Nothing has piqu'd her in the whole
Affair, but the Triumph it gave to *that ill-natur'd
Girl*, as fhe juftly calls her Sifter, who has infulted
her unmercifully on that Account, and yet with fo
low and mean a Spite, that fhe has been vex'd at
herfelf to fhew the leaft Concern on the Occafion.
But ungenerous Teizing is an intolerable thing, as fhe

says; and, often repeated, will vex a Mind naturally above it. Had it, says she, come from any body else, I should not have heeded it, but how can one despise a Sister?

We have been at the Play-house several times; and, give me Leave to say, Madam, (for I have now read as well as seen several) That I think the Stage, by proper Regulations, might be made a profitable Amusement. But nothing more convinces one of the Truth of the common Observation, That the best Things, corrupted, prove the worst, than these Representations. The Terror and Compunction for evil Deeds, the Compassion for a just Distress, and the general Beneficence which those lively Exhibitions are so capable of raising in the human Mind, might be of great Service, when directed to right Ends, and induced by proper Motives: Particularly, where the Actions which the Catastrophe is design'd to punish, are not set in such advantageous Lights, as shall destroy the End of the Moral, and make the Vice that ought to be censured, imitable, where Instruction is kept in View all the Way, and where Vice is punished, and Virtue rewarded.

But give me Leave to say, that I think there is hardly one Play I have seen or read hitherto, but has too much of Love in it, as that Passion is generally treated. How unnatural in some, how inflameing in others, are the Descriptions of it!---In most, rather Rant and Fury, like the Loves of the fiercer Brute Animals, as *Virgil,* translated by *Dryden,* describes them, than the soft, sighing, fearfully-hopeful Murmurs, that swell the Bosoms of our gentler Sex; and the respectful, timorous, submissive Complainings of the other, when the Truth of the Passion humanizes, as one may say, their more rugged Hearts.

In particular, my dear Lady, what strange Indelicates do' these Writers of Tragedy often make of

our Sex ? They don't enter into the Paffion at all,
if I have any Notion of it: But when the Authors
want to paint it ftrongly, (at leaft in thofe Plays I
have feen and read) their Aim feems to be to raife
a Whirlwind, as I may fay, which fweeps down Reafon, Religion, and Decency, and carries every laudable Duty away before it; fo that all the Example
can ferve to fhew, is, how a difappointed Lover
may rage and ftorm, refent and revenge.

The Play I firft faw was the Tragedy of the
*Diftreſs'd Mother*, and a great many beautiful Things
I think there are in it: But half of it is a tempeftu-
ous, cruel, ungoverned Rant of Paffion, and ends in
Cruelty, Bloodfhed, and Defolation, which the Truth
of Story not warranting, as Mr. *B.* tells me, makes
it the more Pity, that the original Author (for it is
a *French* Play tranflated, you know, Madam) had not
conducted it, fince it was in his Choice, with lefs Terror, and with greater Propriety, to the Paffions intended to be raifed, and actually raifed in many Places.

I need not tell your Ladyfhip what the Story is;
and yet it is neceffary, as you demand my Opinion,
that I fhould give a little Sketch of it It is this,
then ‘ *Pyrrhus*, the Son of *Achilles*, is betrothed
‘ to *Hermione*, the Daughter of *Menelaus* ; but
‘ *Hector's* Widow, *Andromache*, with *Aſtyanax*,
‘ her Son by *Hector*, in the Divifion of the *Trojan*
‘ Captives, falls to the Lot of *Pyrrhus*, who flight-
‘ ing *Hermione*, (actually fent to his Court, and in
‘ his Court, waiting his good Pleafure to efpoufe
‘ her) falls in Love with *Andromache*. *Oreftes*, the
‘ Son of *Agamemnon*, in Love with *Hermione*, is
‘ fent Embaffador from the other *Greek* Princes to
‘ demand the Life of *Aſtyanax*, for fear the poor
‘ Infant fhould become another *Hector*, and avenge
‘ his Father's Death, a moft improbable, unprincely,
‘ and bafe-hearted Fear, as *Pyrrhus* himfelf repre-
‘ fents it. *Pyrrhus*, in hopes to gain the Mother's

D 5 ‘ Love,

' Love, which he feeks on honourable Terms, offers
' to break with all his Allies, rather than give up the
' Child, but finding her refolv'd on Widowhood,
' determines to facrifice the Child, and to marry
' *Hermione* This creates a fine Diftrefs in *Andro-*
' *mache*, between a laudable Purpofe to continue the
' Widow of fo great and fo deferving a Prince, and
' her Defire to preferve the Life of her Son, by that
' be'oved Hero, and at laft, overcome by maternal
' Tendernefs, fincing no o her Way, fhe refolves to
' marry *Pyrrhus*, and yet to deftroy herfelf after the
' Marriage Ceremony had intitled her Son to hei new
' Husband's Protection (A very ftrange, and not
' very *certain* Expedient to anfwer her View!) and
' fo to die the Widow of *Hector*, tho' fhe gave her
' Hand to *Pyrrhus*, and vow'd herfelf his at the Altar,
' and of Confequence had a ftill lefs Power over her
' own Life than before ----*Hermione*, a high-fpirited
' Lady, raging in her Love to *Pyrrhus*, and for the
' Slight and Difappointment fhe met with, obliges
' *Oreftes*, on Promife of giving her Heart and Hand
' to him, to murder *Pyrrhus* at the Altar, while the
' Ceremony of Marriage with *Andromache* is per-
' forming He caufes this to be done When done,
' he applies to *Hermione*, expecting her Applaufe,
' who then violently upbraids him for having obey'd
' her, and flying towards the Temple, meets the
' Body of *Pyrrhus*, and ftabs herfelf upon it

' Upon this, *Oreftes* runs mad, and it is faid to be
' the fineft mad Scene in any *Englifh* Play ----*An-*
' *dromache* remains Queen, her Son lives, and
' being diverted from her own bloody Purpofe, fhe
' has nothing to do, but to give Orders for the Fu-
' neral of *Pyrrhus*, and to bring her Son in Triumph
' from a Prifon to a Palace '

This is, in brief, the Story Now, Madam,
fince you expect it from me, I will tell you, in my
artlefs Way, what I think not quite fo pretty, and
what

what is great and beautiful in this Play, which, upon the Whole, however, I was much pleafed with, and fhould have been more, had there been lefs Terror in it, and more Probability, as I prefume to fay, in fome of its Parts, and had not the fofteft Paffion in Nature been treated as fuch a flaming Thing, as cannot be a worthy Example to Female Minds

And firft, I could not but obferve, that the Plea of the Princes of *Greece* for the Murder of *Aftyanax*, a helplefs Infant, to procure which, and for nothing elfe, they fend one of the chief Princes of *Greece* Embaffador to *Pyrrhus*, is a very poor one, and moft eafily anfwer'd ----For thus *Oreftes* fays, among other very pompous Things

*Have you fo foon forgot the mighty* Hector ?
*The* Greeks *remember his high brandifh'd Sword,*
*That fill'd their States with Widows and with Orphans,*
*For which they call for Vengeance on his Son*
*Who knows what he may one Day prove ?*——

And in another Place

Troy *may again revive, and a new* Hector
*Rife in* Aftyanax

And in another Place ·

*Sir, call to mind th' unrivall'd Strength of* Troy,
*Her Walls, her Bulwarks. and her Gates of Brafs,*
*Her Kings, her Heroes, and unbattled Armies.*

What Tragedy Pomp is this! How poor the Plea, from Princes and Heroes, when it is fo eafily anfwer'd by *Pyrrhus*, in this manner!

*I call them all to mind; and fee them all*
*Confus'd in Duft, all mix'd in one wide Ruin;*
*All but a* Child, *and he in Bondage held.*
*What Vengeance can we fear in fuch a* Troy?

And

And a little before:

*Let daſtard Souls be timorouſly wiſe ·*
*But tell them,* Pyrrhus *knows not how to form*
*Far-fanſy'd Ills, and Dangers out of Sight*

And ſtill with greater Contempt ·

——— *I thought your Kings were met*
*On more important Counſels   When I heard*
*The Name of their Embaſſador, I hop'd*
*Some glorious Enterprize was taking Birth*
*Is* Agamemnon's *Son diſpatch'd for this ?*
*And do the* Grecian *Chiefs, renown'd in War,*
*A Race of Heroes, join in cloſe Debate,*
*To plot an Infant's Death ?*———

But, what if this very *Pyrrhus*, after twenty humane
and generous Things, which the Poet makes him
ſay, ſhews, that all this right Thinking is only owing
to his Paſſion for the Mother? And as ſoon as ſhe
gives him to underſtand ſhe is reſolv'd to remain
*Hector's* Widow, he determines to give way to the
Embaſſy and Threats of the *Grecian* Princes, which
he had ſo juſtly deſpiſed, and to deſtroy the Infant.
But firſt he tells her

*'Tis true,* Hermione *was ſent to ſhare*
*My Throne and Bed*———

A fine Errand for a high-ſpirited Lady, and to
wait afterwards his good Pleaſure in his own Court,
thro' a Series of Slights and Contempts, for the Performance of his Vows ! And he generouſly, like a
true inſulting Man, boaſts

———*And would with Tranſport hear*
*The Vows which you neglect*

To which *Andromache* nobly anſwers.

———*She has no* Troy,
No Hector, *to lament ·  She has not loſt*
*A Husband by your Conqueſts ·  Such a Husband,*
*Torn with Thought !  whoſe Death alone has made*
*Your Sire immortal !*———                 This

This enrages the Hero; and what he fhould have admir'd her for, had his Soul been half as noble as hers, he thus refents:

*I've been too tame ; I will awake to Vengeance!*
*The Son fhall anfwer for his Mother's Scorn.*
*The Greeks demand him · Nor will I indanger*
*My Realms, to pleafure an ungrateful Woman.*

Accordingly he refolves to-facrifice the Child; to do Juftice to Hermione, out of Spite to Andromache: And, moft ungeneroufly, knowing Oreftes loves Hermione to Diftraction, tells him, he fhall grace his Nuptial Rites, and he will receive Hermione from his Hands.

But now again, fee what fucceeds to this · One Look of Favour from Andromache reverfes all his new Refolves, makes him throw new Indignities on Hermione, new Contempts upon the Greek Princes, and fhew, that if he acts right in one Point, the faving of the Child, it is from wrong and unjuftifiable Motives , and yet the Poet feems to defign him an amiable Character.

Now, Madam, could not a Diftrefs have been formed in this Story from more laudable and proper Motives ? Should this Paffion of unbridled Love be reprefented in fuch a ftrong, fuch an irrefiftible Light, to an Audience, who muft be taught, that the higheft Ingratitude, the moft rageful Extreme of fenfual Paffion, the moft unjuftifiable Actions, and the Sacrifice of all Confiderations of publick Good, and private Right, had Examples all in this Piece to warrant them ?

'Tis true, Pyrrhus is punifh'd by a cruel Affaffination—Hermione falls by her own Hand for caufing Oreftes to procure him to be murdered, and the Phrenfy of Oreftes becomes his Punifhment : But what a Scene of Terror does all this raife ? How unlikely to be an Exemplar either to publick or private

vate Life? And what a hard Fate is that of *Hermione*, slighted, despised, insulted, by the Man she lov'd, to whom she was betrothed, and whose Resentment therefore was warranted, had it shewn itself in almost any Act short of the Murder, which, in the Violence of her Passion, she commanded *Orestes* to perperrate?

Then, Madam, the Love of *Hermione* for *Pyrrhus* is not, I think, of that delicate Sort which ought to be set before our Sex for an Example ----'Tis Rage, not Love, that of a Woman slighted, and, however just, supposing our Sex to have such revengeful Hearts, when slighted by the Man they love, is not so exemplary as one would wish: And besides, she is represented as sometimes *sighing and wishing for* Orestes, when a true Love bears not the Thought of any Object, but that one it sighs for, even should that one be ungrateful　Thus it is said of *Orestes* by her Confidante

Orestes, *whose Return you oft had wish'd,*
*The Man whose Suff'rings you so oft lamented,*
*And often prais'd his Constancy and Love*

Then *Hermione* repeats her Woman's Words :

*That Love, that Constancy, so ill requited----*
Upbraids *me to myself　I blush, to think*
*How I have us'd him, and would shun his Presence*

The Motive for this, however, is neither Justice nor Generosity, but Pride, indeed, it must be own'd, a Pride very natural to a Female Mind, in such Circumstances as hers :

*What will be my Confusion, when he sees me*
*Neglected and forsaken, like himself?*
'. Her *Insolence at last is well repaid!*"
*I cannot bear the Thought*

And then, the Moment she sees him,---this is her blunt Question to him, notwithstanding all her Shame to see him.

*How am I to interpret, Sir, this Visit?*
*Is it a Compliment of Form, or Love?*

Does this, Madam, shew any thing of the Delicacy of Sex or Condition?— And would one think it right, after she has thus extorted from him a repeated Confession of his Love, or *Weakness*, as he calls it, to upbraid him, that it ill becomes the Embassador of *Greece*, *to talk of Love or Dying?*

In short, Madam, I think none of the Love in this Piece is such a Love, however suited to *Hermione*'s Character and Circumstances, as is fit to be recommended to our Example 'Tis a Love that shocks one, and is rather Rage and Tumult than Love, and succeeds accordingly So that of *Pyrrhus* is ungovern'd, wild, unjust, ungenerous Caprice *Hermione*'s is founded in confess'd Ingratitude to *Orestes*, and she perseveres in it to *Pyrrhus*, when the Indignities put upon her should have made her sooner wish for Death, than for so perjur'd a Man, and yet, I think, she shews an inconsistent Tenderness for *Orestes*, (as I have hinted) while her Passion for *Pyrrhus* flames out with so much Violence.

The Motive of *Andromache*, (for hers is the most perfect Character in the Piece, and designed to be so by the Poet) to save her Son, is the best a Woman could have to excuse her for marrying the Man who had slaughter'd all her Relations But the Uncertainty of securing that Point, by the mere Formality of joining Hands with *Pyrrhus*, and her Resolution to destroy herself, in Defiance of her Vows just plighted to be his, was a strange Expedient to preserve her Widowhood, and her Child For was it very likely, that a Man so wildly in Love with her, as to forego all other just and prudent Considerations for her, (and who had shewn, that he would have destroy'd her Son, but for the sake of *her* Person) would, when disappointed by so great a Rashness, have hazarded his Realms in Defence of her Son?

But

But of all Things, commend me to the noble Regard for *Self*, in her Woman and Confidante *Cephifa*, to whom *Andromache* communicates her rafh Purpofe, injoining her a willing Secrecy, the only way the Poet had to let us know it, fince it was not put in Execution, for fhe fhews that Regard to her dear Self, in this tragick Performance, which, in a Comedy, would have raifed a Laugh, no doubt, as a Satire on Ladies Women:

*Alas! I fear,--I--never fhall outlive you!*

Thefe Things ftruck me, Madam, when I faw the Play, and when I came to read it, I was more confirm'd in my Sentiments   But now I will tranfcribe fome Paffages, which pleafed me much.

The Storms, and Doubts, and Uncertainty of wild ungovern'd Love, are very naturally, I humbly think, painted in feveral Scenes of this Play, in the Characters of *Hermione* and *Pyrrhus*, and no-where more affectingly than in the Upbraidings of *Hermione* to *Oreftes*, after fhe found her bloody Purpofes too weil comply'd with.   Thus.

*What, if tranfported by my boundlefs Paffion,*
*I could not bear to fee him wed another?*
*Were you t' obey a jealous Woman's Phrenfy?*
*You fhould have div'd into my inmoft Thoughts*
*My Heart, tho' full of Rage, was free from Malice;*
*And all my Anger was Excefs of Love*
*Why did you take me at my Word? You faw*
*The Struggles of my Soul, you heard me rave.*
*You fhould have queftion'd me a thoufand times;*
*Yet ftill have doubted, ftill have queftion'd on,*
*Before you ventur'd on a Life fo precious.*
*Why did you not return? Why not confult me*
*A fecond time? And, undetermin'd ftill,*
*Again return, and ftill find new Delays?*

The

The Scene between *Andromache* and *Hermione,* when the former fuppofes the latter on the Point of marrying *Pyrrhus,* and befpeaks her Intereft for her Son's Life, affected me much, and was nobly acted by Mrs *Oldfield,* who, after affuring her, that her Love to her flain Lord, was the only Love fhe could ever indulge, as *Hermione* flies her, cries——

*Ah ! Madam, whither, whither do you fly ?*
*Where can your Eyes behold a Sight more pleafing*
*Than* Hector's *Widow, fuppliant, and in Tears ?*
*I come not an alarm'd, a jealous Foe,*
*To envy you the Heart your Charms have won.——*
*But oh ! I have a Son:——And you, one Day,*
*Will be no Stranger to a Mother's Fondnefs.*

Was not this, Madam, a moving and interefting Plea? And is not what follows affectingly noble?

*But Heav'n forbid, that you fhould-ever know*
*A* Mother's *Sorrow for an* only *Son,*
*Her Joy ! her Blifs ! her laft furviving Comfort !*
*When ev'ry Hour fhe trembles for his Life.*
*Your Pow'r o'er* Pyrrhus *may relieve my Fears.*
*Alas ! what Danger is there in a Child,*
*Sav'd from the Wreck of a whole ruin'd Empire ?*
*Let me go hide him in a defart Ifle.*
*You may rely upon my tender Care*
*To keep him far from Perils of Ambition ·*
*All he can learn of me, will be to weep.*

This is fweetly moving, nobly pathetick. But I am angry at the Poet, if he could have help'd it, for drawing in *Hermione* fuch an ungenerous and unprincely Infult upon the Royal Mourner, when in the Height of her own Profperity, as fhe imagin'd, and her Rival fubjected beneath her Feet —Fie upon him, thus to make her fay, like a true Woman, as our Cenfurers will reflect !

*Madam,,*

*Madam, if* Pyrrhus *must be wrought to Pity,*
*No Woman does it better than yourself.*
*If you gain him, I shall comply of course.*

This from one Woman to another, much more
from one Princess to another, from the Elated to
the Captive, could not be said, surely ---Nor do I
see there was any need of it For had the Poet made
*Hermione* on this Occasion (her own Empire secured,
as she thought) give a more generous and humane
Answer, would it not have heighten'd the Distress,
when such a Character should sink, as she had been
basely injur'd by the Man she lov'd, and whose
Crime was owing to the Rage of slighted Love?
Why should he chuse to make *Andromache's* Part
thus nobly moving, at the Expence of the other
Character, in a Point, where Justice, Generosity,
and Humanity, were so much concern'd? And
would not a fine Instruction have lain here for the
Audience, to have had Compassion for the Distresses
of another, and so much the more, as that other was
a Rival sunk at the Feet of the Prosperous?---Indeed
*Hermione*, which by the way Mrs *Porter* acted
incomparably, is a Character full of Rage and Violence, of Jealousy, and great Cause she had for it
But what then? Could she not, a Princess as she
was, when her own Love was secured, for so she
thought, have been made capable of feeling a Distress
so nobly pleaded, by Motives so becoming a Mother's
Lips, and a basest Virgin's Prospects?--- But I am
upon the Author's Beauties

*Andromache's* Plea to *Pyrrhus*, when, thus insulted
by *Hermione*, she sees no Hope of any way to preserve her Son, but by soothing the proud Heart of
the Prince, whom her Refusal had incensed, is very
sweet in the Mouth of Captive Royalty

　　　　　*---Oh, Sir, excuse*
*The Pride of Royal Blood, that checks my Soul,*

　　　　　　　　　　　　　　　　　　　*And*

*And knows not how to be importunate.*
*You know, alas! I was not born to kneel,*
*To sue for Pity, and to own a Master.*

And afterwards:

*Behold, how low you have reduc'd a Queen!*
*These Eyes have seen my Country laid in Ashes;*
*My Kindred fall in War; my Father slain;*
*My Husband dragg'd in his own Blood, my Son*
*Condemn'd to Bondage; and myself a Slave*
*Yet, in the midst of these unheard-of Woes,*
*'Twas some Relief to find myself your Captive;*
*And that my Son, deriv'd from antient Kings,*
*Since he must serve, had Pyrrhus for his Master.*
*When Priam kneel'd, the great Achilles wept;*
*I hop'd I should not find his Son less noble*
*I thought the Brave were still the most compassionate.*
*O do not, Sir, divide me from my Child,*
*If he must die——*

Then there is a fine Scene recollected by *Andromache* to her Woman, between *Hector* and herself, on the Morning he set out for the Action in which he was slain

*That Morn, Cephisa! that ill fated Morn!*
*My Husband bid thee bring Astyanax*
*He took him in his Arms; and, as I wept,*
*My Wife, my dear Andromache, said he,*
*(Heaving with stifled Sighs, to see me weep)*

Finely said, and the Hero all preserv'd! He sigh'd, not for Fear of the Foe, but to see his beloved Lady weep!—From that Humanity, which should always be inseparable, I think, whether in Fiction or Fact, from true Heroism And that other Inseparable, Piety; as follows·

*What Fortune may attend my Arms, the Gods*
*Alone can tell To thee I give the Boy,*

*Preserve him as the Token of our Loves.*
*If I should fall, let him not miss his Sire,*
*While thou surviv'st, but, by thy tender Care,*
*Let the Son see, that thou didst love his Father*

And the Advice, left by *Andromache* with *Cephisa*, for her Son, when she resolves to kill herself, after the Nuptial Ceremony is perform'd, is very worthy, after a Scene of passionate Fondness well express'd:

*————— Let him know,*
*I dy'd to save him———And would die again ——*
*Season his Mind with early Hints of Glory ·*
*Make him acquainted with his Ancestors,*
*Trace out their shining Story in his Thoughts:*
*Dwell on th' Exploits of his immortal Father;*
*And sometimes———*

Very pretty

*————let him hear his Mother's Name:*
*Let him reflect upon his Royal Birth*
*With modest Pride    Pyrrhus will prove a Friend:*
*But let him know, he has a Conqu'ror's Right.*
*He must be taught to stifle his Resentments,*
*And sacrifice his Vengeance to his Safety.*

And to his *Gratitude* too, Madam, should it not have been said, when he was so generously protected against the Demand and Menaces of confederate Kings?

*Should he prove headstrong, rash, or unadvis'd,*
*He then would frustrate all his Mother's Virtue,*
*Provoke his Fate; and I shall die in vain!*

Very nobly said! But I cannot forbear making one Observation on Occasion of Self-murder, which, however the Poets may be justify'd by the Examples of the *Greeks* and *Romans*, when they draw their Stories from them, yet, in such a gloomy, saturnine

Nation

Nation as ours, where Self-murders are more frequent, than in all the Chriſtian World beſides, methinks all thoſe Stories ſhould be avoided, for publick Entertainment: Or, where there is a Neceſſity, as in the Play of *Cato,* for Inſtance, to introduce ſuch a wicked Practice, the bad Example ſhould be obviated, and the Poiſon it may adminiſter, antidoted by more forcible Leſſons than what theſe few doubtful Words expreſs:

*I fear I've been too haſty!*——

So, in this Tragedy I am ſpeaking of, when *Hermione* deſtroys herſelf, and *Andromache* deſigns to do the like, ſhould the *Engliſh* Poet have left this Practice unguarded or unaccompany'd by proper Leſſons and Cenſures in ſuch a Country as ours?

The ſtaggering Doubts and Diſtreſs of *Hermione,* after ſhe had engaged *Oreſtes* in the Murder of *Pyrrhus,* between her Love and her Reſentment, her Queſtions to her Woman, whether, as he approach'd the Temple to marry her Rival, in Breach of his Vows of Betrothment to her, his Countenance ſhewed not ſome Tokens of Remorſe, are very natural to one in her amorous Circumſtance, I fanſy:

*But, ſay,* Cleone, *didſt thou mark him well?*
*Was his Brow ſmooth? Say, did there not appear*
*Some Shade of Grief? Some little Cloud of Sorrow?*
*Did he not ſtop? Did he not once look back?*
*Didſt thou approach him? Was he not confounded?*
*Did he not——Oh! be quick, and tell me all.*

This, Madam, I think, is charmingly natural. And on *Cleone*'s Anſwer, That he went to the Temple all Joy and Tranſport, unguarded, and all his Cares imploy'd to gratify *Andromache* in her Son's Safety, it is the leſs to be wonder'd at, that ſhe ſhould be quite exaſperated, and forgetting all her Love for the ingrateful Prince, ſhould ſay:

*Enough!*

*Enough! he dies!—the Traitor!—Where's* Oreſtes?

There are ſeveral Circumſtances of Horror in this Play, that made me ſhudder, but I think none like the Deſcription the Poet puts into the Mouth of *Pylades*, the inſeparable Friend of *Oreſtes*, who, far from avoiding to ſhock the Soul of his Friend, by gently inſinuating the Fate of that *Hermione*, on whom he had fixed his Happineſs, thus terribly, with all the Aggravations that could attend ſuch a Tragedy, points out the horrid Action, taking care even to make her as impious in her Reproaches of the Deity for her own Raſhneſs, as ſhe was in the Violence by which ſhe dies, and ſo leaving a dreadful Example, (which I preſume was not needful to be left) of final Impenitence, eſpecially in a ſuffering Character, that had not merited the Evils ſhe met with.

Thus it is decrib'd; and I am affected with the Tranſcription of a Paſſage, which the Poet has labour'd more than he ought, I think, to ſhew the Force of his deſcriptive Vein.

*Full of Diſorder, Wildneſs in her Looks,*
*With Hands expanded and diſhevell'd Hair,*
*Breathleſs and pale, with Shrieks ſhe ſought the Temple.*
*In the Mid-way ſhe met the Corps of* Pyrrhus.
*She ſtartled at the Sight. Then, ſtiff with Horror,*
*Gaz'd frightful! Waken'd from the dire Amaze,*
*She rais'd her Eyes to Heav'n, with ſuch a Look,*
*As ſpoke her Sorrows, and* reproach'd *the Gods.*
*Then plung'd a Poniard deep within her Breaſt,*
*And fell on* Pyrrhus, *graſping him in Death.*

This, from a Friend, to a Lover of the miſerable *Hermione*, tho' the Poet might think it the only Way he had left to make *Oreſtes* run quite diſtracted, yet was not, I preſume to ſay, very judiciouſly put into the Mouth of a beloved Friend anxious for his Safety,

and

and to get him off, after the Murder; and whofe Part, till now, had been rather that of foothing, like a true Friend, the Sorrows of his Mind.

The Moral of the whole only regards *Andromache*; nor is there, indeed, any thing but Violence and Terror in the reft of the Story and Characters, as if the Poet was determin'd to fink all into one, and make that great, at the Expence of the reft 'Tis, however, in my humble Opinion, a good one, to fhew, that Perfons in Diftrefs ought never to defpond, be their Afflictions what they *will*, and ought to have weigh'd with *Andromache* herfelf, to make her avoid the Crime of Suicide, which fhe had refolved upon, fince this Moral is put into her Mouth; but fo late, that it feems rather to make her good by an Event fhe could not forefee, than by the Prudence of her Reflections, which would not, without that Event, have prevented her from a rafh Action, that muft have render'd the Moral ineffectual.

*Tho' plung'd in Ills, and exercis'd in Care,*
*Yet never let the noble Mind defpair.*
*Where prefs'd by Dangers, and befet with Foes,*
*The Gods their timely Succour interpofe,*
*And when our Virtue finks, o'erwhelm'd with Grief,*
*By unforefeen Expedients bring Relief*

Now, Madam, good as this Moral is, I fhould rather, in Generofity, have had it recommended from any Mouth than that of *Andromache* For what is the Confolation fhe receives? What are the Expedients fhe fo much rejoices in? Why, in the firft place, the Murder of a Prince who lov'd her more than his own Glory, and to whom fhe had juft given her Faith, as a fecond Hufband, tho' forced to it, from a laudable Motive. And next, The Self-murder of *Hermone*, the Diftraction of *Oreftes*, and the Profpect of fucceeding with her Son to the Throne of the murder'd Prince, from which, however,

ever, she could not expect but to be driven, and her Son at last to be destroy'd, by those vengeful Confederates, who had joined, by a solemn Embassy, to demand his Life, and who now, by his Elevation, had stronger Reasons to apprehend Danger from him, and less Difficulty to effect his Ruin, since *Pyrrhus* was no more

But, judge, my dear Lady, what, after the Play was over, I must think of the Epilogue, and indeed of that Part of the Audience, which called out for it

An Epilogue spoken by Mrs *Oldfield* in the Character of *Andromache*, that was more shocking to me, than the most terrible Parts of the Play, as by lewd, and even senseless *Double-entendre*, it could be calculated only to efface all the tender, all the virtuous Sentiments, which the Tragedy was design'd to raise

The Pleasure this was receiv'd with by the Men, was equa'ly barbarous and insulting, every one turning himself to the Boxes, Pit, and Galleries, where Ladies were, to see how they look'd, and how they stood an emphatical and too-well pronounc'd Ridicule, not only upon the Play in general, but upon the Part of *Andromache* in particular, which had been so well sustain'd by an excellent Actress, and I was extremely mortify'd to see my favourite (and the only perfect) Character, debas'd and despoil'd, and the Widow of *Hector* Prince of *Troy*, talking Nastiness to an Audience, and setting it out with all the wicked Graces of Action, and affected Archness of Look, Atitude, and Emphasis

I stood up—Dear Sir!—Dear Miss!—said I

What's the matter, my Love? said Mr *B* smileing, who expected, as he told me afterwards, to see me mov'd by this vile Epilogue—for it is always call'd for, it seems

Why have I wept the Distresses of the injur'd *Hermione*? whisper'd I. Why have I been mov'd by

4

by the Murder of the brave *Pyrrhus*, and shock'd by
the Madness of *Oreftes* ? Is it for this ? See you not
*Hector's* Widow, the noble *Andromache*, inverting
the Design of the whole Play, satirizing her own Sex,
but indeed most of all ridiculing and shaming, in
*my* Mind, that Part of the Audience, who have call'd
for this vile Epilogue, and those who can be delighted
with it, after such Scenes of Horror and Distress ?

He was pleas'd to say, smiling, I expected, my
Dear, that your Delicacy, and Miss's too, would be
shock'd on this preposterous Occasion. I never saw
this Play, Rake as I was, but the Impropriety of the
Epilogue sent me away dissatisfy'd with it, and with
human Nature too: And you only see, by this one
Instance, what a Character that of an Actor or
Actress is, and how capable they are to personate
any thing for a sorry Subsistence.

Well, but, Sir, said I, are there not, think you,
extravagant Scenes and Characters enough in most
Plays, to justify the Censures of the Virtuous upon
them, that the wicked Friend of the Author must
crown the Work in an Epilogue, for fear the Audience should go away improv'd by the Representa-
tion? It is not, I see, always Narrowness of Spirit,
as I have heard some say, that opens the Mouths of
good People against these Diversions

In this wild way, talk'd I; for I was quite out of
Patience at this unnatural and unexpected Piece of
Ridicule, tack'd to so serious a Play, and coming
after such a Moral

Here is a Specimen, my dear Lady, of my Observations on the first Play I saw How just, or
how impertinent, I must leave to your better Judgment I very probably expose my own Ignorance
and Folly in them , but I will not say, Presumption,
because you have put me upon the Task, which
otherwise I should hardly have attempted I have
very little Reason therefore to blame myself on this

score; but, on the contrary, (if I can escape your Ladyship's Censure) have Cause to pride myself in the Opportunity you have thereby given me to shew my Readiness to obey you, and the rather, since I am sure of your kindest Indulgence, now you have given me Leave to style myself

> *Your Ladyship's obliged Sister,*
> *and humble Servant,*

P. B

---

# LETTER XII.

*My dear Lady,*

I GAVE you in my last, my bold Remarks upon a TRAGEDY---*The Distress'd Mother* I will now give you my shallow Notions of a COMEDY---*The Tender Husband*

I lik'd this Part of the Title; tho' I can't say I was pleas'd at all with the other, explanatory of it, Or,---*The Accomplish'd Fools* But when I was told it was written by Sir *Richard Steele,* and that Mr *Addison* had given some Hints towards it, if not some Characters, O dear Sir, said I, give us your Company to this Play, for the Authors of the *Spectators* cannot possibly produce a faulty Scene.

Mr B indeed smil'd, for I had not then read the Play And the Earl of *F* his Countess, Miss *Darnford,* Mr *B* and myself, agreed to meet with a Niece of my Lord's in the Stage Box, which was taken on purpose

There seems to me, my dear Lady, to be a great deal of Wit and Satire in the Play But, upon my Word, I was grievously disappointed as to the Morality of it Nor, in some Places, is *Probability* preserved, and there are divers Speeches so very free, that I could not have expected to meet with such, from the Names I mention'd.

I should

I fhould be afraid of being cenfur'd for my Prefumption, were I to write to any body lefs indulgent
to me, than your Ladyfhip. But I will make no
Apologies to you, Madam —Let me fee, then, can
I give you the brief Hiftory of this Comedy, as I
did of the Tragedy?—I profefs I hardly know, whether I can or not, at leaft, whether I fhould or not.
—But I'll try.

The Tender Husband, MR. CLERIMONT, has
for his Wife a Lady who has travelled, and is far
gone in all the *French* Fafhions ' She brought me,'
fays he, ' a noble Fortune ; and I thought, fhe had
' a Right to fhare it ; therefore carry'd her to fee
' the World, forfooth, and make the Tour of *France*
' and *Italy*, where fhe learn'd to lofe her Money
' gracefully, to admire every Vanity in *our* Sex, and
' contemn every Virtue in *her own*, which, with
' Ten thoufand other Perfections, are the ordinary
' Improvements of a travell'd Lady.'

Tender as the Husband was to be fuppos'd to the
Wife, which, by the way, is not extremely apparent,
in *proper* or *right* Inftances of Tendernefs, I prefume to think, he fhews no great Politenefs to the
Sex in general in this Speech, and the Poet will be
the lefs excufable for it, if he has not drawn a general
Character of travell'd Ladies ; and much lefs ftill, if
it fhall appear, that that of Mrs *Clerimont*, on which
this general Reflection is founded, is carry'd beyond
Nature, and Probability too

But what is the Method the Tender Husband takes
to reclaim the Lady ?—Why this. He fets a former
Miftrefs of his own to work, in Man's Cloaths, to
infnare her And thus he declares himfelf---' Now I
' can neither mortify her Vanity, that I may live at
' Eafe with her, nor quite *difcaid* her, till I have
' catch'd her a little inlarging her innocent Free-
' doms, as fhe calls them. For this End I am con-
' tent to be a *French* Husband, tho', now-and-hen,

' with

' with the fecret Pangs of an *Italian* one; and
' therefore, Sir, or Madam,' (to his Miftrefs Lucy,
under the Name of Mr Fainlove, in the Drefs
of a young Coxcomb) ' you are thus equipp'd to
'attend and accoft her Ladyfhip.' A Speech unneceffary to *Fainlove*, who was drefs'd before for that
Purpofe, and had actually won Money, in that Character, of Mrs *Clerimont*. But the Poet had no
other way to let the Audience know it, as it fhould
feem—' It concerns you,' continues he, ' to be dili-
' gent. If we (*i e* Himfelf and his Lady) wholly
' part—I need fay *no more*: If we do *not*— I'll fee
' thee *well provided* for '

Here's a fine moral Scene open'd, my Lady, with
regard to Mr *Clerimont*, his Lady, and his kept
Miftrefs! Mr. *Fainlove*, alias Mrs *Lucy*, undertakes
the Task, in Hopes to live with Mr *Clerimont*, in
cafe of a Divorce from his Wife, or to be provided
for, in cafe the Plot does not fucceed. Which
makes it apparent, that, to fay nothing of his Morality, poor *Lucy* had not met with a generous Man
in Mr *Clerimont*, fince, after the Forfeiture of her
Honour, fhe was ftill to do a more infamous Jobb,
if poffible, to procure for herfelf a Provifion from
him

Then Mr. *Clerimont* proceeds to inftruct the new-
made Man, how to behave like a Coxcomb, in
order to engage his Lady's Attention, and to join in
all her Foibles, till fhe can furnifh him with an Op
portunity to detect them in fuch a way, as fhall give
a Pretence for a Divorce (a Hint that has been
fcandaloufly improved, and made *more* fafhionable,
fince this Play was written), and this he does in fuch
free Language and Action, as muft difguft any modeft
Perfon of either Sex

Then the Poet caufes this faithful Miftrefs, in order
to make her Character fhine above that of the Wife,
and indeed above his own likewife, to prefent her
Imployer

Imployer with Bills for 500 *l* which she tells him she won of his Wife the preceding Night, and makes up 2000 *l* which Mr *Clerimont* says, this unprovided-for Miftrefs of his has won from his Lady, and honeftly given him; or elfe he could not, he owns, have fupply'd her Gaming Loffes And *Lucy* declares, she will gain him for ever from his Lady, if she can · Yet, you'll fee, by-and-by, that it is not Love to his particular Perfon, more than *any* other, that is *Lucy's* Inducement· Of courfe then, it muft be Wickednefs for Wickednefs fake!

The next Character is CAPTAIN CLERIMONT, Brother to the other Gentleman, a Man of Fafhion and of the World, who being a younger Brother, has his Fortune to make; and we shall fee prefently, how he propofes to make it.

The next is POUNCE, an infamous Jobber or Broker of Stocks, Marriages, or any thing—whofe Character be pleas'd to take in his own Words. ' Now 'tis my Profeffion to affift a *free-hearted* ' young Fellow againft an *unnatural long-liv'd* Father ' —to difincumber Men of Pleafure of the Vexation ' of unwieldy Eftates; to fupport a feeble Title to ' an Inheritance!'— One that Mr *Clerimont* fays, by way of *Praife*, he has feen prompting a ftammering Witnefs in *Weftminfter-hall*, that wanted Inftruction, and could venture his Ears with great Bravery for his Friend

A worfe Character than this, can there be? Yet is it not produced to be punifhed, neither.

The next Perfon introduc'd is HEZEKIAH TIPKIN, a Banker in *Lombard-ftreet*, a Man of an infamous and fordid Character, and a vile Ufurer. Who has a beautiful Niece, Mifs BRIDGET TIPKIN, over-run with Affectation and Romance, with a great Fortune in Money, which fo attracts the Captain, that he fuppofes, in a fordid, but witty manner enough, all imaginable Perfections in her Perfon, before he has

E 3      a Sight

a Sight of it This young Lady, by a Treaty between her Uncle *Tipkin* and Sir HARRY GUBBIN,
a tyrannical, positive, hot-headed Country Gentleman, is design'd to be marry'd to HUMPHREY the
Son of Sir *Harry*, a Creature so savage, so rough,
and so stupid, that there cannot be drawn a stronger
Contraste between his Character and that of Miss
*Bridget's*

Mr *Pounce*, who is imploy'd as a Broker in *their*
Match, is, for a Reward of 1000 *l* to cheat them
and poor *Humphrey*, and to procure this young Lady
for Captain *Clermont* Admirable Justice and Morality all round! you say, my Lady —For this Purpose it was necessary, that Mr *Pounce* should find
Mr *Humphrey* so great a Fool, that, tho' he never
saw him before, he very easily sets him against his
Father, and against his Cousin *Bridget*, and all this
on the Wedding-day, in order to induce him to make
Court to a Person he tells him of, but never saw:
And who should this Person be, as he tells him, but
the Sister of *Fainlove*, *Clermont's* Man-dress'd Mistress, which Sister, however, was to be *Fainlove*,
or *Lucy* herself, with a worthy Intent to impose upon
poor *Humphrey*, as a Wife, this cast-off Mistress
of *Clermont*? A just, a generous, an exemplary
Plot this!

The next Character is an old Maiden Gentlewoman, AUNT to Miss *Bridget*, an antiquated Virgin,
who, as *Pounce* says, has a mighty Affectation for
Youth, and is a great Lover of Men and Money—
and she is set over her Niece as a Promoter of the
Match with *Humphrey*—Over this Lady Mr *Pounce*
has a great Ascendant, half for sordid Reasons, and
half for amorous ones, and she makes a thorough
ridiculous and improbable Character. *Pounce* intro-
duces Captain *Clermont* into the Company of th i
Aunt and her Niece, and entertains the former,
while the Captain engages the latter on the Subject of
her

her beloved Romance. Thefe, with Mrs *Clermont's* Maid JENNY, are the principal Characters.

I need not, my Lady, take up much of your Time, or my own, to tell you how they proceed.

Mr. *Clermont,* then, after bearing from his Wife, what hardly any Gentleman could bear, furprifes *Fainlove* as a Man (and a very wicked Scene it is, in every Part) taking fhocking Freedoms with her. And falling into a feigned Rage, threatens to kill *Fainlove* The Lady at firft menaces, and is haughty and arrogant; but finding by her Husband's Behaviour to *Lucy,* whom he then addreffes with Fondnefs before her Face, that fhe is trick'd by a Woman in Man's Habit, in her Turn would kill the Impoftor as *Lucy,* whom as *Fainlove* fhe try'd to fave, and a Scene on this Occafion occurs, to my thinking, very ridiculous Mr *Clermont* then upbraids her with her Guilt, and, what was hardly ever known in Nature, fhe reforms *inftantly* on the Spot, and expreffes all the Signs of Contrition imaginable He forgives and receives her, guilty as fhe is in her Intention, her Perfon only untainted, and an Adultrefs in her Mind, as fhe would have been in Fact, had *Fainlove* been a Man · And a moving Scene, had it been from proper Motives, follows *Yet,* (ftill more prepofterous, excufe me, Madam) afterwards fhe refumes all her travell'd and nonfenfical Airs, all her improbable Follies, to help to fupport the Plot in favour of Captain *Clermont* upon Mifs *Bridget,* and the infamous one of *Pounce's* and Mr *Clermont's* againft poor *Humphry,* the only *innocent* Character in the Play, and the only *fuffering* one; and this latter, as well as the former Plot, being brought about, a laughing Scene is produced, by Sir *Harry's* foundly cudgelling his ftupid Son, for permitting himfelf to be fo foolifhly drawn in.

Now, my good Lady, can you fee one Character, and, I think, I have given them juftly, fit to be fet

E 4 up

up for an Example in this celebrated Play of an Author so celebrated? I must own, as I said before, I was greatly disappointed in my Expectations of it There is, indeed, a great deal of sprightly Wit, and Knowlege of the wicked Part of the World, display'd in it, as it seems to me, by what I have heard Mr *B* talk sometimes, but there is not one Character in it, but what is shockingly immoral, and, at the same time, either *above* or *below* Nature; so that the Ridicule which is intended in it, on the bad Characters, cannot, in my poor Opinion, be just or efficacious.

For, first, there never, I believe, could be a Gentleman, so foolishly tender, yet so plottingly cruel, to his Lady, as Mr *Clerimont*

There never could be such a very fantastical Lady, as Mrs *Clerimont* ----And there is such an Improbability in the intimate Access, which *Lucy* in Man's Cloaths has to her, in that Creature's lewd Views, yet faithful and generous Conduct in giving back to *Clerimont*, who had not provided for her, 2000 *l* won of the fantastical Lady, and yet in her being so little delicate in her *Love* to *Clerimont*, which one would expect should be her Motive, as to join to trick and marry one of the greatest Fools in the World, that it was surprising to me, that it could pass on her Author or Audience.

Then *Tipkin*'s Character is unnaturally, stupidly, yet knavishly bad

S. *Harry Gubbin* is a Father, who never could have his Fellow, and after furiously beating his Son, is reconciled to his Marriage, as instantly as Mrs *Clerimont* is converted, and that to an unknown Person, who appears to *him* in Man's Cloaths, for the sake of 3000 *l*. Fortune only, altho' he had been quarrelling with *Tipkin*, about 1000 *l*. which he would not give up, out of 10,000 *l*. which his Son was to have had with *Bridget*.

*Numps*,

*Numps*, his Son, is a Character, take it all together, quite out of Nature and Probability. 'Tis hardly
possible, that a Savage, brought up in a Wood, who
never convers'd with Man or Woman, could be so
stupid, and easily might a Poet form a Plot for a
Play, if such a Character could be admitted, as
*Numps's*

The Aunt is credulous and affected beyond Probability also.

Miss *Bridget* delicately indelicate in many Places,
and improbably fantastick in all

*Pounce* shamelesly glorying, and *succeeding* in his
Villainy, and deeming the Imputation of the worst
of Rogueries to him, as a Panegyrick And such Im-
moralities, mingled with Obscenities, all thro', that I
was glad when the Play was over.

But yet, to say Truth, there are very pretty Descriptions, and a great deal of Wit and Humour in
it. The Dialogue is lively; the Painter's Scene
entertaining; and that between Sir *Harry* and *Tipkin*,
diverting, tho' low; which, together with the fantastick Airs of Mrs *Clerimont*, and Miss *Bridget*, and
the farcical Humours of *Numps*, make it the less
Wonder, that such as did not attend to Nature, Probability, and Morality, were struck with the Life
and Spirit of the Performance. And especially as
Mr *Wilks*, who acted Captain *Clerimont*, and Mrs.
*Oldfield*, who acted Miss *Bridget*, so incomparably
perform'd their Parts, as must have saved a Play even
of a worse Tendency than the *Accomplish'd Fools*

The Moral I will transcribe, altho', I doubt, it is a
very inapplicable one to the Characters; and so is
far from making Amends for a long Performance,
that in such a Variety of Characters has not *one* moral one in it, nor, indeed, is there so much as one just
or generous Design pursued throughout the Play.

*You've seen th' Extremes of the domestick Life,*
*A Son too much confin'd——too free a Wife*
*By gen'rous Bonds you either should restrain,*
*And only on their Inclinations gain*

This I call inapplicable, because it was needless
Advice to such Husbands as Mr *Clermont*, for whom
it seems design'd, for he was generous to Excess,
carrying her abroad to *Italy* and *France*, and paying
all her Debts of Honour implicitly  Whence the
Name of the Play, *The Tender Husband*

*Wives, to obey, must* LOVE——

*Clermont* did every thing to make a grateful Woman
love him, before his strange Plot to reclaim her.

——— *Children* REVERE,
*While only* SLAVES *are govern'd by their Fear.*

Mrs *Clermont* was not treated like a *Slave*, yet is
reclaim'd only by *Fear*  So that the Moral seems to
be calculated for the *Numps*'s (the Fools and Idiots)
and the *Sir Harries*, two Characters, that, as I humbly apprehend, never were in Nature, any more, it
is to be hoped, than are the rest

It looks to me, in short, as if the Author had forgot the Moral all the way, and being put in mind
of it by some kind Friend, (Mr *Addison*, perhaps)
was at a Loss to draw one from such Characters and
Plots as he had produc'd; and so put down what
came uppermost, for the sake of Custom, without
much regard to Propriety  And truly, I should
imagine likewise, that the Play was begun with a
Design to draw more amiable Characters, answer-
able to the Title of *The Tender Husband*, but that
the Author being carried away by the Luxuriancy of
a Genius, which he had not the Heart to prune, on
a general Survey of the Whole, distrusting the Propriety of that Title, added the under-one. With
an——OR, *The Accomplish'd Fools*, in Justice to his
Piece,

Piece, and Compliment to his Audience. And, pardon me, Madam, had he called it *The Accomplish'd Knaves*, I would not have been angry at him, becaufe there would have been more Propriety in the Title

I wifh I could, for the fake of the Authors, have praifed every Scene of this Play I hoped to have Reafon for it. Judge then, my dear Lady, what a Moftification it was to me, not to be able to fay I liked above one, the *Painter's Scene*, which too was out of Time, being on the Wedding-day, and am forc'd to difapprove of every Character in it, and the Views of every one. I am, deareft Madam,

*Your moft obliged Sifter, and Servant,*

P B.

## LETTER XIII.

*My dear Lady,*

ALTHO' I cannot tell how you receiv'd my Obfervations on the Tragedy of *The Diftrefs'd Mother*, and the Comedy of *The Tender Husband*, yet will I proceed to give your Ladyfhip my Opinion of the Opera I was at laft Night

But what can I fay, when I have mention'd what you fo well know, the fine Scenes, the genteel and fplendid Company, the charming Voices, and delightful Mufick?

If, Madam, one were all Ear, and loft-to every Senfe but that of Harmony, furely the *Italian* Opera would be a tranfporting Thing!-- -But when one finds good Senfe, and Inftruction, and Propriety, facrific'd to the Charms of Sound, what an unedifying, what a mere temporary Delight does it afford! For what does one carry home, but the Remembrance of having been pleas'd fo many Hours by the mere

E 6 Vibra-

Vibration of Air, which being but Sound, you cannot bring away with you, and muft therefore enter the Time pafs'd in fuch a Diverfion, into the Account of thofe blank Hours, from which one has not reap'd fo much as one improving Leffon?

I fpeak this with regard to myfelf, who know nothing of the *Italian* Language · But yet I may not be very unhappy, that I do not, if I may form my Opinion of the Sentiments by the enervating Softnefs of the Sound, and the unmanly Attitudes and Geftures made ufe of to exprefs the Paffions of the Men-Performers, and from the amorous Complainings of the Women, as vifible in the foft, the toofoft, Action of each

Then, tho' I cannot but fay, That the Mufick is moft melodious, yet to fee a Hero, as an *Alexander*, or a *Julius Cæfar*, warbling out his Atchievements in War, his military Conquefts, as well as his Love, in a Song, it feems to me to be making a Jeft of both ·

And how much more abfurd is it ftill, to hear fome dying Chieftain, fome unfortunate Hero, chanting forth his Woes and his Calamities, and taking his Leave of the World, with lefs Propriety than our *Englifh* Criminals at the fatal Tree ' What can this move, how can this *pierce*, be the Story ever fo difmal, any thing but one's Ears?

Every Nation, Mr *B.* fays, has its peculiar Excellence The *French* Tafte is Comedy and Harlequinery · the *Italian*, Mufick and Opera, the *Englifh*, mafculine and nervous Senfe, whether in Tragedy or Comedy ----Why can't one, methinks, keep to one's own particular national Excellence, and let others retain theirs? For Mr *B* obferves, That when once Sound is preferr'd to Senfe, we fhall depart from all our own Worthinefs, and, at beft, be but the Apes, yea, the Dupes, of thofe whom we may

*ftrive*

*ſtrive* to imitate, but never can reach, much leſs excel

Mr B. ſays, ſometimes, that this Taſte is almoſt the only good Fruit our young Nobility gather, and bring home from their foreign Tours, and that he found the *Engliſh* Nation much ridicul'd on this Score by thoſe very People who are benefited by the Depravity. And if this be the beſt, what muſt the other Qualifications be, which they bring home? ----Yet every one does not return with ſo little Improvement, it is to be hop'd.

But what have I ſaid, what can I ſay, of an *Italian* Opera?----Only, little to the Purpoſe as it is, I wonder how I have been able to ſay ſo much· For who can deſcribe Sound? Or what Words ſhall be found to imbody Air?----And when we return, and are ask'd our Opinion of what we have ſeen or heard, we are only able to anſwer, as I hinted above, The Scenery is fine; The Company ſplendid and genteel, The Muſick charming for the Time;---- The Action not extraordinary, The Language unintelligible, and, for all theſe Reaſons---The Inſtruction none at all

This·is all that the Thing itſelf gives me Room to ſay of the *Italian* Opera; very probably, for want of a polite Taſte, and a Knowlege of the Language.

In my next, I believe I ſhall give you, Madam, my Opinion of a Diverſion or Amuſement, which, I doubt, I ſhall like ſtill leſs; and that is a *Maſquerade*, for I fear I ſhall not be excus'd going to one, altho' I have no manner of Liking to it, eſpecially in my preſent Way I am, Madam,

*Your Ladyſhip's moſt obliged and faithful*

P. B.

I muſt add another Half-ſheet to this Letter on the Subject-matter of it, the Opera, and am
ſure

sure your Ladyship will not be difpleafed with the Addition

Mr. *B* coming up, juft as I had concluded my Letter, asked me, What was my Subject ? I told him, I was giving your Ladyship my Notions of the *Italian* Opera    Let me fee what they are, my Dear; for this is a Subject, that very few of thofe who admire thefe Performances, and fewer ftill of thofe who decry them, know any thing of.

He read the above, and was pleafed to commend it   Operas, faid he, are very fad Things in *England*, to what they are in *Italy* , and the Tranflations given of them, abominable . And, indeed, our Language will not do them Juftice.

Every Nation, as you take notice, has its Excellencies, and you fay well, that ours fhould not quit the manly nervous Senfe, which is the Diftinction of the *Englifh* Drama.   One Play of our celebrated *Shakefpeare* will give infinitely more Pleafure to a fenfible Mind, than a dozen *Englifh Italian* Operas. But, my Dear, in *Italy* they are quite another Thing · And the Senfe is not, as here, facrific'd fo much to the Sound, but that they are both very compatible

Be pleafed, Sir, to give me your Obfervation on this Head in Writing, and then I fhall have fomething to fend worthy of Lady *Davers's* Acceptance Do, Sir, pray do

I will, my Dear , and he took a Pen, and wrote the inclofed , which I beg your Ladyship to return me, becaufe I will keep it by me, for my Inftruction, if I fhould be led to talk of this Subject in Company   You muft let my Sifter know, faid he, that I have given myfelf no Time to re perufe what I have written   She will do well therefore to correct it, and return it to you.

‡ In

' In *Italy*, Judges of Operas are so far from think-
' ing the Drama a Poetical Part of their Opera's
' Nonsense, as the Unskill'd in *Italian* rashly con-
' clude in *England*, that if the *Libretto*, as they call
' it, is not approved, the Opera, notwithstanding the
' Excellence of the Musick, will be condemned. For
' the *Italians* justly determine, that the very Musick
' of an Opera cannot be complete and pleasing, if
' the Drama be incongruous, as I may call it, in its
' Composition , because, in order to please, it must
' have the necessary Contraste of the Grave and
' the Light, that is, the Diverting, equally blended
' through the Whole. If there be too much of the
' first, let the Musick be composed ever so masterly in
' that Style, it will become heavy and tiresome ;
' if the latter prevail, it will surfeit with its Levity :
' Wherefore it is the Poet's Business to adapt the
' Words for this agreeable Mixture · For the Musick
' is but secondary and subservient to the Words ; and
' if there be an artful Contraste in the Drama, there
' will be the same in the Musick, supposing the Com-
' poser to be a skilful Master.

' Now, since in *England*, the Practice has been
' to mutilate, curtail, and patch up a Drama in
' *Italian*, in order to introduce favourite Airs, selected
' from different Authors, the Contraste has always
' been broken thereby, and the Opera damn'd,
' without every one's knowing the Reason And since
' ignorant mercenary Prompters, tho' *Italians*, have
' been imploy'd in the Hotch-potch, and in translate-
' ing our Drama's from *Italian* into *English*, how
' could such Opera's appear any other than incon-
' gruous Nonsense ?

### Recitativo's

' To avoid the natural Dissonance and Irregularity
' in common Speech, Recitativo's in Musick and
' dramatical

5

' dramatical Performances were invented; and, altho'
' the Time in pronouncing the Words contained in
' them, is scarce longer, than in common Conver-
' sation, yet the Harmony of the Chords of the
' Thorough-Base, which then accompanies the Voice,
' delights the Ears of discerning Judges. Wherefore
' Recitative is a regular way of speaking musically, as
' I may say, in order to avoid and correct the Irregu-
' larities of Speech, often found in Nature, and to
' express the Variety of Passions, without Offence
' to the Ear.'

Permit me, dear Madam, to repeat my Assurances,
that I am, and must ever be,

*Your obliged Sister, and Servant,*

P B.

## LETTER XIV.

WELL, now, my dear Lady, I will give you my
poor Opinion of a Masquerade, to which Mr *B.*
persuaded me to accompany Miss *Darnford*, for, as
I hinted in my former, I had a great Indifference,
or rather Dislike, to go, and Miss therefore wanted
so powerful a Second, to get me with her; because
I was afraid the Freedoms which I had heard were
used there, would not be very agreeable to my apprehensive Temper, at *this* Time especially

But finding Mr. *B* chose to have me go, if, as
he was pleased to say, I had no Objection, I said, I
will have none. Sir, I *can* have none, when you tell
me it is your Choice, and so send for the Habits
you like, and that you would have me appear in,
and I will chearfully attend you

The Habit Mr. *B*. pitch'd upon, was that of a
*Spanish* Don, and it well befitted the Majesty of his
Person

Perfon and Air, and Mifs chofe that of a young Widow , and Mr *B* recommended that of a Quaker
for me  We all admir'd one another in our Drefles;
and Mr *B* promifing to have me always in his Eye,
we took Coach, and went thither

But I never defire to be prefent at another  Mr. *B.*
was fingled out by a bold Nun, who talk'd *Italian*
to him with fuch free Airs, that I did not much like
it, tho' I knew not what fhe faid; for I thought the
dear Gentleman no more kept to his *Spanifh* Gravity, than fhe to the Requifites of the Habit fhe
wore: When I had imagin'd, that all that was tolerable in a Mafquerade, was the acting up to the
Character each Perfon affum'd . And this gave me
no Objection to the Quaker's Drefs , for I thought
I was prim enough for that naturally.

I faid foftly, Dear Mifs, (for Mr *B* and the Nun
were out of Sight in a Moment) What is become
of that Nun ?-----Rather, whifper'd fhe, What is
become of the *Spaniard* ?

A Cardinal attack'd me inftantly in *French*  But
I anfwer'd in *Englifh*, not knowing what he faid,
Quakers are not fit Company for Red-hats

They are, faid he, in the fame Language , for a
Quaker and a Jefuit is the fame Thing

Mifs was addrefs'd by the Name of the fprightly
Widow · Another ask'd, How long fhe intended to
wear thofe Weeds ? And a Footman, in a rich Livery,
anfwer'd for her Eyes, thro' her Mask, that it would
not be a Month.

But I was ftartled, when a Presbyterian Parfon
came up to me, and bid me look after my *Mufido-
rus*----So that I doubted not by this, it muft be fomebody who knew my Name to be *Pamela* , and I
prefently thought of one of my Lawyers, whofe
Characters I gave in a former Letter

Indeed, he needed not to bid me , for I was
forry, on more Accounts than that of my Timorouf-
nefs,

nefs, to have loft Sight of him. Out upon thefe nafty Mafquerades! thought I, I can't abide them already!

An egregious beauifh Appearance came up to Mifs, and faid, You hang out a very pretty *Sign*, Widow.------

Not, reply'd Mifs, to invite fuch Fops as you to my Shop

Any Cuftomer would be welcome, return'd he, in my Opinion —I whifper this as a Secret.

And I whifper another, faid Mifs, That no Place warrants ill Manners

Are you angry, Widow?

She affected a Laugh · No indeed; it i'n't worth while

He turn'd to me—and I was afraid of fome fuch Hit as he gave me----I hope, Friend, thou art prepar'd with a Father for the Light within thee?-----That was his free Word

Is this Wit? faid I, turning to Mifs: I have enough of this Diverfion, where nothing but coarfe Jefts appear *barefac'd*

At laft Mr *B* accofted us, as if he had not known us: So lovely a Widow, and fo fweet a Friend! no wonder you do not feparate · For I fee not in this various Affemblée a third Perfon of your Sex fit to join with you

Not one, Sir!---faid I---Will not a penitent Nun make a good Third with a mournful Widow, and a prim Quaker?

Not for more than Ten Minutes, at moft.

Inftantly the Nun, a fine Perfon of a Lady, with a noble Air, tho' I did not like her, join'd us, and fpoke in *Italian* fomething very free, as it feem'd by her Manner, and Mr. *B*'s fmiling Anfwer, but neither Mifs nor I underftood that Language, and Mr *B*. would not explain it to us.

But

But she gave him a Signal to follow her, seeming to be much taken with his Person and Air ; for tho' there were three other *Spanish* Habits there, he was call'd *The stately Spaniard* by one, and *The handsome Spaniard* by another, in our Hearing, as he pass'd with us to the Dessert, where we drank each of us a Glass of Champaign, and eat a few Sweet-meats, with a Croud about us, but we appear'd not to know one another. While several odd Appearances, as One *Indian* Prince, One *Chinese* Mandarin, several Domine's, of both Sexes, a *Dutch* Skipper, a *Jewish* Rabbi, a *Greek* Monk, a Harlequin, a *Turkish* Bashaw, and a *Capuchin* Frier, glided by us, as we return'd into Company, signifying, that we were Strangers to them, by squeaking out, *I know you !*----Which is half the Wit of the Place

Mr. *B* had more Attacks made upon him by Ladies, than we had by Gentlemen, and his fine Person, noble Air, and a Deportment so suited to his Habit, (only in the Encounter of the Nun, when he had more of the *French* Freedom, as I thought, than the *Spanish* Gravity) made him many Admirers ; and more, when the *Spanish* Minister, who was there in a *French* Dress, spoke to him in *Spanish*, and receiv'd a polite Answer from him in the same ; while there were several who personated Foreign Characters, and knew nothing of the Language of the Country, whose Habits they assumed.

There were divers Antick Figures, some with Caps and Bells, one dress'd like a Punch ; several Harlequins, and other ludicrous Forms, that jump'd and ran about like mad, and seem'd as if they would have it thought, that all their Wit lay in their Heels

Two Ladies, one in a very fantastick party-colour'd Habit, with a Plume of Feathers, the other in a rustick one, with a Garland of Flowers round her Head, were much taken notice of for their Freedom, and having something to say to every body. They were

were as seldom separated as Miss and I, and were followed by a Croud, where-ever they went.

The Party-colour'd one came up to me: Friend, said she, there is something in thy Person, that attracts every one's Notice: But if a Sack had not been a profane Thing, it would have become thee almost as well

I thank thee, Friend, said I, for thy Counsel; but if thou hadst been pleased to look at home, thou would't not have taken so much Pains to join such Advice, and such an Appearance, together, as thou makest!

This made every one that heard it, laugh---One said, The Butterfly had met with her Match

She return'd, with an affected Laugh----Smartly said----Put art thou come hither, Friend, to make thy Light shine before Men or Women?

Verily, Friend, neither, reply'd I, but out of mere Curiosity to look into the *Minds* of both Sexes, which I read in their *Dresses*

A general Satire on the Assemblee, by the Mass! said a fat Monk

The Nun whisk'd to us We're all concern'd in my Friend's Remark----

And no Disgrace to a fair Nun, return'd I, if her Behaviour answer her Dress----Nor to a Reverend Friar, turning to the Monk, if his Mind be not a Discredit to his Appearance- ---Nor yet to a Country Girl, turning to the party-colour'd Lady's Companion, if she has not Weeds in her Heart to disgrace the Flowers on her Head.

An odd Figure, representing a *Merry Andrew*, took my Hand, and said, I had the most piquant Wit he had met with that Night: And, Friend, said he, let us be better acquainted!

Forbear, said I, withdrawing my Hand, not a Companion for a Jack-pudding neither!

A *Roman*

A *Roman* Senator juft then accofted Mifs ; and Mr *B.* feeing me fo much engag'd, 'Twere hard, faid he, if our Nation, in Spite of *Cervantes,* produc'd not one Cavalier to protect a fair Lady thus furrounded.

Tho' furrounded, not diftrefs'd, my good Knight-Errant, faid the Nun The fair Quaker will be too hard for half a dozen Antagonifts, and wants not your Protection.----But your poor Nun befpeaks it, whifper'd fhe, who has not a Word to fay for herfelf

Mr. *B.* anfwer'd her in *Italian,* (I wifh I underftood *Italian !*)---and fhe had recourfe to her Beads.

You can't imagine, Madam, how this Nun haunted the dear Gentleman!----Indeed, my Lady, you can't imagine it!

I muft needs fay, I don't like thefe Mafquerades at all Many Ladies, on thefe Occafions, are fo very free, that the Cenforious will be apt to blame the whole Sex for *their* Conduct, and to fay, their Hearts are as faulty as thofe of the moft culpable Men, fince they fcruple not to fhew as much, when they think they cannot be known by their Faces. But it is my humble Opinion, that could there be a Standard fix'd, by which one could determine readily what *is,* and what is *not* Wit, Decency would not be fo often wounded, by Attempts to be witty, as it is. For here every one, who can give himfelf the Liberty to fay Things that fhock a modefter Perfon, not meeting with due Rebuke, but perhaps a Smile, (without confidering whether it be of Contempt or Approbation) miftakes Courage for Wit, and every thing facred or civil becomes the Subject of his frothy Jeft.

How elfe can one account for the Liberties of Expreffion and Behaviour taken by fome of thofe who perfonated Bifhops, Cardinals, Priefts, Nuns, &*c. ?*---For the freeft Things I heard faid, were from

Perfons

Perfons in thofe Habits; who behav'd with fo much
Levity and Indecorum, as if they were refolved,
as much as in them lay, to throw thofe venerable
Characters into Ridicule, for no other Reafon, than
becaufe they are by the Generality of the World
deem'd *venerable*: But if it was once determin'd,
that nothing fhould be call'd true Wit, as nothing
certainly ought, but what will ftand the Teft of
Examination, but what is confiftent with Decency
and good Manners, and what will make an innocent
Heart brilliant and chearful, and give its Sanction to
the happy Expreffion, by trying to keep up and
return the Ball in like virtuous and lively Raillery,
then we fhould have our publick Entertainments
fuch as the moft Scrupulous might join to countenance and applaud.

But what a Moralizer am I! will your Ladyfhip
fay. Indeed I can't help it ·—And efpecially on fuch
a Subject as a *Mafquerade*, which I diflike more than
any thing I ever faw I could fay a great deal more
on this Occafion ; but, upon my Word, I am quite
out of Humour with it ; for I liked my *Englifh* Mr. *B*
better than my *Spaniard* ; and the Nun I approved
not by any means ; tho' there were fome who ob
ferved, that fhe was one of the gracefulleft Figures
in the Place. And indeed, in fpite of my own
Heart, I could not help thinking fo too

Your Ladyfhip knows fo well what *Mafquerades*
are, that I may well be excus'd faying any thing
further on a Subject I am fo little pleafed with · For
you only defire my Notions of thofe Diverfions,
becaufe I am a Novice in them, and this, I doubt
no·, will doubly ferve to anfwer that Purpofe

I fhall only therefore add, That after an hundred
other Impertinencies fpoken to Mifs and me, and
retorted with Spirit by Mifs, and as well as I could
by myfelf, quite fick of the Place, I feigned to be more
indifpofed than I was, and fo got my beloved *Spa-*
*niard*

*niard* to go off with us, and reached Home by Three in the Morning And so much for *Masquerades.* I hope I shall never have Occasion to mention them again to your Ladyship I am, my dearest Lady,

*Your ever-oblig'd Sister, and Servant,*

P B.

## LETTER XV.

*My dearest Lady,*

MY Mind is so wholly ingross'd by Thoughts of a very different Nature from those which the Diversions of the Town and Theatres inspire, that I beg to be excused, if, for the present, I say nothing further of those lighter Matters But yet, since your Ladyship does not disapprove of my Remarks, I intend, if it please God to spare my Life, to make a little Book, which I will present to your Ladyship, containing my poor Observations on all the Dramatick Entertainments I have seen, and shall see, this Winter, and for this Purpose I have made brief Notes in the Margin of the printed Plays I have bought, as I saw them, with a Pencil ; by referring to which, as Helps to my Memory, I shall be able to tell your Ladyship what my Thoughts were at the Time of seeing them, pretty nearly with the same Advantage, as if I had written them at my Return from each.

I have obtained of Sir *Simon,* and Lady *Darnford,* the very great Pleasure of their Permission to Miss to stay with me, till it shall be seen how it will please God to deal with me, and I owe this Favour partly to a kind Letter written in my Behalf to Sir *Simon,* by Mr *B* and partly to Miss's earnest Request to her Papa, to oblige me, Sir *Simon* having made some Difficulty to comply, as Mr. *Murray* and his Bride have left them, saying, he could not

live

live long, if he had not the Company of his beloved Daughter.

I cannot but fay, I have many more Anxieties and Apprehenfions, than perhaps I ought to have, on the approaching Occafion, but I was always a fad Coward, and too thoughtful a good deal. But I have fo *much* to lofe ; fuch a dear Gentleman to part with, if I *muft* part with him, fuch generous Friends and Lovers, as I may fay, of both Sexes. And then the Circumftance itfelf has fo many Terrors to an apprehenfive Mind, attending it, that I am out of Breath fometimes at the Thoughts of it, and want to run away from myfelf, if I could ----But it cannot be, and when I charge my Mind with the Reflections which Religion infpires, and afk myfelf, Who it was that gave me all thefe Bleffings, and who it is that has a Right to recall them, if He pleafes, and *when*, and in *what way*, He pleafes ? and that if I leave them not *now*, I muft be feparated from them *another* Day, I endeavour to bring my Mind to a Refignation to the Divine Will.

But what fhall I fay, Madam, when I find my Frailty is fo much increafed, that I cannot, with the fame Intenfenefs of Devotion, that I ufed to be bleft with, apply myfelf to the Throne of Grace, nor, of Confequence, find my Invocations anfwer'd by that Delight, and inward Satisfaction, with which I ufed to pleafe myfelf, when the prefent near Profpect was more remote ?

I hope I fhall not be deferted in the Hour of Trial, and that this my Weaknefs of Mind will not be punifh'd with a fpiritual Dereliction, for fuffering myfelf to be too much attach'd to thofe worldly Delights and Pleafures which no Mortal ever enjoy'd in a more exalted Degree than myfelf. And I befeech you, my deareft Lady, let me be always remember'd in your Prayers----*Only* for a Refignation to the Divine Will, a *chearful* Refignation I prefume

prefume not to prefcribe to His gracious Providence ; for if one has but *that*, one has every thing that one need to have. Yet, my dear Lady, there is fuch a natural Repugnance between Life and Death, that Nature will fhrink, when one comes to the Trial, let one have never fo much Fortitude at a Diftance. Yet, I hope, I may be forgiven ; for now-and-then I comfort myfelf with the Divine Exemplar, who prayed in bloody Sweats for the bitter Cup to be removed ; but gave us the Example of Refignation, that I am wifhing to be able to follow : *However, not mine, but thy Will be done !*

Forgive me, my deareft Lady, for being fo deeply ferious. I have juft now been contending with a fevere Pang, that is, for the prefent, gone off ; what Effect its Return may have, God only knows. And if this is the laft Line I fhall ever write, it will be the more fatisfactory to me, as (with my humble Refpects to my good Lord *Davers*, and my dear Countefs, and praying for the Continuance of all your Healths and Happinefs, both here and here-after) I am permitted to fubfcribe myfelf,

*Your Ladyfhip's obliged Sifter, and humble Servant,*

P. B.

---

## LETTER XVI.

*From* Lady DAVERS *to* Mr. B.

*My deareft Brother,*

ALTHO' I believe it is needlefs to put a Gentleman of your generous Spirit in mind of doing a worthy Action , yet, as I do not know whether you have thought of what I am going to hint to you, I cannot forbear a Line or two with regard to the good old Couple in *Kent*

I am

I am sure, if, for our Sins, God Almighty should take from us my incomparable Sister, (forgive me, my dear Brother, but to intimate what *may* be, altho' I hourly pray, as her trying Minute approaches, that it will not) you will, for her sake, take care that her honest Parents have not the Loss of your Favour, to deepen the inconsolable one, they will have, in such a Case, of the best of Daughters

I say, I am sure you will do as generously by them as ever. And I dare say, your sweet *Pamela* doubts it not  Yet as you know how sensible she is of every Favour done to them, it is the Countess's, Opinion, and mine, and Lady *Betty*'s too, that you give *her* this Assurance in some *legal* Way, for, as she is naturally apprehensive, and thinks more of her present Circumstances, than, for your sake, she chuses to express to you, it will be like a Cordial to her dutiful and grateful Heart, and I do not know, if it will not contribute, more than any *one* Thing, to make her go thro' her Task with Ease and Safety

I know how much your Heart is wrapp'd up in the dear Creature ⋅ And you are a worthy Brother, to let it be so!----You will excuse me therefore, I am sure, for this my Officiousness

I have no Doubt, that God will spare her to us, because, altho' we may not be worthy of so much Excellence, yet we now all unite so gratefully to thank Him for such a worthy Relation, that I hope we shall not be depriv'd of an Example so necessary to us all

I can have but one Fear; and that is, that, young as she is, she seems ripen'd for Glory, she seems to have liv'd long enough for *Herself* But for *You*, and for *Us*, that God will *still* spare her, shall be the hourly Prayer of,

*My dear worthy Brother,*
　　*Your ever-affectionate Sister,*
　　　　B DAVERS

Have

Have you got her Mother with you? I hope you
have God give you a Son and Heir, if it be
his bleſſed Will! But however that be, preſerve
your PAMELA to you! For you never can have
ſuch *another* Wife.

---

# LETTER XVII.

## *From Mrs.* B. *to Mr.* B.

*My ever dear, and ever honoured Mr* B --

SINCE I know not how it may pleaſe God Almighty to diſpoſe of me on the approaching
Occaſion, I ſhould think myſelf inexcuſable, if I
could not find one or two ſelect Hours to dedicate
to you, out of the very many, in the Writing way,
in which your Goodneſs has indulged me, becauſe
you ſaw I took Delight in it

But yet think not, O beſt Beloved of my Heart!
that I have any Boon to beg, any Favour to ask,
either for myſelf, or for my Friends, or ſo much as
the *Continuance* of your Favour to the one or the
other As to them, you have prevented and exceeded
all my Wiſhes . As to myſelf, if it pleaſe God to
ſpare me, I know I ſhall always be rewarded beyond
my Deſert, let my Deſervings be what they will.
I have only therefore to acknowlege, with the deepeſt
Senſe of your Goodneſs to me, and with the moſt
Heart-affecting Gratitude, that from the happy, the
thrice happy Hour, that you ſo generouſly made
me yours, till *this* Moment, you have not left me
one Thing, on my own Part, to wiſh for, but the
Continuance and Increaſe of your Felicity, and that
I might be worthier and worthier of the unexampled
Goodneſs, Tenderneſs, and Condeſcenſion, where-
with you have always treated me.

No, my deareſt, my beſt beloved Maſter, Friend, Husband, my *firſt*, my *laſt*, and *only* Love<sup>1</sup> beſieve me, I have nothing to wiſh for but your Honour and Felicity, temporary and eternal, and I make no doubt, that God, in his infinite Goodneſs and Mercy, will perfect his own good Work, begun in your dear Heart; and whatever may now happen, give us a happy Meeting, never more to part from one another. For, altho', as you were pleaſed to queſtion t'other Day, when you were reſolving ſome of my Doubts——(and, Oh! what a ſweet Expoſitor have you been to me upon all thoſe Occaſions, on which my diffident Mind led me to you for Information and Direction!) whether the Happineſs of the Bleſſed was not too exalted a Happineſs to be affected with the poor Ties of Relationſhip and Senſe, which now delight, and attach ſo much to them, our narrow Minds and Conceptions; yet cannot I willingly give up the pleaſing, the *charming* Hope, that I ſhall one Day rejoice, *diſtinguiſhingly* rejoice, in the Society of my beſt beloved Husband and Friend, and in that of my dear Parents; and I will keep and encourage this dear Hope, ſo conſolatory to me in the Separation which deareſt Friends *muſt* experience, ſo long as it can ſtand me in any ſtead, and till I ſhall be all Intellect, and above the ſoothing Impreſſions which are now ſo agreeable to Senſe, and to conjugal and filial Piety.

Let me then beg of you, my deareſt Protector and beſt Friend, to pardon all my Imperfections and Defects, and if, ever ſince I have had the Honour to be yours, I have in *Looks*, or in *Word*, or in *Deed*, given you Cauſe to wiſh me other than I was, that you will kindly put it to the Score of natural Infirmity (for in *Thought* or *Intention*, I can truly boaſt, I have never wilfully err'd) Your Tenderneſs for me, and your generous Politeneſs to me, always gave me Apprehenſion, that I was not what
*you*

you wifh'd me to be, becaufe you would not find Fault with me, fo often as I fear I deferved · And this makes me beg of you to do, as I hope God Almighty will, pardon all my involuntary Errors and Omiffions

You have enabled me, Sir, to do all the Good to my poor Neighbours, and to diftreffed Objects, which was in my own Heart to do, and I hope I have made ufe of the Power you have fo generoufly intrufted me with, in a manner, that may fhew I had a Regard to your Honour, and to the Exigency of the particular Cafes recommended to me, without Extravagance or Vanity But yet, as it is neceffary I fhould render fome Account of my Stewardfhip, in relation to the large Sums you have put into my Hands for charitable Ufes, you will find, my beloved *Mafter,* and beft *Friend,* your poor *Steward's* Accounts of every thing, in the Cabinet that was my honour'd Lady's, till your Goodnefs made it mine, in a † Vellom Book, on the firft Leaf of which, is written, Title-page-wife, Humble RETURNS for DIVINE MERCIES, and you will fee a Balance ftruck, down to this very Day, and the *little Surplus* in the green Purfe upon the Book And if you will be pleafed, Sir, to perfect, by your Generofity, the Happinefs of the Cafes I have marked with a Star, [thus, *] which are fuch as are not fully recovered, and will be fo good as to keep up my little School, I dare ask no more; for, my deareft Mr B if I fhould be called from *your Service* to my *new Place,* your *next* Steward (and long, I hope, for your honourable Family's fake, you will not be without one) may find out another and *better* Method for your Honour and her own, to difpenfe your Bounty, than that I have taken.

† *See* Vol II *p* 353.

F 3. The

The rich Jewels and Equipage, with which your generous Goodness adorned my Unworthiness, will be found in the fame Cabinet, in the private Drawer And if I may be pardon'd for one extravagant Wish, (your Circumstances, dear Sir, are very great) and your future Lady will not wear any thing that was mine) it is, that my dear Miss *Darnford* may be defir'd, as the Effect of your own Goodness, and generous Confideration for my Memory, to wear the Diamond Necklace, which, I know, fhe admires, but is far from wifhing for it, or expecting it, if the Neck that it was given to adorn, and to make more worthy of you, fhould be laid low by the irrefiftible Leveller

In the loweft Drawer, on the Left-hand of the Cabinet, you will find, Sir, all my unfinifh'd Scribble, and amongft the reft, a little Parcel, indorfed, Mr *H* and *P Barlow* The Title will furprife you, but as I know not what may happen to make Doubts and Puzzles in the Affair mentioned in thofe Papers, when I cannot explain them, I thought it was beft to give a brief Hiftory of it in Writing, with his Letter to me on the Occafion, and I humbly beg, the Whole may be kept within your own Breaft, unlefs that vile Affair, which has much difturb'd me, fhou'd be reviv'd Altho' I have no Reafon to apprehend it will, becaufe the poor Girl, I hope, is fincerely penitent, and Mr *H* himfelf feems in another way of thinking, as to her.

Will you be pleafed, Sir, to beftow on my deareft Mifs *Goodwin*, as a Remembrance of her Aunt's true Love, the Diamond Solitaire, and the fecond Pair of Ear-rings? Perhaps, my deareft Lady *Davers* will not difdain to wear, as a Prefent from her beloved Brother, my beft Diamond Ring And if my moft beloved and moft valued Ring of all, the dear firft Pledge of my Happinefs, were, for the firft

Since I was honoured with it, by your own putting it on, taken from my Finger and inamel'd,

it

it would he a mournful, yet a pleafing Token for
my poor Mother, and a fweet *Memento* of your
Bounty to them, and of your inexpreffible Goodnefs and Favour to her poor Daughter !------But how
I prefume ! And yet juft now faid, I had nothing.
to ask !

Now I am, unawares to myfelf, upon the Subject
of petitioning, how it would pleafe me, could I know
it, if the dear Child I have juft named, were given
to the Care and Example of my excellent Mifs
*Darnford,* if fhe would be pleafed to accept of the
Truft, and if Lady *Davers* has no Objection, and
would not chufe to take the pretty Soul under her
own Wing !

I had once great Pleafure in the Hope of having.
this dear Mifs committed to my Care----But what
Pleafures, what Happinefs, have I not had crouded
into this laft, and this firft happy, thrice happy
Year—even more than moft of my Sex have had
to boaft of, and thofe not unhappy neither, in a
long, long Life ! Every Day has brought with it fome
new Felicity, fome new Happinefs, as unlook'd for,
as undeferv'd, for, Oh ! beft Beloved of my Heart,
how have you always met me in your Comings-in,
left me at your Goings-out, with Smiles and Complacency, the *latter* only diftinguifh'd from the *former,* by a kind Regret, as the *other* was from *that,*
by a Joy, next to Tranfport, when all *your* dear
generous Heart appear'd in your noble Countenance,
and fet *my* faithful one into refponfive Flutters, to
meet and receive it with all the grateful Emotions
that the chafteft conjugal Flame could infpire !

But I muft not dwell upon thefe charming, charming Reflections !----My prefent Doubts will not permit me to indulge them ! For, if I were----how
would my Defires be rivetted to this Earth !---With
what Regret fhould I transfer my Thoughts to a
*ftill* more important and more neceffary Subject !

F 4         and

and with what Ingratitude look up to a diviner, and
ftill more noble Mafter, who ought to be the Ulti-
mate of all our Wifhes and Defircs! And who has
given me You, my deareft Mr *B* and *with* You, all
that this World can make defirable!----And has therefore a Right to take away, what he has given ----And
if I now die, what a Glory will it be to me, to be
permitted to difcharge Part of my Obligations to the
worthieft of Gentlemen, by laying down my Life
in the Service of his honourable Family!

But let me fay one Word for my dear worthy
Mrs *Jervis* Her Care and Fidelity will be very
neceffary for your Affairs, dear Sir, while you remain
fingle, which I hope will not be long But, whenever, Sir, you make a fecond Choice, be pleafed to
allow her fuch an Annuity as may make her independent, and pafs away the Remainder of her Life
with Eafe and Comfort And this I the rather prefume to requeft, as my late honour'd Lady * once
intimated the fame thing to you. If I were to name
what that may be, it would not be with the Thought
of *heightening*, but of *limiting* rather, the natural
Bounty of your Heart, and Fifty Pounds a Year
wou'd be a rich Provifion, in her Opinion, and
will intail upon you, dear Sir, the Bleffings of one
of the faithfulleft and worthieft Hearts in the Kingdom.

Nor will Chriftian Charity permit me to forget
the once wicked, but now penitent *Jewkes* I underftand by Mifs *Darnford*, that fhe begs for nothing
but to have the Pleafure of dying in your Service,
and of having, by that means, an Opportunity given
her of atoning for fome fmall Slips and Miftakes in
her Accounts, which fhe had made formerly, as fhe
accufes herfelf, for fhe will have it, that Mr *Longman* has been better to her than fhe deferv'd, in paf-

* *See* Vol. III. *p* 203

king

sing one * Account particularly, to which he had, with too much Reason, objected, Do, dear Sir, if your *future* happy Lady has no *great* Dislike to the poor Woman, be pleased to grant her Request, except her own Mind should alter, and she desire her Dismission. And be pleased to present her with my little Book of select Devotions, with my Notes in the Inter-leaves · It is in the bottom Drawer of the Right-hand, among my devotional Miscellanies: Or-rather, much rather, be pleased to order a Copy of it to be made out for her, and to give the Original, it being mostly in my own Hand-writing, to my dear Father  This is a better Thought by much; for the dear good Man will esteem it the more for that  I wonder I did not think of this before

To the other Servants, I have only to leave my Thanks, and best Wishes, for their respectful Love and dutiful Behaviour to one, who from being once hardly the Equal to some of them, has been exalted to the honourable Station of their Mistress, by your superlative Goodness and Favour  No Servants, my dear Mr. *B.* ever deserved a Mistress's Thanks, if yours do not, for they, every one of them, most chearfully came into all my little Schemes and Regulations; and they have encouraged me, by their ready Obedience, and their respectful Loves, to pursue the natural Dictates of my own Heart, and have made all Assumings and Pride as unnecessary, as they would have been grievous to me, and censurable by every one else  For was it not my high Concern so to behave myself to all, Low as well as High, that my best beloved Benefactor should not, by *my* Arrogance or Inattention, have Censurers of *him*, added to Enviers of *me*, for the Step he had taken, so derogatory to his own Honour, and to that of his antient and splendid Family?

* *See, for a Hint of this,* Vol I. *p.* 87.

To

To the Favour of the beſt of Maſters I therefore leave them, with this Teſtimony of their Merits, and of my kird Regard to them, which makes me venture to call them, without one Exception, from my Silver-hair'd *Jonathan*, to the loweſt Menial, *The beſt Set of Servants* that any Gentleman ever had Nor, by Miſs *Darnford's* Account of the Behaviour of thoſe at the Hall, do I find them at all unworthy of being claſs'd with theſe here, in the happy Character  And let me ſay, my deareſt Mr *B* that I have been not a little attentive to their reſpective Behaviours, and have taken Mrs *Jervis's* Obſervations, as a Help to my own, in this Particular, becauſe I thought it my Duty, to do ſo, as well in Juſtice to your dear Self, as to them

As to *Polly Barlow*, to whom I was willing to behave with an Eye to my dear good Lady's Kindneſs to myſelf, I have nothing to ſay, by way of Diſtinction from the reſt, having hinted to Mrs. *Jervis* to give her *her* Advice, from time to time, and that if an honeſt Husband ſhould offer, ſhe ſhould adviſe the poor Girl not to decline it

Forgive me, deareſt Sir, for thus mentioning to you, in this ſolemn Letter, ſo particularly, your Servants  But the Pleaſure which their Regularity and Worthineſs have given me, together with the Knowlege I have of their Fidelity and affectionate Duty to You, methinks call for this Teſtimony of my Satisfaction in them, and for my Recommendation of them to your Favour

And now, what have I farther to ſay, but to beg of God to ſhower down his moſt precious Bleſſings upon you, my deareſt, my *firſt*, my *laſt*, and my *only* Love' and to return to You an hundred-fold, the Benefits, which you have conferr'd upon Me and Mine, and upon ſo many poor Souls, as you have bleſs'd 'bro' my Hands' And that you may in your next Choice be happy with a Lady, who may have

*ever*

every thing I want; and who may love and honour
you, with the same affectionate Duty, which has
been my Delight, and my Glory to pay you. For
in this, I am sure, no one *can* exceed me!— And
after having giving you long Life, Prosperity, and
Increase of Honour, translate you into a blessed
Eternity, where, through the Merits of our common
Redeemer, I hope I shall be allowed a Place, and be
permitted (O let me indulge that pleasing, that *con-
solatory* Thought!) to receive and rejoice in my
restored Spouse, for ever and ever; are the Prayers,
the *last* Prayers, if it so please God! of, my dearest
dear Mr. *B*

*Your dutiful and affectionate Wife,*
*and faithful Servant,*

P. B.

---

## LETTER XVIII.

*From Miss* DARNFORD *to Lady* DARNFORD,

*My honoured Mamma,*

YOU cannot conceive how you and my dear
Papa have delighted the Heart of my good
Mrs *B* and obliged her Mr *B* by the Permission you
have given me to attend her till the important Hour
shall be over with her, for the dear Lady is exceedingly apprehensive, and one can hardly blame her;
since there is hardly such another happy Couple in
the World

I am glad to hear, that the Ceremony is over, so
much to both your Satisfactions. May this Matrimony
be but a *Tenth Part* as happy, as that I am Witness
to here, and Mr and Mrs *Murray* will have that to
boast of, which few married People have, even
among those we call happy!

F 6

For

For my Part, I believe I shall never care to marry at all, for tho' I cannot be so deserving as Mrs *B.* yet I shall not bear to think of a Husband much less excellent than hers    Nay, by what I see in *her* Apprehensions, and conceive of the Condition she hourly expects to be in, I don't think a Lady can be requited with a *less* worthy one, for all she is likely to suffer on a Husband's Account, and for the sake of *his* Family and Name

Mrs. *Andrews*, a discreet worthy Soul, as ever I knew, and who in her Aspect and Behaviour, is far from being a Disgrace even to Mr *B*'s Lady, is with her dear Daughter, to her no small Satisfaction, as you may suppose, who now-and-then says, What a foolish Creature, my dear Mother, have you for a Daughter!— *You* did not behave so weakly as I do, when you were in the same Circumstances, I dare say, and yet you had a dear good Husband, tho' not a rich one, to hope to live for!—But, come, I will have a good Heart, to make myself as worthy of the Company and Chearings of Three such Friends, as I am bless'd with, in my Mother, my Miss *Darnford*, and Mrs *Jervis!*

Mr *B* ask'd my Advice Yesterday, about having in the House a Midwife, to be at hand, at a Moment's Warning    I told him, I fear'd the Sight of such a Person would terrify her ·  And so he instantly started an Expedient, of which her Mother, Mrs *Jervis*, and myself, approved, and have put into Practice, for, this Day, Mrs *Harris*, a distant Relation *of mine*, tho' not of yours, Sir and Madam, is arrived from *Essex*, to make me a Visit, and Mr *B.* has been so good as to prevail upon her, in *Compliment to me*, as he pretended, to accept of her Board in his House, while she stays in Town, which, she says, will be about a Week.

Now, you must know, that this Mrs *Harris* being a discreet, modest, matron-like Person, Mrs *B*
took

took a Liking to her at firft Sight, and is already very familiar with her; and underſtanding that ſhe is a Gentlewoman who was a Doctor of Phyſick's Lady, and takes as much Delight in adminiſtring to the Health of her own Sex, as her Husband uſed to do to that of both, Mrs. *B.* ſays, It is very fortunate, that ſhe has ſo experienc'd a Lady to conſult, as ſhe is ſuch a Novice in her own Caſe.

Mr. *B* however, to carry on the honeſt Impoſture better, juſt now, in Preſence of Mrs. *Harris,* and Mrs *Andrews,* and me, ask'd the former, If it was not neceſſary to have in the Houſe the good Woman? This frighted Mrs. *B* who turn'd pale, and ſaid ſhe could not bear the Thoughts of it. Mrs *Harris* ſaid, It was highly neceſſary, that Mrs. *B.* if ſhe would not permit the Gentlewoman to be in the Houſe, ſhould ſee her; and that then, ſhe apprehended, there would be no Neceſſity, as ſhe ſuppos'd ſhe did not live far off, to have her in the Houſe, ſince Mrs *B* was ſo uneaſy upon that Account This pleas'd Mrs *B* much, and Mrs. *Thomas* was admitted to attend her.

Now, you muſt know, that this is the Aſſiſtant of my new Relation, and ſhe, being appris'd of the Matter, came, but never did I ſee ſo much Shyneſs and Apprehenſion as Mrs *B.* ſhew'd all the time Mrs *Thomas* was with her, holding ſometimes her Mother, ſometimes Mrs *Harris,* by the Hand, and being ready to ſweat with Terror.

Mrs. *Harris* ſcrap'd Acquaintance with Mrs *Thomas,* who, pretending to recollect her, gave Mrs. *Harris* great Praiſes, which increas'd Mrs *B* 's Confidence in her. And ſhe undertakes to govern the Whole ſo, that the dreaded Mrs *Thomas* need not come till the very Moment, which is no ſmall Pleaſure to the over-nice Lady. And ſhe ſeems every Hour to be better pleas'd with Mrs *Harris,* who, by her prudent Talk, will more and more familiarize

her

her to the Circumstance, unawares to herself in a
manner. But notwithstanding this Precaution, of a
Midwife in the House, Mr. *B* intends to have a
Gentleman of the Profession in Readiness, for fear
of the worst

I tell Mr *B* He is very happy, in this Stratagem;
but that, I suppose, he has been more us'd to Contrivances of this sort, than he ought to have been,
and was so free as to add, That I presum'd his Lady
is hardly the first he has cheated into a Child. And,
indeed, I think, Mrs *B*'s Merit to the rest of her
Sex, is very great, were it only in reforming such
an uncommonly agreeable and manly Rake as this, for
no doubt he has done, and would have done, a world
of Mischief among the Thoughtless and Indiscreet in
Upper Life, for, it seems, when he was at the worst,
he never made the Vulgar the Subjects of his vile
Attempts

Mrs. *B* has written a Letter, and the Superscription following will tell you to whom it is directed:
' To the ever-honour'd and ever-dear Mr *B* with
' Prayers for his Health, Honour, and Prosperity in
' this World, and everlasting Felicity in that to come
' *P B*' It is seal'd with black Wax, and she gave
it me this Moment, on her being taken ill, to give
to Mr. *B* if she dies  But GOD, of his Mercy,
avert that' and preserve the dear Lady, for the
Honour of her Sex, and the Happiness of all who
know her, and particularly for that of your *Polly
Darnford*, for I cannot have a greater Loss, I am
sure, while my honour'd Papa and Mamma are
living  And may that be for many, very many, happy
Years !

I will not close this Letter, till all is over · Happily, as I hope '—Mrs. *B* is better again, and has,
occasionally, made some fine Reflections, directing
herself to me, but design'd for the Benefit of her
*Polly*,

*Polly*, on the Subject of the Inconfideration of fome of our Sex, with regard to the Circumftances fhe is in; inferring, that if *fuch* are *her* Apprehenfions; tho' a lawful Wife, and *fuch* the Danger attending this Cafe, how muft it leave a poor Creature deftitute of all fpiritual Confolation, (as well as of the Affiftance and Comfortings of the neareft Friends, and of a kind Husband) when fhe has facrific'd her Honour; and cannot think of any thing fo probable, as the Moment approaches, but that GOD will punifh her *in Kind*, as fhe call'd it; that is to fay, added fhe, by the very Sufferings, which are the natural Confequences of the Sin fhe has fo wickedly committed!

I knew what her Defign was, and faid, Ay, *Polly*, let you and I, and every fingle young Body, bear thefe Reflections in Mind, pronounced by fo excellent a Lady, in Moments fo arduous as thefe!

· The Girl wept, and very movingly fell down by the Door, on her Knees, praying to GOD to preferve her dear Lady, and fhe fhould be happy for ever! —*That*, as Mrs. *B.* fo often prettily writes, *was her Word*

Mrs *B* is exceedingly pleas'd with my new Relation, Mrs *Harris*, as we call her, who behaves with fo much Prudence, that fhe fufpects nothing, and told Mrs. *Jervis*, She wifh'd nobody elfe was to come near her. And as fhe goes out (being a Perfon of Eminence in her way) two or three times a Day, and laft Night ftaid out late, Mrs. *B* faid, fhe hop'd fhe would not be abroad, when fhe fhould wifh her to be at home

I have the Pleafure, the very great Pleafure, my dear Papa and Mamma, to acquaint you, and I know you will rejoice with me upon it, that juft half an Hour ago, my dear Mrs. *B.* was brought to-bed of a fine Boy

We

We are all out of our Wits for Joy almoſt. I ran down to Mr *B.* myſelf, who receiv'd me with trembling impatience. A Boy! a fine Boy! dear Mr *B* ſaid I: A Son and Heir, indeed!

But how does my *Pamela*? Is *ſhe* ſafe? Is *ſhe* like to do well? We hope ſo, ſaid I. Or I had not come down to you, I'll aſſure you. He folded me in his Arms, in a joyful Rapture: How happy you make me, deareſt Miſs *Darnford!* If my *Pamela* is ſafe, the Boy is welcome, welcome indeed!— But when may I go up to thank my Jewel?

Mrs *Andrews* is ſo overjoy'd, and ſo thankful, that there's no getting her from her Knees.

A Man and Horſe is diſpatch'd already to Lady *Davers*, and another order'd to *Kent*, to the good old Man.

Mrs *Jervis*, when I went up, ſaid, ſhe muſt go down, and releaſe the good Folks from their Knees, for, half an Hour before, they declar'd they would not ſtir from that Poſture, till they heard how it went with their Lady, and when the happy News was brought them of her Safety, and of a young Maſter, they were quite ecſtatick, ſhe ſays, in their Joy, and not a dry Eye among them, ſhaking Hands, and congratulating one another, Men and Maids. Which muſt make it one of the moſt affecting Sights that can be imagin'd. And Mr *Longman,* who had no Power to leave the Houſe for Three Days paſt, (tho' Buſineſs requir'd his Preſence in *Bedfordſhire*) haſted to congratulate his worthy Principal, and never was ſo much moving Joy ſeen, as this honeſt-hearted Steward ran over with.

I cannot draw theſe affecting Scenes of Joy, as Mrs *B* could have done, had ſhe been in my Caſe. —Let me only ſay, I never ſaw ſuch a Family-Joy in my Life. And who would care for Royalty, or any of its Pageantry, when Virtue can thus intereſt every body in its Concerns, and, on ſuch an Occafion

fion as this, give that general and fincere Joy to all within its Circle, which could fill a Nation on the Birth of a firft-born Prince from Sovereigns the moft beloved?

I did a foolifh thing in my Joy—I gave Mr. *B.* the Letter defign'd for him, had an unhappy Event follow'd, and he won't give it me again; but fays, he will obtain Mrs *B* 's Leave, when fhe is better, to open it; and the happier Turn will augment his Thankfulnefs to God, and Love to her, when he fhall, by this means, be bleft with Sentiments fo different from what the other Cafe would have afforded. But I will get it from him, if I can, and give it her back, for one knows not what it may contain, yet her Innocence and Purity make one lefs apprehenfive a good deal, for, I dare fay, fhe has no Excufes to make for Failings he knows nothing of

Mrs. *B* had a very fharp Time. Never more, my dear Papa, talk of a Husband to me Indeed, in the Mind I am in, I will never be marry'd.— Place all your Expectations on *Nancy!* Not one of thefe Men, that I have yet feen, Mr *B* excepted, (and you know what a Chance it was, that he would be fo good) is worth running thefe Rifques for! But his Indearments and Tendernefs to his Lady, his thankful and manly Gratitude and Politenefs, when he was admitted to pay his Refpects to her, and his Behaviour to Mrs *Andrews*, and to us all, tho' but for a Vifit of Ten Minutes, was alone worthy of all her Rifque!

I would give you a Defcription of it, had I Mrs *B* 's Pen, and of Twenty agreeable Scenes and Converfations befides · But, for want of that, muft conclude, with my humble Duty, as becomes, honour'd Sir and Madam,

*Your ever-grateful*
POLLY DARNFORD.

I have

I have been Three Days writing this Letter, Piece by Piece

---

# LETTER XIX.

*From the same.*

*My honour'd Papa and Mamma,*

WE have nothing but Joy and Festivity in this House, and it would be endless to tell you the Congratulations the happy Family receives every Day, from Tenants and Friends Mr *B* you know, was always deem'd one of the kindest Landlords in *England*, and his Tenants are overjoy'd at the happy Event which has given them a young Landlord of his Name For all those who live in that large Part of the Estate, which came by Lady *B.* his Mother, were much afraid of having any of Sir *Jacob Swynford's* Family for their Landlord, who, they say, are all made up of Pride and Cruelty, and would have racked them to Death Insomuch that they had a voluntary Meeting of about Twenty of the principal of them, to rejoice on the Occasion, and it was unanimously agreed to make a Present of a Piece of gilt Plate to serve as a Bason for the Christening, to the Value of One hundred Guineas, on which is to be engraven the following Inscription.

*In Acknowlegement of the Humanity and Generosity of the Best of Landlords, and as a Token of his Tenants Joy on the happy Birth of a Son and Heir, who will, it is hoped, inherit his Father's Generosity, and his Mother's Virtues, this Piece of Plate, is, with all due Gratitude, presented, as a Christening Bason to all the Children that shall proceed from such worthy Parents, and their Descendants, to the End of Time.*

By

*By the obliged and joyful Tenants of the maternal Estate in* Bedfordshire *and* Gloucestershire, *the Initials of whose Names are under-engraven,* VIZ.

Then are to follow the first Letters of each Persons Christian and Surname.

What an Honour is this to a Landlord! In my Opinion far, very far, surpassing the *mis-nomer'd* Free-gifts which we read of in some Kingdoms on extraordinary Occasions, some of them like this! For here it is all truly spontaneous------ A Free-gift *indeed*, and Mr. *B* took it very kindly, and has put off the Christening for a Week, to give Time for its being completed and inscribed as above.

Such good Tenants, such a good Wife, such Blessings from Heaven following him, nobody, I tell Mr *B* has so much Encouragement to be good, as he has, and if hereafter he should swerve, he would not have the least Excuse, and would be the ungratefullest Man breathing.

The Earl and Countess of *C----*, and Lord and Lady *Davers*, are here, to stand in Person at the Christening, and you cannot conceive how greatly my Lady *Davers* is transported with Joy, to have a Son and Heir to the Estate · She is, every Hour almost, thanking her dear Sister for him; and reads in the Child all the great Qualities she forms to herself in him 'Tis, indeed, a charming Boy, and has a great deal (if one may judge of a Child so very young) of his Father's manly Aspect. The dear Lady herself is still but weak, but the Joy of all around her, and her Spouse's Tenderness and Politeness, give her chearful and free Spirits, and she is all Serenity, Ease, and Thankfulness.

Mrs *B* as soon as the Danger was over, asked me for her Letter with the black Seal I had been very earnest to get it from Mr *B* but to no Purpose: So I was forced to tell her who had it. She said,

said, but very composedly, She was sorry for it, and hop'd he had not open'd it.

He came into her Chamber soon after, and I demanded it before her. He said, He had design'd to ask her Leave to break the Seal, which he had not yet done, nor would, without her Consent.

You will see nothing in it, Sir, said the dear Lady, but a grateful Heart, a faithful Love, and my Prayers, that GOD will be as good to You, as you have been to Me

Will you give me Leave, my Dear, said he, to break the Seal? If you do, Sir, let it not be in my Presence, but it is too serious Not, my Dear, now the Apprehension is so happily over It may now add to my Joy and my Thankfulness on that Account Then do as you please, Sir. But I had rather you would not

Then here it is, Miss *Daraford*, I had it from you It was put in o your Hands, and there I place it again. That's something like, said I, considering the Gentleman Mrs. *B.* I hope we shall bring him into good Order between us in time

So I return'd it to the dear Writer; who lifted up her Eyes, and her Lips moving, shew'd a thankful Ejaculation, that she was spared to receive it back again and put it in her Bosom

I related to Lady *Davers*, when she came, this Circumstance. and she, I believe, has got Leave to take it with her She is very proud of all Opportunities now of justifying her Brother's Choice, and doing Honour to his Spouse, with Lady *Betty C* who is her great Favourite, and who delights to read Mrs *B's* Letters

You desire to know, my honoured Papa, how Mr *B* passes his Time, and whether it be in his Lady's Chamber? No, indeed! Catch Gentlemen, the best of them, in too great a Complaisance that way, if you can. What then, does he pass his Time

*with*

*with me*, you are pleafed to ask? What a Difadvantage a Man lies under, who has been once a Rake! But I am fo generally with Mrs. B. that when I tell you, Sir, that his Vifits to her are pretty much of the polite Form, I believe I anfwer all you mean by your Queftions, and efpecially when I remind you, Sir, that Lord and Lady *Davers*, and the Earl and Countefs, and your unworthy Daughter, are at Dinner and Supper-time generally together; for Mrs. *Andrews*, who is not yet gone back to *Kent*, breakfafts, dines, and fups with her beloved Daughter, and is hardly ever out of her Room.

Then, Sir, Mr B and the Earl, and Lord *Davers*, give pretty conftant Attendance to the Bufinefs of Parliament; and, now-and-then, fup abroad----So, Sir, we are all upon Honour, and I could wifh, (only that your Facetioufnefs always gives me Pleafure, as it is a Token, that you have your much-defired Health and Freedom of Spirits) that, even in Jeft, my *Mamma*'s Daughter might pafs unqueftioned.

But I know *why* you do it: It is only to put me out of Heart to ask to ftay longer. Yet I wifh--- But I know you won't permit me to go thro' the whole Winter here --- Will my dear Papa grant it, do you think, my honoured Mamma, if you were to lay the higheft Obligation upon your dutiful Daughter, and petition for me? And fhould you care to try?

I dare not hope it myfelf, you fee, Madam: But when one fees a Gentleman here, who denies his Lady nothing that fhe asks, it makes one be ready to wifh, methinks, that Lady *Darnford* was as happy in that Particular as Lady B

*Your* Indulgence, for this Winter, this *one* Winter, or, rather this fmall *Remainder* of Winter, I make not fo much doubt of, you fee, Madam. I know you'll call me a bold Girl, but then you always, when you do, condefcend to grant my Requeft

And

And I will be as good as ever I can be afterwards
I will fetch up all the loſt Time ; riſe an Hour ſooner
in the Morning, go to-bed an Hour ſooner at Night,
flower my Papa any thing he pleaſes, read him to
ſleep, when he pleaſes, put his Gout into good Humour, when it will be ſoothed---And Mrs *B* to
crown all, will come down with me, by Permiſſion
of her ſovereign Lord, who will attend her, you
may be ſure. And will not *all* this do, to procure
me a Month or two more ?---If it won't, why then,
I will thank you for your paſt Goodneſs to me, and,
with all Duty and Chearfulneſs, bid Adieu to this
dear *London*, this dearer Family, and attend a *ſtill*
dearer Papa and Mamma, whoſe dutiful Daughter I
will ever be, whilſt

POLLY DARNFORD.

---

## LETTER XX.

### *To the ſame.*

*My honoured Papa and Mamma,*

I Have received your joint Commands, and intend
to ſet out on *Wedneſday* next Week   I hope I
ſhall find my Papa in better Health than he is at
preſent, and in better Humour too, for I am very
ſorry he is diſpleaſed with my petitioning for a little
longer Time in *London*.   It is very ſevere to impute
to me Want of Duty and Affection to you both,
which would, if deſerved, make me very unworthy
of your Favour to me.

Mr *B* and his Lady are reſolved to accompany
me in their Coach, till your Chariot meets me, if
you will be pleaſed to permit it ſo to do, and even
ſet me down at your Gate, if it do not ; but he
vows, that he will not alight at your Houſe, nor let
his Lady neither.   But I ſay, that this is a miſplaced
Reſent-

Resentment, because I ought to think it a Favour, that you have indulg'd me so much as you have done. And yet even this is likewise a Favour on *their* Side to me, because it is an Instance of their Fondness for your unworthy Daughter's Company.

Mrs *B.* is, if possible, more lovely since her Lying-in, than before. She has so much Delight in her Nursery, that I fear it will take her off from her Pen, which will be a great Loss to all whom she used to oblige with her Correspondence. Indeed, this new Object of her Care is a charming Child, and she is exceedingly pleased with her Nurse,—for she is not permitted, as she very much desired, to suckle it herself.

She makes a great Proficiency in the *French* and *Italian* Languages; and well she may, for she has the best Schoolmaster in the World, and one whom she loves better than Lady ever lov'd a Tutor. He is lofty, and will not be disputed with, but I never saw a more polite and tender Husband, for all that; and well may a Lady, bless'd as she is, bear with a little Imperiousness sometimes, which, however, she nips in the Bud, by her Sweetness of Temper, and ready Compliance. But then he is a Man of Sense, and a Lady need be the less concern'd to yield a Point to a Man of Sense, and of Generosity, as he is: Who is incapable of treating her the worse for her Resignation and Complacency. Whenever I marry, it shall be to a Man of Sense, and a generous Man, against the World, for such an one cannot treat a Woman ill, as Mrs *B.* often observes.

We had a splendid Christening, exceedingly well order'd, and every body was highly delighted at it. The Quality Gossips went away but on *Tuesday*, and my Lady *Davers* took Leave of her charming Sister, with all the Blessings, and all the Kindness, and affectionate Fondness, that could be express'd

Mr.

Mr. *Andrews*, that worthy old Man, came up to see his Grandfon Yesterday, and in order to attend his Wife down. You would never have forgotten the good Man's Behaviour (had you feen it) to his Daughter, and to the charming Child: I wish I could defcribe it to you; but I am apt to think Mrs B will take Notice of it to Lady *Davers*; and if fhe enters into the Defcription of it while I ftay, I will beg a Copy of it, to bring down with me; becaufe I know you were pleas'd with the fenfible, plain, good Man, and his Ways, when at the Hall in your Neighbourhood.

The Child is named *William*, that I fhould have told you, but I write without any manner of Connection, juft as things come uppermoft: But don't, my dear Papa, conftrue this, too, as an Inftance of Difrefpect I wifh you were not fo angry with me; it makes me almoft afraid to fee you!--As I faid, I fhall fet out next *Wednefday* in Mr. *B*'s Coach, and as we fhall keep the main Road all the Way, I fhall fee, by my being met, how I am to be received, or whether pardon'd or not. Mr. *B*. fays, He will take me back again, if my dear Papa frown at me ever fo little; and he will not deliver me up into any other Hands but his, neither.

We have been at feveral Plays, and at the Opera divers times, for we make the beft of our Time, fince it is fo fhort, and we fear'd how it would be; tho' I hoped I fhould not have Anger neither. Mrs. *B* is taken up between whiles, with writing Remarks upon the Plays, *&c.* fhe fees, in a little Book, for Lady *Davers* She fent that Lady her Remarks upon one or two, with which fhe is fo well pleafed, that fhe will not let even her Nurfery excufe her from proceeding upon thofe Subjects, and this will fo ingrofs the dear Lady's Pen, that I fhall not be favour'd fo much as I ufed to be, but Lady

*Davers*

I

*Davers* promises me to lend me the Book, when she has read it, so that will be some Satisfaction.

I see but one thing that can possibly happen to disturb the Felicity of this charming Couple, and that I will mention, in Confidence. Mr. *B.* and Mrs *B.* and myself, were at the Masquerade, before she lay-in: There was a Lady greatly taken with Mr. *B.* She was in a Nun's Habit, and followed him where-ever he went; and Mr *Turner*, a Gentleman of one of the Inns of Court, who visits Mr. *B.* sometimes, and is an old Acquaintance of his, tells me, by the bye, that the Lady took an Opportunity to unmask to Mr *B.* Mr. *Turner* has since found she is the young Countess Dowager of⸺⸺, a fine Lady, but not the most reserv'd in her Conduct of late, since her Widowhood. And he has since discovered, as he says, that a Letter or two have passed between Mr *B* and that Lady, if not more.

Now Mrs. *B.* with all her Perfections, has, as she *owns*, a little Spice of Jealousy, and should she be once alarm'd, I tremble for the Consequences to both their Happiness.

It is my Opinion, that if ever any thing makes a Misunderstanding between them, it will be from some such Quarter as this. But 'tis a thousand Pities it should. And I hope, as to the actual Correspondence begun, Mr. *Turner* is mistaken.

But be it as it will, I would not for the World, the first Hints of this Matter should come from me. --Mr *B* is a very enterprising and gallant Gentleman, is a fine Figure of a Man, and very genteel, and I don't wonder a Lady may like him. But he seems so pleas'd, so satisfy'd with his Lady, and carries it to her with so much Tenderness and Affection, that I hope her Merit, and this his Affection for her, will secure his conjugal Fidelity.

If it prove otherwise, and she discovers it, I know no one that would be more miserable than Mrs B. as well from Motives of Piety and Virtue, as from the excessive Love she bears him ---- But I hope for better Things, for both their sakes.

My humble Thanks for all your Indulgences to me, with Hopes, that you will not, my dear Papa and Mamma, hold your Displeasure against me, when I throw myself at your Feet, as I now soon hope to do, conclude me

*Your dutiful Daughter,*

M Darnford.

---

## LETTER XXI.

### *From Mrs.* B. *to Lady* Davers.

*My dear Lady,*

WE are just return'd from accompanying the worthy Miss *Darnford* as far as *Bedford*, in her Way home, where her Papa and Mamma met her in their Coach  Sir *Simon* put on his pleasant Airs, and schooled Mr *B* for persuading his Daughter to stay so long from him, *me* for putting her upon asking to stay longer; and *Miss* for being persuaded by us

I think he is worse than ever, in his way of Talk, and for my Rebukes to him, for he ran on a deal of Stuff about me, and my late Lying-in, and would have it, that I am so much improv'd, that I ought to make a Court'sy to Mr *B* once an Hour  He said, when I was angry at him, and his Lady blam'd him, that it was all pure Revenge for my Letter *, and for keeping Miss so long from him.

*  See Vol. III *p* 101.

We

We tarry'd Two Days together at *Bedford*, for we knew not how to part, and then we took a most affectionate Leave of each other

We struck out of the Road a little, to make a Visit to the dear House, where we tarry'd one Night, and next Morning, before any body could come to congratulate us, (designing to be *incog*) we proceeded on our Journey to *London*, and found my dearest, dear Boy, in charming Health.

What a new Pleasure has God Almighty's Goodness bestow'd upon me; which, after every little Absence, rises upon me, in a true maternal Tenderness, every Step I move toward the dear little Blessing! --Yet sometimes, I think your dear Brother is not so fond of him, as I wish him to be. He says, 'tis time enough for him to mind him, when he can return his Notice, and be grateful ---- A negligent Word, i'n't it, Madam?---Considering---

My dear Father came to Town, to accompany my good Mother down to *Kent*, and they set out three or four Days after your Ladyship left us. It is impossible to describe the Joy with which his worthy Heart overflow'd, when he congratulated us on the happy Event  And as he had been apprehensive for his Daughter's Safety, judge, my Lady, what his Transports must be, to see us all safe and well, and happy, and a Son given to Mr B by his greatly honoured Daughter

I was in the Nursery when he came  So was my Mother  Miss *Darnford* also was there  And Mr B who was in his Closet at his Arrival, after having received his most respectful Congratulations himself, brought him up (tho' he has not been there since. indeed he han't') · *Pamela*, said the dear Gentleman, see who's here'

I sprang to him, and kneeled for his Blessing  O my Father! said I, see (pointing to the dear Baby at
the

the Nurfe's Breaft) how God Almighty has anfwer'd all our Prayers!

He dropp'd down on his reverend Knees by me, clafping me in his indulgent Arms O my Daugh ter!---My bleffed Daughter!---And do I once more fee you! And fee you fafe and well!---I do! I do! . Bleffed be thy Name, O gracious GOD, for thefe thy Mercies!

While we were thus joined, happy Father, and happy Daughter, in one Thankfgiving, the fweet Baby having fallen afleep, the Nurfe had put it into the Cradle, and when my Father rofe from me, he went to my Mother, God blefs my dear *Betty*, faid he I long'd to fee you, after this Separation Here's Joy! Here's Pleafure! O how happy are we! And taking her Hand, he kneeled down on one Side the Cradle, and my Mother on the other, both looking at the dear Baby, with Eyes running over, and, Hand in Hand, he prayed, in the moft fervent manner, for a Bleffing upon the dear Infant, and that God Almighty would make him an Honour to his Father's Family, and to his Mother's Virtue (that was his Word); and that, in the Words of Scripture, *he might grow on, and be in Favour both with the Lord, and with Men!*

They both rofe, and Mr. *B* taking my Hand, and Mifs *Darnford's* (your Ladyfhip may guefs how we were moved! for Mifs is a fweet-natur'd Lady, you know, Madam), My dear *Pamela!* How thefe kind, thefe grateful Hearts affect one!---- Do you often, my dear Mifs *Darnford*, fee Scenes wrough up by the Poets to this moving Height?---Here we behold and admire that noble Simplicity, in which Nature always triumphs over her Hand maid Art!- And which makes a Scene of Joy as affecting to a noble Mind, as that of the deepeft Diftrefs Elfe, how could it difplay its Force thus fweetly on

your

your lovely Cheek! And he saluted Miss, and me too

Mr *B* has just put into my Hands Mr *Locke's* Treatife on Education, and he commands me to give him my Thoughts upon it in Writing. He has a very high Regard for this Author, and tells me, That my Tendernefs for *Billy* will make me think fome of the first Advice given in it, a little harfh, perhaps, but altho' he has not read it through, only having dipp'd into it here and there, he believes, from the Name of the Author, I cannot have a better Directory And my Opinion of it, after I have well confidered it, will inform him, he fays, of my own Capacity and Prudence, and how far he may rely upon both in the Point of a *first Education*

I ask'd, If I might not be excus'd Writing, only making my Obfervations here and there, to himfelf, as I found Occafion? But he faid, You will yourfelf, my Dear, better confider the Subject, and be more a Miftrefs of it, and I fhall the better attend to your Reafonings, when they are put into Writing. And furely, *Pamela*, added he, you may, in fuch an important Point as this, as well oblige *me* with a little of your Penmanfhip, as your other dear Friends

After this, your Ladyfhip will judge I had not another Word to fay He cuts one to the Heart, when he fpeaks fo ferioufly

I have look'd a little into it It is a Book quite accommodated to my Cafe, being written to a Gentleman, the Author's Friend, for the Regulation of his Conduct towards his Children But how fhall I do, Madam, if in fuch a fam'd and renowned Author, I fee already fome few things, which I think want clearing up? Won't it look like intolerable Vanity, in fuch a one as me, to find Fault with fuch a Genius as Mr. *Locke* ?

But

But I will confider of the Matter thoroughly, before I fet Pen to Paper; for, altho' he writes in a very familiar and intelligible Style, perhaps I may not underftand him at once reading.

I muft, on this Occafion, give your Ladyfhip the Particulars of a fhort Converfation between your Brother and me, which, however, perhaps, will not be to my Advantage, becaufe it will fhew you what a teizing Body I can be, if I am indulged ----- But Mr B will not fpoil me neither in that way No fear of that, I dare fay ---- Your Ladyfhip will fee this in the very Dialogue I fhall give you

Thus it was I had been reading in Mr. *Locke's* Book, and Mr B ask'd me, How I lik'd it? Exceedingly well, Sir But I have a Propofal to make, which, if you will be pleafed to comply with, will give me a charming Opportunity of underftanding Mr *Locke*

What is your Propofal, my Dear? I fee it is fome very particular one, by that fweet Earneftnefs in your Look.

Why fo it is, Sir And I muft know, whether you are in high good Humour, before I make it I think you look grave upon me, and my Propofal will not then do, I'm fure

You have all the amufing Ways of your Sex my dear *Pamela* But tell me what you would fay? You know I don't love Sufpenfe

May be you're bufy, Sir Perhaps I break in upon you I believe you were going into your Clofet.

True Woman ----How you love to put one upon the Tenters! Yet, my Life for yours, by your Parade, what I juft now thought important, is fome pretty Trifle.----Speak it at once, or I'll be angry with you, and tapp'd my Cheek

Well, I wifh I had not come juft now ---- I fee you are not in a quite good Humour enough for my Propofal --- So, pray, Sir, excufe me, till To-morrow.                                                    He

He took my Hand, and led me to his Clofet, calling me his pretty Impertinent, and then urging me, I faid----You know, Sir, I have not been us'd to the Company of Children  Your dear *Billy* will not make me fit, for a long time, to judge of any Part of Education  I can learn of the charming Boy nothing but the Baby Conduct: But now, if you would permit me to take into the Houfe fome little Mafter of Three or Four Years old, or Mifs of Five or Six, I fhould watch over all their little Ways; and now reading a Chapter in the *Child,* and now a Chapter in the *Book,* I fhall be enabled to look forward, and with Advantage, into the Subject; and to go thro' all the Parts of Education tolerably, for one of my Capacity; for, Sir, I can, by my own Defects, and what I have wifhed to mend, know how to judge of, and fupply that Part of Life, which carries a Child up to Eleven or Twelve Years of Age, which was mine, when my Lady took me.

A pretty Thought, *Pamela!* But tell me, Who will part with their Child, think you? Would *you* do it, if it were your own Cafe, altho' you were ever fo well affur'd of the Advantages your Little-one would reap by it?----- For, don't you confider, my Dear, that the Child ought to be wholly fubjected to your Authority? That its Father or Mother ought feldom to fee it; becaufe it fhould think itfelf abfolutely dependent upon you?— And where, my Dear, will you meet with Parents fo refign'd?— Befides, one would have the Child defcended of genteel Parents, and not fuch as could do nothing for it, otherwife the Turn of Mind and Education you would give it, might do it more Harm than Good.

All this is true, Sir, very true  But have you no other Objection, if one could find a genteelly defcended young Mafter? And would you join to perfuade his Papa to give me up his Power, only from three Months to three Months, as I lik'd, and

G 4　　　　the

the Child lik'd, and as the Papa approv'd of my Proceedings?

This is so reasonable, with these last Conditions, *Pamela*, that I should be pleased with your Notion, if it could be put in Practice, because the Child would be benefited by your Instruction, and you would be improved in an Art, which I could wish to see you an Adept in

But, perhaps, Sir, you had rather it were a Miss, than a Master?

I had, my Dear, if a Miss could be found, whose Parents would give her up to you But I suppose you have some Master in your Head, by your putting it upon that Sex at first.

Let me see, Sir, You say you are in a good Humour Let me see, if you be '--- Looking boldly in his Face

What now, with some little Impatience, would the pretty Fool be at?

Only, Sir, that you have nothing to do, but to speak the Word, and there is a Miss whose Papa, and Mamma too, I am sure, would consent to give up to me, for my own Instruction, as well as for her sake, and if, to speak in the Scripture Phrase, I have found *Grace in your Sight*, kind Sir, speak this Word to the dear Miss's Papa

And have you thus come over with me, *Pamela*'.. Go, I am half angry with you, for leading me on in this manner against myself This looks so artful, that I won't love you '— Dear Sir '— And dear Madam' too ' Begone, I say '—You have surpris'd me by Art, when your Talent is Nature, and you should keep to that '

I was sadly balk'd, and had neither Power to go nor stay '---At last, seeing I had put him into a kind of Flutter, as now he had put me, I moved my unwilling Feet towards the Door ---He took a Turn about the Closet mean time —Yet stay, said he, there is something so generous in your Art, that, on Re-collection, I cannot part with you

He took Notice of the starting Tear— I am to blame!— You had surpris'd me so, that my hasty Temper got the better of my Consideration  Let me kiss away this pearly Fugitive  Forgive me, my dearest Love! What an inconsiderate Brute am I, when compar'd to such an Angel as my *Pamela!* I see, at once now, all the Force, and all the Merit, of your amiable Generosity  And to make you amends for this my Hastiness, I will cooly consider of the Matter, and will either satisfy you by my Compli-ance, or by the Reasons which I will give for the contrary.

But say, my *Pamela*; can you forgive my Harsh-ness?—Can I! Yes, indeed, Sir, pressing his Hand to my Lips, and bid me Go, and Begone, twenty times a Day, if I am to be thus kindly called back to you, thus nobly and condescendingly treated, in the same Breath!— I see, dear Sir, continued I, that I must be in Fault, if ever you are lastingly dis-pleased with me — For as soon as you turn yourself about, your Anger vanishes, and you make me rich Amends for a few harsh Words  Only one thing, dear Sir, let me add  If I have dealt artfully with you, impute it to my Fear of offending you, thro' the Nature of my Petition, and not to Design, and that I took the Example of the Prophet, to King *David*, in the Parable of the *Ewe-Lamb*.

I remember it, my Dear— and you have well pointed your Parable, and had nothing to do, but to say, *Thou art the Man!*

I am called upon by my dear Benefactor for a little Airing; and he suffers me only to conclude this long Letter, knowing to whom I have the Ho-nour to write, this being Post-day.  And so I am obliged, with greater Abruptness than I had design'd,

to

to mention thankfully your Ladyfhip's Goodnefs to me, particularly in that kind, kind Letter *, in behalf of my dear Parents, had a certain Event taken place  Mr B fhew'd it to me *this Morning*, and not before --I believe, for fear I fhould have been fo much opprefs'd by the Senfe of your Ladyfhip's unmerited Goodnefs to me, had he let me know of it before your Departure from us, that I fhould not have been able to look up at you, heaping Favours and Bleffings upon me, as you hourly were doing befides.  What a happy Creature am I! --- But my Gratitude runs me into Length, and forry I am, that I cannot have time juft now to indulge it

But yet I am apt fometimes to doubt, whether I ought to think myfelf fo very happy, and whether it is not an Argument of a mean Spirit, becaufe I am under Obligations, *unreturnable* Obligations, to every living Soul, as well as to your Ladyfhip, and yet can rejoice in them, as if it was fuch a glorious Thing to be obliged, when it is not in one's Power to oblige again.

Is there nothing, my dear Lord and Lady *Davers*, is there nothing, my dear Lady Countefs, and my good Lord C. that I can do, to fhew, at leaft, that I have a *Will*, and am not an ingrateful, and a fordid Creature?

And yet, if you give me Power to do any thing that will have the *Appearance* of a Return, even that *Power* will be laying a frefh Obligation upon me-- Which, however, I fhould be very proud of, becaufe I fhould thereby convince you, by fomething more than Words, how much I am (moft particularly, my deareft Lady *Davers*, my Sifter, my Friend, my Patronefs)

*Your moft obliged, and faithful Servant,*

P B

* *See Letter* xvi *in this Volume,* p 97

Your

Your dear Brother joins in refpectful Thankfulnefs to his Four noble Goffips And I made
my *Billy*, by his Lips, fubfcribe his. I hope fo
to direct his earlieft Notions, as to make him
fenfible of his dutiful Obligations to fuch noble
and good God-papa's and Mamma's

---

## LETTER XXII.

### *From Lady* DAVERS *to Mrs.* B.

*My deareft* PAMELA,

TALK not to us of unreturnable Obligations,
and all that, as in your laft Letter. You do
more for us, in the Entertainment you give us all,
by your Letters, than we *have* done, or ever *can* do,
for you And as to me, I know no greater Pleafure in the World, than that which my Brother's
Felicity and yours gives me GOD continue this
Felicity to you both. I am fure it will be *his* Fault,
and not yours, if it be at all diminifh'd

We have heard fome idle Rumours here, as if
you were a little uneafy of late; and having not had
a Letter from you for this Fortnight paft, it makes
me write, to afk, How you all do? and, Whether
you expected an Anfwer from me to your laft?

I hope you won't be punctilious with me, my
*Pamela* For we have nothing to write to you about,
except it be, how much we all love and honour you,
and that you believe already, or elfe you don't do
us Juftice.

I fuppofe you'll be going out of Town foon, now
the Parliament is rifing My Lord is refolv'd to
put his Proxy into another Hand, and intends, I believe, to take my Brother's Advice in it Both the
Earl and his Lordfhip are highly pleas'd with my
Brother's moderate and independent Principles. He

has got great Credit among all unprejudic'd Men,
by the Part he acted throughout the laft Seffions,
in which he has fhewn, that he would no more join
to diftrefs and clog the Wheels of Government, by
an unreafonable Oppofition, than he would do the
dirty Work of any Adminiftration   As he has fo
noble a Fortune, and wants nothing of any body,
he would be doubly to blame, to take any other
. Part than that of his Country, in which he has fo
great a Stake

May he act *out* of the Houfe, and *in* the Houfe,
with equal Honour, and he will be his Country's
Pride, and your Pride, and mine too ! Which is the
Wifh of

*Your affectionate Sifter,*

B. DAVERS.

If you want a Pretence to kifs my dear Boy, give
him, now-and-then, one for me   I hope he
improves, under the Eye of fo careful a Mamma,
the little Rogue will elfe be unworthier than I
wifh him to be   I hope you proceed with my
Book   I muft fee your Obfervations on *Locke*
too   'Twas a charming pretty Thought of yours,
that of Mifs *Goodwin*   A hafty Wretch ! How
could he be angry ?----'Twas well he fo foon
confidered of the Matter, and afk'd Pardon. *

---

# LETTER XXIII.

*My deareft Lady,*

I Have been a little in Diforder, that I have.  Some
few Rubs have happen'd   I hope they will be
happily removed   But I am unwilling to believe all
that is faid   This is a wicked Town, though I
wifh we were out of it   But I fee not when that
will

will be I wifh Mr. *B* would permit me and my *Billy* to go into *Kent:* But I don't care to leave him behind me, neither, and he is not inclin'd to go. Excufe my Brevity, my deareft Lady — But I muft break off, with only affuring your Ladyfhip, that I am, and ever will be,

*Your obliged and grateful*

P B.

## LETTER XXIV.

*My deareft* PAMELA,

I Underftand Things go not fo well as I wifh If you think my coming up to Town, and refiding with you, while you ftay in it, will be of Service to you, or help to get you out of it, I will fet out directly I will pretend fome Indifpofition, and a Defire of confulting your *London* Phyficians, or any thing you fhall think fit to be done, by

*Your affectionate Sifter,*

*and faithful Friend,*

B DAVERS.

## LETTER XXV.

*My deareft Lady,*

A Thoufand Thanks for your Goodnefs to me But I hope all will be well I hope God will enable me to act fo prudent a Part, as will touch his generous Breaft. Be pleafed to tell me what your Ladyfhip has heard, but it becomes not me, I think, till I cannot help it, to make any Appeals; for, I know, thofe will not be excus'd; and I do all I can to fupprefs my Uneafinefs before him. But I

pay

4

pay for it, when I am alone. My Nurfery, and my Reliance on God, (I fhould have faid the latter firft) are all my Confolation ---- God preferve and blefs you, my good Lady, and my Noble Lord, (but I am apt to think your Ladyfhip's Prefence will not avail) prays,

*Your affectionate and obliged*

P B

## LETTER XXVI.

WHY does not my fweet Girl fubfcribe *Sifter,* as ufual ? I have done nothing amifs to you ! I love you dearly, and ever will. I can't help my Brother's Faults But I hope he treats you with Politenefs and Decency He fhall be none of my Brother, if he don't I reft a great deal upon your Prudence, and it will be very meritorious, if you can overcome yourfelf, fo as to act unexceptionably, tho' it may not be deferv'd, on this Occafion · For in doing fo, you'll have a Triumph over Nature itielf; for, my dear Girl, as you have formerly own'd, you have a little Touch * of Jealoufy in your Compofition

What I have heard, is no Secret to any body. The injured Party is generally the laft who hears in thefe Cafes, and you fhall not firft be told any thing by me that muft *afflict* you, but cannot *you,* more than it does *me* God give you Patience and Comfort ! The wicked Lady has a deal to anfwer for, to difturb fuch an uncommon Happinefs But no more, than that I am

*Your ever affectionate Sifter,*

B. DAVERS

* *See p* 44 *of this* Volume.

I am

I am all Impatience to hear how you conduct yourself upon this trying Occasion. Let me know *what* you have heard, and *how* you came to hear it.

---

## LETTER XXVII.

WHY don't I subscribe Sister? asks my dearest Lady *Davers?*----I have not had the Courage to do it of late. For my Title to that Honour, arises from the dear, thrice dear Mr *B.* And how long I may be permitted to call him mine, I cannot say. But since you command it, I will call your Ladyship by that beloved Name, let the rest happen as God shall see fit.

Mr *B* cannot be unpolite, in the main; but he is cold, and a little cross, and short in his Speeches to me. I try to hide my Grief from every body, and most from him, for, my dear Lady, neither my Father, Mother, nor Miss *Darnford,* know any thing from me. Mrs. *Jervis,* from whom I seldom hide any thing, as she is on the Spot with me, hears not my Complainings, nor my Uneasiness; for I would not lessen the dear Gentleman. He may *yet* see the Error of the Way he is in. God grant it, for his own sake, as well as mine!---I am even sorry your Ladyship is afflicted with the Knowlege of the Matter.

The poor unhappy Lady, God forgive her! is to be pity'd. She loves him, and having strong Passions, and being unus'd to be controul'd, is lost to a Sense of Honour and Justice, poor, poor Lady!---O these wicked Masquerades! From them springs all my Unhappiness! My *Spaniard* was too amiable, and met with a Lady who was no Nun, but in Habit. Every one was taken with him in that Habit, so
suited

fuited to the natural Dignity of his Perfon!---O thefe wicked, wicked Mafquerades!

I am all Patience in Appearance, all Uneafinefs in Reality  I did not think I could, efpecially in *this* Point, this moft *affecting* Point, be fuch an Hypocrite  It has coft me---Your Ladyfhip knows not what it has coft me! to be able to affume that Character! Yet my Eyes are fwell'd with crying, and look red, altho' I am always breathing on my Hand, and patting them with that, and my warm Breath, to hide the Diftrefs that will, from my over-charged Heart, appear in them.

Then he fays, What's the matter with the little Fool! You're always in this Way of late! What ails you, *Pamela*?

Only a little vapourifh, Sir!--- Nafty Vapours! Don't be angry at me!----Then *Billy*, I thought, was not very well!

This Boy will fpoil your Temper  At this Rate, what fhould be your Joy, will become your Misfortune  Don't receive me in this manner, I charge you

In what manner, Sir? I always receive you with a grateful Heart! If any thing troubles me, it is in your Abfence  But fee, Sir, (then I try to fmile and feem pleafed) I am all Sunfhine now you are come! ----Don't you fee I am?

Yes, your Sunfhine of late is all thro' a Cloud!--- I know not what's the matter with you  Your Temper will alter, and then---

It fhan't alter, Sir---It fhan't---if I can help it. ----And then I kifs'd his Hand, that dear Hand, that, perhaps, was laft about his more beloved Countefs's Neck----Diftracting Reflection!

But come, may-be I think the worft!----To be fure I do!---For my Apprehenfions were ever afore-hand with Events, and bad muft be the Cafe, if it is worfe than I think it.  But it will ripen of itfelf,

it

it is a corroding Evil It will increase to its Crisis, and then it may dissipate happily, or end in Death!

All that grieves me, (for I have had the Happiness of a whole Life crouded thick upon me into a few past Months, and so ought to be grateful for the Good I have reaped) is for his own dear sake, for his Soul's sake ----But, come, he is a young Gentleman, and may see his Error ----This may be a Trial to *him*, as well as to *me* And if he *should* conquer it, what a charming, charming Thing would that be!

You command me to let you know *what* I have heard, and how I *came* to hear it I told your Ladyship, in one of my former *, that two Gentlemen, brought up to the Law, but above the Practice of it, tho', I doubt, not above Practices less honourable, had visited us, on coming to Town

They have been often here since, Mi *Turner* particularly; and sometimes by himself, when Mr *B* has happen'd to be out, and he it was, as I guess'd, that gave me, at the wicked Masquerade, the Advice to look after my *Musidorus* †

I did not like their Visits, and *his* much less. For he seem'd to me a Man of an intriguing Spirit. But about Three Weeks ago, Mr. *B.* setting out upon a Party of Pleasure to *Oxford,* he came, and pretending great Business with me, and I happening to be at Breakfast in the Parlour, only *Polly* attending me, admitted him to drink a Dish of Chocolate with me. And when *Polly* had stept out, he told me, after many Apologies, that he had discover'd who the Nun was at the Masquerade, that had engaged Mr *B.*

I said, It was very indifferent to me, who the Lady was.

* *See this* Vol *p* 6.    † Ibid *p.* 89.

He

He reply'd, (making ftill more Apologies, and pretending great Reluctance to fpeak out) That it was no lefs a Lady than the young Countefs Dowager of——, a Lady noted for her Wit and her Beauty, but of a gay Difpofition, tho' he believ'd not yet culpable.

I was alarm'd, but would not let him fee it, and he ran into the Topick of the Injuftice of marry'd Gentlemen, who had virtuous Wives, and gave themfe'ves up to Intrigues of this kind

I remember'd fome of Mr. *B*'s Leffons formerly, of which I once gave your Ladyfhip a Tranfcript\*, particularly, that of drawing a kind Veil over his Faults, and extenuating thofe I could not hide, and, ftill more particularly, that Caution, that if ever Rakes attempted a marry'd Lady, their Encouragement proceeded from the Slights and Contempts with which they endeavour'd to poffefs her againft her Husband, and I told Mr *Turner*, That I was fo well fatisfy'd in Mr. *B*'s Affection for, me, and his well-known Honour, that I could not think myfelf obliged to any Gentleman, who fhould endeavour to give me a lefs Opinion of either, than I ought to have.

He then bluntly told me, that the very Party Mr *B* was upon, was with the Countefs for one, and the Lord——, who had marry'd her Sifter

I faid, I was glad he was in fuch good Company, and wifhed him all manner of Pleafure in it

He hoped, he faid, he might truft to my Difcretion, that I would not let Mr *B* know from whom I had the Information: That, indeed, his Motive in mentioning it to me, was Self-intereft, for that he had prefum'd to make fome Overtures of an honourable Nature to the Counfefs, in his own Behalf, which had been rejected fince that Mafquerade

* *See* Vol. II *p* 318.

Night

Night: And that he hoped the prudent Ufe I would make of the Intimation, might, fome-how, be a Means to break off that Correfpondence, before it was attended with bad Confequences

I told him, coldly, tho' it ftung me to the Heart, That I fhould not interfere in the Matter at all: That I was fully affur'd of Mr B's Honour, and was forry, he, Mr. *Turner*, had fo bad an Opinion of a Lady, for whom he profeffed fo high a Confideration And rifing up, Will you excufe me, Sir, that I cannot attend at all to fuch a Subject as this, and think I ought not, and fo muft withdraw?

Only, Madam, one Word He offer'd to take my Hand, but I would not permit it—And then he fwore a great Oath, that he had told me his true and his only Motive And that Letters had paffed between the Countefs and Mr B, adding, That one Day I wou'd blame myfelf, for not endeavouring to ftifle a Flame, that might now perhaps be kept under, but which, if it got Head, would be of more fatal Confequence to my Repofe, than I at prefent imagin'd—But, faid he, I beg you'll keep it within your own Breaft, elfe, from two fuch hafty Spirits, as his and mine, it may poffibly be attended with ftill worfe Confequences

I will never, Sir, enter into a Subject, that is not proper to be communicated, every Tittle of it, to Mr B, and this muft be my Excufe for withdrawing And away I went from him

Your Ladyfhip will judge with how uneafy a Heart, which became more fo, when I fat down to reflect upon what he had told me But I was refolved to give it as little Credit as I could, or that any thing would come of it, till Mr B's own Behaviour fhould convince me, to my Affliction, that I had fome Reafon to be alarmed: So I open'd not my Lips about it, not even to Mrs. *Jervis.*

At Mr *B*'s Return, I received him in my usual affectionate and unreserved Manner, and he behaved himself to me with his accustomed Goodness and Kindness, or, at least, with so little Difference, that had not the Gentleman's Officiousness made me more watchful, I should not have perceived it

But, next Day, a Letter was brought by a Footman from Mr *B* He was out So *John* gave it to me The Superscription was a Lady's Writing The Seal, the Dowager Lady's, with a Coronet This gave me great Uneasiness And when Mr *B* came in, I said, Here is a Letter for you, Sir, and from a Lady too!

What then?—said he with Quickness

I was balk'd, and withdrew For I saw him turn the Seal about and about, as if he would see whether I had endeavour'd to look into it

He needed not to have been so afraid, for I would not have done such a Thing, had I known my Life was to depend upon it

I went up, and could not help weeping at his quick Answer, yet I did my Endeavour to hide it, when he came up

Was not my Girl a little inquisitive upon me, just now?

I spoke pleasantly, Sir — But you were very quick upon your Girl.

'Tis my Temper, my Dear—You know I mean nothing You should not mind it

I should not, Sir, if I had been *used* to it

He look'd at me with Sternness —Do you doubt my Honour, Madam?

*Madam* ' did you say, Sir '—I won't take that Word '—Dear Sir, call it back—' won't be call'd *Madam* '—Call me your Girl, your Rustick, your *Pamela*—Call me any thing but *Madam* '

My Charmer, then, my Life, my Soul, will any of those do? and saluted me But whatever you do,

let

let me not fee, that you have any Doubts of my Honour to you

The very Mention of the Word, dear Sir, is a Security to me, I want no other, I cannot doubt. But if you fpeak fhort to me, how fhall I bear that?

He withdrew, fpeaking nothing of the Contents of his Letter, as I dare fay he would, had the Subject been fuch as he chofe to mention to me.

We being alone, after Supper, I took the Liberty to ask him, Who was of his Party to *Oxford?* He nam'd the Vifcountefs————and her Lord, Mr *Howard* and his Daughter, Mr *Herbert* and his Lady. And I had a Partner too, my Dear, to reprefent you

I am much obliged to the Lady, Sir, be fhe who fhe would

Why, my Dear, you are *fo* engag'd in your Nurfery! Then this was a fudden Thing, as, you know, I told you.

Nay, Sir, as long as it was agreeable to you, I had nothing to do, but to be pleafed with it

He watched my Eyes, and the Turn of my Countenance—You look, *Pamela,* as if you'd be glad to return the Lady Thanks in Perfon. Shall I engage her to vifit you? She longs to fee you

Sir,—Sir,—hefitated I—as you pleafe—I can't be —I can't be—difpleafed ---

*Difpleafed!*—interrupted he, why that Word? and why that Hefitation in your Anfwer? You fpeak very volubly, my Dear, when you're not moved.

Dear Sir, faid I, almoft as quick as himfelf, Why fhould I be moved? What Occafion is there for it? I hope you have a better Opinion of me, than——

Than what, *Pamela?*—What would you fay? I know you're a little jealous Slut    I know you are

But, dear Sir, why fhould you think of imputing Jealoufy to me on *this* Score?----What a Creature muft I be, if you could not be abroad with a Lady,

but

but I muſt be jealous of you?---No, Sir, I have Reaſon to rely upon your Honour, and I *do* rely upon it, and——

And what? Why, my Dear, you are giving me Aſſurances, as if you thought the Caſe requir'd it!

Ah! thought I, ſo it does, I ſee too plainly, or apprehend I do; but I durſt not ſay ſo, nor give him any Hint about my Informant; tho' now I was enough confirmed of the Truth of what Mr *Turner* had told me

Yet, I reſolved, if poſſible, not to alter my Conduct But my frequent Weepings, when by myſelf, could not be hid as I wiſhed, my Eyes not keeping my Heart's Counſel.

And this gives Occaſion to ſome of the ſtern Words which I have mention'd above

All that he further ſaid, at this Time, was, with a negligent, yet a determin'd Air——Well, *Pamela*, don't be doubtful of my Honour. You know how much I love you But, one Day or other, I ſhall gratify this Lady's Curioſity, and will bring her to pay you a Viſit, and you ſhall ſee you need not be aſham'd of her Acquaintance.---Whenever you pleaſe, Sir,---was all I car'd to ſay farther, for I ſaw he was upon the Catch, and looked ſtedfaſtly upon me whenever I moved my Lips; and I am not a finiſh'd Hypocrite, and he can read the Lines of one's Face, and the Motions of one's Heart, I think

I am ſure mine is a very uneaſy one But 'till I reflected, and weighed well the Matter, it was worſe. and my natural Imperfection of this ſort made me ſee a Neceſſity to be the more watchful over myſelf, and to doubt my own Prudence And thus I reaſon'd when he withdrew.

Here, thought I, I have had a greater Proportion of Happineſs, without Alloy, fallen to my Share, than any of my Sex, and I ought to be prepar'd for ſome Trials

T is

'Tis true, this is of the foreft Kind, 'tis worfe than Death itfelf to me, who had an Opinion of the dear Gentleman's Reformation, and prided myfelf not a little on that Account. So that the Blow is full upon my fore Place 'Tis on the Side I could be the moft eafily penetrated But *Achilles* could be touched only in his Heel; and if he was to die by an Enemy's Hand, muft not the Arrow find out that only vulnerable Place?----My Jealoufy is that Place with me, as your Ladyfhip obferves *, but it is feated deeper than the Heel: It is in my *Heart* The barbed Dart has found that out, and there it fticks up to the very Feathers

Yet, thought I, I will take care, that I do not exafperate him by Upbraidings, when I fhould try to move him by Patience and Forbearance For the Breach of *his* Duty cannot warrant the Neglect of *mine* My Bufinefs is to reclaim, and not to provoke And when, if it pleafe God, this Storm fhall be over-blown, let me not, by my prefent Behaviour, leave any Room for Heart-burnings, but, like a fkilful Surgeon, fo heal the Wound to the Bottom, tho' the Operation be painful, that it may not fefter, and break out again with frefh Violence, on future Mifunderftandings, if any fhall happen.

He is a young Gentleman, has been ufed to have his own Will, thought I. This may be a permitted Stumbling-block in his Way, to make him ftand the firmer, when recover'd The Lady may be unhappy, that fhe cannot conquer her faulty Love They may both fee their Error, and ftop fhort of Crime. If not, he is a Gentleman of fine Senfe, he may run an undue Length, but may reclaim; and then I fhall be *his* Superior, by my preferved Virtue and Duty, and have it in my Power to *forgive* the dear Gentleman, and fo repay him fome of thofe Obli-

* *See this* Vol. p 134.

gations

gations which I shall never otherwise have it in my Power to repay,----nor indeed wish to have it, in this way, if it please God to prevent it.

Then, thought I, how much better is it to be the *suffering* than the *offending* Person ?----But yet, Madam, to have so *fine* a Gentleman, who had advanced so far up the Hill of Virtue, to slide back all at once, and (between your Ladyship and me) to have him sink down to the Character he had despised, and, at last, if his precious Life should be spared (as is my hourly Prayer), to have him carry his Vice, into advanced Years, and become such a poor Gentleman, as we see Sir *Simon Darnford*, retaining a Love of his juvenile Follies, even after the Practice has left him, how my Heart shudders at such a Thought for my Mr *B*. '

Well, but, thought I, let the worst come to the worst, he may perhaps be so good as to permit me to pass the Remainder of my Days, with my dear *Billy*, in *Kent*, with my Father and Mother, and so, when I cannot rejoice in Possession of a virtuous Husband, I shall be imployed in praying for him, and enjoy a two fold Happiness, that of doing my own Duty to my dear Baby----and a pleasing Entertainment that will be !----and that of comforting my worthy Parents, and being comforted by them;---- and no small Consolation this '----And who knows, but I may be permitted to steal a Visit now-and-then to dear Lady *Davers*, and be called Sister, and be deemed a *faultless* Sister too '----and that will be a fine thing ' But, remember, my dear Lady, that if ever it come to this, I will not bear, that for my sake, you shall, with too much Asperity, blame your dear Brother, for I will be ingenuous to find Excuses or Extenuations for him, and I will now-and-then, in some disguised Hint, steal the Pleasure of seeing him, and his happier Countess, and gave him, with

a silent

a silent Tear, my Blessing for the Good I and mine have reaped at his Hands.

But, oh! if he takes from me my dear *Billy*, who must, after all, be his Heir, and gives him to the cruel Countess, he will at once burst asunder the Strings of my Heart! For, Oh my happy Rivaless! if you tear from me my Husband, he is in his own Disposal, and I cannot help it.—Nor can I indeed, if he will give you my *Billy*. But this I am sure of, that my Child and my Life must go together!

Your Ladyship will think I rave. Indeed I am almost crazed at times. For the dear Gentleman is so negligent, so cold, so haughty, that I cannot bear it. He says, just now, You are quite alter'd, *Pamela*. I believe I am, Madam. But what can I do? He knows not, that I know so much I dare not tell him. For he will have me then reveal my Intelligencer· And what may be the Case between them?

I weep in the Night, when he is asleep, and in the Day, when he is absent· And I am happy, when I can, unobserved, steal this poor Relief I believe already I have shed as many Tears as would drown my poor Baby How many more I may have to shed, God only knows! ---For, O Madam, after all my Fortitude, and my Recollection, to fall from so much Happiness, and so soon, is a trying Thing!

But I will still hope the best, and resign to God's Will, and his, and see how far the dear Gentleman will be permitted to exercise me. So don't, my good Lady, be over-much concerned for me---For you know I am apt to be too apprehensive. And should this Matter blow over, I shall be asham'd of my Weakness, and the Trouble I must give to your generous Heart, for one so undeservedly favour'd by you, as is

*Your obliged Sister, and most humble Servant,*

P. B

D.ar

Dear my Lady, let no Soul see any Part of this our
present Correspondence, for your dear Brother's
sake, and your sake, and my sake

## LETTER XXVIII.

*My dearest* PAMELA,

YOU need not be afraid of any body's knowing
what passes between us on this cutting Subject.
Tho' I hear of it from every Mouth, yet I pretend
'tis all Falshood and Malice   Yet Lady *Betty* will
have it, that there is more in it than I will own,
and that I know my Brother's Wickedness, by my
pensive Looks   She will make a Vow, she says,
never to marry any Man living

I am greatly moved by your affecting Periods
Charming *Pamela !* what a Tempest do you raise in
one's Mind, when you please, and lay it too, at
your own Will ! Your Colourings are strong ; but,
I hope, your Imagination carries you much farther
than it is possible ne should go.

I am pleased with your prudent Reasonings, and
your wise Resolutions.   I see nobody can advise or
help you   God only can ! And his Direction you
beg *so* hourly, that I make no doubt you will
have it

What vexes me is, that when the noble Uncle of
this vile Lady---(why don't you call her so as well as
I ?)---expostulated with her on the Scandals she
brought upon her Character and Family, she pretended to argue, foolish Creature ! for Polygamy,
and said, She had rather be a certain Gentleman's
second Wife, than the first to the greatest Man in
*England*

I leave you to your own Workings , but if I find
your Prudence unrewarded by the Wretch, the Storm

you

you faw raifed at the Hall, fhall be nothing to the Hurricane I will excite, to tear up by the Roots all the Happinefs the two Wretches propofe to themfelves

Don't let my Intelligence, which is undoubted, grieve you over-much  Try fome way to move the Wretch.  What muft be done, muft be by touching his Generofity : He has that in fome Perfection. But how in *this* Cafe to move it, is beyond my Power or Skill to prefcribe

God blefs you, my deareft *Pamela* !  You fhall be my *only* Sifter   And I will never own my Brother, if he be fo bafe to your fuperlative Merit.  Adieu once more,

*From your Sifter and Friend,*

B. DAVERS.

## LETTER XXIX.

*My deareft Lady*,

A Thoufand Thanks for your kind, your truly Sifterly Letter and Advice   Mr B. is juft returned from a Tour to *Portfmouth*, with the Countefs, I believe, but am not fure

Here I am forced to leave off

Let me fcratch thro' this laft Surmife   It feems, fhe was not with him   This is fome Comfort, however

He is very kind; and *Billy* not being well, when he came in, my Grief paffed off without Blame. He has faid a great many tender Things to me  But added, That if I gave myfelf fo much Uneafinefs every Time the Child ailed any thing, he would hire the Nurfe to over-lay him   Blefs me, Madam ! what hard-hearted, what fhocking Things are thefe Men capable of faying !—The fartheft from their

H 2 Hearts,

Hearts, indeed; so they had need ---For he was as glad of the Child's being better as I could be

In the Morning he went out in the Chariot for about an Hour, and return'd in a very good Humour, saying twenty agreeable Things to me, which makes me so proud, and so pleas'd !

He is gone out again

Could I but find this Matter happily conquered, for his own Soul's sake! --But he seems, by what your Ladyship mentions, to have carry'd this Polygamy Point with the Lady

Can I live with him, Madam,---*Ought* I----if this be the Case? I have it under his Hand, that the Laws of his Country were sufficient to deter him from this Practice  But oh! he knew not this Countess then!

But here I must break off.

He is returned, and coming up.  Go into my Bosom, for the present, 'O Letter dedicated to dear Lady *Davers*· --Come to my Hand, the Play Imployment, so unsuited to my present afflicted Mind! ---Here he comes !

O but, Madam, Madam! my Heart is almost broken !- -Just now Mr. *B* tells me, That the Countess Dowager, and the Viscountess her Sister, are to be here to see my *Billy*, and to drink Tea with me, this very Afternoon!

I was all Confusion, when he told me this. I looked around and around, and upon every thing but him

Will not my Friends be welcome, *Pamela*? said he, sternly.

O yes, Sir, very welcome !---But I have these nasty Vapours so, that I wish I might be excus'd -- I wish I might be allowed to take an Airing in the Chariot for two or three Hours, for I shall not be fit to be seen by such- -Ladies---said I, half out of Breath

You'll be fit to be seen by nobody, my Dear, if you go on thus -- But, do as you please.

He was going, and I took his Hand · Stay, dear Sir, let me know what you would have me do. If you would have me stay, I will.

To be sure I would

Well, Sir, then I will. For it is hard, thought I, if an innocent Person cannot look up, in her own House too, as it is at present, as I may say, to a guilty one !----Guilty in her Heart, at least ! --Tho', poor Lady, I hope she is not so in Fact; and, if God hears my Prayers, never will, for all Three of our sakes

But, Madam, think for me, what a Task I have ! How my Heart throbs in my Bosom ! How I tremble ! How I struggle with myself ! What Rules I form for my Behaviour to this naughty Lady ! How they are dashed in Pieces as soon as formed, and new ones taken up ! And yet I doubt myself, when I come to the Test

But one thing will help me  I *pity* the poor Lady, and as she comes with the Heart of a Robber, to invade me in my lawful Right, I pride myself in a Superiority over this Countess, and will endeavour to shew her the Country Girl in a Light which would better become *her* to appear in

I must be forced to leave off here, for Mr B is just come in to receive his Guests, and I am in a sad Flutter upon it.  All my Resolution fails me What shall I do !--- O that this Countess was come, and gone !---I tremble so, that I shall behave like a Guilty one before the Guilty, who will enjoy their Minds, I'll warrant, as if they were innocent !--- Why should that be ?---But, surely, if all was bad, as this *Turner* has said, they could not act thus bar-

baroufly

barously by me! For I have not deserved to be given up to be insulted! I hope I have not!----For what have I done?

I have one Comfort, however, in the midst of all my Griefs, and that is in your Ladyship's Goodness, which gives me Leave to assume the honoured Title, that, let what will happen, will always give me equal Pride and Pleasure, in subscribing myself,

*Your Ladyship's obliged Sister,*

*and humble Servant,*

P B

## LETTER XXX.

*My dear Lady,*

I Will now pursue my last affecting Subject; for the Visit is over, but a sad Situation I am in with Mr B. for all that. But, bad as it is, I'll try to forget it, till I come to it in course

At Four in the Afternoon Mr B came in to receive his Guests, whom he expected at Five. He came up to me I had just closed my last Letter, but put it up, and set before me your Ladyship's Play Subjects

So, *Pamela!*—How do you now?

Your Ladyship may guess, by what I wrote before, that I could not give any extraordinary Account of myself ----As well----As well, Sir, as possible ---Half out of Breath.

You give yourself strange melancholy Airs of late, my Dear ----You don't do well ---All that Chearfulness which used to delight me whenever I saw you, I'm sorry for it, is quite vanish'd of late ---You and I must shortly have a little serious Talk together

When you please, Sir ---I believe it is only not being us'd to this smoaky thick Air of *London!*---I shall
be

be better when you carry me into the Country---I dare fay I fhall — But I never was in *London* fo long before, you know, Sir

All in good time, *Pamela* !---But is this the beft Appearance you chufe to make, to receive fuch Guefts ?

If it difpleafe you, Sir, I will drefs otherwife in a Minute

You look well in any thing ---But I thought you'd have had your Jewels---Yet they would never have lefs become you , for of late your Eyes have loft that Brilliancy that ufed to ftrike me with a Luftre, much furpaffing that of the fineft Diamonds

I am forry for it, Sir ---But as I never could pride myfelf in deferving fuch a kind Compliment, I fhould be too happy, forgive me, my deareft Mr. *B* if the Failure be not rather in *your* Eyes than in *mine*

He looked at me ftedfaftly.--- I fear, *Pamela*---- But, don't be a Fool.

You are angry with me, Sir !

No, not I

Would you have me drefs better ?

No, not I---If your Eyes looked a little more brilliant, you want no Addition.

Down he went.

Strange, fhort Speeches, thefe, my Lady, to what you have heard from his dear Mouth !---Yet they fhall not rob me of the Merit of a patient Sufferer, I am refolved, thought I.

Now, my Lady, as I doubted not, my Rival would come adorned with every outward Ornament, I put on only a white Damask Gown, having no Defire to vie with her in Appearance , for a virtuous and honeft Heart is my Glory, I blefs God ! I wifh the Countefs had the fame to boaft of !

About Five, their Ladyfhips came in the Countefs's new Chariot, for fhe has not been long out of her tranfitory Mourning, and drefs'd as rich as Jewels, and a Profufion of Expence, could make her.

I faw them from the Window alight O how my Heart throbbed!---Lie ftill, faid I, bufy Thing! Why all this Emotion?---Thofe fhining Ornaments cover not fuch a guilelefs Flutterer as thou. Why then, all this Emotion?

I would not be fo officious as to be below to receive them Polly Barlow came up inftantly, from Mr B

I haftened down, tremble, tremble, tremble, went my Feet, in fpite of all the Refolution I had been endeavouring fo long to collect together

Mr B prefented the Countefs to me, both of us cover'd with Blufhes; but from very different Motives, as I imagine

The Countefs of—, my Dear

She faluted me and looked, as I thought, half with Envy, half with Shame: But one is apt to form Peoples Countenances by what one judges of their Hearts

O too lovely, too charming Rivalefs! thought I. ---Would to Heaven I faw lefs Attractions in you! - For indeed, indeed, Madam, fhe is a charming Lady! ---Yet fhe could not help calling me Mrs B that was fome Pride to me Every little Diftinction is a Pride to me now----and faid, She had heard me fo much praifed, that fhe quite long'd to fee me.

O thefe villainous Mafquerades, thought I! - You would never have wanted to fee me, but for them, poor naughty Nun, that was!

Mr B. prefented alfo the Vifcountefs to me. I faluted her Ladyfhip, her Sifter faluted me

She is a graceful Lady, better, as I hope, in Heart, but not equal in Perfon to her Sifter.

You have taken no Pains, my Dear, in your Drefs To-day.

The

The Ladies will excufe it, Sir, I am fo often in the Nurfery, when you are abfent.

Mrs *B* anfwers her Character, faid the Countefs; fhe wants no Ornaments You have a charming little Mafter, I am told, Madam, but no Wonder, from fuch a Pair!

O dear Heart, thought I, i'n't it fo! --Your Lady-fhip may guefs, what I thought farther

Will your Ladyfhip fee him now? faid Mr *B*

He did not look down, no, not one bit!---tho' the Countefs play'd with her Fan, and looked at him, and looked at me, and then looked down, by Turns, a little confcioufly. While I wrapt up myfelf in my Innocence, my firft Flutters being over, and thought I was fuperior, by reafon of that, even to a Countefs

With all my Heart, Mr *B* faid fhe

I rang *Polly*, bid Nurfe bring *my Billy* down--- *My*, faid I, with an Emphafis.

I met the Nurfe at the Stairs Foot, and brought in my dear Baby in my Arms· Such a Child, and fuch a Mamma, faid the Vifcountefs!

Will you give Mafter to my Arms, one Moment, Madam? faid the Countefs.

Yes, thought I, much rather than my dear naughty Gentleman fhould any other.

I *yielded* it to her· I thought fhe would have ftifled it with her warm Kiffes Sweet Boy! Charming Creature! And preffed it to her too lovely Bofom, with fuch Emotion, looking on the Child, and on Mr *B* that I liked it not by any means

Go, you naughty Lady! thought I ---But I durft not fay fo And go, naughty Man, too! thought I, for you feem to look too much gratify'd in your Pride, by her Fondnefs for your Boy I wifh I did not love you fo well as I do! --But neither, your Ladyfhip may believe, did I fay this

Mr. *B* looked at me, but with a Bravery, I thought, too like what I had been Witnefs to, in fome former Scenes, in as bad a Cause ---But, thought I, God deliver'd me *then* I will confide in Him --- He will *now*, I doubt not, restore thy Heart to my Prayers, un-tainted, I hope, for thy own dear sake, as well as mine

The Viscountess took the Child from her Sister, and kissed him with great Pleasure She is a marry'd Lady Would to God, the Countess was too! for Mr. *B* never corresponded, as I told your Lady-ship once *, with marry'd Ladies · So I was not afraid of *her* Love to my *Billy*.----But let me, said the Viscountess, have the Pleasure of restoring Ma-fter to his charming Mamma I thought, added she, I never saw a lovelier Sight in my Life, than when in his Mamma's Arms

Why. I *can't say*, said the Countess, but Master and his Mamma do Credit to one another Dear Madam, let us have the Pleasure of seeing him still on your Lap, while he is so good

I wonder'd the dear Baby was so quiet, tho', indeed, he is generally so But *he* might surely, if but by Sympathy, have complained for his poor Mamma, tho' she durst not for herself.

How apt one is to engage every thing in one's Distress, when it is deep¹ And one wonders too, that Things animate and inanimate look with the same Face, when we are greatly moved by any extraordinary and interesting Event¹

I sat down with my Baby on my Lap, looking, I believe, with a righteous Boldness (I will call it so, for well says the Text, *The Righteous is as bold as a Lion*¹) now on my *Billy*, now on his dear Papa, and now on the Countess, with such a *Triumph* in my Heart! for I saw her blush, and look down, and the dear Gentleman seemed to eye me with a kind of conscious Tenderness, as I thought

---

* *See her Journal of Saturday Morning, Letter* XXIII Vol III　　　　　　　　　　　　A

A Silence of five Minutes, I believe, succeeded, we all Four looking upon one another; and the little Dear was awake, and stared full upon me, with such innocent Smiles, as if he promised to love me, and make me Amends for all.

I kissed him, and took his pretty little Hand in mine---You are very good, my Charmer, in this noble Company! said I

I remember'd, Madam, a Scene, which made greatly for me in the Papers you have seen *, when, instead of recriminating, as I might have done, before Mr *Longman,* for harsh Usage, (for, O my Lady, your dear Brother has a hard Heart, indeed he has, when he pleases) I only prayed for him on my Knees

And I hope I was not now too mean; for I had Dignity and a proud Superiority in my vain Heart, over them all ---Then, it was not my Part to be upon Defiances, where I loved, and where I hoped to reclaim Besides, what had I done by it, but justified, seemingly, by After-Acts in a passionate Resentment, to their Minds, at least, their too wicked Treatment of me? Moreover, your Ladyship will remember, that Mr B knew not, that I was acquainted with his Intrigue, for I must call it so --- If he had, he is too noble to insult me by such a Visit, and he had told me, I should see the Lady he was at O. *ford* with

And this, breaking Silence, he mention'd; saying, I gave you Hope, my Dear, that I should procure you the Honour of a Visit from the Lady who put herself under my Care at O*xford*

I bow'd my Head to the Countess, but my Tears being ready to start, I kissed my *Billy* Dearest Baby, said I, you are not going to cry, are you?---I would have had him just then to cry, instead of me

---

* *See* Vol. I. *p.* 90

H 3                    The

The Tea Equipage was brought in  *Polly*, carry the Child to Nurse  I gave it another Kiss, and the Countess desired another.  I grudged it, to think her naughty Lips should so closely follow mine.  Her Sister kissed it also, and carry'd him to Mr *B*  Take him away, *Polly*, said he. I owe him my Blessing

O these young Gentlemen Papa's ! said the Countess---They are like young unbroken Horses, just put into the Traces !---Are they so, thought I? ---Matrimony must not expect your good Word, I doubt.

Mr. *B*. after Tea, at which I was far from being talkative, (for I could not tell what to say ; tho' I try'd, as much as I could, not to appear sullen) desir'd the Countess to play one Tune upon the Harpsichord. She did, and sung, at his Request, an *Italian* Song to it, very prettily , too prettily, I thought  I wanted to find some Faults, some great Faults in her  But O Madam ! she has too many outward Excellencies ! Pity she wants a good Heart!

He could ask nothing, that she was not ready to oblige him in ! Indeed he could no !

She desired *me* to touch the Keys  I would have been excus'd · but could not.  And the Ladies commended my Performance . But neither my Heart to play, nor my Fingers in playing, deserv'd their Praises  Mr *B said* indeed, You play better sometimes, my Dear ---Do I, Sir ? was all the Answer I made.

The Countess hoped, she said, I would return her Visit, and so said the Viscountess.

I reply'd, Mr *B* would command me whenever he pleas'd.

She said, She hoped to be better acquainted---(I hope not, thought I) and that I would give her my Company for a Week or so, upon the Forest. It seems she has a Seat upon *Windsor* Forest.

Mr.

Mr. *B.* fays, added fhe, you can't ride a fingle Horfe, but we'll teach you there. 'Tis a fweet Place for that Purpofe.

How came Mr *B* thought I, to tell *you* that, Madam? I fuppofe you know more of me than I do myfelf. Indeed, my Lady, this may be too true, for fhe may know what is to become of me!

I told her, I was very much oblig'd to her Lady-fhip, and that Mr. *B.* directed all my Motions.

What fay *you*, Sir? faid the Countefs

I can't promife that, Madam; for Mrs. *B.* wants to go down to *Kent*, before we go to *Bedfordfhire*, and I am afraid I can't give her my Company thither

Then, Sir, I fhan't chufe to go without you

I fuppofe not, my Dear But, if you are dif-pofed to oblige the Countefs for a Week, as you never were at *Windfor*---

I believe, Sir, interrupted I, what with my little Nurfery, and *one* thing or *another*, I muft deny my-felf that Honour, for this Seafon

Well, Madam, then I'll expect you in *Pallmall.*

I bowed my Head, and faid, Mr. *B.* would com-mand me

They took Leave with a Politenefs natural to them

Mr *B* as he handed them to their Chariot, faid fomething in *Italian* to the Countefs: The Word *Pamela* was in what he faid . She anfwer'd him, with a downcaft Look, in the fame Language, half pleas'd, half ferious, and the Chariot drove away.

I would give, faid I, a good deal, Sir, to know what her Ladyfhip faid to you; fhe look'd with fo particular a Meaning, if I may fo fay.

I'll tell you, truly, *Pamela* · I faid to her, Well, now your Ladyfhip has feen my *Pamela*--- Is fhe not the charming'ft Girl in the World?

She

She anfwer'd, Mrs B is very grave, for fo young a Lady But I muft needs fay, She is a lovely Creature

And did you fay fo, Sir? And did her Ladyfhip fo anfwer?--- And my Heart was ready to leap out of my Bofom for Joy

But my Folly fpoil'd all again, for, to my own Surprize, and great Regret, I burft out into Tears, tho' I even fobb'd to have fuppref'd them, but could not, and fo I loft a fine Opportunity to have talked to him while he was fo kind For he was more angry with me than ever.

What made me fuch a Fool, I wonder! But I had fo long ftruggled with myfelf, and not expecting fo kind a Queftion from the dear Gentleman or fuch a favourable Anfwer from the Countefs, I had no longer any Command of myfelf

What ails the little Fool? faid he, with a wrathful Countenance This made me worfe, and he added, Take care, take care, *Pamela* !---- You'll drive me from you in fpite of my own Heart

So he went into the beft Parlour, and put on his Sword, and took his Hat ---I follow'd him, Sir, Sir with my Arms expanded, was all I could fay, but he avoided me, putting on his Hat with an Air, and out he went, bidding *Abraham* follow him

This is the Dilemma, into which, as I hinted at the Beginning of this Letter, I have brought myfelf with Mr B How ftrong, how prevalent, is the Paffion of Jealoufy, that thus it will fhew itfelf uppermoft, when it *is* uppermoft, in fpite of ones moft watchful Regards!

My Mind is fo perplex'd, that I muft lay down my Pen And, indeed, your Ladyfhip will wonder, all Things confider'd, that I could write the above Account as I have done, in this cruel Sufpenfe, and with fuch Apprehenfions But Writing is all the Diverfion I have, when my Mind is opprefs'd

I b

'Tis a temporary Relief; and this Interview was so interesting, that it took up a great deal of my Attention while I wrote  But now I am come to a Period of it, (and so unhappy an one, as has resulted from my ungovern'd Passion) my Apprehensions are return'd upon me with double Strength  Why did I drive the dear Gentleman from me upon such a promising Appearance?---Why did I?---But all this had been prevented, had not this nasty Mr Turner put into my Head worse Thoughts  For now I can say with the Poet

> Since Knowlege is but Sorrow's Spy,
>   'Twere better NOT to know

How shall I do to look up to him now on his Return! To be sure, he plainly sees, to what my Emotion is owing!---Yet I dare not tell him either my Information, or my Informant, because if he knows the one, he will know the other, and then what may be the Consequence!---

*Past Ten o'Clock at Night*

I have only Time to tell your Ladyship, (for the Postman waits) that Mr B is just come in  He is gone into his Closet, and has shut the Door, and taken the Key on the Inside, so I dare not go to him there  In this Uncertainty and Suspense, pity and pray for

*Your Ladyship's afflicted Sister, and Servant,*

P. B

---

# LETTER XXXI.

*My dear Lady,*

I Will now proceed with my melancholy Account.
Not knowing what to do, and Mr B not coming near me, and the Clock striking Twelve, I ventur'd to send this Billet to him, by *Polly*

*Dear*

*Dear Sir,*

' I Know you chuse not to be invaded, when you
' retire into your Closet, and yet, being very uneasy
' on account of your abrupt Departure, and heavy
' Displeasure, I take the Liberty to write these few
' Lines

' I own, Sir, that the sudden Flow of Tears which
' involuntarily burst from me, at your kind Expres-
' sions to the Countess in my Favour, when I had
' thought for more than a Month past, you were
' angry with me, and which had distress'd my weak
' Mind beyond Expression, might appear unaccount-
' able to you But had you kindly waited but one
' Moment, till this Fit, which was rather owing to
' my Gratitude, than to Perverseness, had been over,
' (and I knew the Time when you would have gene-
' rously soothed it') I should have had the Happi-
' ness of a more serene and favourable Parting

' Will you suffer me, Sir, to attend you? (*Polly*
' shall wait your Answer) I dare not come *without*
' your Permission, for should you be as angry as you
' were, I know not how I shall bear it But if you
' say I may come down, I hope to satisfy you, that
' I intended not any Offence Do, dear Sir, permit
' me to attend you. I can say no more, than that
' I am

*Your ever dutiful,*

P B

*Polly* return'd with the following — So, thought
I, a Letter!— I could have spared that, I am sure
I expected no Favour from it So, tremblingly,
open'd it

*My Dear,*

' I Would not have you sit up for me We are
' getting apace into the matrimonial Recrimina-
' tions. *You knew the Time!*— So did I, my Dear!—
' But

‘ But it feems that Time is over with both; and I have
‘ had the Mortification, for fome paſt Weeks, to
‘ come home to a very different *Pamela*, than I uſed
‘ to leave all Company and all Pleaſure for ---I hope
‘ we ſhall better underſtand one another. But you
‘ cannot ſee me at preſent with any Advantage to
‘ yourſelf, and I would not, that any thing farther
‘ ſhould paſs, to add to the Regrets of both I wiſh
‘ you good Reſt. I will give your Cauſe a fair
‘ Hearing, when I am more fit, than at preſent, to
‘ hear all your Pleas, and your Excuſes I cannot
‘ be inſenſible, that the Reaſon for the Concern you
‘ have lately ſhewn, muſt lie deeper than, perhaps,
‘ you’ll own, at preſent As ſoon as you are pre-
‘ pared to ſpeak all that is upon your Mind, and I
‘ to hear it with Temper, then, we may come to
‘ an Eclairciſſement. ’Till when I am

> *Your affectionate,* &c.

My buſy Apprehenſion immediately ſuggeſted to
me, that I was to be terrified, with a high Hand, into
a Compliance with ſome new Scheme or other that
was projecting But I had reſolved to make their
Way as clear to one another as was in my Power,
if they would have it ſo, and ſo I try’d to allay my
Grief as much as I could, and it being near One,
and hearing nothing from Mr *B* I bid *Polly* go to
Bed, thinking ſhe would wonder at our Intercourſe
by Letter, if I ſhould ſend again

So down I ventur’d, my Feet, however, trembling all the Way, and tapp’d at the Door of his
Cloſet

Who’s that ?

I, Sir. One Word, if you pleaſe Don’t be more
angry, however, Sir

He open’d the Door Thus poor *Heſter*, to her
Royal Husband, ventur’d her Life, to break in upon
him

him unbidden  But that *Eastern* Monarch, great as he was, extended to the fainting Suppliant the golden Sceptre!

He took my Hand  I hope, my Dear, by this Tragedy Speech, we are not to expect any sad Catastrophe to our present Misunderstanding.

I hope not, Sir  But 'tis all as God and You shall please  I am resolv'd to do my Duty, Sir, if possible.  But, indeed, I cannot bear this cruel Suspense  Let me know what is to become of me --- Let me know but what is design'd for me, and you shall be sure of all the Acquiescence that my Duty and Conscience can give to your Pleasure

What *means* the dear Creature!  What *means* my *Pamela*!--- Surely your Head, Child, is a little affected!

I can't tell, Sir, but it may!--- But let me have my Trial, that you write about.  Appoint my Day of Hearing, and speedily to, for I would not bear such another Month, as the last has been, for the World.

Come, my Dear, said he, let me attend you to your Chamber  But your Mind has taken much too solemn a Turn, to enter further now upon this Subject  Think as well of me, as I do of you, and I shall be as happy as ever

I wept---Be not angry, dear Sir·  Your kind Words have just the same Effect upon me now, as in the Afternoon

Your Apprehensions, my Dear, must be very strong, that a kind Word, as you call it, has such an Effect upon you!  But let us wave the Subject for a few Days, because I am to set out on a little Journey at Four, and had not intended to go to Bed for so few Hours.

When we came up, I said, I was very bold, Sir, to break in upon you; but I could not help it, if

my

my Life had been the Forfeit And you receiv'd
me with more Goodnefs than I could have expected.
But will you pardon me, if I ask, Whither you go
fo foon? And if you had intended to have gone
without taking Leave of me?

I go to *Tunbridge*, my Dear I fhould have ftept
up, and taken Leave of you, before I went

Well, Sir, I will not ask you, Wlo is of your
Party?---I will not--- No, putting my Hand to his
Lips---Don't tell me, Sir It mayn't be proper.

Don't fear, my Dear, I won't tell you· Nor am
I certain whether it be *proper* or not, till we are
come to a better Underftanding ---Only, once more,
think as well of me, as I do of you

Would to Heaven, thought I, there was the fame
Reafon for the one, as for the other!

I intended (for my Heart was full) to enter further into this Subject, fo fatal to my Repofe· But
the dear Gentleman had no fooner laid his Head on
the Pillow, but he fell afleep, or feign'd to do fo,
and that was as prohibitory to my Talking, as if he
had So I had all my own entertaining Reflections
to myfelf; which gave me not one Wink of Sleep;
but made me of fo much Service to him, as to
tell him, when the Clock ftruck Four, that he fhould
not (tho' I did not fay fo, you may think, Madam)
make my ready Rivalefs (for I doubted not her
being one of the Party) wait for him

He arofe, and was drefs'd inftantly; and faluting
me, bid me be eafy and happy, while it was *yet* in
my own Power

He faid, He fhould be back on *Saturday* Night,
as he believ'd And I wifh'd him, moft fervently, I
am fure! Health, Pleafure, and Safety

Here, Madam, muft I end this Letter. My next
will, perhaps, contain my Trial, and my Sentence·
God give me but Patience and Refignation, and
then, whatever occurs, I fhall not be unhappy Efpecially

cially while I can have, in the laſt Reſource, the Pleaſure of calling myſelf

*Your Ladyſhip's moſt obliged Siſter and Servant,*

P B.

---

## LETTER XXXII.

*My dear Lady,*

I Will be preparing to write to you, as I have Opportunity, not doubting but this preſent Leter muſt be a long one, and having ſome Apprehenſions, that, as things may fall out, I may want either Head or Heart to write to your Ladyſhip, were I to defer it till the Cataſtrophe of this cruel, cruel Suſpenſe

O what a Happineſs am I ſunk from!--- And in ſo few Days too!--- O the wicked, wicked Maſquerades! They ſhall be always followed with the Execrations of an injured Wife in me, who, but for that wretched Diverſion, had ſtill been the happieſt of her Sex!

But I was too ſecure! It was fit, perhaps, that I ſhould be humbled and mortified, and I muſt try to make a Virtue of the cruel Neceſſity, and ſee, if, by the Divine Grace, I cannot bring *real* Good out of this *appearing* Evil

The following Letter, in a Woman's Hand and ſign'd, as you'll ſee, by a Woman's Name, and ſpelt as I ſpell it, will account to your Ladyſhip for my beginning ſo heavily   It came by the Peny-Poſt

*Madame,*

I Ame unknowne to yowe ; but yowe are not ſo altogathar to mee, becaus I haue bene edefy'd by yowre pius Behafior att Church, whir I ſee yowe with Plaiſir everie Sabbaoth Day.   I ame welle acquaintid

quaintid with the Famely of the Coumpteffe of------;
and yowe maie poffiblie haue hard what yowe wifhid
not to haue hard concerninge hir   Butt this verie
Morninge, I can affur yowe, hir Ladifhippe is gon
with yowre Spowfe to *Tonbrigge*; and theire they are
to take Lodginges, or a Hous; and Mr. *B* is after
to come to Towne, and fettel Matters to goe downe
to hir, where they are to liue as Man and Wiffe.
Make what Ufe yowe pleas of thifs Informafion, and
belieue me to haue noe other Motife, than to ferue
yowe, becaufe of yowre Vartues, whiche make yowe
deferue a better Retorne.   I ame, thof I fhall not
fett my trewe Name,

*Yowre grete Admirer and Seruant,*

*Wednefday* Morninge,         Thomafine Fuller.
9 o'Clock.

Juft above I called my State, a State of *cruel
Sufpenfe !* But I recall the Words: For now it is no
longer Sufpenfe; fince, if this Letter fays Truth, I
know the worft. And there is too much Appearance,
that it does, let the Writer be who it will, or his
or her Motive what it will, for, after all, I am apt
to fanfy this, a Contrivance of Mr. *Turner's*, tho', for
fear of ill Confequences, I will not fay fo.

And now, Madam, I am endeavouring, by the
Help of Religion, and cool Reflection, to bring my
Mind to bear this heavy Evil, and to recollect what
I *was*, and how much more honourable an Eftate I
am *in*, than I could ever have expected to be in;
and that my Virtue and good Name are fecured;
and I can return innocent to my dear Father and
Mother. And thefe were once the only Pride of my
Heart

Then, additional to what I was, at that Time, (and
ye' I pleafed myfelf with my Profpects, poor as they
were) I have honeft Parents bountifully provided for,
thank God, and your ever dear Brother, for this
Bleffing!

Blessing!--- and not only provided for--- but made useful to him, to the Amount of their Provision, well nigh! There is a Pride, my Lady!

Then I shall have better Conditions from his Generosity to support myself, than I can wish for, or make use of

Then I have my dear, charming *Billy*--- O be contented, too charming, and too happy Rivaless, with my Husband, and tear not from me my dearest Baby, the Pledge, the beloved Pledge, of our happier Affections, and the dear Remembrance of what I once was!--- But if, my dear Mr B. you doubt the Education I can give him, fit for the Heir to your great Fortune, (for such he must be, despised or abandon'd as his poor Mother may be!) and will remove him from me, and Grief kill me not before that sad Hour, let me have some Office, not incompatible with that of his Tutor, to instil Virtue into his ductile Mind, for Tutors, altho' they may make Youth learned, do not always make him virtuous, and let me watch over his Steps, and where-ever *he* goes, let *me* go I shall value no Dangers nor Risques; the most distant Clime shall be native to me, where-ever my *Billy* is; so that I may be a Guard, under God, to his Morals, that he make no Virgin's Heart sigh, nor Mother's bleed, as mine has done in both States.

But, how I rave! will your Ladyship be apt to say ---This is no good Symptom, you'll think, that I have reap'd at present that Consolation from religious Considerations, which, to a right Turn of Mind, they will afford in the heaviest Misfortunes But this was only in fear they should take my *Billy* from me A thousand pleasing Prospects, that had begun to dawn on my Mind, I can bear to have dissipated; but I cannot, indeed I cannot! permit my dear Mr. *B*'s Son and Heir to be torn from me.

Yet

I

Yet I hope they will not be so cruel; for I will give them no Provocation to do it, if I can help No Law-suits, no Complainings, no Asperities of Expression, much less bitter Reflections, shall they ever have from me. I will be no Conscience to them They will be punished too much, greatly too much, in their own, for what I wish, and they shall *always* be follow'd by my Prayers I shall have Leisure for that Exercise, and shall be happy and serene, when, I doubt, I doubt, they will not be so

But still I am running on in a Strain that shews my Impatience, rather than my Resignation · Yet some Struggles must be allow'd me, I could not have loved, as I love, if I could easily part with my Interest in so beloved a Husband ---For, Madam, my Interest I *will* part with, and will sooner die, than live with a Gentleman, who has another Wife, tho' I was the first ---Let Countesses, if they can, and Ladies of Birth, chuse to humble themselves to this Baseness---The low-born *Pamela* cannot stoop to it Pardon me, Madam, you know I only write this with a View to this poor Lady's Answer to her noble Uncle, of which you wrote me Word

### F R I D A Y

Is now concluding I hope I am calmer a great deal For, being disappointed, in all Likelihood, in twenty agreeable Schemes and Projects, I am now forming new ones, with as much Pleasure to myself, as I may For, my Lady, 'tis one's Duty, you know, to suit one's Mind to one's Condition, and I hope I shall be enabled to do Good in *Kent*, if I cannot in *London*, and *Bedfordshire*, and *Lincolnshire* God every-where provides us with Objects, on which to exercise one's Gratitude and Beneficence

I am thinking to try to get good Mrs. *Jervis* with me.

Come,

Come, Madam, you muſt not be too much con
cern'd for me. After a while, I ſhall be no unhappy
Perſon, for tho' I was thankful for my ſplendid Fortunes, and ſhould have been glad, to be ſure I ſhould,
of continuing in them, with ſo dear a Gentleman,
yet a high Eſtate had never ſuch dazling Charms
with me, as it has with ſome: If it had, I could not
have reſiſted ſo many Temptations, poſſibly, as God
enabled me to reſiſt.

### SATURDAY Night.

Is now come. 'Tis Nine, and no Mr B.———O
why, as *Deborah* makes the Mother of *Siſera* ſay,
is his Chariot ſo long in coming? Why tarry the
Wheels of his Chariot?
I have this Note now at Eleven o'Clock:

*My deareſt* PAMELA,

'  I Diſpatch this Meſſenger, leſt, expecting me this
'    Night, you ſhould be uneaſy I ſhall not be
'  with you till *Monday*, when I hope to dine with
'  my deareſt Life.

*Ever affectionately Yours*

So I'll go up and pray for him, and then to Bed.
Yet 'tis a ſad thing!— I have had but poor Reſt for
a great while; nor ſhall have any till my Fate is decided. Hard-hearted Gentleman, he knows under
what Uneaſineſs he left me!

### MONDAY Eleven.

If God Almighty hears my Yeſterday's, and indeed my hourly Prayers, the dear Gentleman will
be good ſtill But my aking Heart, every Time I
think what Company he is in, (for I find the Coun
teſs is *certainly* one of the Party) bodes me little
Satisfaction.

He'

He's come! He's come! now, juſt now, come!
I will have my Trial over before this Night be
paſt, if poſſible. I'll go down, and meet him with
Love unfeigned, and a Duty equal to my Love,
altho' he may forget his to me  If I conquer myſelf on this Occaſion, I conquer Nature, as your
Ladyſhip ſays, and then, by GOD's Grace, I can
conquer every thing.  They have taken their Houſe,
I ſuppoſe.---But what need they, when they'll have
one in *Bedfordſhire*, and one in *Lincolnſhire?* But they
know beſt.  GOD bleſs him, and reform her!  That's
all the Harm I wiſh them, or will wiſh them!

The dear Gentleman has receiv'd me with great
Affection and Tenderneſs.  Sure he cannot be ſo
bad!---Sure he cannot!

I know, my Dear, ſaid he, I left you in great
Anxiety; but 'tis an Anxiety you have brought
upon yourſelf, and I have not been eaſy ever ſince
I parted from you.

I am ſorry for it, Sir.

Why, my dear Love, there is ſtill a melancholy
Air in your Countenance: Indeed it ſeems mingled
with a kind of Joy, I hope at my Return to you.
But 'tis eaſy to ſee which of the two is the moſt
natural

You ſhould ſee nothing, Sir, that you would not
wiſh to ſee, if I could help it

I am ſorry you cannot  But I am come Home
to hear all your Grievances, and to redreſs them, if
in my Power.

When, Sir, am I to come upon my Trial? I
have a great deal to ſay to you  I will tell you
every thing I think  And as it may be the laſt *Grievances*, as you are pleaſed to call them, I may ever
trouble you with, you muſt promiſe to anſwer me
not one Word till I have ſaid all I have to ſay.  For,
if it does but hold, I have great Courage; I have

indeed ¹--You don't know half the Sauciness that is in your Girl yet, but when I come upon my Trial, you'll wonder at my Boldness

What means my Dearest? taking me into his Arms You alarm me exceedingly, by this moving Sedateness

Don't let it alarm you, Sir ¹ I mean you nothing but Good ¹--- But I have been preparing myself to tell you all my Mind And as an Instance of what you may expect from me, sometimes, Sir, I will be your Judge, and put home Questions to you, and sometimes you shall be mine, and at last pronounce Sentence upon me, or, if you won't, I will upon myself, a severe one to me, it shall be, but an agreeable one, perhaps, to you!---- When comes on the Trial, Sir?

He loooked steadily upon me, but was silent And I said, But don't be afraid, Sir, that I will invade your Province, for tho' I shall count myself your Judge, in some Cases, you shall be Judge Paramount still

Dear Charmer of my Heart, said he, and clasped me to his Bosom, what a *new* PAMELA have I in my Arms! A mysterious Charmer ¹ Let us instantly go to my Closet, or yours, and come upon our mutual Trial, for you have fir'd my Soul with Impatience!

No, Sir, if you please, we will dine first I have hardly eaten any thing these Four Days, and your Company will give me an Appetite perhaps I shall be pleas'd to sit down at Table with you, Sir, taking his Hand, and trying to smile upon him, for the Moments I shall have of your Company, may be, some Time hence, very precious to my Remembrance

I was forced then to turn my Head, to hide from him my Eyes, brimful, as they were, of Tears

He took me again into his Arms --- My dearest *Pamela*, if you love me, distract not my Soul thus,

Dy

by your dark and mysterious Speeches You are displeased with *me*, and I thought I had Reason, of late, to take something amiss in *your* Conduct, but, instead of your suffering by my Anger, you have Words and an Air, that penetrate my very Soul

O Sir, Sir, treat me not thus kindly! Put on an angrier Brow, or how shall I retain my Purpose! How shall I!

Dear, dear Creature! make not use of *all* your Power to melt me! *Half* of it is enough. For there is Eloquence in your Eyes I cannot resist; but in your present solemn Air, and affecting Sentences, you mould me to every Purpose of your Heart; so that I am a mere Machine, a passive Instrument, to be play'd upon at your Pleasure

Dear, kind Sir! how you revive my Heart, by your Goodness! Perhaps I have only been in a frightful Dream, and am but just now awaken'd !----But we will not anticipate our Trial Only, Sir, give Orders, that you are not to be spoken with by any body, when we have din'd, for I must have you *all* to myself, without Interruption

Just as I had said this, a Gentleman called on him, and I retir'd to my Chamber, and wrote to this Place.

Mr B. dismiss'd his Friend, without asking him to dine with him· So I had him all to myself at Dinner But we said little, and sat not above a Quarter of an Hour, looking at each other, he with Impatience, and some seeming Uneasiness, I, with more Steadiness, I believe, but now-and-then a Tear starting

I could eat but little, tho' I try'd all I could, and especially as he help'd me, and courted me by Words of Tenderness and Sweetness----- O why were ever such Things as *Masquerades* permitted in a Christian Nation!

I chose

I chofe to go into *my* Clofet rather than into *his*; and here I fit, waiting the dear Gentleman's coming up to me  If I keep but my Courage, I fhall be pleafed  I know the *worft*, and that will help me, for he is too noble to ufe me roughly, when he fees I mean not to provoke him by Upbraidings, any more than I will act, in this Cafe, beneath the Character I ought to affume as his Wife.

For, my dear Lady, this is a Point of high Importance  It has touch'd and rais'd my Soul beyond its Pitch  I am a *new Pamela*, as he fays, and a *proud Pamela*, as he will find---- For, Madam, the Perfon who can fupport herfelf under an Injury like this, and can refolve to forgive it, has a Superiority to the Injurer, let him be a Prince, tho' fhe were but a Beggar-born.  But the Difficulty will be, how to avoid being melted by my own Softnefs, and Love for the Man, more dear to me than Life, yea, more dear to me, than my *Billy*, and than all my Hopes in the charming Boy.  But here he comes!

Now, *Pamela*---Now, fee what thou canft do!--- Thou knoweft the worft! Remember that!---And may'ft not be unhappy, even *at* the worft, if thou trufteft in GOD

I am commanded, my dear Lady, now to write particularly my Trial, for a Reafon I fhall mention to you in the Conclufion of this Letter, and I muft beg you to favour me with the Return of all my Letters to you, on this affecting Subject ----- The Reafon will appear in its Place---And, Oh! congratulate me, my dear, dear Lady, for I am happy, and fhall be happier than I ever was, and that I thought, fo did every body, was impoffible. But I will not anticipate the Account of my Trial, and the Effects, the bleffed Effects, it has produced. Thus, then, it was

Mr *B.* came up, with great Impatience in his Looks.  I met him at my Chamber-door, with as
fedate

ledate a Countenance, as I poffibly could put on, and my Heart was high with my Purpofe, and fupported me better than I could have expected —Yet, on Recollection, now, I impute to myfelf fomething of that kind of Magnanimity, that was wont to infpire the innocent Sufferers of old, for a ftill worthier Caufe than mine, though their Motives could hardly be more pure, in that one Hope I had to be an humble Means of faving the Man I love and honour, from Errors that might be fatal to his Soul.

I took his Hand with Boldnefs: Dear Sir, leading him to my Clofet, Here is the Bar, at which I am to take my Trial, pointing to the Backs of Three Chairs, which I had placed in a join'd Row, leaveing juft Room to go by on each Side— You muft give me, Sir, all my own Way, this is the firft, and perhaps the laft Time, that I fhall defire it — Nay, dear Sir, turning my Face from him, look not upon me with an Eye of Tendernefs: If you do, I may lofe my Purpofes, important to me as they are, and however fantaftick my Behaviour may feem to you, I want not to move your Paffions, (for the good Impreffions made upon them, may be too eafily diffipated, by the Winds of *Senfe*)—but your *Reafon* And if that can be done, I am fafe, and fhall fear no Relapfe.

What means all this Parade, my Dear? Let me perifh, that was his Word, if I know how to account for *You*, or your *Humour*

You *will* prefently, Sir But give me all my Way— I pray you do, this once—this one Time only!

Well, fo, this is your Bar, is it? There's an Elbowchair, I fee, take your Place in it, *Pamela*, and here I ll ftand to anfwer all your Queftions.

No, Sir, that muft not be So I boldly led *him* to the Elbow-chair You are the Judge, Sir, it is I that am to be try'd. Yet I will not fay I am a

I 3 Criminal.

Criminal I know I am not But that muſt be proved, Sir, you know

Well, take your Way, but I fear for your Head, my Dear, in all this.

I fear only my Heart, Sir, that's all: But there you muſt ſit— So here (retiring to the Three Chairs, and leaning on the Backs, here) I ſtand

And now, my deareſt Mr *B.* you muſt begin firſt When you ſhew'd me the Houſe of Peers, their Bar, at which Cauſes are heard, and ſometimes Peers are try'd, look'd awful to me, and the preſent Occaſion requires, that this ſhould Now, dear Sir, you muſt be my Accuſer, as well as my Judge

I have nothing to accuſe you of, my Dear, if I *muſt* give into your moving Whimſy You are every thing I wiſh you to be. But for the laſt Month you have ſeem'd to be uneaſy, and have not done me the Juſtice to acquaint me with your Reaſons for it

I was in hopes, my Reaſons might prove to be no Reaſons, and I would not trouble you with my ungrounded Apprehenſions But now, Sir, we are come directly to the Point; and methinks I ſtand here as *Paul* did before *Felix*, and, like that poor Priſoner, if I, Sir, reaſon of *Righteouſneſs*, *Tempe rance* and *Judgment to come*, even to make you, as the great *Felix* did, tremble, don't put me off to *another Day*, to a *more convenient Seaſon*, as that Governor did *Paul*, for you muſt bear patiently with all I have to ſay

Strange, uncommon Girl! how unaccountable is all this!—Pr'ythee, my Dear, and he pulled a Chair by him, Come and ſit down by me, and without theſe romantick Airs let me hear all you have to ſay, and teize me not with this Parade

No, Sir, let me ſtand, if you pleaſe, while I can ſtand; when I am weary, I will ſit down at my Bar

Now, Sir, ſince you are ſo good as to ſay, you have nothing but Change of Temper to accuſe me of, I am to anſwer to that, and aſſign a Cauſe; and I will do it without Evaſion, or Reſerve· But I beſeech you, ſay not one Word, but Yes, or No, to my Queſtions, 'till I have ſaid all I have to ſay, and then you ſhall find me all Silence and Reſignation

Well, my ſtrange Dear!—But ſure your Head is a little turn'd!—What is your Queſtion?

Whether, Sir, the Nun—I ſpeak boldly, the Caſe requires it— who follow'd you at the Maſquerade every where, is not the Counteſs of ------?

What then, my Dear? (ſpeaking with Quickneſs)—I *thought* the Occaſion of your Sullenneſs and Reſerve was this!---But, *Pamela*---

Nay, Sir, interrupted I, only Yes, or No, if you pleaſe I will be all Silence by-and-by.

Yes, then

Well, Sir, then let me *tell* you, for I *aſk* you not, (it may be too bold in me to multiply Queſtions) that ſhe *loves* you; that you correſpond by Letters with her ---- Yes, Sir, *before* that Letter from her Ladyſhip came, which you receiv'd from my Hand in ſo ſhort and angry a manner, for fear I ſhould have had a Curioſity to ſee its Contents, which would have been inexcuſable in me, I own, if I had  You have talked over to her all your Polygamy Notions, and her Ladyſhip ſeems ſo well convinced of them, that ſhe has declar'd to her noble Uncle, (who expoſtulated with her on the Occaſions ſhe gave for Talk) that ſhe had rather be a certain Gentleman's ſecond Wife, than the firſt to the greateſt Man in *England*, and you are but juſt return'd from a Journey to *Tunbridge*, in which that Lady was a Party, and the Motive for it, I am acquainted with, by a Letter here in my Hand.

He was diſpleaſed, and frowned: I look'd down, being reſolv'd not to be terrified, if I could help it.

I have caution'd you, *Pamela*---

I know

I know you have, Sir, interrupted I; but be pleased to answer me, Has not the Countess taken a House or Lodgings at *Tunbridge*?

She has:---And what then?

And is her Ladyship there, or in Town?

There---And what then?

Are you to go to *Tunbridge*, Sir, soon, or not? Be pleased to answer me but that one Question.

I will know, rising up in Anger, your Informants, *Pamela*

Dear Sir, so you shall in proper Time: You shall know all, as soon as I am convinc'd, that your Wrath will not be attended with bad Consequences to yourself and others. That is wholly the Cause of my Reserve in this Point, for I have not a Thought, and never had, since I have been yours, that I wish to be concealed from you --- But, dear Sir, your Knowlege of the Informants makes nothing at all as to the Truth of the Information ---Nor will I press you too home   I doubt not, you are soon to go down to *Tunbridge* again

I am· And what then?--- Must the Consequence be Come enough to warrant your Jealousy?

Dear Sir, don't be so very angry, still looking down, for I durst not trust myself to look up   I don't do this, as you charged me in your Letter, in a Spirit of matrimonial Recrimination. If you don't *tell* me, that you see the Countess with Pleasure, I *ask* it not of you, nor have I any thing to say by way of Upbraiding   'Tis my Misfortune, that she is too lovely, and too attractive, and it is the less Wonder, that a fine young Gentleman as you are, and a fine young Lady as she is, should engage one another's Affections

I knew every thing, except what this Letter, which you shall read presently, communicates, when you brought the Two noble Sisters to visit me. Hence proceeded my Grief, and should I, Sir, have deserv'd

to

to be what I am, if I was *not* griev'd? Religion has help'd me, and GOD has answer'd my Supplications, and enabled me to act this new and uncommon Part before you, at this imaginary Bar. You shall see, Sir, that as, on one hand, I want not, as I said before, to move your Passions in my Favour, so, on the other, I shall not be terrify'd by your Displeasure, dreaded by me as it us'd to be, and as it will be again, the Moment that my rais'd Spirits sink down to their usual Level, or are diverted from this my long meditated Purpose, to tell you all my Mind

I repeat then, Sir, that I knew all this, when the Two noble Sisters came to visit your poor Girl, and to see your *Billy*  Yet, *grave*, as the Countess call'd me, (dear Sir I might I not well be grave, knowing what I knew?) did I betray any Impatience of Speech or Action, any Discomposure?

No, Sir, patting my Hand on my Breast, *here* all the Discomposure lay, struggling, vehemently struggling, now-and-then, and wanting that Vent at my Eyes, which, it seems, (overcome by my Joy, to hear myself favourably spoken of by You and the Lady) it *too soon* made itself  But I could not help it---You might have seen, Sir, I could not!

But I want neither to recriminate, nor expostulate, nor yet, Sir, to form Excuses for my general Conduct, for that you accuse not in the main ---- But be pleased, Sir, to read this Letter  It was brought by the Peny-Post, as you'll see by the Mark  Who the Writer is, I know not. And did *you*, Sir, that Knowlege, and your Resentment upon it, will not alter the Fact, or give it a more favourable Appearance

I stepp'd to him, and giving him the Letter, came back to my Bar, and sat down on one of the Chairs while he read it, drying my Eyes, for they would overflow as I talked, do what I could

He was much moved at the Contents of this Letter: Called it d---n'd Malice, and hop'd he might

I 5

find

find out the Author of it, saying he would advertise 500 Guineas Reward for the Discoverer

He put the Letter in his Pocket, Well, *Pamela*, you believe all that you have said, no doubt, and this Matter has a black Appearance indeed, if you do  But who was your *first* Informant ? Was that by Letter, or personally ? That d---n'd *Turner*, I doubt not, is at the Bottom of all this  The vain Coxcomb has had the Insolence to imagine the Countess would favour an Address of his, and is enraged to meet with a Repulse , and has taken Liberties upon it, that have given Birth to all the Scandals which have been scatter'd about on this Occasion  Nor do I doubt, but he has been the Serpent at the Ear of my *Eve*

I stood up at my Bar, and said, Don't be too hasty, Sir, in your Judgment --You *may* be mistaken

But *am* I mistaken, *Pamela* ?--- You never yet told me an Untruth in Cases the most important to you to conceal  *Am* I mistaken?

Dear Sir, if I should tell you it is *not* Mr *Turner*, you'll guess at somebody else . And what avails all this to the Matter in hand ? You are your own Master, and must stand and fall by your own Conscience  God grant, that *that* may acquit you !--- But my Intention is not either to accuse or upbraid you

But, my Dear, to the Fact then  This is a malicious and a villainous Piece of Intelligence ! given you, perhaps, for the sake of Designs and Views, that may not yet be proper to be avow'd

By GOD's Grace, Sir, I defy all Designs and Views of any one, upon my Honour !

But, my Dear, the Charge is basely false  We have not agreed upon any such way of Life

Well, Sir, all this only proves, that the Intelligence may be a little premature  But now let me, Sir, sit down one Minute or two, to recover my
failing

failing Spirits, and then I'll tell you all I purpofe to do, and all I have to fay, and that with as much Brevity as I can, for fear neither my Head nor my Heart fhould perform the Parts I have been fo long endeavouring to prevail upon them to perform.

I fat down then, he taking the Letter out of his Pocket, and looking upon it again, with much Vexation and Anger in his Countenance, and after a few Tears and Sobs, that would needs be fo officious as to offer their Service, unbidden and undefired, to introduce what I had to fay, I rofe up, my Feet trembling, as well as my Knees, which however, leaning againft the Seats of the Chairs, which made my Bar, as my Hand held by the Back, tolerably fupported me, I cleared my Voice, wiped my Eyes, and faid ·

You have all the Excufes, dear Mr *B* that a Gentleman can have, in the Object of your prefent Paffion.

Prefent Paffion, *Pamela !*

Dear Sir, hear me out, without Interruption

The Countefs is a charming Lady She excels your poor Girl in all thofe outward Graces of Form, which your kind Fancy (more valu'd by me than the Opinion of all the World befides) had made you attribute to me And fhe has all thofe additional Advantages, as Noblenefs of Birth, of Alliance, and Deportment, which I want (Happy for you, Sir, that you had known her Ladyfhip fome Months ago, before you difgrac'd yourfelf by the Honours you have done me !) This, therefore, frees you from the aggravated Crime of thofe, who prefer to their own Ladies lefs amiable and lefs deferving Perfons, and I have not the Sting which thofe muft have, who are contemn'd and ill-treated for the fake of their Inferiors Yet cannot the Countefs love you better than your Girl loves you, not even for your Perfon, which muft, I doubt, be *her* principal Attachment;

when

when I can truly fay, all noble and attracting to the
outward Eye as it is, that is the leaft Confideration
by far with me. No, Sir, it is your Mind, your
generous and beneficent Mind, that is the principal
Object of my Affection, and the Pride I took in
hoping, that I might be an humble Means, in the
Hands of Providence, to blefs you *hereafter* as well
as *here*, gave me more Pleafure than all the Bleffings
I reaped from your Name or your Fortune Judge
then, my deareft Mr *B.* what my Grief and my
Difappointment muft be!

But I will not expoftulate; I *will not*, becaufe it
*muft* be to no Purpofe, for could my Fondnefs for
you, and my watchful Duty to you, have kept you
fteady, I fhould not now have appear'd before you
in this folemn manner; and I know the Charms of
my Rival are too powerful for me to contend with
Nothing but Divine Grace can touch your Heart,
and that I expect not, from the Nature of the Cafe,
fhould be inftantaneous.

I will therefore, Sir, dear as you are to me (—
Don't look with fuch tender Surprize upon me )
give up your Perfon to my happier, to my *worthier*
Rival For, fince fuch is your Will, and fuch feem
to be your Engagements, what avails it me to oppofe them?

I have only to beg, therefore, that you will be
fo good as to permit me to go down to *Kent*, to
my dear Parents, who, with many more, are daily
rejoicing in your Favour and Bounty.

I will there (folding up my folded Hands) pray
for you every Hour of my Life, and for every
one, who fhall be dear to you, not excepting your
charming Countefs

I will never take your Name into my Lips, nor
fuffer any other in my Hearing, but with Reverence
and Gratitude, for the Good I and mine *have* reap'd
at your Hands, nor will I wifh to be freed from my
Obliga-

Obligations to you, except you shall chuse to be divorced from me, and if you should, I will give your Wishes all the Forwardness that I honourably can, with regard to my own Character, and yours, and that of your beloved Baby.

But you must give me something worth living for along with me, your *Billy* and mine!--- Unless it is your Desire to kill me quite, and then, 'tis done, and nothing will stand in your happy Countess's Way, if you tear from my Arms my *second* earthly Good, after I am depriv'd of You, my *first*.

I will there, Sir, dedicate all my Time to my first Duties, happier far, than once I could have hoped to be! And if, by any Accident, any Misunderstanding, between you, you should part by Consent, and you will have it so, my Heart shall be ever yours, and my Hopes shall be resum'd of being an Instrument still for your future Good, and I will receive your returning ever-valu'd Heart, as if nothing had happen'd, the Moment I can be sure it will be wholly mine

For, think not, dear Sir, whatever be your Notions of Polygamy, that I will, were my Life to depend upon it, consent to live with a Gentleman, dear as, GOD is my Witness, (lifting up my tearful Eyes) you are to me, who lives in what I cannot but think open Sin with another! You *know*, Sir, and I appeal to you for the Purity, and I will aver Piety, of my Motives, when I say this, that I *would not*, and as you do know this, I cannot doubt, but my Proposal will be agreeable to you both And I beg of you, dear Sir, to take me at my Word, and don't let me be tortur'd, as I have been so many Weeks, with such Anguish of Mind, that nothing but religious Considerations can make supportable to me.

And are you in Earnest, *Pamela?* coming to me, and folding me in his Arms over the Chair's Back,
the

the Seat of which fupported my trembling Knees.
Can you fo eafily part with me?

I can, Sir, and I will!---rather than divide my
Intereft in you, knowingly, with any Lady upon
Earth. But fay not, however, Can I part with You,
Sir, it is You that part with Me · And tell me, Sir,
tell me but, what you had intended fhould become
of me?

You talk to me, my deareft Life, as if all you had
heard againft me was true ; and you would have me
anfwer you, (would you?) as if it was?

I want nothing to convince me, Sir, that the
Countefs loves you : You know the reft of my Information : Judge for me, what I can, what I ought
to believe !---You know the Rumours of the World
concerning you : Even I, who ftay fo much at
home, and have not taken the leaft Pains to find out
my Wretchednefs, nor to confirm it, fince I knew
it, have come to the Hearing of it ; and if you know
the Licence taken with both your Characters, and
yet correfpond fo openly, muft it not look to me,
that you value not your Honour in the World's
Eye, nor my Lady hers ? I told you, Sir, the Anfwer fhe made to her Uncle.

You told me, my Dear, as you were told. Be
tender of a Lady's Reputation---for your own fake.
No one is exempted from Calumny, and even
Words faid, and the Occafion of faying them not
known, may bear a very different Conftruction from
what they would have done, had the Occafion been
told

This may be all true, Sir · I wifh my Lady would
be as tender of her Reputation as I would be, let
her injure me in your Affections as fhe will. But
can you fay, Sir, that there is nothing between you,
that fhould *not* be, according to *my* Notions of
Virtue and Honour, and according to your *own*,
which I took Pride in, before that fatal Mafquerade?

You

You anfwer me not, continu'd I, and may I not fairly prefume you are not able to anfwer me as I wifh to be anfwered? But come, deareft Sir, (and I put my Arms round his Neck) let me not urge you too boldly. I will never forget your Benefits and your paft Kindnefs to me   I have been a happy Creature· No one, till within thefe few Weeks, was ever fo happy as I.   I will love you ftill with a Paffion as ardent as ever I loved you   Abfence cannot leffen fuch a Love as mine   I am fure it cannot

I fee your Difficulties.   You have gone too far to recede   If you can make it eafy to your Confcience, I will wait with Patience my happier Deftiny, and I will wifh to live, (if I can be convinc'd you wifh me not to die) in order to pray for you, and to be a Directrefs to the firft Education of my deareft Baby

You figh, dear Sir; repofe your beloved Face next to my fond Heart   'Tis all your own: And ever fhall be, let it, or let it not, be worthy of the Honour in your Eftimation.

But, yet, my dear Mr *B.* if one could as eafily, in the Prime of fenfual Youth, look Twenty Years forward, as one can Twenty Years backward, what an empty Vanity, what a mere Nothing, will be all thofe groffer Satisfactions, that now give Wings of Defire to our debafed Appetites?

Motives of Religion *will* have their due Force upon *your* Mind one Day, I hope; as, bleffed be God, they have enabled *me* to talk to you on fuch a touching Point (after infinite Struggles, I own) with fo much Temper and Refignation; and then, my deareft Mr *B* when we come to that laft Bed, from which the Piety of our Friends fhall lift us, but from which we fhall never be able to raife ourfelves; for, dear Sir, your Countefs, and You, and your poor *Pamela,* muft all come to this'---we fhall find what it is will give us the true Joy, and
                                                        enable

enable us to fupport the Pangs of the dying Hour —.
Think you, my deareft Sir, (and I preffed my Lips
to his Forehead, as his Head was reclin'd on my
throbbing Bofom) that *then*, in that important Moment, what now gives us the greateft Pleafure, will
have any Part in our Confideration, but as it may
give us Woe or Comfort in the Reflection ?

But, I will not, I will not, O beft Beloved of my
Soul, afflict you farther ¹---Why fhould I thus fadden
all your gaudy Profpects ? I have faid enough to fuch
a Heart as yours, if Divine Grace touches it    And
if not, all I can fay, will be of no Avail ¹---I will
leave you therefore to That, and to your own Reflections.    And after giving you ten thoufand Thanks
for your kind, your indulgent Patience with me, I
will only beg, that I may fet out in a Week for
*Kent*, with my dear *Billy*, that you will receive one
Letter, at leaft, from me, of Gratitude and Bleffings,
it fhall not be of Upbraidings and Exclamations

But my Child you muft not deny me; for I fhall
haunt, like his Shadow, every Place wherein you
fhall put my *Billy*, if you fhould be fo unkind to
deny him to me ¹---And if, moreover, you will permit me to have the dear Mifs *Goodwin* with me, as
you had almoft given me room to hope, I will read
over all the Books of Education, and digeft them as
well as I am able, in order to fend you my Scheme,
and to fhew you how fit I hope your *Indulgence*,
at leaft, will make you think me, of having two fuch
precious Trufts repofed in me !

I was filent, waiting in Tears his Anfwer    But
his generous Heart was touch'd, and feem'd to labour
within him for Expreffion.

He came round to me at laft, and took me in his
Arms · Exalted Generofity ! faid he, Noble-minded
*Pamela* ! Let no Bar be put between us henceforth !
No Wonder, when one looks back to thy firft pro-
mifing Dawn of Excellence, that thy fuller Day
fhould

should thus irrefiftibly dazle such weak Eyes as mine. Whatever it cofts me, and I have been inconfiderately led on by blind Paffion for an Object too charming, but which I never thought equal to my *Pamela,* I will (for it is yet, I blefs God, in my Power) reftore to your Virtue a Husband all your own.

O Sir, Sir ! (and I fhould have funk down with Joy, had not his kind Arms fupported me) what have you faid ?---Can I be fo happy as to behold you innocent as to Deed, God, of his infinite Goodnefs, continue you both fo !---And Oh ! that the dear Lady would make me as truly love her, for the Graces of her Mind, as I admire her for the Advantages of her Perfon !

You are Virtue itfelf, my deareft Life; and from this Moment I will reverence you as my tutelary Angel I fhall behold you with Awe, and implicitly give up myfelf to all your Dictates ; for what you *fay,* and what you *do,* muft be ever right.---But I will not, my deareft Life, too lavifhly promife, left you fhould think it the fudden Effect of Paffions thus movingly touch'd, and which may fubfide again, when the Soul, as you obferved in your own Cafe, finks to its former Level But this I promife you, (and I hope you believe me, and will pardon the Pain I have given you, which made me fear, more than once, that your Head was affected, fo *uncommon,* yet fo *like yourfelf,* has been the manner of your Acting) that I will break off a Correfpondence, that has given you fo much Uneafinefs . And my *Pamela* may believe, that if I can be as good as my Word in this Point, fhe will never more be in Danger of any Rival whatever.

But fay, my dear Love, (added the charming, charming Man) fay you forgive me ; and refume but your former Chearfulnefs, and affectionate Regards to me, elfe I fhall fufpect the Sincerity of your Forgivenefs :

nefs . And you fhall indeed go to *Kent*; but not without me, nor your Boy neither, and, if you infift upon it, the poor Mifs, you have wifhed fo often, and fo generoufly to have, fhall be given up abfolutely to your Difpofal.

Do you think, my Lady, I could fpeak any one diftinct Sentence ? No indeed I could not—Pardon, Pardon *You*, dear Sir !—and I funk down on my Knees, from his Arms—All I beg—All I hope—*Your* Pardon -- *my* Thankfulnefs —O fpare me — fpare me but Words —— And indeed I was juft choak'd with my Joy; I never was fo in my whole Life before. And my Eyes were in a manner fixed, as the dear Gentleman told me afterwards, and that he was a little ftartled, feeing nothing but the Whites, for the Sight was out of its Orbits, in a manner, lifted up to Heaven—in Ecftafy for a Turn fo fudden, and fo unexpected !

We were forced to feparate foon after; for there was no bearing each o her, fo exceffive was my Joy, and his Goodnefs He left me, and went down to his own Clofet

Judge my Imployment you will, I am fure, my dear Lady I had new Ecftafy *to be bleft with*, in a Thankfulnefs fo exalted, that it left me all light and pleafant, as if I had fhook off Body, and trod in Air, fo much Heavinefs had I loft, and fo much Joy had I received !—From two fuch Extremes, how was it poffible I could prefently hit the Medium !--- For when I had given up my beloved Husband, as loft to me, and had dreaded the Confequences to his future State, to find him not only untainted as to Deed, but, in all Probability, mine upon better and furer Terms than ever---O, Madam ! muft not this give a Joy beyond all Joy, and furpaffing all Expreffion !

About Eight o'Clock Mr *B.* fent me up thefe Lines from his Clofet, which will explain what I
meant,

meant, as to the Papers I muſt beg your Ladyſhip
to return me

*My dear* PAMELA,

‘ I HAVE ſo much real Concern at the Anguiſh
‘ I have given you, and am ſo much affected with
‘ the Recollection of the uncommon Scenes which
‘ paſſed between us, juſt now, that I write, becauſe I
‘ know not how to look ſo excellent a Creature in the
‘ Face ---You muſt therefore ſup without me, and
‘ take your Mrs *Jervis* to Bed with you ; who, I
‘ doubt not, knows all this Affair , and you may tell
‘ her the happy Event

‘ You muſt not interfere with me juſt now, my
‘ Dear, while I am writing upon a Subject which
‘ takes up all my Attention , and which requiring
‘ great Delicacy, I may, poſſib'y, be all Night, before
‘ I can pleaſe myſelf in it

‘ I am determined, abſolutely, to make good my
‘ Promiſe to you. But if you have written to your
‘ Mother, to Miſs *Darnford*, or to Lady *Davers,*
‘ any thing of this Affair, you muſt ſhew me the
‘ Copies of your Letters, and let me into every
‘ Title how you came by your Information ----
‘ I ſolemnly promiſe you, on my Honour, (that
‘ has not yet been violated to you, and I hope never
‘ will) that not a Soul ſhall know or ſuffer by the
‘ Communication, not even *Turner* , for I am con-
‘ fident he has had ſome Hand in it This Requeſt
‘ you muſt comply with, if you can confide in me ;
‘ for I ſhall make ſome Uſe of it, (as prudent an one
‘ as I am able) for the ſake of every one concern'd,
‘ in the Concluſion of the Correſpondence between
‘ the Lady and myſelf. Whatever you may have
‘ ſaid, in the Bitterneſs of your Heart, in the Letters
‘ I require to ſee, or whatever any of thoſe, to
‘ whom they are directed, ſhall ſay, on the bad
‘ Proſpect,

' Profpect, fhall be forgiven, and look'd upon as
' deferved, by

*Your ever obliged and faithful,* &c.

I return'd the following ·

*Deareft, dear Sir,*

' I WILL not break in upon you, while you are
' fo importantly imploy'd  Mrs *Jervis* has indeed
' feen my Concern for fome time paft, and has
' heard Rumours, as I know by Hints fhe has from
' time to time given me, but her Prudence, and
' my Referves, have kept us from faying any thing
' to one another of it  Neither my Mother, nor
' Mifs *Darnford*, know a Tittle of it from me  I
' have received a Letter of Civility from Mifs, and
' have anfwered it, taking and giving Thanks for
' the Pleafure of each other's Company, and beft
' Refpects from her, and the *Lincolnfhire* Families,
' to your dear Self  Thefe, my Copy, and her
' Original, you fhall fee when you pleafe.  But, in
' Truth, all that has paffed, is between Lady *Davers*
' and me, and I have not kept Copies of mine, but
' I will difpatch a Meffenger to her Ladyfhip for
' them, if you pleafe, in the Morning, before 'tis
' Light; not doubting your kind Promife of excufing
' every Thing, and every Body

' I beg, dear Sir, you will take care your Health
' fuffers not by your fitting up, for the Nights are
' cold and damp

' I will, now you have given me the Liberty, let
' Mrs *Jervis* know how happy you have made me,
' by diffipating my Fears, and the idle Rumours, as
' I fhall call them to her, of Calumniators

' God blefs you, dear Sir, for your Goodnefs and
' Favour to

' *Your ever dutiful*

' P B '

He

'He was pleafed to return me this :

' *My dear Life*,

' YOU need not be in fuch hafte to fend. If
' you write to Lady *Davers*, how the Matter
' has ended, let me fee the Copy of it · And be
' very particular in *your*, or rather *my* Trial. It
' fhall be a ftanding Leffon to me for my future In-
' ftruction; as it will be a frefh Demonftration of
' your Excellence, which every Hour I more and
' more admire ' I am glad Lady *Davers* only knows
' the Matter. I think I ought to avoid feeing you,
' till I can affure you, that every thing is accommo-
' dated to your Defire. *Longman* has fent me fome
' Advices, which will make it proper for me to meet
' him at *Bedford* or *Gloucefter* I will not go to *Tun-*
' *bridge*, till I have all your Papers , and fo you'll
' have three Days time to procure them Your Boy,
' and your Penmanfhip, will find you no difagreeable
' Imployment till I return Neverthelefs, on fecond
' Thoughts, I will do myfelf the Pleafure of break-
' fafting with you in the Morning, to re-affure you
' of my unalterable Purpofe to approve myfelf,

' *My deareft Life*,

' *Ever faithfully Yours* '

Thus, I hope, is happily ended this dreadful
Affair My next fhall inform your Ladyfhip of the
Particulars of our Breakfaft Converfation. But I
would not flip this Poft, without acquainting you
with this bleffed Turn , and to beg the Favour of
you to fend me back my Letters, which will lay a
new Obligation upon,

*Dear Madam,*

*Your obliged Sifter, and humble Servant,*

P B.

LETTER

## LETTER XXXIN.

*My deareſt Lady,*

YOUR joyful Correſpondent has obtained Leave
to get every thing ready to quit *London* by
*Friday* next, when your kind Brother promiſes to
carry me down to *Kent*, and allows me to take my
Charmer with me   There's Happineſs for you,
Madam! To ſee, as I hope I ſhall ſee, upon one
bleſſed Spot, a dear faithful Husband, a beloved
Child, and a Father and Mother, whom I ſo much
love and honour!

· Mr. *B.* told me this voluntarily, this Morning at
Breakfaſt, and then, in the kindeſt manner, took
Leave of me, and ſet out for *Bedfordſhire*

But I ſhould, according to my Promiſe, give
your Ladyſhip a few Particulars of our Breakfaſt
Conference

I bid *Polly* withdraw, when her Maſter came up
to Breakfaſt; and I ran to the Door to meet him,
and threw myſelf on my Knees · O forgive me,
deareſt, dear Sir, all my Boldneſs of Yeſterday! --
My Heart was ſtrangely affected---or I could not
have acted as I did.  But never fear, my deareſt
Mr *B.* that my future Conduct ſhall be different
from what it uſed to be, or that I ſhall keep up to
a Spirit, which you hardly thought had Place in the
Heart of your dutiful *Pamela*, till ſhe was thus
ſeverely tried

I have weighed well your Conduct, my dear Life,
raiſing me to his Boſom, and I find an Uniformity
in it, that is ſurpriſingly juſt.

There is in your Compoſition indeed, the ſtrangeſt
Mixture of Meekneſs and high Spirit, that ever I
met with   Never was a ſaucier dear Girl, than you,
in your Maiden Days, when you thought your Honour in Danger   Never a more condeſcending Goodneſs,

ness, when your Fears were at an End. Now again, when you had Reason, as you believed, to apprehend a Conduct in me, unworthy of my Obligations to you, and of your Purity, you rise in your Spirit, with a Dignity that becomes an injured Person, and yet you forget not, in the Height of your Resentments, that angelick Sweetness of Temper, and Readiness to forgive, which so well become a Lady who lives as you live, and practises what you practise. My dearest *Pamela*, I see, continued he, serves not GOD for nought: In a better Sense I speak it, than the Maligner spoke it of *Job*: Since in every Action of yours, the heavenly Direction you so constantly invoke, shews itself thus beautifully

And now again, this charming Condescension, the Moment you are made easy, is an Assurance, that your affectionate Sweetness is return'd. And I cannot fear any thing, but that I shall never be able to deserve it

He led me to the Tea-Table, and sat down close by me. *Polly* came in. If every thing, said he, be here, that your Lady wants, you may withdraw; and let Mr. *Colbrand* and *Abraham* know, I shall be with them presently. Nobody shall wait upon me, but you, my Dear.

*Polly* withdrew.

You are all Goodness, Sir: And how generously, how kindly, do you account for that Mixture in my Temper you speak of!—Depend upon it, dear Sir, that I will never grow upon this your Indulgence

I always *lov'd* you, my Dearest, said he, and that with a passionate Fondness, which has not, I dare say, many Examples in the marry'd Life. But I *revere* you now. And so great is my Reverence for your Virtue, that I chose to sit up all Night, as I now do, to leave you for a few Days, until, by disengaging myself from all Intercourses that have

given

given you Uneafinefs, I can convince you, that I have render'd myfelf as worthy as I can be, of fuch an Angel, even upon your own Terms. I will account to you, continued he, for every Step I *fhall* take, and will reveal to you every Step I *have* taken. For this I *can* do, becaufe the Lady's Honour is untainted, and wicked Rumour has treated her worfe than fhe could deferve.

I told him, that fince *he* had been pleafed to name the Lady, I would take the Liberty to fay, I was glad, for her own fake, to hear that. Changing the Subject a little precipitately, as if it gave him Pain, he told me, as above, that I might prepare on *Friday* for *Kent*; and I parted with him, with greater Pleafure than ever I did in my Life. So neceffary fometimes are Afflictions, not only to teach one how to fubdue one's Paffions, and to make us, in our happieft States, know we are ftill on Earth, but even when they are over-blown, to augment and redouble our Joys!

I am now giving Orders, my dear Lady, for my beloved Journey, and quitting this undelightful Town, as it has been, and is, to me. My next will be from *Kent*, I hope; and perhaps I fhall then have an Opportunity to acquaint your Ladyfhip with the Particulars, and (if GOD anfwers my Prayers) the Conclufion of the Affair, which has given me fo much Uneafinefs.

Mean time, I am, with the greateft Gratitude, for the kind Share you have taken in my paft Afflictions, my good Lady,

*Your Ladyfhip's*
*Moft obliged Sifter and Servant,*

P. B

LETTFR

## LETTER XXXIV.

*My dearest* PAMELA,

INclofed are all the Letters you fend for   I rejoice with you upon the Turn this afflicting Affair has taken, thro' your inimitable Prudence, and a Courage I thought not in you ---A Wretch '---to give you fo much Difcompofure ?----But I will not, if he be good now, rave againft him, as I was going to do---I am impatient to hear what Account he gives of the Matter.  I hope he will be able to abandon this--- I won't call her Names, for fhe loves the Wretch, and that, if he be juft to *you*, will be her Punifh-ment

What Care ought thefe young Widows to take of their Reputation ?---And how watchful ought they to be over themfelves ?---She was hardly out of her Weeds, and yet muft go to a Mafquerade, and tempt her Fate, with all her Paffions about her, with an Independence, and an Affluence of Fortune, that made her able to think of nothing but gratifying them.

Then her Lord and fhe had been marry'd but barely Two Years; and one of them, fhe was forc'd, with the gayeft Temper in the World, to be his Nurfe. For, always inclin'd to a confumptive Indifpofition, he languifhed, without Hope, a Twelvemonth, and then died

She has good Qualities---is generous-- noble---but has ftrong Paffions, and is thoughtlefs and precipi-tant

My Lord came home to me laft *Tuefday*, with a long Story of my Brother and her, for I had kept the Matter as fecret as I could, for his fake and yours It feems, he had it from Sir *John*---Uncle to the young Lord C who is very earneft to bring on a Treaty of Marriage between her and his Nephew, who is in Love with her, and is a fine young Gentleman but has held back, on the Liberties she has lately given herself with my Brother

I hope she is innocent, as to Fact, but I know not what to say to it He ought to be hang'd, if he did not say she was Yet I have a great Opinion of his Veracity And yet he is so bold a Wretch!... And her Inconsideration is so great! ——

But left I should alarm your Fears, I will wait till I have the Account he gives you of this dark Affair, till when, I congratulate you upon the Leave you have obtained to quit the Town, and on your setting out for a Place so much nearer to *Tunbridge* Forgive me, *Pamela*, but he is an intriguing Wretch, and I would not have you to be too secure, left the Disappointment should be worse for you, than what you knew before But assure yourself, that I am, in all Cases and Events,

*Your affectionate Sister and Admirer,*

B DAVERS.

P S Your *Bar*, and some other Parts of your Conduct in your Trial, as you call it, make me ( as, by your Account, it seemed to do him) apprehensive, that you would hardly have been able to have kept your Intellect so untouched as were to be wish'd, had this Affair proceeded And this, as it would have been the moft deplorable Misfortune that could have befallen us, who love and admire you so justly, redoubles my Joy, that it is likely to end so happily GOD send it may!

LETTER

## LETTER XXXV.

### *From Mrs.* B. *to Lady* DAVERS.

*My deareſt Lady,*

MR B came back from *Bedfordſhire* to his Time Every thing being in Readineſs, we ſet out, my Baby, and his Nurſe, and *Polly,* and *Rachel,* in the Coach, Mr B and myſelf in the Chariot. The other Maids are to go down with Mrs *Jervis,* when every thing in *London* is ſettled by her Direction, to *Bedfordſhire,* and all the Men-ſervants too, except Mr. *Jonathan,* and *Abraham* and *John,* who went down with us on Horſeback; as alſo did Mr. *Colbiand*

We were met by my Father and Mother in a Chaiſe and Pair, which your kind Brother had preſented to them, unknown to me, that they might often take the Air together, and go to Church in it, (which is at ſome Diſtance from them) on *Sundays* The Driver is cloathed in a good brown Cloth Suit, but no Livery, for that my Parents could not have borne, as Mr. *B*'s Goodneſs made him conſider.

Your Ladyſhip muſt needs think, how we were all overjoy'd at this Meeting· For my own Part, I cannot expreſs how much I was tranſported when we arrived at the Farm-houſe, to ſee all I delighted in, upon one happy Spot together !

Mr B is much pleaſed with the Alterations made here *, and it is a ſweet, rural, and convenient Place

We were welcomed into theſe Parts by the Bells, and by the Miniſter, and People of moſt Note; and were at Church together on *Sunday.*

* *See* Vol. III. *Letter* I

M1.

Mr *B* is to set out on *Tuesday* for *Tunbridge*, with my Papers A happy Issue attend that Affair, I pray God' He has given me the following Particulars of it, to the Time of my Trial; beginning at the Masquerade.

He says, That at the Masquerade, when, pleased with the fair Nun's Shape, Air, and Voice, he had followed her to a Corner most unobserved, she said, in *Italian*, Why are my Retirements invaded, audacious *Spaniard*?

Because, my dear Nun, I hope you would have it so

I can no otherwise, returned she, strike dead thy bold Presumption, than to shew thee my Scorn and Anger thus----And unmasking, she surpris'd me, said Mr *B* with a Face as beautiful, but not so soft, as my *Pamela's* ---- And I, said Mr *B* to shew I can defy your Resentment, will shew you a Countenance as intrepid, as yours is lovely And so he drew aside his Mask too.

He says, he observed his fair Nun to be followed, where-ever she went, by a Mask habited like *Testimony* in *Sir Courtly Nice*, whose Attention was fixed upon her and him , and he doubted not, that it was Mr *Turner* So he and the fair Nun took different Ways, and he joined me and Miss *Darnford*, and found me engaged in the manner I related to your Ladyship, in a former Letter , and his Nun at his Elbow, unexpected

That afterwards, as he was engag'd in *French* with a Lady who had the Dress of an *Indian* Princess, and the Mask of an *Ethiopian*, his fair Nun said, in broken *Spanish*, Art thou at all Complections? ·· By St *Ignatius*, I believe thou'rt a Rover !

I am trying, reply'd he, in *Italian*, whether I can meet with any Lady comparable to my lovely Nun

And

And what is the Result?

Not one, no, not one

I wish you could not help being in Earnest, said she; and slid from him

He engag'd her next at the Side-board, drinking under her Veil a Glass of Champaign   You know, *Pamela*, said he, there never was a sweeter Mouth in the World, than the Countess's, except your own   She drew away the Glass, as if, unobserved by any body, to shew me the lower Part of her Face

I cannot say, continued he, but I was struck with her charming Manner, and an Unreservedness of Air and Behaviour, that I had not before seen so becoming --The Place, and the Freedom of Conversation and Deportment allowed there, gave her great Advantages, in my Eye, altho' her Habit requir'd, as I thought, continued he, a little more Gravity and Circumspection·  And I could not tell how to resist a secret Pride and Vanity, which is but too natural to both Sexes, when they are taken notice of by Persons so worthy of Regard

Naturally fond of every thing that carry'd the Face of an Intrigue, I long'd to know, proceeded he, who this charming Nun was --And next Time I engag'd her, My good Sister, said I, how happy should I be, if I might be admitted to a Conversation with you at your Grate?

Answer me, said she, thou bold *Spaniard*, (for that was a Name she seem'd fond to call me by, which gave me to imagine, that Boldness was a Qualification with which she was not displeased: 'Tis not unusual with our vain Sex, observed he, to construe even Reproaches to our Advantage) Is the Lady here, whose Shackles thou wearest?

Do I look like a Man shackled, my fairest Nun?

N---No! not much like such an one   But I fansy thy Wife is either a *Widow*, or a *Quaker*?

Neither,

Ne ther, reply'd I, taking, by Equivocation, her Queſtion literally.

And art thou not a marry'd Wretch? Anſwer me quickly '--We are obſerv'd.

No---ſaid I

Swear to me, thou art not ---

By St *Ignatius* then. For, my Dear, I was no *Wretch*, you know.

Enough' ſaid ſhe---and ſlid away; and the Fanatick wou'd fain have engaged her, but ſhe avoided him as induſtriouſly

Before I was aware, continued Mr *B* ſhe was at my Elbow, and, in *Italian*, ſaid, That fair Quaker yonder is the Wit of the Aſſemblée Her Eyes ſeem always directed to thy Motions And her Perſon ſhews ſome Intimacies have paſſed with ſomebody: Is it with thee?

It would be my Glory if it was, ſaid I, were her Face anſwerable to her Perſon

Is it not?

I long to know, replied Mr *B.*

I am glad thou doſt not

I am glad to hear my fair Nun ſay that.

Doſt thou, ſaid ſhe, hate Shackles? Or is it, that thy Hour is not yet come?

I wiſh, reply'd he, this be not the Hour, the very Hour----pretending (naughty Gentleman!--- What Ways theſe Men have '---) to ſigh

She went again to the Side-board, put her Handkerchief upon it Mr *B* followed her, and obſerved all her Motions She drank a Glaſs of Lemonade, as he of Burgundy, and a Perſon in a Domine, who was ſuppoſed to be the King, paſſing by, took up every one's Attention but Mr *B*'s, who eyed her Handkerchief, not doubting but ſhe laid it there on purpoſe to forget to take it up Accordingly ſhe left it there, and ſlipping by him, he, unobſerved, as he believes, put it in his Pocket, and at one Corner
found

found the Cover of a Letter, To the Right Honourable the Countess Dowager of——

That after this, the fair Nun was so shy, so reserved, and seem'd so studiously to avoid him, that he had no Opportunity to return her Handkerchief, and the Fanatick observing how she shunned him, said, in *French*, What, Monsieur, have you done to your Nun?

I found her to be a very Coquet, and told her so,——and she is offended

How could you affront a Lady, reply'd he, with such a *charming Face*?

By that, I had Reason to think, said Mr *B* that he had seen her unmask, and I said——It becomes not any Character, but that you wear, to pry into the Secrets of others, in order to make ill natur'd Remarks, and perhaps to take ungentlemanlike Advantages

No Man would make that Observation, returned he, whose Views would bear prying into

I was nettled, said Mr *B* at this warm Retort, and drew aside my Mask· Nor would any Man, who wore not a Mask, tell me so!

He took not the Challenge, and slid from me, and I saw him no more that Night

So! thought I, another Instance this might have been of the glorious Consequences of Masquerading ——O my Lady, these Masquerades are abominable Things!

The King, they said, met with a free Speaker that Night In Truth, I was not very sorry for it, for if Monarchs will lay aside their sovereign Distinctions, and mingle thus in Masquerade with the worst as well as the highest (I cannot say *best*) of their Subjects, let 'em take the Consequence ——Perhaps they might have a Chance to hear more Truth here than in their Palaces——the only Good that possibly can accrue from them--that is to say--If they made a good

Use

Ufe of it when they heard it. For, you fee, my
Monarch, tho' told the Truth, as it happen'd, receive the Hint with more Refentment than Thankfulnefs—So, as too likely, did the Monarch of us
both

And now, my Lady, you need not doubt, that
fo polite a Gentleman would find an Opportunity
to return the Nun her Handkerchief—To be fure
he would For what Man of Honour wou'd rob a
Lady of any Part of her Apparel? And fhould He
who wanted to fteal a Heart, content himfelf with
a Handkerchief?—No, no, that was not to be expected—So what does he do, but refolve, the very
next Day, after Dinner, the foonest Opportunity he
could well take, becaufe of the late Hours the Night
before, to purfue this Affair! Accordingly, the poor
Quaker little thinking of the Matter, away goes her
naughty Spaniard, to find out his Nun at her Grate,
or in her Parlour rather

He afks for the Countefs Is admitted into the
outward Parlour—Her Woman comes down, requires his Name, and Bufinefs His Name he mention'd not His Bufinefs was, to reftore into her
Lady's own Hands, fomething fhe had dropt the
Night before — Was defir'd to wait.

I fhould have told your Ladyfhip, that he was
drefs'd very richly—having no Defign at all, to make
Conquefts, no, not he!— O this wicked Love of
Intrigue!----- A kind of Olive-colour'd Velvet, and
fine brocaded Waiftcoat I faid, when he took Leave
of me, You're a charming Mr. *B* — and faluted him,
more preffingly than he return'd it, but little did I
think, when I plaited fo fmooth his rich-lac'd Ruffles,
and Bofom, where he was going, or what he had in
his plotting Heart — He went in his own Chariot,
that he did So that he had no Defign to conceal
who he was — But Intrigue, a new Conqueft, Vanity,
Pride!--- O thefe Men!--- They had need talk of
Ladies!

Ladies!---But it is half our own Fault, indeed it is, to encourage their Vanity

Well, Madam, he waited till his Statelinefs was moved to fend up again, That he would wait on her Ladyfhip fome other Time --- So down fhe came, drefs'd moft richly, Jewels in her Breaft, and in her Hair, and Ears--- But with a very referved and ftately Air--- He approached her --- Methinks I fee him, dear faucy Gentleman You know, Madam, what a noble manner of Addrefs he has!

He took the Hankerchief, from his Bofom, with an Air, and kiffing it, prefented it to her, faying, This happy Eftray, thus reftor'd, begs Leave, by me, to acknowlege its lovely Owner!

What mean you, Sir?--- Who be you, Sir?--- What mean you?

Your Ladyfhip will excufe me · But I am incapable of meaning any thing but what is honourable. ---(*No to be fure!*)--- This, Madam, you left laft Night, when the Domine took up every one's Attention but mine, which was much better engag'd; and I take the Liberty to reftore it to you.

She turn'd to the Mark, a Coronet, at one Corner. 'Tis true, Sir, I fee now it is one of mine: But fuch a Trifle was not worthy of being brought by fuch a Gentleman as you feem to be, nor of my Trouble to receive it in Perfon Your Servant, Sir, might have deliver'd the Bagatelle to mine

Nothing fhould be called fo, that belongs to the Countefs of ———.

She was no Countefs, Sir, that dropt that Handkerchief, and a Gentleman would not attempt to penetrate *unbecomingly*, through the Difguifes that a Lady thinks proper to affume, efpecially at fuch a Place, where every Inquiry fhould begin and end

This, Madam, from a Lady, who had unmasked ---becaufe *fhe would not be known!*---Very pretty, indeed!---Oh! thefe flight Cobweb Airs of Modefty·

fo eafi'y feen thro'---Hence fuch Advantages againft us are taken by the Men

She had looked out of her Window, and feen no Arms quarter'd with his own, for you know, my Lady, I would never permit any to be procured for me So, fhe doubted not, it feems, but he was an unmarried Gentleman, as he had intimated to her the Night before

He told her, it was impoffible, after having had the Opportunity of feeing the fineft Lady in the World, not to wifh to fee her again, and that he hop'd, he did not, *unbecomingly*, break thro' her Lad,fhip's Referves Nor had he made any Inqui res either on the Spot, or off of it, having had a much better Direction by Accident

As how, Sir? faid fhe, as he told me, with fo bewitching an Air, between Attentive and Pleafant, that, bold Gentleman, forgetting all manner of Diftance, fo early too! he claiped his Arms round her Waift, and faluted her, ftruggling with Anger and Indignation, he fays But I think little of that!

Whence this Infolence?---How-now, Sir!---Begone! were her Words, and fhe rung the Bell; but he fet his Back againft the Door—(I never heard fuch Boldnefs in my Life, Madam!)—till fhe would forgive him —And it is plain, fhe was not fo angry as fhe pretended, for her Woman coming, fhe was calmer *Nelthorpe*, faid fhe, fetch my Snuff box, with the Lavender in it

Her Woman went, and then fhe faid, You told me, Sir, laft Night, of your Intrepidnefs · I think you are the boldeft Man I ever met with · But, Sir, furely you ought to know, that you are not now in the *Hay-market*

I think, tru'y, Madam, the Lady might have fav'd herfelf that Speech, for, upon my Word, they nether of them were Masks —Tho' they ought both to be put on one of Bluſhes —I am fure I do for them, while I am writing

Her

Her irrefiſtible Lovelineſs ſerved for an Excuſe, that ſhe could not diſapprove from a Man ſhe diſliked not, and his irreſiſtible—may I ſay, Aſſurance, Madam?—found too ready an Excuſe

Well, but, Sir, ſaid I, pray, when her Ladyſhip was made acquainted. that you were a marry'd Gentleman, how then?—I long to hear, how then!—Pray, did *ſhe* find it out, or did *you* tell her?

Patience, my Dear!

Well pray, Sir, go on—What was next?

Why, next, I put on a more reſpectful and tender Air I would have taken her Hand indeed, but ſhe would not permit it, and when ſhe ſaw I would not go, till her Lavender Snuff came down, (for ſo I told her, and her Woman was not in Haſte) ſhe ſeated herſelf, and I took my Place by her, and began upon a Subject of a charming Lady I ſaw the Night before, after I had parted with her Ladyſhip, but not equal by any means to her And I was confident this would engage her Attention; for I never knew the Lady, who thought herſelf handſome, that was not taken by this Topick Flattery and Admiration, *Pamela,* are the Two principal Engines by which our Sex make their firſt Approaches to yours; and if you liſten to us, we are ſure, either by the Sap or the Mine, to ſucceed, and blow you up, whenever we pleaſe, if we do but take care to ſuit ourſelves to your particular Foibles, or, to carry on the Metaphor, point our Batteries to your weak Side For the ſtrongeſt Fortreſſes, my Dear, are weaker in one Place than another — A fine thing, Sir, ſaid I, to be ſo learned a Gentleman!—I wiſh, however, thought I, you had always come honeſtly by your Knowlege.

When the Lavender Snuff came down, continu'd he, we were engaged in an agreeable Diſputation, which I had raiſed on purpoſe to excite her Oppoſition, ſhe having all the Advantage in it, and in order to my

K 6 giving

giving it up, when she was intent upon it, as a Mark
of my Consideration for her

I the less wonder, Sir, said I, at your Boldness
(pardon the Word') with such a Lady, in your first
Visit, because of her Freedoms, when mask'd, her
Unmasking, and her Handkerchief, and Letter-cover.
To be sure the Lady, when she saw next Day, such
a fine Gentleman, and such an handsome Equipage,
had little Reason, after her other Freedoms, to be
so very nice with you, as to decline an insnaring
Conversation, calculated on purpose to engage her
Attention, and to lengthen out your Visit. But did
she not ask you, who you were?

Her Servants did of mine ---And her Woman
(for I knew all afterwards, when we were better acquainted) came, and whisper'd her Lady, that I was
Mr. *B* of *Bedfordshire*, and had an immense Estate,
to which they were so kind as to add two or three
thousand Pounds a Year, out of pure Good will to
me. I thank them

But pray, dear Sir, what had you in View in all
this? Did you intend to carry this Matter at first,
a far as ever you could?

I had, at first, my Dear, no View, but such as
Pride and Vanity suggested to me I was carried
away by Inconsideration, and the Love of Intrigue,
without so much as giving myself any Thought about
the Consequences The Lady, I observed, had
abundance of fine Qualities I thought I could con-
verse with her, on a very agreeable Foot, and her
Honour, I knew, at any Time, would preserve me
mine, if ever I should find it in Danger And, in
my Soul, I preferr'd my *Pamela* to all the Ladies
on Earth and question'd not, but that, and your
Virtue, would be another Barrier to my Fidelity.

As to the Notion of *Polygamy*, I never, but in
the Levity of Speech, and the Wantonness of Argument, like other lively young Fellows, who think
they

they have Wit to shew, when they advance something out of the common way, had it in my Head. I thought myself doubly bound by the Laws of my Country, to discourage that way of Thinking, as I was a Five hundredth Part of one of the Branches of the Legislature, and, inconsiderable as that is, yet it makes one too considerable, in my Opinion, to break those Laws, one should rather join all one's Interest to inforce

In a Word, therefore, Pride, Vanity, Thoughtlessness, were my Misguiders, as I said The Countess's Honour and Character, and your Virtue and Merit, my Dear, and my Obligations to you, were my Defences: But I find one should avoid the first Appearances of Evil. One knows not one's own Strength 'Tis presumptuous to depend upon it, where Wit and Beauty are in the Way on one Side, and Youth and strong Passions on the other

You certainly, Sir, say right But be pleased to tell me, what her Ladyship said, when she knew you were marry'd?

The Countess's Woman was in my Interest, and let me into some of her Lady's Secrets, having a great Share in her Confidence, and particularly acquainted me, how loth her Lady was to believe I was marry'd I had paid her Three Visits in Town, and attended her once to her Seat upon the Forest, before she heard that I was But when she was assured of it, and directed her *Nelthorpe* to ask me about it, and I readily own'd it, she was greatly incensed, tho' nothing but general Civilities, and Intimacies not inconsistent with honourable Friendship, had passed between us The Consequence was, she forbad me ever seeing her again, and set out with her Sister, and the Viscount, for *Tunbridge*, where she stay'd about Three Weeks

I thought I had already gone too far, and blam'd myself for permitting her Ladyship so long to believe

me

me a fingle Man, and here the Matter had dropp'd,
in all Probability, had not a Ball, given by Lord----,
to which, unknown to each other, we were both,
as alfo the Vifcountefs, invited, brought us again
into one another's Company  The Lady withdrew,
after a while, with her Sifter, to another Apartment;
and being refolved upon perfonal Recrimination,
(which is what a Lady, who is refolved to break with
a favoured Object, fhould never truft herfelf with)
fent for me, and reproached me on my Conduct, in
which her Sifter join'd

I own'd frankly, that it was rather Gaiety than
Defign, that made me give Caufe at the Mifque-
rade, for her Ladyfhip to think I was not marry'd,
for that I had a Wife, who had a thoufand Excellencies, and was my Pride, and my Boaft  That I
held it very poffible for a Gentleman and Lady to
carry on an innocent and honourable Friendfhip, in
a *Family* way, and I was fure, when fhe and her
Sifter faw my Spoufe, they would not be difpleafed
with her Acquaintance, and all that I had to reproach myfelf with, was, that after having, at the
Mafquerade, given Reafon to think I was not marry'd, I had been loth, *officioufly*, to fay I was, altho'
it never was my Intention to conceal it

In fhort, I acquitted myfelf fo well to both Ladies,
that a Family Intimacy was confented to

I renew'd my Vifits, and we accounted to one
another's Honour, by entering upon a kind of *Pla-
tonic* Syftem, in which Sex was to have no manner
of Concern

But, my dear *Pamela*, I muft own myfelf extremely blameab'e, becaufe I knew the World and
human Nature, I will fay, better than the Lady,
who never before had been trufted into it upon her
own Feet, and who, notwithftanding that Wit and
Vivacity which every one admires in her, gave herfelf little Time for Confideration, as fhe had met
with

with a Man whofe Perfon and Converfation fhe did not diflike, and whofe Circumftances and Spirit fet him above fordid or mercenary Views: And befides, I made myfelf ufeful to her in fome of her Affairs, wherein fhe had been grofly abufed , which brought us into more intimate and frequent Converfations, than otherwife we fhould have had Opportunities for

I ought therefore to have more carefully guarded againft Inconveniencies, which I knew were fo likely to arife from fuch Intimacies , and the rather, as I hinted, becaufe the Lady had no Apprehenfion at all of any So that, my Dear, if I have no Excufe from human Frailty, from Youth, and the Charms of the Object, I am intirely deftitute of any

I fee, Mr B faid I, there is a great deal to be faid for the Lady I wifh I could fay there was for the Gentleman But fuch a fine Lady had been fafe, with all her Inconfideration, and fo, forgive me, Sir, would the Gentlemen, with all his intriguing Spirit, had it not been for thefe vile Mafquerades. Never, dear Sir, think of going to another.

Why, my Dear, he was pleafed to fay, thofe are leaft of all to be trufted at thefe Diverfions, who are moft defirous to go to them ——Of this I am now fully convinced.

Well, Sir, I long to hear the further Particulars of this Story . For this generous Opennefs, now the Affair is over, cannot but be grateful to me, as it fhews me you have no Referves ; and as it tends to convince me, that the Lady was lefs blameable than I apprehended fhe was For dearly do I love, for the Honour of my Sex, to find Ladies of Birth and Quality innocent, who have fo many Opportunities of knowing and practifing their Duties, above what meaner Perfons can have——E'fe, while the *one* fails thro' Surprize and Ignorance, it will look as if the *others* were faulty from Inclination . And what a Difa Difgrace is that upon the Sex in general? And what a Triumph to the wicked ones of yours?

Well obferved, my Dear. This is like your generous and deep way of Thinking

Well, but, dear Sir, proceed, if you pleafe ---Your Reconciliation is now effected. A Friendfhip Quadrupartite is commenced. And the Vifcounrefs and myfelf are to find Cement for the erecting of an Edifice, that is to be devoted to *Platonik* Love. What, may I afk, came next? And what did you defign fhould come of it?

The O*xford* Journey, my Dear, followed next, and it was my Faulr, that you were not a Party in it. For both Ladies were very defirous of your Company. But it being about the Time you were going abroad, after your Lying in, I excufed you to them. Yet they both long'd to fee you, efpecially, as by this Time, you may believe, they knew all your Story. And befides, whenever you were mention'd, I always did Juftice, as well to your Mind, as to your Perfon; and this, not only for the Sake of Juftice, but, to fay Truth, becaufe it gave the Two Sifters, and the Vifcount, (whofe foftly Character, and his Lady's prudent and refpectful Conduct to him, notwithftanding that, are both fo well known) lefs Caufe of Sufpicion, that I had any difhonourable Defigns upon the Dowager Lady

Mifs *Darnford* will have it, permit me, my good Lady, to obferve, that I fhall have fome Merit, with regard to the reft of my Sex, if I can be a means to reform fuch a dangerous Spirit of Intrigue, as that of your dear Brother. And the Hiftory of this Affair from his own Mouth, made me begin to pride myfelf on this Head. For was he not, think you, my Lady, in this Cafe, a fad Genrleman!---- And how deeply was he able to lay his Mifchiefs! And how much had this fine Lady been to be pity'd,

had

had she fallen by his Arts, as he was almost the only Man, who, by reason of the Gracefulness of his Person, his Generosity, Courage, ample Fortunes, and Wit, could have made her unhappy ----- G o d be praised, that it was stopt in Time, (altho', as it seems, but just in Time) as well for the poor Lady's sake, as for Mr *B's*, and my own!

Excuse me, Madam, for this Digression But yet, for what I am going to repeat, I shall still want farther Excuse; for I cannot resist a little rising Vanity, upon a Comparison (tho' only as to Features) drawn, by Mr *B* between the Countess and me; which, however the Preference he gives me in it, may be undeserv'd, yet it cannot but be very agreeable, in this particular Case of a Rivalry, to one who takes so much Pride in his good Opinion, and who makes it her chief Study, by all honest and laudable Means, to preserve it, but who, else, I hope, am far from considering such a transitory Advantage, (had I it in as great a Degree as his kind Fancy imputes it to me) but as it deserves I will give it, as near as I can, in his own Words:

It may not be altogether amiss, my Dear, now I have mention'd the Justice I always did your Character and Merit, to give you a brief Account of a Comparison, which once the Countess's Curiosity drew from me, between your Features and hers

She and I were alone in the Bow-window of her Library, which commands a fine View over *Windsor* Forest, but which View we could not enjoy, for it rain'd, and blew a Hurricane almost, which detain'd us within, altho' we were ready dress'd to go abroad

I began a Subject, which never fails to make the worst of Weather agreeable to a fine Lady; that of praising her Beauty, and the Symmetry of her Features, telling her, how much I thought every graceful one in her Face adorn'd the rest, as if they were

all

all form'd to give and receive Advantage from each other. I added, approaching her, as if the more attentively to perufe her fine Face, that I believ'd it poffible, from the tranfparent Whitenefs of her Skin, and the clear Bluenefs of her Veins, to difcover the Circulation, without a Microfcope

Keep your Diftance, Mr *B* faid fhe   Does your magnifying thus egregioufly the *Graces* you impute to my outward Form, agree with your *Platonick* Scheme? Your Eye, penetrating as you imagine it to be, pierces not deep enough for a *Platonick*, if you cannot look farther than the White and the Blue, and difcover the Circulation of the Spirit, for our Friendfhip is all Mind, you know

True, Madam, but if the Face is the Index of the Mind, when I contemplate yours, I fee and revere the Beau-ies of both in one   And what *Platonick* Laws forbid us to do Juftice to the one, when we admire the other?

Well, fit you down, bold Mr. *B.* fit you down, and anfwer me a Queftion or two on this Subject, fince you will be always raifing my Vanity upon it.

I did, faluting her Hand *only*, that was his Word, which I took Notice of in the dear *Platonick*, tho' I faid nothing

Tell me now of a Truth, with all the Charms your too agreeable Flattery gives me, Which is the moft lovely, your *Pamela*, or myfelf?

I told her, you were both incomparable, in a different Way

Well, faid fhe, I give up the Perfon and Air in general, becaufe I have heard, that fhe is flenderer, and better fhap'd, than moft Ladies, but for a few Particulars, as to *Face*, (invidious as the Comparifon may be, and concern'd as you are to juftify your Choice) I'll begin with the *Hair*, Mr *B*   Whofe HAIR is of moft Advantage to her Complection? -- Come, I fanfy, I fhall, at leaft, divide Perfections with your *Pamela*.                *Your*

Your Ladyſhip's delicate light Brown is extremely beautiful, and infinitely better becomes your Complexion and Features, than would that lovely ſhineing Auburn, which ſuits beſt with my Girl's

You muſt know, *Pamela,* I always called you my Girl, to her, as I do frequently to yourſelf and others.

So ſhe excels me there, I find!

I don't ſay ſo.

Well, but, as to the FOREHEAD, Mr B. ?

Indeed, Madam, my Girl has ſome Advantage, I preſume to think, in her Forehead She has a noble Openneſs and Freedom there, which beſpeaks her Mind, and every body's Favour, the Moment ſhe appears. Not but that your Ladyſhip's, next to hers, is the fineſt I ever ſaw

So!---*Next* to hers! rubbing her Forehead---Well, BROWS, Mr B ?

Your Ladyſhip's fine Arch-Brow is a Beauty in your fair Face, that a Pencil cannot imitate, but then your fairer Hair ſhews it not to that Advantage, I muſt needs ſay; which her darker Hair gives to hers; for, as to COMPLEXION, you are both ſo charmingly fair, that I cannot, for my Life, tell to which to give the Preference

Well, well, fooliſh Man, ſaid ſhe, peeviſhly, thou art ſtrangely taken with thy Girl!----- I wiſh thou wouldſt go about thy Buſineſs!-----What ſignifies a little bad Weather to Men?—But if her Complexion is as good as mine, it muſt look better, becauſe of her dark Hair —I ſhall come poorly off, I find!—Let's have the EYES, however.

For black Eyes in my Girl, and blue in your Ladyſhip, they are both the lovelieſt I ever beheld — And, *Pamela,* I was wicked enough to ſay, That it would be the ſweeteſt Travelling in the World, to have you both placed at Fifty Miles Diſtance from each other, and to paſs the Prime of one's Life from Black to Blue, and from Blue to Black, and

it

it would be impossible to know which to prefer, but the present

Ah! naughty Mr *B* said I, were you not worse than the Countess a great deal?

The Countess is not bad, my Dear. I only was in Fault.

But what, Sir, did she say to you?

Say! why, the saucy Lady did what very few Ladies have ever done. She made the Powder fly out of my Wig, by a smart Cuff, with her nimble Fingers.

And how, Sir, did you take that?

How, my Dear!---Why I kiss'd her in Revenge. Fine Doings between Two *Platonicks*! thought I.

But I will own to you, Madam, that my Vanity in this Comparison, was too much soothed, not to wish to hear how it was carried on.

Well, Sir, did you proceed further in your Comparison?

I knew, my Dear, you would not let me finish at half your Picture — O *Pamela*— Who says, you are absolutely perfect? Who says, there is no *Sex* in your *Mind*? and tapp'd my Neck.

All is owing, Sir, to the Pride I take in your Opinion. I care not how indifferent I appear in the Eyes of all the World besides.

The CHEEK came next, proceeded Mr *B* I allow'd her Ladyship to have a livelier Carmine in hers; and that it was somewhat rounder, her Ladyship being a little plumper than my Girl, but that *your* Face, my Dear, being rather smaller featur'd of the two, there was an inimitably finer Turn in your Cheek, than I had ever seen in my Life, in any Lady's.

Her Ladyship, he said, stroked her Cheek-bones, which, however, Madam, I think, are far from being high, (tho' to be sure, she is a little larger featur'd, a excellent Proportion, for all that, as she is of a

taller

taller and a larger Make than me) and said, Very
well, Sir, you are determin'd to mortify me  But,
added her Ladyship, (which shewed, Madam, she
little depended upon *Platonicism* in him) if you
have a *View* in this, you will be greatly mistaken,
I'll assure you  For, let me tell you, Sir, the Lady
who can think meanly of herself, is any Man's Pur-
chase

The NOSE I left in doubt, said Mr *B.* but allow'd, that each were exquisitely beautiful on its
own proper Face

Her Ladyship was sure of a Preference in her
MOUTH  I allow'd, that her LIPS were somewhat
plumper—and, saluting her by Surprize, (for which
I had much ado to preserve my Wig from another
Disorder—) a little softer, of Consequence , but not
quite so red—for, said I, I never saw a Lip of so
rich and balmy a Red in my Life, as my Girl's.

But *your* SMILES, Madam, are more bewitch-
ingly free and attractive, for my Girl is a little too
grave

As to TEETH, charming as your Ladyship's are,
I think hers not a whit inferior in Whiteness and
Regularity

Her CHIN, is a-sweet Addition to her Face, by
that easy soft half Round, that looks as if Nature
had begun at Top, and gave that as her finishing
Stroke to the rest  While, my dear Lady, yours is
a little, little too strong featur'd , but such as so infinitely becomes your Face, that my Girl's Chin
would not have half the Beauty upon your Face.

Her EARS, my Lady, are just such as your own :---
Must they not be beautiful then ?  Her NECK, tho'
it must not presume—let me see, Madam, approaching her—(Keep your Distance, Sir   I was forc'd to
do so)—tho' it must not pretend to excel yours for
Whiteness, yet, except yours, did I never see any
Neck so beautiful  But your Ladyship, it must be
con-

confefs'd, being a little plumper in Perfon, has the Advantage *here*

I had a fmart Rap on my Knuckles with her Fan And fhe would hear no more. But was refolv'd fhe would fee you, fhe faid.

And, my Dear, I am the more particular in re pearing this comparative Defcription of the Two charming'ft Perfons in *England*, becaufe you will fee the Reafon, (and that it was not to infult you, as you rightly judg'd in your Letter to my Sifter *, but to your Advantage) that I gave way to the Im portunity of the Countefs to fee you, for I little thought you were fo well acquainted with our In ti macy, much lefs, that we had been made more intimate, to you, than ever, in Truth, we were, or perhaps, might have been And when I asked you, Why you were not more richly drefs'd, and had not your Jewels, you may believe, (as I had no Reafon to doubt, that the Countefs would come in all her Ornaments) I was not willing my Girl fhould give way to the noble Emulatrefs in any thing, being concern'd for your own Honour, as well as mine, in the Superiority of Beauty I had fo juftly given you

Well, Sir, to be fure, this was kind, very kind; and little was I difpofed (knowing what I knew) to pafs fo favourable a Conftruction on your Genero fity to me.

My Queftion to her Ladyfhip, continu'd Mr B. at going away, Whether you were not the charming'ft Girl in the World, which, feeing you together at one View, rich as fhe was dreft, and plain as you, gave me the double Pleafure (a Pleafure fhe faid afterwards I exulted in) of deciding in your Favour, my Readinefs to explain to you what we both faid, and her not ungenerous Anfwer, I thought would

† *See p* 155. *l* 26.

have

have intitled me to a better Return than a Flood of Tears, which confirm'd me, that your past Uneasiness was a Jealousy, I was not willing to allow in you, tho' I should have been more indulgent to it, had I known the Grounds you thought you had for it · And this was the Reason of my leaving you so abruptly as I did

Here, Madam, Mr *B* broke off, referring to another time the Conclusion of his Narrative  And, having written a great deal, I will here also close this Letter (tho' possibly I may not send it, till I send the Conclusion of this Story in my next) with the Assurance, that I am

*Your Ladyship's obliged Sister and Servant,*

P. B.

## LETTER XXXVI.

*My dear Lady,*

NOW I will proceed with my former Subject; and with the greater Pleasure, as what follows makes still more in Favour of the Countess's Character, than what went before, altho' that set it in a better Light, than it had once appeared to me in. I began, as follows

Will you be pleased, Sir, to favour me with the Continuation of our last Subject? I will, my Dear. You left off, Sir, with acquitting me (as knowing what I knew) for breaking out into that Flood of Tears, which occasioned your abrupt Departure But, dear Sir, will you be pleased to satisfy me about that affecting Information, of your Intention and my Lady's, to live at *Tunbridge* together?

'Tis absolutely Malice and Falshood  Our Intimacy had not proceeded so far, and, thoughtless as my Sister's Letters suppose the Lady, she would have spurn'd at such a Proposal, I dare say.

Well,

Well, but then, Sir, as to the Expreſſion to her Uncle, that ſhe had rather have been a certain Gentleman's ſecond Wife?

I believe, ſne might, in a Paſſion, ſay ſomething like it to him. He had been teizing her (from the time that I held an Argument in Favour of that fooliſh Topick *Polygamy*, in his Company, and his Niece's, and in that of her Siſter and the Viſcount) with Cautions againſt converſing with a Man, who, having, as he was pleaſed to ſay behind my Back, marry'd beneath him, wan ed to engage the Affections of a Lady of Birth, in order to recover, by doubling the Fault upon her, the Reputation he had loſt.

She deſpis'd his Inſinuation enough to anſwer him, That ſhe thought my Arguments in Behalf of *Polygamy* were convincing. This ſet him a raving, and he threw ſome coarſe Reflections upon her, which could not be repeated, if one may gueſs at them, by her being unable to tell me what they were; and then, to vex him more, and to revenge herſelf, ſhe ſaid ſomething like what was reported. And this was Handle enough for her Uncle, who took care to propagate it with an Indiſcretion peculiar to himſelf, for I heard of it in three different Companies, before I knew any thing of it from herſelf, and when I did, it was ſo repeated, as you, my Dear, would hardly have cenſur'd her for it, the Provocation conſider'd.

Well, but then, dear Sir, there is nothing at all amiſs, at this Rate, in the Correſpondence between my Lady and you?

Not on her Side, I dare ſay, if her Ladyſhip can be excuſed to Punctilio, and for having a greater Eſteem for a marry'd Man, than he can deſerve, or than may be ſtrictly defended to a Perſon of your Purity and Niceneſs.

Well, Sir, this is very noble in you. I love to hear the Gentlemen generous in Points where the Honour
of

of our Sex is concern'd. But, pray, Sir, what then was there on *your* Side, in that Matter, that made you give me so patient and so kind a Hearing?

Now, my Dear, you come to the Point: At first it was, as I have said before, nothing in me but Vanity, Pride, and Love of Intrigue, to try my Strength, where I had met with some Encouragement, as I thought, at the Masquerade; where the Lady went farther too than she would have done, had she not thought I was a single Man For, by what I have told you, *Pamela,* you will observe, that she endeavour'd to satisfy herself on that Head, as soon as she well could Mrs *Nelthorpe* acquainted me afterwards, when we were better known to each other, That her Lady was so partial in my Favour, (Who can always govern their Fancies, my Dear?) as to think, so early as at the Masquerade, that if every thing answer'd Appearances, and that I were a single Man, she, who has a noble and independent Fortune, might possibly be induc'd to make me happy in her Choice.

Supposing then, that I was unmarry'd, she left a Signal for me in her Handkerchief. I visited her; had the Honour, after the customary first Shyness, of being well receiv'd by her, and continued my Visits, till, perhaps, she would have been glad I had not been marry'd But, when she found I was, she avoided me, as I have told you, till the Accident I mention'd, threw us again upon each other, which renew'd our Intimacy upon Terms, which you would think too inconsiderate on one Side, and too designing on the other.

For myself, what can I say? Only that you gave me great Disgusts (without Cause, as I thought) by your unwonted Reception of me Ever in Tears and Grief; the Countess ever chearful and lively. And apprehending, that your Temper was intirely changing, I believ'd I had no bad Excuse to endea-

vour to make myfelf eafy and chearful abroad, fince
my Home became more irkfome to me, than ever
I believ'd it could be   Then, as we naturally love
thofe, who love us, I had Vanity, and fome Reafon
for my Vanity, (indeed all vain Men believe they
have) to think the Countefs had more than an Indifference for me   She was fo exafperated by the wrong
Methods taken with an independent Lady of her
generous Spirit, to break off the Acquaintance with
me, that, in Revenge, fhe deny'd me lefs than ever
Opportunities of her Company.   The Pleafure we
took in each other's Converfation, was reciprocal
The World's Reports had united us in one common
Caufe, and you, as I faid, had made Home lefs delightful to me, than it us'd to be. What might not
then have been apprehended from fo many Circumftances concurring with the Lady's Beauty, and my
Frailty?

I waited on her to *Tunbridge*.   She took a Houfe
there.   Where Peoples Tongues will take fo much
Liberty, when they have no Foundation for it at all,
and where the utmoft Circumfpection is us'd, what
will they not fay, where fo little of the latter is obferv'd? No wonder then, that Terms were faid to
be agreed upon between us. From her Uncle's Story,
of *Polygamy* propos'd by me, and feemingly agreed
to by her, no wonder that all your *Thomafine Fuller's*
Information was furmifed.

And thus ftood the Matter, when I was determin'd to give your Caufe for Uneafinefs a Hearing,
and to take my Meafures according to what fhould
refult from that Hearing

From this Account, dear Sir, faid I, it will not
be fo difficult, as I was afraid it would be, to end
this Affair even to her *Ladyfhip's* Satisfaction

I hope not, my Dear.

But, if, now, Sir, the Countefs fhould ftill be defirous not to break with you, from fo charming a Lady,
who knows what may happen !                    Very

Very true, *Pamela*  But, to make you ftill eafier, I will tell you, That her Ladyfhip has a firft Coufin marry'd to a Perfon going with a publick Character to feveral of the *Italian* Courts, and had it not been for my Perfuafions, fhe would have accepted of their earneft Invitations, and pafs'd a Year or two in *Italy,* where fhe once refided for Three Years together, which makes her fo perfect a Miftrefs of *Italian.*

Now I will let her know, additionally to what I have written to her, the Uneafinefs I have given you, and, fo far as it is proper, what is come to your Ears, and your generous Account of her, and the Charms of her Perfon, of which fhe will not be a little proud, for fhe has really noble and generous Sentiments, and thinks well (tho' her Sifter, in Pleafantry, will have it, a little envioufly) of you. And when I fhall endeavour to perfuade her to go, for the fake of her own Character, to a Place and Country of which fhe was always fond, I am apt to think fhe will come into it, for fhe has a greater Opinion of my Judgment, than it deferves  And I know a young Lord, who may be eafily perfuaded to follow her thither, and bring her back his Lady, if he can obtain her Confent  And what fay you, *Pamela,* to this?

O, Sir! I believe I fhall begin to love the Lady dearly, and that is what I never thought I fhould. I hope this will be brought about

But I fee, give me Leave to fay, Sir, how dangeroufly you might have gone on, both You and the Lady, under the Notion of this *Platonick* Love, till two precious Souls might have been loft: And this fhews one, as well in Spirituals as Temporals, from what flight Beginnings the greateft Mifchiefs fometimes fpring , and how eafily at firft a Breach may be ftopp'd, that, when neglected, the Waves of Paffion will widen, till they bear down all before them.

Your Obfervation, my Dear, is juft, reply'd Mr. *B.* and tho' I am confident the Lady was more in Earr-

neft

neft than myfelf in the Notion of *Platonick* Love, yet am I convinc'd, and always was, That *Platonick* Love is *Platonick* Nonfenfe: 'Tis the Fly buzzing about the Blaze, till its Wings are fcorch'd Or, to fpeak ftill ftronger, It is a Bait of the Devil to catch the Unexperienc'd and Thoughtlefs Nor ought fuch Notions to be pretended to, till the Parties are Five or Ten Years on the other Side of their Grand Clima-ɛterick. For Age, Old-age, and nothing elfe, muft eftablifh the Barriers to *Platonick* Love But, continu'd he, this was my comparative Confolation, though a very bad one, that had I fwerv'd, I fhould not have given the only Inftance, where Perfons more fcrupulous than I pretend to be, have begun Friendfhips even with fp'ritual Views, and ended them as grofly as I could have done, were the Lady to have been as frail as her Tempter

Here, Madam, Mr *B.* finifhed his Narrative. He is now fet out for *Tunbridge* with all my Papers I have no Doubt in his Honour, and kind Affurances, and hope my next will be a joyful Letter; and that I fhall inform you in it, that the Affair which went fo near my Heart, is abfolutely concluded to my Satisfaction, to Mr *B*'s, and to the *Countefs*'s, for if it be fo to all Three, my Happinefs, I doubt not, will be founded on a permanent Bafis. Mean time I am, my dear good Lady,

*Your moft affectionate and*

*obliged Sifter and Servant*

P. B.

---

## LETTER XXXVII.

A New Misfortune, my dear Lady !---But this is of GOD Almighty's fending, fo muft bear it patiently. My dear Baby is taken with the Small pox!

pox! To how many Troubles are the happieft of us
fubjected, in this Life! One need not multiply them
by one's own wilful Mifmanagements!--- I am able
to mind nothing elfe!

I had fo much Joy (as I told your Ladyfhip in
the Beginning of my laft Letter but one) to fee, on
our Arrival at the Farm-houfe, my dearest Mr *B.*
my beloved Baby, and my good Father and Mother,
all upon one happy Spot together, that I fear I was
too proud ---Yet I was truly thankful---I am fure I
was!---But I had, notwithftanding, too much Pride,
and too much Pleafure, on this happy Occafion

I told your Ladyfhip, in my laft, that your dear
Brother fet out on *Tuefday* Morning for *Tunbridge*
with my Papers: And I was longing to know the
Refult, hoping that every thing would be concluded
to the Satisfaction of all Three: For, thought I,
if this be fo, my Happinefs muft be permanent But,
alas! alas! there is nothing permanent in this Life
I feel it by Experience now!---I knew it before by
Theory! But that was not fo near and fo interesting by half!

For, in the Midft of all my Pleafures and Hopes;
in the Midft of my dear Parents Joy and Congratulations on our Arrival, and on what had paffed fo
happily fince we were laft here together, (in the
Birth of the dear Child, and my Safety, for which
they had been fo apprehenfive) the poor Baby was
taken ill It was on that very *Tuefday* Afternoon,
his Papa fet out for *Tunbridge* · But we knew not it
would be the Small-pox till *Thurfday* O Madam!
how are all the Pleafures I had form'd to myfelf, fick-
en'd now upon me! for my *Billy* is very bad

They talk of a kind Sort, but, alas! they talk at
random for they come not out at all! How then
can they fay they are kind?---I fear the Nurfe's Conftitution is too hale and too rich for the dear Baby!
·Had I been permitted---But, hufh! all my repining

L 3                                            *Ifs*

*Ifs!*---Except one *If*, and that,---*If* it be got happily over, it will be beſt he had it ſo young, and while at the Breaſt!

Oh! Madam, Madam! The ſmall Appearance that there was, is gone in again· And my Child, my dear Baby, will die!---The Doctors ſeem to think ſo

They want to ſend for Mr. *B* to keep me from him!---But I forbid it!---For what ſignifies Life or any thing, if I cannot ſee my Baby, while he is ſo dangerouſly ill?

My Father and Mother are, for the firſt time, quite cruel to me, they have forbid me, and I never was ſo deſirous of diſobeying them before, to attend the Darling of my Heart And why?---For fear of this poor Face!---For fear I ſhould get it myſelf!--But I am living low, very low, and have taken proper Precautions by Bleeding, and the like, to leſſen the Diſtemper's Fury, if I ſhould have it. And the reſt I leave to Providence. And if Mr. *B*'s Value is confin'd ſo much to this poor tranſitory Sightlineſs, he muſt not break with his Counteſs, I think; and if I am ever ſo deform'd in Perſon, my poor Intellects, I hope, will not be impair'd, and I ſhall, if GOD ſpare my *Billy*, be uſeful in his firſt Education, and be helpful to dear Miſs *Goodwin* --- or to any Babies --- with all my Heart --- he may make me an humble Nurſe to!---How peeviſh, ſinfully ſo, I doubt, does this Accident, and their affectionate Contradiction, make one!

I have this Moment received the following from Mr *B*

  ' *My deareſt Love*,            *Maidſtone*

' I AM greatly touched with the dear Boy's Ma-
' lady, of which I have this Moment heard I
' deſire you inſtantly to come to me hither, in the
' Chariot, with the Bearer, Mr *Colbrand*. I know
' what your Grief muſt be. But as you can do the
                   ' Child

' Child no Good, I beg you'll oblige me. Every
' thing is in a happy Train; but I can think of no-
' body but you, and (for *your* fake principally, but
' not a little for *my own*) my Boy. I will fet out
' to meet you; for I chufe not to come myfelf, left
' you fhould endeavour to perfuade me to permit
' your tarrying about him, and I fhould be forry to
' deny you any thing   I have taken here handfome
' Apartments for you, till the Event, which I pray
' GOD may be happy, fhall better determine me
' what to do.   I will be ever

*Your moſt affectionate and faithful*

*Maidſtone* indeed is not fo very far off, but one
may hear every Day once or twice, by a Man and
Horfe, fo I will go, to fhew my Obedience, fince
Mr B is fo intent upon it --- But I cannot live, if I
am not permitted to come back --- Oh! let me be
enabled, gracious Father! to clofe this Letter more
happily than I have begun it!

I have been fo dreadfully uneafy at *Maidſtone*,
that Mr B. has been fo good as to return with me
hither, and I find my Baby's Cafe not yet quite
defperate --- I am eafier now I fee him, in Prefence
of his beloved Papa --- who lets me have all my Way,
and approves of my preparative Method for myfelf,
and he tells me, that, fince I will have it fo, he will
indulge me in my Attendance on the Child, and
endeavour to imitate my Reliance on GOD --- that is
his kind Expreffion,---and leave the Iffue to Him.
And on my telling him, that I feared nothing in the
Diftemper, but the Lofs of his Love, he faid, in
Prefence of the Doctors, and my Father and Mother, preffing my Hand to his Lips, My deareft Life,
make yourfelf eafy under this Affliction, and apprehend nothing for yourfelf: I love you more for your
Mind than for your Face   That and your Perfon

L 4

will

will be the fame, and were that fweet Face to be cover'd with Seams and Scars, I will value you the more for the Misfortune  And glad I am, that I had your Picture fo well drawn in Town, to fatisfy thofe who have heard of your Lovelinefs, what you were, and hitherto are  For myfelf, my Admiration lies deeper, and, drawing me to the other End of the Room, whifperingly he faid, The laft Uneafinefs between us, I now begin to think, was neceffary, becaufe it has turned all my Delight in you, more than ever, to the Perfections of your Mind, and fo GOD preferves to me the Life of my *Pamela*, I care not, for my own Part, what Ravages the Diftemper makes here, and tapp'd my Cheek

How generous, how noble, how comforting was this! --- I will make this Ufe of it, I will now be refigned more and more to this Difpenfation, and prepare myfelf for the worft; for it is the Difpenfation of that GOD, who gave me my Baby, and all I have!

When I retir'd, the Reflections which I made, on fuppofing the worft, gave Birth to the following ferious Lines, (for I cannot live without a Pen in my Hand) written, as by a third Perfon, fuppofe a good Minifter  Your Ladyfhip will be pleafed to give them your favourable Allowances

Tell me, fond, weeping Parent, why
Thou fear'ft fo much thy Child fhould die?
'Tis true, tho' human Frailty may,
Yet Reafon can't, have much to fay
What is it thou thyfelf haft found
In this dull, heavy, tirefome Round
Of Life --- to make thee wifh thy Son
Should thro' the like dark Mazes run?

Suppofe the worft! --- 'Twill end thy Fears,
And free thee from a world of Cares.

*For, Oh! what anxious Thoughts arise*
*From hopefull'st Youths, to damp our Joys?*
*Who, from the Morning's brightest Ray,*
*Can promise, what will be the Day?*

When I went from my Apartment, to go to my Child, my dear Mr *B* met me at the Nursery Door, and led me back again. You must not go in again, my Dearest: they have just been giving the Child other Things to try to drive out the Malady; and some Pustules seem to promise on his Breast. I made no Doubt, my Baby was then in Extremity, and I would have given the World to have shed a few Tears; but I could not.

With the most soothing Goodness he led me to my Desk, and withdrew to attend the dear Baby himself,—to see his last Gaspings, poor little Lamb, I make no doubt!

This Suspense, and my own strange Hardness of Heart, that would not give up one Tear, (for the Passage from *that* to my *Eyes* seemed quite choak'd up, which used to be so open and ready on other Occasions, affecting ones too) produced these Lines.

*Why does my full-swoln Heart deny*
*The Tear, relief-ful, to my Eye?*
*If all my Joys are pass'd away,*
*And thou, dear Boy, to Parent Clay*
*Art hasting, the last Debt to pay,*
*Resign me to thy Will, my* GOD
*Let me, with Patience, bear this Rod.*
*However heavy be the Stroke,*
*If thou wilt not his Doom revoke,*
*Let me all sinful Anguish shun,*
*And say, resign'd, Thy Will be done!*

Two Days have pass'd, dreadful Days of Suspense! and now, blessed be GOD! who has given me Hope that our Prayers are heard, the Pustules

come

come kindly out, very thick in his Breaſt, and on his Face; but of a good Sort, they tell me — They won't let me ſee him; indeed they won't! — What cruel Kindneſs is this! One muſt believe all they tell one!

But, my dear Lady, my Spirits are ſo weak; I have ſuch a violent Head-ach, and have ſuch a ſtrange ſhivering Diſorder all running down my Back, and I was ſo hot juſt now, and am ſo cold at this preſent—Aguiſhly inclin'd—I don't know how!— that I muſt leave off, the Poſt going away, with the Aſſurance, that I am, and will be to the laſt Hour of my Life,

*Your Ladyſhip's grateful and*

*obliged Siſter and Servant,*

P. B.

---

## LETTER XXXVIII.

### *From Mr. B. to Lady* DAVERS.

*My dear Siſter,*

I Take very kind'y your Solicitude for the Health of my beloved *Pamela* The laſt Line ſhe wrote, was to you; for ſhe took to her Bed the Moment ſhe laid down her Pen.

I told her your kind Meſſage, and Wiſhes for her Safety, by my Lord's Gentleman; and ſhe begg'd I would write a Line to thank you in her Name for your affectionate Regards to her

She is in a fine way to do well: For, with her accuſtomed Prudence, ſhe had begun to prepare herſelf by a proper Regimen, the Moment ſhe knew the Child's Illneſs was the Small-pox

The worſt is over with the Boy, which keeps up her Spirits, and her Mother is ſo excellent a Nurſe

to

to both, and we are so happy likewise in the Care of a skilful Physician, Dr *M* (who directs and approves of every thing the good Dame does) that it is a singular Providence, this Malady seized them here, and affords no small Comfort to the dear Creature herself.

When I tell you, that, to all Appearance, her charming Face will not receive any Disfigurement by this cruel Enemy to Beauty, I am sure you will congratulate me upon a Felicity so desirable : But were it to be otherwise, if I were capable of slighting a Person, whose principal Beauties are much deeper than the Skin, I should deserve to be thought the most unworthy and superficial of Husbands

Whatever your Notions have been, my ever-ready censuring Lady *Davers*, of your Brother, on a certain Affair, I do assure you, That I never did, and never can, love any Lady as I love my *Pamela*

It is indeed impossible I can ever love her better than I do, and her outward Beauties are far from being indifferent to me, yet, if I know myself, I am sure I have Justice enough to love her *equally*, and Generosity enough to be *more tender* of her, were she to suffer by this Distemper. But, as her Humility, and her Affection to me, would induce her to think herself under greater Obligation to me, for such my Tenderness to her, were she to lose any the *least* valuable of her Perfections, I rejoice, that she will have no Reason for Mortification on that Score

My Respects to Lord *Davers*, and all your noble Neighbours. I am,

*Your affectionate Brother,*
*and humble Servant.*

## LETTER XXXIX.

*From Lady* DAVERS, *in Answer to the
preceding.*

*My dear Brother,*

I DO most heartily congratulate you on the Recovery of Master *Billy*, and the good Way my Sister is in. I am the more rejoic'd, as her sweet Face is not likely to suffer by the Malady, for, be the Beauties of the Mind what they will, those of Person are no small Recommendation, with some Folks, I am sure, and I began to be afraid, that when it was hardly possible for *both conjoined* to keep a roving Mind constant, that *one only* would not be sufficient.

This News gives me the more Pleasure, because I am well inform'd, that a certain gay Lady was pleased to give herself Airs upon hearing of my Sister's Illness, as, That she could not be sorry for it, for now she should look upon herself as the prettiest Woman in *England*. She meant only, I suppose, as to *outward* Prettiness, Brother!

You give me the Name of a *ready Censurer*. I own, I think myself to be not a little interested in all that regards my Brother, and his Honour. But when some People are not readier to *censure*, than others to *trespass*, I know not whether they can with Justice be stiled *censorious*.

But however that be, the Rod seems to have been held up, as a Warning—and that the Blow, in the irreparable Deprivation, is not given, is a Mercy, which I hope will be deserved; though you never can those very signal ones you receive at the Divine Hands, beyond any Gentleman I know. For even (if I shall not be deemed censorious again) your very

Vices

Vices have been turned to your Felicity, as if GOD
would try the Nobleness of the Heart he has given
you, by overcoming you (in Anfwer to my Sifter's
conftant Prayers, as well as mine) by Mercies rather
than by Judgments.

I might give Inftances of the Truth of this Obfervation, in almoft all the Actions and Attempts of
your paft Life . And take care, (if you *are* difpleafed,
I *will* fpeak it, take care) thou bold Wretch, that
if this Method be ingratefully flighted, the uplifted
Arm fall not down with double Weight on thy devoted Head !

I muft always love and honour my Brother, but
cannot help fpeaking my Mind Which, after all,
is the natural Refult of that very Love and Honour,
and which obliges me to ftyle myfelf

*Your truly affectionate Sifter,*

B. DAVERS.

---

## LETTER XL.

### *From Mrs.* B. *to Lady* DAVERS,

*My deareft Lady,*

MY firft Letter, and my firft Devoirs, after thofe
of Thankfulnefs to that gracious GOD, who has
fo happily conducted me thro' two fuch heavy Trials,
as my Child's and my own Illnefs, muft be directed
to your Ladyfhip, with all due Acknowlegement of
your generous and affectionate Concern for me

We are now preparing for our Journey to *Bedfordfhire*, and there, to my great Satisfaction, I am to
be favoured with the Care of Mifs *Goodwin*

After we have tarry'd about a Month there, Mr. *B*
will make a Tour with me thro' feveral Counties,
(taking the Hall in the Way, for about a Fortnight)
and

and fhew me what is remarkable every-where as we pafs, for this, he is pleafed to think, will better contribute to my Health, than any other Method; for the Diftemper has left upon me a kind of Wearinefs and Liftleffnefs · And he propofes to be out with me till the *Bath* Seafon begins, and by the Aid of thofe healing and balfamick Waters, he hopes, I fhall be quite eftablifhed Afterwards he propofes to return to *Bedfordfhire* for a little while; then to *London*, then to *Kent*, and, if nothing hinders, has a great mind to carry me over to *Paris*

Thus moft kindly does he amufe and divert me with his agreeable Schemes and Propofals But I have made one Amendment to them, and that is, that I muft not be deny'd to pay my Refpects to your Ladyfhip, at your Seat, and to my good Lady Countefs, in the fame Neighbourhood; and this will be far from being the leaft of my Pleafures.

I have had Congratulations without Number, upon my Recovery, but one, among the reft, I did not expect, from the Countefs Dowager · Could you think it, Madam ? Who fent me, by her Gentleman, the following Letter, from *Tunbridge*.

' *Dear Mrs* B.

' I Hope, among the Congratulations of your nume-
' rous Admirers, on your happy Recovery, my
' very fincere ones, will not be unacceptable I have
' no other Motive for making you my Compliments
' on this Occafion, on fo flender an Acquaintance,
' than the Pleafure it gives me, that the Publick, as
' well as your private Friends, have not been deprived
' of a Lady whofe Example, in every Duty of Life,
' is of fo much Concern to both. May you, Madam,
' long rejoice in an uninterrupted State of Happi-
' nefs, anfwerable to your Merits, and to your own
' Wifhes, are thofe of

*Your moft obedient humble Servant.*

To

To this kind Letter I return'd the following:

' *My good Lady*,

I AM under the higheft Obligation to your generous Favour, in your kind Compliments of
Congratulation on my Recovery. There is fomething fo noble and fo condefcending in the Honour you have done me, on fo flender an Acquaintance, that it befpeaks the exalted Mind and
Character of a Lady, who, in the Principles of
Generofity, and in true Noblenefs of Nature, has
no Example. May God Almighty blefs you, my
dear Lady, with all the Good you wifh me, and
with Increafe of Honour and Glory, both here
and hereafter, prays, and will always pray,

*Your Ladyfhip's*

*Moft obliged and obedient Servant,*

P.B.

This leads me to mention to your Ladyfhip, what
my Illnefs would not permit me to do before, that
Mr *B* met with fuch a Reception and Audience
from the Countefs, when he attended her, in all he
had to offer and propofe to her, and in her patient
Hearing of what he thought fit to read her from
your Ladyfhip's Letters and mine, that he faid, Don't
be jealous, my dear *Pamela*, but I muft admire her,
as long as I live

He gave me the Particulars, fo much to her Ladyfhip's Honour, that I told him, He fhould not only
be welcome to admire her Ladyfhip, but that I
would admire her too.

They parted very good Friends, and with great
Profeffions of Efteem for each other---And as Mr. *B.*
had undertaken to infpect into fome exceptionable
Accounts

Accounts and Managements of her Ladyſhip's Bai-
liff, one of her Servants brought a Letter for him
on *Monday* laſt, wholly written on that Subject.
But her Ladyſhip was ſo kindly conſiderate, as to
ſend it unſealed, in a Cover directed to me When
I opened it, I was frighted, to ſee it begin, to
Mr *B* and I haſtened to find him, in the Walk up
to the new-rais'd Mount ----Dear Sir---Here's ſome
Miſtake---You ſee the Direction is to Mrs *B* - Tis
very plain----But upon my Word, I have not read it

Don't be uneaſy, my Love - - I know what the
Subject muſt be, but I dare ſwear there is nothing
nor will there ever be, but what you or any body
may ſee

He read it, and giving it to me to peruſe, ſaid
Anſwer you ſelf the Poſtſcript, my Dear---I har
was--' If, Sir, the Trouble I give you is likely to
' ſubject you or your Lady to Uneaſineſs or Appre
' henſions, I beg you will not be concerned in it
' I will then ſet about the Matter myſelf, for my
' Uncle I will not trouble Yet, Women enter into
' theſe Particulars with as little Advantage to them-
' ſelves, as Inclination '

I told him, I was intirely eaſy and unapprehen-
ſive ; and, after all his Goodneſs to me, ſhould be
ſo, if he ſaw the Counteſs every Day That's kindly
ſaid, my Dear, returned he, but I will not truſt
myſelf to ſee her every Day, or at all, for the preſent I'll aſſure you, I will not ------ But I ſhall be
obliged to correſpond with her for a Month or ſo,
on this Occaſion Unleſs you prohibit it, and it
ſhall be in your Power to do ſo

I ſaid, With my whole Heart, he might, and I
ſhould be quite eaſy in both their Honours

Yet will I not, *Pamela*, ſaid he, unleſs you ſee our
Letters, for I know ſhe will always, now ſhe has
begun, ſend in a Cover to you, what ſhe will write
to me, unſeal'd, and whether I am at home or
abroad,

abroad, I shall take it unkindly, if you do not read them.

He went in with me, and wrote an Answer, which he sent by the Messenger, but would make me, whether I would or not, read it, and seal it up with his Seal But all this needed not to me now, who think so much better of the Lady than I did before, and am so well satisfy'd in his own Honour and generous Affection for me, for you saw, Madam, in what I wrote before, that he always loved me, tho' he was angry, at times, at my Change of Temper, as he apprehended it, not knowing, that I was appris'd of what passed between him and the Countess

I really am better pleased with this Correspondence, than I should have been, had it not been carry'd on, because the Servants, on both Sides, will see, by my Deportment on the Occasion, (and I will officiously, with a smiling Countenance, throw myself in their Observation) that it is quite innocent ; and this may help to silence the Mouths of those who have so freely censur'd their Conduct

Indeed, Madam, I think I have received no small Good myself by that Affair, which once lay so heavy upon me · For I don't believe I shall ever be jealous again, indeed, I don't think I shall. And won't that be an ugly Foible overcome? I see what may be done, in Cases not favourable to our Wishes, by the Aid of proper Reflection , and that the Bee is not the only Creature that may make Honey out of the bitter Flowers, as well as the sweet

My best and most grateful Respects and Thanks to my good Lord *Davers*, to the Earl, and his excellent Countess, and, most particularly, to Lady *Betty*, (with whose kind Compliments your Ladyship acquaints me ) and to Mr *H* for all your united Congratulations on my Recovery What Obligations do I lie under to such noble and generous Well-wishers!---I can make no Return, but by my Prayers,

ers, that God, by *his* Goodnefs, will fupply all my
Defects   And thefe will always attend you, from,
my dea-eft Lady,

*Your ever obliged Sifter, and humble Servant,*

P B.

Mr *H* is juft arrived   He fays, He comes a
fpecial Meffenger, to make a Report how my
Face has come off   He makes me many
Compliments upon it.   How kind your Ladyfhip is, to enter fo favourably into the minuteft
Concerns, which you think may any way affect
my future Happinefs in your dear Brothers
Opinion !----I want to pour out all my Joy and
my Thankfulnefs to God, before your Lady
fhip, and my good Lady Counress of *C*----'
For I am a happy, yea, a bleffed Creature---
Mr *B*'s Boy, your Ladyfhip's Boy, and my
Boy, is charmingly well, quite ftrong, and very
forward, for his Months, and his Papa is delighted with him more and more.

## LETTER XLI.

*My dear Mifs* DARNFORD,

I HOPE you are happy and well.   You kindly fay
you can't be fo, till you hear of my perfect Recovery.   And this, bleffed be God ' you have heard
already from Mr *B*

As to your Intimation of the fair Nun, 'tis all
happily over.   Bleffed be God, for that too ! And
I have a better and more indearing Husband than
ever.   Did you think that could be ?

My *Billy* too improves every Day . And my dear
Father and Mother feem to have their Youth renew'd
like

like the Eagle's. How many Bleſſings have I to be thankful for!

We are about to turn Travellers, to the Northern Counties, I think, quite to the Borders and afterwards to the Weſtern, to *Bath*, to *Briſtol*, and I know not whither myſelf: But among the reſt, to *Lincolnſhire*, that you may be ſure of Then how happy ſhall I be in my dear M ſs *Darnford!*

I long to hear whether poor Mrs *Jewkes* is better or worſe for the Advice of the Doctor, whom I order'd to attend her from *Stamford*, and in what Frame her Mind is.

Do, my dear Miſs, vouchſafe her a Viſit, in my Name ; tell her, if ſhe be low-ſpirited, what GOD has done for me, as to *my* Recovery, and comfort her all you can ; and bid her ſpare neither Expence nor Attendance, nor any thing her Heart can wiſh for, nor the Company of any Relations or Friends ſhe may deſire to be with her

If ſhe is in her *laſt Stage*, poor Soul! how noble will it be in you to give her Comfort and Conſolation in her dying Hours !

Altho' we can merit nothing at the Hand of GOD, yet I have a Notion, that we cannot deſerve more of one another, and, in ſome Senſe, for that Reaſon, of HIM, than in our Charities on ſo trying an Exigence ! When the poor Soul ſtands ſhivering, as it were, on the Verge of Death, and has nothing ſtrong, but its Fears and Doubts!---Then a little Balm pour'd into the Wounds of the Mind, a little comforting Advice to rely on GOD's Mercies, from a good Perſon , how conſolatory muſt it be! And how, like Morning Miſts before the Sun, muſt all Diffidences, and gloomy Doubts, be chaſed away by it!

But, my dear Miſs, the great Occaſion of my writing to you juſt now, is, by Lady *Davers*'s Deſire, on a quite different Subject. She knows how we love one another. And ſhe has ſent me the following-

ing

ing Lines by her Kinsman, who came to *Kent*, purposely to inquire how my Face fared in the Small-pox, and accompany'd us from *Kent* hither, [i e to *Bedfordshire*] and sets out To-morrow for Lord *Davers's*

*My dear* P A M E L A,

'*JACKEY* will tell you the Reason of his Jour-
' ney, my Curiofity, on your own Account And
' I fend this Letter by him, but he knows not the
' Contents My good Lord *Davers* wants to have
' his Nephew marry'd, and fettled in the World ·
' And his noble Father leaves the whole Matter to
' my Lord, as to the Person, Settlements, &c

' Now I, as well as my Lord, think fo highly of
' the Prudence, the Person, and Family of your
' Mifs *Darnford*, that we fhall be obliged to you, to
' found that young Lady on this Score

' I know Mr *H* would wifh for no greater Hap-
' pinefs. But if Mifs is engag'd, or cannot love my
' Nephew, I don't care, nor would my Lord, that
' fuch a Propofal fhould be received with undue
' Slight His Birth, and the Title and Eftate he is Heir
' to, are Advantages that require a Lady's Confi-
' deration. He has not indeed fo much Wit as Mifs;
' but he has enough for a Lord, whofe Friends are
' born before him, as the Phrafe is, is very good-
' humour'd, no Fool, no Sot, no Debauchee And,
' let me tell you, thefe are Circumftances not to be
' met with every Day in a young Man of Quality.

' As to Settlements, Fortune, &c. I fanfy there
' would be no great Difficulties The Bufinefs is, If
' Mifs could love him well enough for a Husband?
' *That* we leave to you to found the young Lady,
' and if fhe thinks fhe can, we will directly begin
' a Treaty with Sir *Simon* on that Subject I am,
' my deareft *Pamela*,

Your ever affectionate Sifter,

B. D A V E R S.

Now, my dear Mifs, as my Lady has fo well ſtated the Caſe, I beg you to enable me to return an Anſwer I will not ſay one Word *pro* or *con.* till I know your Mind----Only, that I think he is good-humour'd,.and might be eaſily perſuaded to any thing a Lady ſhould think reaſonable

And now, I muſt tell you another Piece of News in the matrimonial way Mr *Williams* has been here to congratulate us, on our multiply'd Bleſſings ; and he has acquainted Mr. *B* that an Overture has been made him by his new Patron, of a Kinſwoman of his Lordſhip's, a Lady of Virtue and Merit, and a Fortune of 3000 *l.* to make him Amends, as the Earl tells him, for quitting a better Living to oblige him , and that he is in great Hope of obtaining the Lady's Conſent, which is all that is wanting Mr. *B.* is very much pleaſed with ſo good a Proſpect in Mr. *Williams's* Favour, and has been in the Lady's Company formerly at a Ball, at *Gloucefter* , and he ſays, ſhe is a prudent and deſerving Lady ; and offers to make a Journey on Purpoſe to forward it, if he can be of Service to him

I ſuppoſe you know, that all is adjuſted, according to the Scheme I formerly acquainted you with \*, between Mr *Adams*, and that Gentleman ; and both are ſettled in their reſpective Livings But I ought to have told you, that Mr *Williams*, upon mature Deliberation, declin'd the ſtipulated 80 *l per Annum* from Mr. *Adams*, as he thought it would have a Simoniacal Appearance.

But now my Hand's in, let me tell you of a third matrimonial Propoſition, which gives me more Puzzle and Diſlike a great deal. And that is, Mr. *Adams* has, with great Reluctance, and after abundance of baſhful Apologies, ask'd me, If I have any Objection to his making his Addreſſes to *Polly Barlow* ?

\* *See her Journal of* Tueſday, Letter xxxii. Vol. III.

Which,

Which, however, he told me, he had not mention'd to her, nor to any body living, becaufe he would firft know whether I fhould take it amifs, as her Service was fo immediately about my Perfon

This unexpected Motion perplexed me a good deal The Gentleman is a worthy and a pious Man He has now a very good Living; but is but juft enter'd upon it, and, I think, according to his accuftom'd Prudence in other Refpects, had better have turned himfelf about firft.

But that is not the Point with me, neither. I have a great Regard to the Function I think it is as neceffary, in order to preferve the Refpect due to the Clergy, that their Wives fhould be nearly, if not quite, as unblemifh'd, and as circumfpect, as themfelves, and this, for the Gentleman's own fake, as well as in the Eye of the World For how fhall he purfue his Studies with Comfort to himfelf, if he be made uneafy at home ? or how fhall he expect his Female Parifhioners will regard his *publick* Preaching, if he cannot have a due Influence over the *private* Conduct of his Wife ?

I can't fay, excepting in the Inftance of Mr. *H.* but *Polly* is a good fort of Body enough, fo far as I know · But that is fuch a Blot in the poor Girl's Efcutcheon, a Thing not *accidental*, not *furpris'd* into, not owing to *Inattention*, but to cool *Premeditation*, after fhe had flept over and over upon it, that, I think, I could wifh Mr *Adams* a Wife more unexceptionable

'Tis true, Mr *Adams* knows not this;---but *that* is one of my Difficulties. If I acquaint him with it, I fhall hurt the poor Maiden irreparably, and deprive her of a Gentleman for a Husband, to whom fhe may poffibly make a good Wife---For fhe is not very meanly defcended---much better than myfelf, as the World would fay, were a Judgment to be made from my Father's low Eftate, when I was
exalted.

exalted ---I never, dear Miſs, ſhall be aſham'd of theſe Retroſpections [1]

She is genteel, has a very innocent Look, a good Face, is neat in her Perſon, and not addicted to any Exceſs, that I know of But, *ſtill,* my dear Miſs, that one *premeditated* Fault, is ſo ſad a one, that tho' ſhe might make a good Wife, for any middling Man of Buſineſs,---yet ſhe wants, methinks, that Diſcretion, that Purity, which I would always have in the Wife of a good Clergyman

Then, ſhe has not applied her Thoughts to that ſort of Oeconomy, which the Wife of a Country Clergyman ought to know ſomething of. And has ſuch a Turn to Dreſs and Appearance, that I can ſee, if indulg'd, ſhe would not be one that would help to remove the Scandal which ſome ſevere Remarkers are apt to throw upon the Wives of *Parſons,* as they call them

The Maiden, I believe, likes Mr *Adams* not a little She is very courteous to every body, but moſt to him of any body, and never has miſſed being preſent at our *Sunday* Duties ; and five or ſix times, Mrs *Jervis* tells me, ſhe has found her deſirous to have Mr. *Adams* expound this Text, and that Difficulty ; and the good Man is taken with her Piety · Which, and her Reformation, I hope, is ſincere · But, O Miſs ! ſhe is very ſly, very ſubtle, as I have found in ſeveral Inſtances, as fooliſh as ſhe was in the Affair I hint at.

So, ſometimes, I ſay to myſelf, The Girl may love Mr *Adams* : Ay, but then I anſwer, So ſhe did Mr *H.* and on his own very bad Terms too.--- In ſhort---but I wont be too cenſorious neither

So I'll ſay no more, than that I was perplexed ; and yet ſhould be very glad to have *Polly* well marry'd, for, ſince *that* Time, I have always had ſome Diffidences about her---Becauſe, you know, Miſs---her Fault was ſo enormous, and, as I have
ſaid,

said, so premeditated. I wanted you to advise with —But this was the Method I took.

I appointed Mr. *Adams* to drink a Dish of Tea with me in the Afternoon. *Polly* attended, as she generally does; for I can't say I love Men Attendants in these womanly Offices---A Tea-kettle in a Man's Hand, that would, if there was no better Imployment for him, be fitter to hold a Plough, or handle a Flail, or a Scythe, has such a Look with it ¹ —This is like my low Breeding, some would say, perhaps ----But I cannot call Things polite, that I think unseemly; and, moreover, let me tell you, Lady *Davers* keeps me in Countenance in this my Notion , and who doubts her Politeness?

Well, but *Polly* attended, as I said , and there were strange Simperings, and Bowing, and Court'sying, between them , the honest Gentleman seeming not to know how to let his Mistress wait upon him, while she behaved with as much Respect and Officiousness, as if she could not do too much for him.

Very well, thought I; I have such an Opinion of your Veracity, Mr. *Adams*, that I dare say you have not, because you told me you have not, mention'd the Matter to *Polly*: But, between her Officiousness, and your mutual Simperings, and Complaisance, I see you have found out a Language between you, that is full as significant as plain *English* Words *Polly*, thought I, sees no Difficulty in *this* Text, nor need you, Mr *Adams*, have much Trouble to make her understand you, when you come to expound upon *this* Subject.

I was forced, in short, to put on a statelier and more reserv'd Appearance than usual, to make them avoid Acts of Complaisance for one another, that might not be proper to be shewn before me, from one who sat as my Companion, to my Servant

When she withdrew, the modest Gentleman hem'd, and looked on one Side, and turn'd to the right and
left,

left, as if his Seat was uneafy to him, and I faw knew not how to fpeak; fo I began, in mere Compaffion to him, and faid, Mr *Adams*, I have been thinking of what you mentioned to me, as to *Polly Barlow.*

Hem! Hem! faid he; and pull'd out his Handkerchief, and wip'd his Mouth---Very well, Madam; ---I hope, no Offence, Madam!

No, Sir, none at all. But I am at a Lofs how to diftinguifh in this Cafe; whether it may not be from a Motive of too humble Gratitude, that you don't think yourfelf above matching with *Polly*, as you may fuppofe her a Favourite of mine; or whether it be your Value for her Perfon and Qualities, that makes her more agreeable in your Eyes, than any other Perfon would be.

Madam---Madam, faid the bafhful Gentleman hefitatingly---I do---I muft needs fay---I can't but own---that---Mrs *Mary*---is a Perfon---whom I think very agreeable, and no lefs modeft and virtuous.

You know, Sir, your own Circumftances. To be fure you have a very pretty Houfe, and a good Living, to carry a Wife to. And a Gentleman of your Prudence and Difcretion wants not any Advice: But you have reaped no Benefits by your Living It has been an Expence to you, rather, which you will not prefently get up. Do you propofe an early Marriage, Sir? Or were it not better, that you fufpended your Intentions of that fort for a Year or two more?

Madam, if your Ladyfhip chufe not to part with ---

Nay, Mr *Adams*, interrupted I, I fay not any thing for my own fake in this Point, that is out of the Queftion with me I can very willingly part with *Polly*, were it To-morrow, for her Good and yours.

Madam, I humbly beg Pardon, but --- but --- Delays---may breed Dangers.

Oh! very well! thought I, I'll be further, if the artful Girl has not let him know, by some means or other, that she has another humble Servant

And so, Miss, it has proved --- For, dismissing my Gentleman, with assuring him, that I had no Objection at all to the Matter, or to parting with *Polly*, as soon as it suited with their Conveniency--- I sounded her, and asked, If she thought Mr. *Adams* had any Affection for her?

She said, He was a very good Gentleman

I know it, *Polly*; and are you not of Opinion, he loves you a little?

Dear Ma'm, good your Ladyship --- love me! --- I don't know what such a Gentleman, as Mr. *Adams*, should see in me, to love me!

Oh! thought I, does the Doubt lie on *that* Side then? --- I see 'tis not of *thine*.

Well, but, *Polly*, if you have *another* Sweetheart, you should do the fair Thing; it would be wrong, if you encouraged any body else, if you thought of Mr *Adams*.

Indeed, Ma'm, I had a Letter sent me --- A Letter that I received --- from --- from a young Man in *Bedford*, but I never gave an Answer to it.

Oh! thought I, then thou wouldst not encourage *two at once*, this was as plain a Declaration as I wanted, that she had Thoughts of Mr. *Adams*

But how came Mr *Adams*, *Polly*, to know of this Letter?

How came Mr *Adams* to know of it, Ma'm! --- repeated she --- half surpris'd --- Why, I don't know, I can't tell how it was --- but I dropp'd it near his Desk --- pulling out my Handkerchief, I believe, Ma'm; and he brought it after me, and gave it me again

Well, thought I, thou'rt an intriguing Slut, I doubt, *Polly* --- *Delays may breed Dangers*, quoth the poor Gentleman! --- Ah! Girl, Girl! thought I, but did
not

not fay fo, thou deferveft to be blown up, and to
have thy Plot fpoiled, that thou doft — But if thy
Forwardnefs fhould expofe thee afterwards to Evils,
which thou mayft avoid, if thy Scheme takes Place,
I fhould very much blame myfelf  And I fee he
loves thee — So let the Matter takes its Courfe ; I
will trouble myfelf no more about it.  I only wifh,
that thou wilt make Mr. *Adams* as good a Wife
as he deferves.

And fo I difmifs'd her, telling her, That whoever
thought of being a Clergyman's Wife, fhould refolve
to be as good as himfelf , to fet an Example to all her
Sex in the Parifh, and fhew how much his Doctrines
had Weight with her , fhould be humble, circumfpect,
gentle in her Temper and Manners, frugal, not proud,
nor vying in Drefs with the Ladies of the Laity ;
fhould refolve to fweeten his Labours, and to be
obliging in her Deportment to Poor as well as Rich,
that her Husband got no Difcredit thro' her Means,
which would weaken his Influence upon his Auditors ;
and that fhe muft be moft of all obliging to him,
and ftudy his Temper, that his Mind might be more
difengag'd, in order to purfue his Studies with the
better Effect.

And fo much, my dear Mifs *Darnford*, for *your*
humble Servant ; and for Mr. *Williams*'s and Mr.
*Adams*'s matrimonial Profpects — And don't think
me difrefpectful, that I have mention'd my *Polly*'s
Affair in the fame Letter with yours  For in High and
Low, (I forget the *Latin* Phrafe — I have not had
a Leffon a long, long while, from my dear Tutor)
Love is in all the fame ! — But whether you'll like
Mr *H* as well as *Polly* does Mr. *Adams*, that's the
Queftion  But, leaving that to your own Decifion, I
conclude with one Obfervation . That altho' I thought
our Houfe of as little Intriguing as any body's,
Matter of it has left off that Practice ;
any Family can be clear of fome

of

of it long together, where there are Men and Women worth plotting for, as Husbands and Wives.

My beſt Wiſhes and Reſpects attend all your worthy Neighbours  I hope, ere many Months are paſt, to aſſure them, ſeverally, (to wit, Sir *Simon*, my Lady, Mrs. *Jones*, Mr *Peters*, and his Lady, and Niece, whoſe kind Congratulations make me very proud, and very thankful) how much I am obliged to them; and particularly, my dear Miſs, how much I am

> *Your ever-affectionate and*
>
> *faithful Friend and Servant,*
>
> P B

---

## LETTER XLII.

### From Miſs DARNFORD, *in Anſwer to the preceding.*

*My dear Mrs.* B.

I HAVE been ſeveral times (in Company with Mr *Peters*) to ſee Mrs. *Jewkes*. The poor Woman is very bad, and cannot live many Days We comfort her all we can; but ſhe often accuſes herſelf of her paſt Behaviour to ſo excellent a Lady, and, with Bleſſings upon Bleſſings, heaped upon you, and her Maſter, and your charming little Boy, ſhe is continually declaring how much your Goodneſs to her aggravates her former Faults to her own Conſcience

She has her Siſter-in-law and her Niece with her, and has ſettled all her Affairs, and thinks ſhe is not long for this World.

Her Diſtemper is an inward Decay, all at once, as it were, from a Conſtitution that ſeem'd like one

of

of Iron; and fhe is a mere Skeleton: You would not know her, I dare fay.

I will fee her every Day; and fhe has given me up all her Keys, and Accompts, to give to Mr. *Longman*, who is daily expected, and I hope will be here foon, for her Sifter-in-law, fhe fays herfelf, is a Woman of *this World*, as *fhe* has been.

Mr *Peters* calling upon me to go with him to vifit her, I will break off here

Mrs. *Jewkes* is much as fhe was, but your faithful Steward is come. I am glad of it—and fo is fhe—Neverthelefs I will go every Day, and do all the Good I can for the poor Woman, according to your charitable Defires.

I thank you, Madam, for your Communication of Lady *Davers*'s Letter. I am much obliged to my Lord, and her Ladyfhip; and fhould have been proud of an Alliance with that noble Family: But with all Mr *H*'s good Qualities, as my Lady paints them out, and his other Advantages, I could not, for the World, make him my Husband.

I'll tell you one of my Objections, in Confidence, however (for you are only to *found* me, you know); and I would not have it mention'd, that I have taken any Thought about the Matter, becaufe a ftronger Reafon may be given, fuch an one as my Lord and Lady will both allow, which I will communicate to you by and-by.

My Objection arifes even from what you intimate of Mr *H*'s Good-humour, and his Perfuadablenefs, if I may fo call it. Now, Madam, were I of a boifterous Temper, and high Spirit, fuch an one as required great Patience in a Husband, to bear with me, then Mr *H*'s Good-humour might have been a Confideration with me But when I have (I pride myfelf in the Thought) a Temper not wholly unlike your own, and fuch an one as would not want to

contend

contend for Superiority with a Husband, it is no Recommendation to me, that Mr. *H.* is a good-humour'd Gentleman, and will bear with Faults I defign rot to be guilty of.

But, my dear Mrs *B* my Husband muft be a Man of Senfe, and muft give me Reafon to think, he has a fuperior Judgment to my own, or I fhall be unhappy He will otherwife do wrong-headed Things I fhall be forced to oppofe him in them He will be tenacious and obftinate, and will be taught to talk of Prerogative, and to call himfelf a *Man*, without knowing how to behave as one, and I to defpife him of courfe, and fo be deemed a bad Wife, when, I hope, I have Qualities that would make me a tolerable good one, with a Man of Senfe for my Husband You know who fays,

*For Fools* (pardon me this harfh Word,'tis in my Author)
*For Fools are ftubborn in their Way,*
*As Coins are harden'd by th' Allay;*
*And Obftinacy's ne'er fo ftiff,*
*As when 'tis in a wrong Belief*

Now you muft not think I would difpenfe with real Good-humour in a Man. No, I make it one of my *Indifpenfables* in a Husband A good-natur'd Man will put the beft Conftructions on what happens· But he muft have Senfe to *diftinguifh* the beft He will be kind to little, unwilful, undefigned Failings. But he muft have Judgment to diftinguifh what *are* or are *not* fo

But Mr *H*'s Good-humour is Softnefs, as I may call it; and my Husband muft be fuch an one, in fhort, as I need not be afhamed to be feen with in Company, one, who being my Head, muft not be beneath all the Gentlemen he may happen to fall in with, and who, every time he is adjufting his Mouth for Speech, will give me Pain at my Heart, and Blufhes in my Face, even before he fpeaks.

I could

I could not bear, therefore, that every Gentleman, and every Lady, we encounter'd, fhould be prepar'd, whenever he offer'd to open his Lips, by their contemptuous Smiles, to expect fome weak and filly Things from him; and when he *had* fpoken, that he fhould, with a booby Grin, feem pleafed that he had not difappointed them

The only recommendatory Point in Mr *H* is, that he dreffes exceedingly fmart, and is no contemptible Figure of a Man, as you have obferved in a former Letter. But, dear Madam, you know, that's fo much the worfe, *when* the Man's Talent is not Taciturnity, except before his Aunt, or before Mr. *B* or you; *when* he is not confcious of internal Defect, and values himfelf upon outward Appearance.

As to his Attempt upon your *Polly,* tho' I don't like him the better for it, yet it is a Fault fo wickedly common among Gentlemen, that when a Lady refolves never to marry, till a quite virtuous Man addreffes her, it is, in other Words, refolving to die fingle · So that I make not this the *chief* Objection; and yet, I muft tell you, I would abate in my Expectations of half a dozen other good Qualities, rather than that one of Virtue in a Husband.

But, when I reflect upon the Figure Mr. *H* made in that Affair, I cannot bear him; and if I may judge of other Coxcombs by him, what Wretches are thefe fmart, well-dreffing, Querpo-fellows, many of which you and I have feen admiring themfelves at the Plays and Operas!

This is one of my infallible Rules, and I know it is yours too; That he who is taken up with the Admiration of his own fweet Perfon, will never admire a Wife's. His Delights are centred in himfelf, and he will not wifh to get out of that narrow, that exceeding narrow Circle, and, in my Opinion, fhould keep no Company, but that of Tailors, Wig-puffers, and Milaners.

M 4　　　　　　　But

But I will run on no further upon this Subject, but will tell you a Reason, which you *may* give to Lady *Davers*, why her kind Intentions to me cannot be anfwer'd; and which fhe'll take better than what I *have faid*, were fhe to know it, as I hope you won't let her · And this is, My Papa has had a Propofal made to him from a Gentleman you have feen, and have thought polite *. It is from Sir *W G* of this County, who is one of *your* great Admirers, and Mr *B*'s too, and that, you muft fuppofe, makes me have never the worfe Opinion of him, or of his Underftanding; altho' it requires no great Sagacity or Penetration to fee how much you adorn our Sex, and human Nature too.

Every thing was adjufted between my Papa and Mamma, and Sir *William*, on Condition we approv'd of each other, before I came down; which I knew not, till I had feen him here four times; and then my Papa furpris'd me into an half Approbation of him · And this, it feems, was one of the Reafons why I was fo hurried down from you.

I can't fay, but I like the Gentleman as well as moft I have feen; he is a Man of Senfe and Sobriety, to give him his Due, and is in very eafy Circumftances, and much refpected by all who know him, and that's no bad Earneft, you are fenfible, in a Marriage Profpect.

But hitherto, he feems to like me better than I do him. I don't know how it is, but I have often obferv'd, that when any thing is in our own Power, we are not half fo much taken with it, as we fhould be, perhaps, if we were kept in Sufpenfe ! Why fhould this be ?

But this I am convinc'd of, There is no Comparifon between Sir *William* and Mr. *Murray*.

* *See* Vol. III *p* 247

Now

Now I have nam'd this Brother-in-law of mine, what do you think ?

Why, that good Couple have had their House on Fire three times already, and that very dangerously too Once it was put out by Mr *Murray*'s Mother, who lives near them, and twice Sir *Simon* has been forced to carry Water to extinguish it; for, truly, Mrs *Murray* would go home again to her Papa: She would not live with such a surly Wretch: And it was, With all his Heart · A fair Riddance! for there was no bearing the House with such an ill-natur'd Wife.----Her Sister *Polly* was worth a thousand of her!

I am sorry, heartily sorry, for their Unhappiness: But could she think every body must bear with her, and her fretful Ways ?

They'll jangle on, I reckon, till they are better us'd to one another, and when he sees she can't help it, why he'll bear with her, as Husbands generally do with ill-temper'd Wives, that is to say, he'll try to make himself happy abroad, and leave her to quarrel with her Maids, instead of him, for she must have somebody to vent her Spleen upon, poor *Nancy* !

I am glad to hear of Mr *Williams*'s good Fortune.

As Mr *Adams* knows not *Polly*'s Fault, and it was prevented in time, they may be happy enough. She is a *sly* Girl. I always thought her so . Something so innocent, and yet so artful in her very Looks! She is an odd Compound of a Girl. But these worthy and piously turn'd young Gentlemen, who have but just quitted the College, are mere Novices, as to the World indeed, they are *above* it, while *in* it, they therefore give themselves little Trouble to study it, and so, depending on the Goodness of their own Hears, are more liable to be imposed upon, than People of half their Understanding

I think,

I think, since he seems to love her, you do right not to hinder the Girl's Fortune. But I wish she may take your Advice, in her Behaviour to *him*, at least; for as to her Carriage to her Neighbours, I doubt she'll be one of the Heads of the Parish, presently, in her own Estimation.

'Tis pity, methinks, any worthy Gentleman of the Cloth should have a Wife, who, by a bad Example, should pull down, as fast as he, by a good one, can build up.

This is not the Case of Mrs. *Peters*, however; whose Example I wish was more generally follow'd by Gentlewomen, who are made so by marrying good Clergymen, if they were not so before

Don't be surpris'd, if you should hear, that poor *Jewkes* is given over!---She made a very exemplary—Full of Blessings—And more easy and resign'd, than I apprehended she would be

I know you'll shed a Tear for the poor Woman·—I can't help it myself But you will be pleas'd, that she had so much Time given her, and made so good Use of it.

Mr *Peters* has been every thing that one would wish one of his Function to be, in his Attendances and Advice to the poor Woman. Mr. *Longman* will take proper Care of every thing.

So, I will only add, That I am, with the sincerest Respects, in Hopes to see you soon, (for I have a Multitude of things to talk to you about) Dear Mrs B

*Your ever faithful and affectionate*

POLLY DARNFORD.

LETTER

## LETTER XLIII.

### *From Mrs.* B. *to Lady* DAVERS.

*My dear Lady* DAVERS,

I Underſtand from Miſs *Darnford,* that before ſhe went down from us, her Papa had encourag'd a Propoſal made by Sir *W G.* whom you ſaw, when your Ladyſhip was a kind Viſitor in *Bedfordſhire* We all agreed, if your Ladyſhip remembers, that he was a polite and ſenſible Gentleman, and I find it is countenanc'd on all Hands

Poor Mrs *Jewkes,* Madam, as Miſs informs me, has paid her laſt Debt. I hope, thro' Mercy, ſhe is happy! Poor, poor Woman! --- But why ſay I ſo! ----Since in *that* Caſe, ſhe will be richer than an earthly Monarch! At leaſt till he is levell'd with her in Death!

Your Ladyſhip was once mentioning a Siſter of Mrs. *Worden's,* whom you could be glad to recommend to ſome worthy Family ---Shall I beg of you, Madam, to oblige Mr. *B.'s* in this Particular? I am ſure ſhe muſt have Merit, if your Ladyſhip thinks well of her, and your Commands in this, as well as in every other Particular in my Power, ſhall have their due Weight with

*Your Ladyſhip's*
*Obliged Siſter, and humble Servant,*

P. B.

Juſt now, dear Madam, Mr *B.* tells me, I ſhall have Miſs *Goodwin* brought me hither To-morrow!

## LETTER XLIV.

*From Lady* DAVERS *to Mrs.* B. *in Answer
to the preceding.*

*My dear* PAMELA,

I AM glad Miss *Darnford* is likely to be so happy
in a Husband, as Sir *W. G.* will certainly make
her. I was afraid, that the Proposal I made, would
not do with Miss, had she not had so good a Tender
I want *too*, to have the foolish Fellow marry'd ----
for several Reasons; one of which is, He is continually teizing us to permit him to go up to Town,
and to reside there for some Months, in order that
he may *see the World*, as he calls it. But we are convinc'd he would *feel* it, as well as *see* it, if we gave
way to his Request For, in Understanding, Dress,
and inconsiderate Vanity, he is so exactly cut out
and siz'd for a Town Fop, Coxcomb, or Pretty
Fellow, that he will undoubtedly fall into all the
Vices of those People, and, perhaps, having such Expectations as he has, will be made the Property of
Rakes and Sharpers. He complains, that we use him
like a Child in a Go-cart, or a Baby with Leading-
strings, and that he must not be trusted out of our
Sight. 'Tis a sad thing, that these *Bodies* will grow
up to the Stature of Men, when the *Minds* improve
not at all with them, but are still those of Boys and
Children. Yet, he would certainly make a fond
Husband, for, at present, he has no very bad Qualities.
But is such a *Narcissus!* ----- But this between ourselves, for his Uncle is wrapt up in the Fellow ----
And why? Because he is good-humour'd, that's all.
He has vex'd me lately, which makes me write so
angrily about him --- But 'tis not worth troubling you
with the Particulars.

I hope

I hope Mrs *Jewkes* is happy, as you fay ! --- Poor
Woman ! fhe feemed to promife for a longer Life !
But what fhall we fay ?

Your Compliment to me, about my *Beck's* Sifter,
is a very kind one    I am greatly obliged to you for
it    Mrs. *Oldham* is a fober, grave Widow, a little
aforehand in the World, but not much ; has liv'd
well, underftands Houfehold Management thoroughly, is diligent, and has a Turn to ferious Things,
which will make you like her the better

I'll order *Beck* and her to wait on you in a Chaife
and Pair, and fhe will fatisfy you in every thing, as
to what you may, or may not, expect of her.

You can't think how kindly I take this Motion
from you    You forget nothing that can oblige your
Friends.    Little did I think you would remember
me, of (what I had forgotten in a manner) my favourable Opinion and Wifhes for her, exprefs'd fo
long ago --- But you are, what you are --- a dear, obliging Creature

*Beck* is all Joy and Gratitude upon it, and her
Sifter had rather ferve you, than the Princefs    You
need be under no Difficulties about Terms · She
would ferve you for nothing, if you would accept
of her Service

I am glad, becaufe it pleafes you fo much, that
Mifs *Goodwin* will be foon put into your Care    It
will be happy for the Child, and I hope fhe will be
fo dutiful to you, as to give you no Pain for your
generous Goodnefs to her    Her Mamma has fent
me a Prefent of fome choice Products of that Climate, with Acknowlegements of my Kindnefs to
Mifs.    I will fend Part of it to you by your new
Servant, for fo I prefume to call her already.

What a naughty Sifter are you, however, to be
fo far advanc'd again, as to be obliged to fhorten
your intended Excurfions, and yet not to fend me
Word of it yourfelf ? Don't you know how much I
interest

intereſt myſeif in every thing that makes for my Brother's Happineſs and yours?---More eſpecially in ſo material a Point, as is the Increaſe of a Family, that it is my Boaſt to be ſprung from --- Yet I muſt find this out by Accident, and by other Hands!--- Is not this very ſlighting?---But never do ſo again, and I'll forgive you now, becauſe of the Joy it gives me. Who am

*Your truly affectionate and obliged Siſter,*

B DAVERS.

I thank you for your Book upon the Plays you ſaw Incloſed is a Liſt of ſome others, which I deſire you to read, and to oblige me with your Remarks upon them at your Leiſure, tho' you may not perhaps have ſeen them by the Time you will favour me with your Obſervations.

---

## LETTER XLV.

### *From Mrs.* B. *to Lady* DAVERS.

*My dear Lady* DAVERS,

I HAVE a valuable Preſent made me by the ſame excellent Lady And therefore hope you will not take it amiſs, that, with abundance of Thanks, I return yours by Mrs *Worden*; whoſe Siſter I much approve of, and thank your Ladyſhip for your kind Recommendation of ſo worthy a Gentlewoman We begin with ſo much good Liking to one another, that I doubt not we ſhall be very happy together

A moving Letter, much more valuable to me, than the handſome Preſent, was put into my Hands, at the ſame time with that, of which the following is a Copy.

*From*

*From Mrs.* WRIGHTSON (*formerly Miſs* SALLY GODFREY) *to Mrs.* B.

*Happy, deſervedly happy, dear Lady,*

'PErmit theſe Lines to kiſs your Hands, from
' one, who, tho' ſhe is a Stranger to your Per-
' ſon, is not ſo to your Character: *That* has reach'd
' us here, in this remote Part of the World, where
' you have as many Admirers as have heard of you.
' But *I* more particularly am bound to be ſo, by
' an Obligation, which I can never diſcharge, but
' by my daily Prayers for you, and the Bleſſings I
' continually implore upon You and Yours.

' I can write my whole Mind *to* you, tho' I can-
' not, from the moſt deplorable Infelicity, receive
' *from* you the wiſh'd-for Favour of a few Lines
' in Return, written with the ſame Unreſervedneſs:
' So unhappy am I, from the Effects of an Incon-
' ſideration and Weakneſs on one hand, and Tempt-
' ations on the other, which You, at a tenderer
' Age, moſt nobly, for your own Honour, and that
' of your Sex, have eſcaped  Whilſt I --- But let my
' Tears in theſe Blots ſpeak the reſt --- as my Heart
' bleeds, and has conſtantly bled ever ſince, at the
' grievous Remembrance --- But believe me, how-
' ever, dear Madam, that 'tis Shame and Sorrow,
' and not Pride and Impenitence, that make me loth
' to ſpeak out, to ſo much Purity of Life and Man-
' ners, my own odious Weakneſs.

' Nevertheleſs, I ought, and I *will* accuſe myſelf
' by Name: Imagine then, illuſtrious Lady, truly
' illuſtrious, for Virtues, which are infinitely ſuperior
' to all the Advantages of Birth and Fortune! ----
' Imagine, I ſay, that in this Letter, you ſee before
' you the *once* guilty, and therefore, I doubt, *always*
' guilty, but *ever penitent, Sarah Godfrey,* the un-
' happy, tho' fond and tender Mother of the poor
' Infant, to whom your generous Goodneſs, as I am
' inform'd,

'inform'd, has extended itself, in such manner, as
'to make you desirous of taking her under your
'worthy Protection God for ever bless you for it'
'prays an indulgent Mother, who admires, at an
'awful Distance, that Virtue in you, which she could
'not practise herself.

'And will you, my dearest Lady, will you take
'under your own immediate Protection, the poor
'unguilty Infant? Will you love her, for the sake
'of her suffering Mamma, whom you know not,
'for the sake of the Gentleman, now so dear to
'you, and so worthy of you, as I hear, with Plea-
'sure, he is? And will you, by the best Example
'in the World, give me a moral Assurance, that
'she will never sink into the Fault, the Weakness,
'the Crime (I ought not to scruple to call it so)
'of her poor, inconsiderate ------ But Y o u are her
'Mamma *now*: I will not think of a *guilty* one
'therefore And what a Joy is it to me, in the
'midst of my heavy Reflections on my past Mis-
'conduct, that my beloved *Sally* can boast a *vir-*
'*tuous* and *innocent Mamma*, who has withstood
'the Snares and Temptations, that have been so
'fatal --- elsewhere' --- and whose Example, and In-
'structions, next to God's Grace, will be the strongest
'Fences, that can be wish'd for, to her Honour! ---
'Once more I say, and on my Knees I write it'
'God for ever bless you here, and augment your
'Joys hereafter, for your generous Goodness to my
'poor, and, till now, *motherless* Infant

'I hope the dear Child, by her Duty and Oblige-
'ingness, will do all in her little Power to make
'you Amends, and never give you Cause to repent
'of this your *unexampled* Kindness to *her* and to *me*
'She cannot, I hope, (except her Mother's Crime
'has had an Influence upon her, too much like
'that of an original Stain) be of a sordid, or an
'ingrateful Nature. And, O my poor *Sally* ! if you
'                                                    *are,*

' *are,* and if ever you fail in your Duty to your
' new Mamma, to whose Care and Authority I
' transfer my *whole* Right in you, remember that
' you have no more a Mamma in me, nor can you
' be intitled to my Blessing, or to the Fruits of my
' Prayers for you, which I make now, on that *only*
' Condition, your implicit Obedience to all your
' new Mamma's Commands and Directions

' You may have the Curiosity, Madam, to wish
' to know how I live · For no doubt you have
' heard all my sad, sad Story ! --- Know then, that
' I am as happy, as a poor Creature can be, who
' has once so deplorably, so inexcusably fallen    I
' have a worthy Gentleman for my Husband, who
' marry'd me as a Widow, whose only Child by
' my former, was the Care of her Papa's Friends,
' particularly of good Lady *Davers,* and her Bro-
' ther - - Poor, unhappy I! to be under such a *sad*
' Necessity, to disguise the Truth! --- Mr. *Wrightson*
' (whose Name I am unworthily honour'd by) has
' several times earnestly intreated me to send for
' the poor Child, and to let her be join'd as his ---
' killing Thought, that it cannot be! --- with Two
' Children, I have by him! --- Judge, my good Lady,
' how that very Generosity, which, had I been guilt-
' less, would have added to my Joys, must wound
' me deeper, than even ungenerous or unkind Usage
' from him could do! And how heavy that Crime
' must lie upon me, which turns my very Pleasures
' to Misery, and fixes all the Joy I *can* know, in
' Repentance for my past Misdeeds! --- How happy
' are You, Madam, on the contrary, You, who
' have nothing of this sort to pall, nothing to mingle
' with your Felicities! who, bless'd in an Honour
' untainted, and a Conscience that cannot reproach
' you, are enabled to enjoy every well-deserv'd
' Comfort, as it offers itself; and can *improve*
' it too, by Reflection on *your* past Conduct! While
' mine

' *mine* — alas ! — like a Winter Froſt, nips in the
' Bud every riſing Satisfaction !

' My Spouſe is rich, as well as generous, and very
' tender of me — Happy, if I could think *myſelf* as
' deſerving, as *he* thinks me ' — My principal Com-
' fort, as I hinted, is in my Penitence for my paſt
' Faults, and that I have a merciful GOD for my
' Judge, who knows that Penitence to be ſincere !

' You may gueſs, Madam, from what I have ſaid,
' in what Light I *muſt* appear here ; and if you would
' favour me with a Line or two, in Anſwer to the
' Letter you have now in your Hand, it will be one
' of the greateſt Pleaſures I *can* receive: A Pleaſure
' next to that which I *have* receiv'd in knowing, that
' the Gentleman you love beſt, has had the Grace
' to repent of all his Evils, has early ſeen his Errors,
' and has thereby, I hope, freed *two* Perſons from
' being, one Day, mutual Accuſers of each other.
' For now I pleaſe myſelf to think, that the Crimes
' of both may be waſh'd away in the Blood of that
' Saviour G O D, whom both have ſo grievouſly
' offended !

' May that good GOD, who has not ſuffer'd me
' to be abandon'd intirely to my own Shame, as I
' deſerved, continue to ſhower down upon You
' thoſe Bleſſings, which a Virtue like yours may
' expect from his Mercy ! May you long be happy
' in the Poſſeſſion of all you wiſh ! And late, very
' late, (for the Good of Thouſands, I wiſh this ')
' may you receive the Reward of your Piety, your
' Generoſity, and your filial, your ſocial, and con-
' jugal Virtues ! are the Prayers of

*Your moſt unworthy Admirer,*
*and obliged humble Servant,*
SARAH WRIGHTSON.

' Mr *Wrightſon* begs your Acceptance of a ſmall
' Preſent, Part of which can have no Value,
' but

' but what its excelling Qualities, for what it is,
' will give it at so great a Distance as that dear
' *England,* which I once left with so much
' Shame and Regret, but with a laudable Pur-
' pose, *however,* because I would not incur still
' *greater* Shame, and of Consequence give Cause
' for still *greater* Regret!

To this Letter, my dear Lady *Davers,* I have
written the following Answer, which Mr *B.* will
take care to have convey'd to the good Lady.

*Dearest Madam,*

' I Embrace with great Pleasure the Opportunity
' you have so kindly given me, of writing to a
' Lady, whose Person tho' I have not the Honour
' to know, yet whose Character, and noble Qualities,
' I truly revere.

' I am infinitely obliged to you, Madam, for the
' precious Trust you have reposed in me, and the
' Right you make over to me, of your maternal In-
' terest in a Child, on whom I set my Heart, the
' Moment I saw her.

' Lady *Davers,* whose Love and Tenderness for
' Miss, as well for her Mamma's sake, as your late
' worthy Spouse's, had, from her kind Opinion of
' me, consented to grant me this Favour; and I
' was, by Mr *B.'s* Leave, in actual Possession of my
' pretty Ward, about a Week before your kind Let-
' ter came to my Hands

' As I had been long very solicitous for this Fa-
' vour, judge how welcome your kind Concurrence
' was to me; and the rather, as, had I known, that
' a Letter from you was on the Way to me, I should
' have apprehended, that you would have insisted
' upon depriving the surviving Friends of her dear
' Papa, of the Pleasure they take in the sweet Miss.
' Indeed, Madam, I believe we should one and all
' have

' have join'd to difobey you, had *that* been the
' Cafe, and it is a great Satisfaction to us, that we
' are not under fo hard a Neceffity, as to difpute
' with a tender Mamma the Poffeffion of her own
' Child

  ' Affure yourfelf, deareft, worthieft, kindeft Ma-
' dam, of a Care and Tendernefs in me to your
' dear Mifs, truly maternal, and anfwerable, as much
' as is in my Power, to the Truft you repofe in me.
' The little Boy, that God has given me, fhall not
' be more dear to me, than my fweet Mifs fhall be,
' and my Care, by God's Grace, fhall extend to her
' *future* as well as to her *prefent* Profpects, that fhe
' may be worthy of that Piety, and *truly* religious
' Excellence, which I admire in your Character

  ' We all rejoice, dear Madam, in the Account
' you give of your prefent Happinefs  It was im-
' poffible, that God Almighty fhould defert a Lady
' fo exemplarily deferving, and He certainly con-
' ducted you in your Refolutions to abandon every
' thing that you loved in *England*, after the Lofs
' of your dear Spoufe, becaufe it feems to have been
' the Intention of His Providence, that you fhould
' reward the Merit of Mr *Wrightfon*, and meet with
' your own Reward in fo doing

  ' Mifs is very fond of my little *Billy* · She is a
' charming Child, is eafy and genteel in her Shape,
' and very pretty, fhe dances finely, has a fweet
' Air, and is improving every Day in Mufick , works
' with her Needle, and reads, admirably, for her
' Years, and takes a Delight in both, which gives me
' no fmall Pleafure.   But fhe is not very forward in
' her Penmanfhip, as you will fee by what follows ·
' The Inditing too is her own; but in that, and the
' Writing, Mifs took a good deal of Time, on a
' feparate Paper.

                                                    *Deareft*

*Dearest dear Mamma,*

" Your *Sally* is full of Joy, to have any Com-
" mands from her honoured Mamma. I pro-
" mise to follow all your Directions. Indeed, and
" upon my Word, I will. You please me mightily
" in giving me so dear a new Mamma here. Now
" I know, indeed, I have a Mamma, and I will
" love and obey her, as if she was you your own
" Self. Indeed I will. You must always bless me,
" because I will be always good. I hope you will
" believe me, because I am above telling Fibs I
" am, my honoured Mamma, on the other Side of
" the Water, and ever will be, as if you was here,

*Your dutiful Daughter,*

SALLY GOODWIN.

' Miss (permit me, dear Madam, to subjoin) is a
' very good-temper'd Child, easy to be persuaded,
' and, I hope, loves me dearly, and I will endea-
' vour to make her love me better and better; for
' on that Love will depend the Regard which, I
' hope, she will pay to all I shall say and do for her
' Good.

' Repeating my Acknowlegements for the kind
' Trust you repose in me, and with Thanks for the
' valuable Present you have sent me, we all here
' join in Respects to worthy Mr. *Wrightson,* and in
' wishing you, Madam, a Continuance and Increase
' of worldly Felicity; and I, particularly, beg Leave
' to assure you, that I am, and ever will be, with
' the highest Respect and Gratitude, tho' personally
' unknown, dearest Madam,

*The affectionate Admirer of your Piety,*
*and your obliged humble Servant,*

P. B

Your Ladyship will see how I was circumscrib'd
and limited; otherwise I would have told the good
Lady

Lady (what I have mention'd more than once) how I admire and honour her for her Penitence, and for that noble Refolution, which enabled her to do what Thoufands could not have the Heart to do, abandon her Country, her Relations, Friends, Baby, and all that was dear to her, as well as the Seducer, whom fhe too well loved, and hazard the Sea, the Dangers of Pirates, and poffibly of other wicked Attempters of the mifchievous Sex, in a World fhe knew nothing of, among Strangers, and all to avoid repeating a Sin, fhe had been unhappily drawn into, and for which the dear good Lady ftill abhors her-felf

Muft not fuch a Lady as this, dear Madam, have as much Merit, as many even of thofe, who, having not had her Temptations, have not fallen? This, at leaft, one may aver, that next to not committing an Error, is certainly the Refolution to retrieve it all that one may, to repent of it, and ftudioufly to avoid the Repetition of it But who, befides this excellent Mrs *Wrightfon*, having fo fallen, and being ftill fo ardently folicited and purfued (and flatter'd, perhaps, by fond Hopes, that her Spoiler would, one Day, do her all the Juftice he *could* --- For who can do complete Juftice to a Lady he has robb'd of her Honour?) --- could refolve as fhe refolved, and act as fhe acted?

Mifs is a fweet pretty Dear; but permit me to fay, has a little of her Papa's Spirit, hafty, yet gene-rous and acknowleging, when fhe is convinc'd of her Fault, a little haughtier and prouder than I wifh her to be; but in every thing elfe deferves the Cha-racter I give of her to her Mamma.

She is very fond of fine Cloaths, is a little too lively to the Servants --- Told me once, when I took Notice, that Softnefs and Mildnefs of Speech be-came a young Lady, That they were *but* Servants; and fhe could fay no more, than *Pray*, and *I desire*, *defire,* and *I wiſh you'd be ſo kind* ---- to her Uncle, or to me.

I told her, Our Servants were not common Servants, and deſerved any civil Diſtinctions, and that ſo long as they were ready to oblige her in every thing, by a kind Word, it would be very wrong to give them imperative ones, which could ſerve for no other End, but to convince every one of the Haughtineſs of one's own Temper, and looked, as if one would queſtion their Compliance with one's own Will, unleſs we would exact it with an high Hand, which might caſt a Slur upon the Command we gave, as if we thought it was hardly ſo reaſonable, as otherwiſe to obtain their Obſervation of it.

Beſides, my Dear, ſaid I, you don't conſider, that if you ſpeak as haughtily and commandingly to them on common, as on extraordinary Occaſions, you weaken your own Authority, if ever you ſhould be permitted to have any, and they'll regard you no more in the one Caſe, than in the other

She takes great Notice of what I ſay, and when her little proud Heart is ſubdu'd by Reaſonings ſhe cannot anſwer, ſhe will ſit as if ſhe were ſtudying what to ſay, that ſhe may come off as flyingly as ſhe can· And as the Caſe requires, I let her go off eaſily, or I puſh the little Dear to her laſt Refuge, and make her quit her Poſt, and yield up her Spirit, a Captive to Reaſon and Diſcretion, Two excellent Commanders, with whom, I tell her, I muſt bring her to be intimately acquainted.

Yet, after all, till I can be ſure, that I can inſpire her with the Love of Virtue, for *its own* Sake, I will rather try to conduct her Spirit to proper Ends, than endeavour totally to ſubdue it; being ſenſible that our Paſſions are given us for excellent Ends, and that they may, by a proper Direction, be made ſubſervient to the nobleſt Purpoſes.

I tell

I tell her fometimes, there may be a decent Pride in Humility, and that it is very poffible for a young Lady to behave with fo much *true* Dignity, as fhall command Refpect by the Turn of her Eye, fooner than by Afperity of Speech; that fhe may depend upon it, that the Perfon who is always finding Faults, frequently caufes them, and that it is no Glory to be better born than Servants, if fhe is not better behav'd too

Befides, I tell her, Humility is a Grace that fhines in a *high* Condition, but cannot equally in a *low* one, becaufe that is already too much humbled, perhaps. And that, tho' there is a Cenfure lies againft being *poor and proud*, yet I would rather forgive Pride in a poor Body, than in a rich; for in the Rich it is Infult and Arrogance, proceeding from their high Condition, but in the Poor it may be a Defenfative againft Difhonefty, and may fhew a natural Bravery of Mind, perhaps, if properly directed, and manifefted on right Occafions, that the Frowns of Fortune cannot deprefs

She fays, She hears every Day Things from me, which her Governefs never taught her

That may very well be, I tell her, becaufe her Governefs has *many* young Ladies to take care of, I but *one*; and that I want to make her wife and prudent betimes, that fhe may be an Example to other Miffes; and that Governeffes and Mamma's fhall fay to their Miffes, When will you be like Mifs *Goodwin*? Do you ever hear Mifs *Goodwin* fay a naughty Word? Would Mifs *Goodwin*, think you, have done fo or fo?

She threw her Arms about my Neck, on one fuch Occafion as this· Oh, faid fhe, What a charming Mamma have I got! I will be in every thing as like you, Madam, as ever I can!—And then You will love me, and fo will my Uncle, and fo will Everybody elfe.

Mr.

Mr *B.* whom, now-and-then, she says, she loves as well as if he were her own Papa, sees, with Pleasure, how we go on, and loves us both, if possible, better and better. But she tells me, I must not have any Daughter but her, and is very jealous on the Occasion about which your Ladyship so kindly reproaches me

There is a Pride, you know, Madam, in some of our Sex, that serves to useful Purposes, and is a good Defence against improper Matches, and mean Actions; and this is not wholly to be subdu'd, for that Reason; for, tho' it is not *Virtue,* yet, if it can be Virtue's *Substitute,* in high, rash, and inconsiderate Minds, it may turn to good Account So I will not quite discourage my dear Pupil neither, till I see what Discretion, and riper Years, may add to her distinguishing Faculty. For, as some have no Notion of Pride, separate from Imperiousness and Arrogance, so others know no Difference between Humility and Meanness

There is a golden Mean in every thing, and if it please God to spare us both, I will endeavour to point her Passions, and such even of those Foibles, which seem too deeply rooted to be soon eradicated, to useful Purposes, chusing to imitate Physicians, who in certain Chronical Illnesses, as I have read in Lord *Bacon,* rather proceed by Palliatives, than by harsh Extirpatives, which, thro' the Resistance given to 'em by the Constitution, may create such Ferments in it, as may destroy that Health it was their Intention to establish.

But, whither am I running?--- Your Ladyship, I hope, will excuse this parading Freedom of my Pen. For tho' these Notions are well enough with regard to Miss *Goodwin,* they must be very impertinent to a Lady, who can so much better instruct Miss's Tutoress, than that vain Tutoress can her Pupil. And therefore, with my humblest Respects to my good

Lord *Davers*, and your noble Neighbours, and to
Mr. *H.* I haften to conclude myfelf,

*Your Ladyfhip's obliged Sifter,*

*and obedient Servant,*

P. B.

Your *Billy*, Madam, is a charming Dear !--- I
long to have you fee him   He fends you a
Kifs upon this Paper.   You'll fee it ftain'd, juft
here   The Charmer has cut Two Teeth, and
is about more   So you'll excufe the dear, pretty,
flabbering Boy.   Mifs *Goodwin* is ready to eat
him with Love: And Mr *B* is fonder and
fonder of us all.  And then your Ladyfhip, and
my good Lord *Davers*, love us too.  O my
dear Lady, what a blefled Creature am I!

Mifs begs I'll fend her Duty to her *Noble* Uncle
and Aunt, that's her juft Diftinction always,
when fhe fpeaks of you both, which is not
feldom.   She ask'd me, pretty Dear ! juft now,
If I think there is fuch a happy Girl in the
World, as fhe is?  I tell her, GOD always blefles
good Mifles, and makes them happier and
happier.

---

## LETTER XLVI.

*My dear Lady* DAVERS,

I Have Three Marriages to acquaint you with, in
One Letter   In the firft Place, Sir *W. G.* has
fent; by the particular Defire of my dear Friend,
that he was made one of the happieft Gentlemen
in *England*, on the 18th paft; and fo I have no
longer any Mifs *Darnford* to boaft of.  I have a
very good Opinion of the Gentleman; but if he be
but half fo good a Husband, as fhe will make a

Wife,

Wife, they will be exceedingly happy in one another.

Mr *Williams's* Marriage to a Kinfwoman of his Noble Patron, (as you have heard was in Treaty) is the next, and there is great Reafon to believe, from the Character of both, that they will likewife do Credit to the State

The Third is Mr. *Adams* and *Polly Barlow* ; and I wifh them, for both their Sakes, as happy as either of the former. They are fet out to his Liveing, highly pleas'd with one another, and I hope will have Reafon to continue fo to be.

As to the firft, I did not indeed think, the Affair would have been fo foon concluded, and Mifs kept it off fo long, as I underftand, that her Papa was angry with her: And indeed, as the Gentleman's Family, Circumftances, and Character, were fuch, that there could lie no Objection againft him, I think it would have been wrong to have delay'd it.

I fhould have written to your Ladyfhip before, but have been favour'd with Mr *B* 's Company into *Kent,* on a Vifit to my good Mother, who was indifpos'd. We tarry'd there a Week, and left both my dear Parents, to my thankful Satisfaction, in as good Health as ever they were in their Lives

Mrs. *Judy Swynford,* or Mifs *Swynford,* (as fhe refufes not being call'd, now-and-then) has been with us for this Week paft ; and fhe expects her Brother, Sir *Jacob,* to fetch her away about a Week hence.

It does not become me to write the leaft Word, that may appear difrefpectful of any Perfon, who has the Honour to bear a Relation to your Ladyfhip and Mr *B.* Otherwife I fhould fay, That the *B's* and the *S---s* are directly the Oppofites of one another. But yet, as (fhe fays) fhe never faw your Ladyfhip but once, you will forgive me to mention

a Word

a Word or two about this Lady, becaufe fhe is a
Character, that is in a manner new to me

She is a Maiden Lady, as you know, Madam,
and tho' fhe will not part with the green Leaf from
her Hand, one fees by the Grey goofe Down on
her Brows and her Head, that fhe cannot be lefs
than Fifty-five --- But fo much Pains does fhe take,
by Powder, to have never a dark Hair in her Head,
becaufe fhe has one Half of them white, that I am
forry to fee, what is a Subject for Reverence, fhould
be deem'd by the good Lady, Matter of Conceal-
ment

She is often in Converfation, indeed, feemingly
reproaching herfelf, that fhe is an *old Maid*, and an
*old Woman*, but it is very difcernible, that fhe expects
a Compliment, that fhe is *not fo*, every time fhe is
to free with herfelf  And if nobody makes her one,
fhe will fay fomething of that fort in her own Behalf

She takes particular Care, that of all the publick
Tranfactions which happen to be talked of, her Memory will never carry her back above Thirty Years,
and then it is, About Thirty Years ago, when I was
a Girl, or, when I was in Hanging-fleeves, and fo
fhe makes herfelf, for Twenty Years of her Life, a
very ufelefs and infignificant Perfon

If her Teeth, which, for her Time of Life, are
very good, tho' not over-white, (and which, by
the Care fhe takes of them, fhe feems to look upon
as the laft Remains of her better Days) would but
fail her, I imagine it would help her to a Conviction,
that would fet her Ten Years forwarder at leaft  But,
poor Lady' fhe is fo *young*, in Spite of her Wrinkles,
that I am really concern'd for her Affectation, becaufe it expofes her to the Remarks and Ridicule of
the Gentlemen, and gives one Pain for her

Surely, thefe Ladies don't act prudently at all;
fince, for every Year Mrs *Judy* would take from
her

her Age, her Cenſurers add two to it; and, behind her Back, make her going on towards Seventy, whereas, if ſhe would lay Claim to her *Reverentials,* as I may ſay, and not endeavour to conceal her Age, ſhe would have a great many Compliments for look-ing ſo well at her Time of Life And many a young Body would hope to be the better for her Advice and Experience, who now are afraid of affronting her, if they ſuppoſe ſhe has lived much longer in the World than themſelves.

Then ſhe laughs back to the Years ſhe owns, when more flippant Ladies, at the Laughing-time of Life, delight to be frolick She tries to ſing too, altho', if ever ſhe had a Voice, ſhe has outliv'd it ; and her Songs are of ſo antique a Date, that they would betray her, only as ſhe tells us, they were learnt her by her Grandmother, who was a fine Lady at the Reſtoration : She will join in a Dance, and tho' her Limbs move not ſo pliantly, as might be expected of a Lady no older than ſhe would be thought to be, and whoſe Dancing-days are not intirely over, yet that was owing to a Fall from her Horſe ſome Years ago, which, ſhe doubts, ſhe ſhall never recover, ſo as to be quite well, tho' ſhe finds ſhe grows better and better *every Year.*

Thus ſhe loſes the Reſpect, the Reverence, ſhe might receive, were it not for this miſerable Affecta-tion, takes Pains, by aping Youth, to make herſelf unworthy of her Years, and is content to be thought leſs diſcreet than ſhe might otherwiſe be deemed, for fear ſhe ſhould be imagined older, if ſhe appear'd wiſer

What a ſad thing is this, Madam ?----What a miſtaken Conduct ?---We pray to live to old Age ; and it is promiſed as a Bleſſing, and as a Reward, for the Performance of certain Duties, and yet, when we come to it, we had rather be thought as fooliſh as Youth, than to be deemed wiſe, and in

Poffeffion of it. And fo we fhew how little we deferve what we have been fo long coveting; and yet covet on : For what? Why, to be more and more afham'd, and more and more unworthy of what we covet!

How fantaftick a Character is this!——Well may irreverent, unthinking Youth defpife, inftead of re-vering, the hoary Head, which the Wearer is fo much afham'd of

Will you forgive me, Madam? The Lady boafts a Relationfhip to you, and to Mr. *B.* and, I think, I am very bold. But my Reverence for Years, and the Difguft I have to fee any Body behave unworthy of them, makes me take the greater Liberty Which, however, I fhall wifh I had not taken, if it meets not with that Allowance, which I have always had from your Ladyfhip in what I write.

God knows whether ever I may enjoy the Bleffing I fo much revere in others For now my heavy Time approaches But I was fo apprehenfive before, and fo troublefome to my beft Friends, with my vapourifh Fears, that now (with a perfect Refigna-tion to the Divine Will) I will only add, That I am

*Your Ladyfhip's moft obliged Sifter and Servant,*

P B.

My dear *Billy,* and Mifs *Goodwin,* improve both of them every Day, and are all I can defire or expect them to be Could Mifs's poor Mamma be here with a Wifh, and back again, how much would fhe be delighted with one of our After-noon Conferences ; our *Sunday* Imployments, efpecially!——And let me tell your Ladyfhip, that I am very happy in another young Gentle-man of the Dean's recommending, inftead of M. *Adams.*

LET-

# LETTER XLVII.

*My dearest Lady,*

I AM once more, blessed be God for all his Mercies to me! enabled to dedicate to you the first Fruits of my Penmanship, on my Upsitting, to thank you, and my noble Lord, for all your kind Solicitudes for my Welfare *Billy* every Day improves, Miss is all I wish her to be, and my second dear Boy continues to be as lovely and as fine a Baby as your Ladyship was pleased to think him, and their Papa, the best of Gentlemen, and of Husbands!

I am glad to hear Lady *Betty* is likely to be so happy Mr *B* says, her noble Admirer is as worthy a Gentleman as any in the Peerage; and I beg of your Ladyship to congratulate the dear Lady, and her noble Parents, in my Name, if I should be at a Distance, when the Nuptials are celebrated.

I have had the Honour of a Visit from my Lady, the Countess Dowager, on Occasion of her leaving the Kingdom for a Year or two, for which Space she designs to reside in *Italy*, principally at *Naples* or *Florence*; a Design she took up, some time ago, as I believe I mentioned to your Ladyship; but which it seems she could not conveniently put into Execution till now

Mr *B.* was abroad when her Ladyship came, having taken a Turn to *Gloucester* the Day before, and I expected him not till the next Day. Her Ladyship sent her Gentleman, the preceding Evening, to let me know, that Business had brought her as far as *Wooburn*, and if it would not be unacceptable, she would pay her Respects to me, at Breakfast, the next Morning, being speedily to leave *England* I return'd, That I should be very proud of that Honour. And about Ten her Ladyship came.

She was exceedingly fond of my two Boys, the little Man, and the pretty Baby, as she called them, and I had very different Emotions from the Expression of her Love to *Billy*, and her Visit to me, from what I had once before  She was sorry, she said, Mr *B*. was abroad, tho' her Business was principally with me  For, Mrs *B* said she, I come to tell you all that passed between Mr *B* and myself, that you may not think worse of either of us than we deserve, and I could not leave *England*, till I had done myself the Pleasure of waiting on you for this Purpose, and yet, perhaps, from the Distance of Time, you'll think it needless now  And indeed, I should have waited on you before, to have cleared up my Character with you, had I thought I should have been so long kept on this Side of the Water

I said, I was very sorry, I had ever been uneasy, when I had two Persons of so much Honour— Nay, said she, interrupting me, you have no need to apologize · Things looked bad enough, as they were represented to you, to justify greater Uneasiness than you express'd.

She ask'd me, Who that pretty genteel Miss was? ---- I said, a Relation of Lord *Davers*, who was intrusted lately to my Care  Then, Miss, said her Ladyship, and kissed her, you are very happy

Believing the Countess was desirous of being alone with me, I said, My dear Miss *Goodwin*, won't you go to your little Nursery, my Love? For so she calls my last Blessing ---- You'd be sorry the Baby should cry for you --- For Miss was so taken with the charming Lady, that she was loth to leave us --- But on my saying this, withdrew.

When we were alone, the Countess began her Story with a sweet Confusion, which added to her Loveliness  She said, She would be brief, because she should exact all my Attention, and not suffer me to interrupt her till she had done

She

She began with acknowleging, ' That she thought,
' when she first saw Mr *B.* at the Masquerade, that
' he was the finest Gentleman she had ever seen,
' that the allow'd Freedoms of the Place had made
' her take Liberties in following him, and engaging
' him where-ever he went   She blamed him very
' freely for passing for a single Gentleman, for that
' she said, (since she had so splendid a Fortune of her
' own) was all she was solicitous about, having never,
' as she confess'd, seen a Gentleman she could like
' so well; her former Marriage having been in some
' sort forced upon her, at an Age when she knew
' not how to distinguish, and that she was very loth
' to believe him marry'd, even when she had no
' Reason to doubt it   Yet, this I must say, Madam,
' said her Ladyship, I never heard a Gentleman,
' when he owned he was married, express himself of
' a Lady, with more affectionate Regard and Fond-
' ness, than he did of you, whenever he spoke of
' you to me, which made me long to see you.
' For I had a great Opinion of those personal Ad-
' vantages, which every one flatter'd me with · And
' was very unwilling to yield the Palm of Beauty to
' you.

   ' I believe you will censure me, Mrs. *B* for per-
' mitting his Visits, after I knew he was marry'd.
' To be sure, that was a thoughtless and a faulty
' Part of my Conduct --- But the World's saucy Cen-
' sures, and my Friends indiscreet Interposals, in-
' cens'd me, and, knowing the Uprightness of my
' own Heart, I was resolved to disregard both, when
' I found they could not think worse of me than
' they did

   ' I am naturally of a high Spirit, impatient of
' Contradiction, always gave myself Freedoms, for
' which, satisfy'd with my own Innocence, I thought
' myself above being accountable to any body - - -
' And

' And then Mr *B* has fuch noble Sentiments, a
' Courage and Fearleffnefs, which I faw on more
' Occafions than one, that all Ladies, who know
' the Weaknefs of their own Sex, and how much
' they want the Protection of the Brave, are taken
' with    Then his perfonal Addrefs was fo peculiarly
' diftinguifhing, that having an Opinion of his Ho-
' nour, I was imbarafs'd greatly how to deny myfelf
' his Converfation, altho', you'll pardon me, Mrs *B.*
' I began to be afraid, that my Reputation might
' fuffer in the World's Opinion for the Indulgence.

' Then, when I had refolv'd, as I did feveral
' times, to fee him no more, fome unforefeen Acci-
' dent threw him in my way again, at one Enter-
' tainment or other; for I love Balls, and Concerts,
' and publick Diverfions, perhaps, better than I
' ought; and then I had all my Refolves to begin
' again

' Yet this I can truly fay, whatever his Views
' were, I never heard from his Lips the leaft inde-
' cent Expreffion, nor faw in his Behaviour to me,
' aught that might make me very apprehenfive,
' faving, that I began to fear, that by his infinuating
' Addrefs, and noble Manner, I fhould be too much
' in his Power, and too little in my own, if I went
' on fo little doubting, and fo little alarm'd, if ever
' he fhould avow difhonourable Defigns

' I had often lamented, faid her Ladyfhip, that
' our *Sex* were prohibited, by the Defigns of the
' other upon their Honour, and by the World's
' Cenfures, from converfing with the fame Eafe and
' Freedom with Gentlemen, as with one another.
' And when once I asked myfelf, To what this Con-
' verfation might tend at laft? And where the Plea-
' fure each feem'd to take in the other's, might
' poffibly end? I refolved to break it off, and told
' him my Refolution next time I faw him    But he
' ftopp'd my Mouth with a romantick Notion, as I
' ' fince

' fince think it, (tho' a forry Plea will have Weight
' in favour of a Propofal, to which one has no Aver-
' fion) of *Platonick* Love, and we had an Inter-
' courfe by Letters, to the Number of Six or Eight,
' I believe, on that and other Subjects.

' Yet all this time, I was the lefs apprehenfive,
' becaufe he always fpoke fo tenderly, and even with
' Delight, whenever he mention'd his Lady; and I
' could not find, that you were at all alarmed at our
' Acquaintance, for I never fcrupled to fend my
' Letters, by my own Livery, to your Houfe, fealed
' with my own Seal

' At laft, indeed, he began to tell me, that from
' the fweeteft and the eveneft Temper in the World,
' you feem'd to be leaning towards Melancholy, were
' always in Tears, or fhew'd you had been weeping,
' when he came home, and that you did not make
' his Return to you fo agreeable as he ufed to
' find it.

' I ask'd, If it were not owing to fome Alteration
' in his own Temper? If you might not be uneafy
' at our Acquaintance, and at his frequent Abfence
' from you, and the like? He anfwer'd, No!---
' that you were above Difguifes, were of a noble and
' frank Nature, and would have taken fome Oppor-
' tunity to hint it to him, if you had

' This, however, when I began to think ferioufly
' of the Matter, gave me but little Satisfaction, and
' I was more and more convinced, that my Honour
' required it of me, to break off this Intimacy.

' And altho' I permitted Mr *B.* to go with me to
' *Tunbridge,* when I went to take a Houfe there,
' yet I was uneafy, as he faw   And, indeed, fo was
' he, tho' he tarry'd a Day or two longer than he
' defigned, on account of a little Excurfion my
' Sifter and her Lord, and he and I, made into
' *Suffex,* to fee an Eftate that I had Thoughts of
' purchafing, for he was fo good as to look into my

N 6                    ' Affairs

' Affairs for me, and has put them upon an admi-
' rable Eſtabliſhment

' His Uneaſineſs, he told me, was upon your
' Account, and he ſent you a Letter to excuſe him-
' ſelf for not waiting on you on *Saturday*, and to
' tell you, he would dine with you on *Monday*
' And I remember, when I ſaid, Mr *B* you ſeem
' to be chagrin'd at ſomething , you are more
' thoughtful than uſual, his Anſwer was---Madam,
' you are right Mrs *B.* and I have had a little
' Miſunderſtanding She is ſo ſolemn and ſo me-
' lancholy of late, that, I fear, it will be no difficult
' Matter to put her out of her right Mind And I
' love her ſo well, that then I ſhould hardly keep
' my own.

' Is there no Reaſon, think you, ſaid I, to ima-
' gine, that your Acquaintance with me gives her
' Uneaſineſs? You know, Mr. *B* how that Villain
' *T* (a Gentleman, ſaid ſhe, whoſe inſolent Addreſs
' I rejected with the Contempt it deſerv'd) has ſlan-
' der'd us How know you, but he has found a
' way to your Wife's Ear, as he has done to my
' Uncle's, and to all my Friends? And if ſo, it is
' beſt for us both to diſcontinue a Friendſhip, that,
' at the beſt, may be attended with diſagreeable
' Conſequences.

' He ſaid, he ſhould find it out on his Return to
' you And will you, ſaid I, ingenuouſly, acquaint
' me with the Iſſue of your Inquiries? for, added I,
' I never beheld a Countenance in ſo young a Lady,
' that ſeem'd to mean more than Mrs *B* 's, when I
' ſaw her in Town , and notwithſtanding her Pru-
' dence, I could ſee a Reſerve and Thoughtfulneſs
' in it, that, if it was not natural to it, muſt indi-
' cate too much

' He return'd to you, Madam· He wrote to me
' in a very moving Letter, the Iſſue of your Con-
' ference, and referred to ſome Papers of yours, that
' he

'he would fhew me, as foon as he could procure
'them, they being out of your own Hands; and let
'me know, that *T* was the Accufer, as I had fu-
'fpected.

'In brief, Madam, when you went down into
'*Kent*, he came to me, and read fome Part of
'your Account to Lady *Davers*, of your Informant
'and Information, your Apprehenfions, your Pru-
'dence, your Affection for him; the Reafon of
'your Melancholy, and, according to the Appear-
'ance Things bore, Reafon enough you had, efpe-
'cially from the Letter of *Thomafine Fuller*, which
'was one of *T*'s vile Forgeries For tho' we had
'often, for Argument's fake, talked of Polygamy,
'(he arguing for it, I againft it) yet had not Mr *B.*
'*dared*, I will fay, nor was he inclined, I verily be-
'lieve, to propofe any fuch thing to me No, Ma-
'dam, I was not fo much abandon'd of a Senfe of
'Honour, as to give Reafon for any one, but my
'impertinent and foolifh Uncle, to impute fuch a
'Folly to me, and he had fo behaved to me, that
'I cared not what *he* thought

'Then, what he read to me, here and there, as
'he pleafed, gave me Reafon to admire you for
'your generous Opinion of one you had fo much
'feeming Caufe to be afraid of He told me his
'Apprehenfions, from your uncommon Manner,
'that your Mind was in fome Degree affected, and
'your ftrange Propofal of parting with a Husband
'every one knows you fo dearly love And we agreed
'to forbear feeing each other, and all manner of
'Correfpondence, except by Letter, for one Month,
'till fome of my Affairs were fettled, which had
'been in great Diforder, and were in his kind Ma-
'nagement then; and I had not one Relation, whom
'I car'd to trouble with them, becaufe of their
'Treatment of me on Mr. *B*'s Account. And
'this,

‘ this, I told him, should not be neither, but thro’
‘ your Hands, and with your Consent.

‘ And thus, Madam, said her Ladyship, have I
‘ told you the naked Truth of the whole Affair

‘ I have seen Mr. B very seldom since, and when
‘ I have, it has been either at a Horse-race, in the
‘ open Field, or at some publick Diversion, by Ac-
‘ cident, where only distant Civilities have passed
‘ between us

‘ I respect him greatly , you must allow me to
‘ say that. Except in the Article of permitting me
‘ to believe, for some Time, that he was a sing’e
‘ Gentleman, which is a Fault he cannot be excused
‘ for, and which made me heartily quarrel wih
‘ him, when I first knew it, he has behaved towards
‘ me with so much Generosity and Honour, that I
‘ could have wished I had been of his Sex, since he
‘ had a Lady so much more deserving than myself,
‘ and then, had he had the same Esteem for me, there
‘ never would have been a more perfect Friendship

‘ I am now going, continu’d her Ladyship, to
‘ embark for *France*, and shall pass a Year or two
‘ in *Italy* , and then I shall, I hope, return, as solid,
‘ as grave, as circumspect, tho’ not so wise, as
‘ Mrs B ’

In this manner the Countess concluded her Nar-
rative, and I told her, That I was greatly obliged
to her Ladyship for the Honour she did me in this
Visit, and the kind and considerate Occasion of it :
But that Mr B had made me intirely happy in every
Particular, and had done her Ladyship the Justice
she so well deserv’d, having taken upon himself the
Blame of passing as a single Gentleman, at his first
Acquaintance with her Ladyship.

I added, That I could hope her Ladyship might
be prevented, by some happy Gentleman, from
leaving

leaving a Kingdom to which she was so great an Ornament, as well by her Birth, her Quality, and Fortune, as by her Perfections of Person and Mind.

She said, She had not been the happiest of her Sex in her former Marriage, altho' nobody, her Youth consider'd, thought her a bad Wife; and her Lord's Goodness to her, at his Death, had demonstrated his own favourable Opinion of her by Deeds, as he had done by Words, upon all Occasions· But that she was yet young, a little too gay and unsettled; and had her Head turn'd towards *France* and *Italy*, having pass'd some Time in those Countries, which she thought of with Pleasure, tho' then but a Girl of Twelve or Thirteen : That for this Reason, and having been on a late Occasion still more unsettled, (looking down with Blushes, which often overspread her lovely Face, as she talked) she had refused some Offers, not despisable : That, indeed, Lord *C----* threatened to follow her to *Italy*, in hopes of meeting better Success there, than he had met with here; but if he did, tho' she would make no Resolutions, she believed she should be too much offended with him, to give him Reason to boast of his Journey, and this the rather, as she had Grounds to think, he had once entertained no very honourable Notions of her Friendship for Mr. *B*

She wished to see M⁚ *B.* and to take Leave of him, but not out of my Company, she was pleased to say Your Ladyship's Consideration for me, reply'd I, lays me under high Obligation, but, indeed, Madam, there is no Occasion for it, from any Diffidences I have in yours or in Mr *B*'s Honour And if your Ladyship will give me the Pleasure of knowing when it will be most acceptable, I will beg of Mr *B.* to oblige me with his Company to return this Favour, the first Visit I make abroad.

You are very kind, my dear Mrs *B* said she . But I think to go to *Tunbridge* for a Fortnight, when I
have

have difposed of every thing for my Imbarkation, and fo fet out from thence  And if you fhould then be both in *Kent*, I fhould be glad to take you at your Word

To be fure, I faid, Mr *B* at leaft, would attend her Ladyfhip there, if any thing fhould happen to deprive me of that Honour , and if it would be agreeable to her Ladyfhip, I made no doubt he would, with as high a Pleafure, as I fhould receive in his doing fo, attend her Ladyfhip on board, and fee her fafe on the other Side

You are a generous Lady, faid the Countefs···. I take great Concern to myfelf, for having been the Means of giving you a Moment's Uneafinefs formerly  But I muft now endeavour to be circumfpect, in order to retrieve my Character, which has been fo bafely traduced by that prefumptuous Fellow *Turner*, who hoped, I fuppofe, by that means, to bring me down to his Level

Her Ladyfhip would not be prevailed upon to ftay Dinner, and faying, She fhould be at *Wooburn* all the next Day, took a very kind and tender Leave of me, wifhing me all manner of Happinefs, as I did her.

Mr *B* came home in the Evening, and next Morning rode to *Wooburn*, to pay his Refpects to the Countefs, and came back in the Evening

Thus happily, and to the Satisfaction of all Three, as I hope, ended this perplexing Affair.

Mr *B* asks me, Madam, How I relifh Mr *Locke's Treatife of Education ?* which he put into my Hands fome time fince, as I told your Ladyfhip  I anfwerd, Very well , and I thought it an excellent Piece, in the main

I'll tell you, faid he, what you fhall do  You have not fhewed me any thing you have written for a good while  I would be glad, you would fill up your Leifure-time, fince you cannot be without a Pen, with your Obfervations on that Treatife, that

I may

I may know what you can object to it, for you say, *In the main*, which shews, that you do not intirely approve of every Part of it

But will not that be presumptuous, Sir?

I admire Mr *Locke*, reply'd he, and I admire my *Pamela*. I have no Doubt of his Excellencies, but I want to know the Sentiments of a young Mother, as well as of a learned Gentleman, upon the Subject of Education; because I have heard several Ladies censure some Part of his Regimen, when I am convinc'd, that the Fault lies in their own overgreat Fondness for their Children.

As to myself, Sir, who, in the early Part of my Life, have not been brought up too tenderly, you will hardly meet with any Objection to the Part which I imagine you have heard most objected to by Ladies who have been more indulgently treated in their first Stage. But there are a few other Things that want clearing up to my Understanding, but which, however, may be the Fault of that.

Then, my Dear, said he, suppose me at a Distance from you, cannot you give me your Remarks in the same manner, as if you were writing to Lady *Davers*, or to Miss *Darnford*, that was?

Yes, Sir, depending on your kind Favour to me, I believe I could.

Do then, and the less Restraint you write with, the more I shall be pleased with it But I confine you not to Time or Place We will make our Excursions as I once proposed to you, and do you write me a Letter now-and-then upon the Subject, for the Places and Remarkables you will see, will be new only to yourself, nor will either of those Ladies expect from you an Itinerary, or a particular Description of Countries, which they will find better described by Authors, who have made it their Business to treat upon those Subjects By this Means, you will be usefully imploy'd in your own way,
which

which may turn to good Account to us both, and to the dear Children, which it may pleafe God to beftow upon us

You don't expect, Sir, any thing regular or digefted from me?

I don't, my Dear  Let your Fancy and your Judgment be both imploy'd, and I require no Method, for I know, in your eafy, natural way, that would be a Confinement, which would cramp your Genius, and give what you write a ftiff, formal Air, that I might expect in a Pedagogue, but not in my *Pamela.*

Well, but, Sir, altho' I may write nothing to the Purpofe, yet if Lady *Davers* is defirous to give it a Reading, will you allow me to tranfmit what I fhall write, to her Hands, when you have perus'd it yourfelf? For your good Sifter is fo indulgent to my Scribble, that fhe will expect to be always hearing from me; and this way I fhall oblige her Ladyfhip, while I obey her Brother.

With all my Heart, he was pleafed to fay.

So, my Lady, I fhall now-and-then pay my Refpects to you in the writing way, tho' I muft addrefs myfelf, it feems, to my deareft Mr *B*; and I hope I fhall be received on thefe my own Terms, fince they are your Brother's Terms alfo, and, at the fame time, fuch as will convince you, how much I wifh to approve myfelf, to the beft of my poor Ability,

*Your Ladyfhip's moft obliged Sifter,*

*and humble Servant,*

P. B.

LET.

# LETTER XLVIII.

*My dearest Mr.* B.

I HAVE been confidering of your Commands, in relation to Mr. *Locke's* Book; and fince you are pleas'd to give me Time to acquit myfelf of the Task, I fhall take the Liberty to propofe to include in a little Book my humble Sentiments, as I did to Lady *Davers,* in that I fhew'd you in relation to the Plays I had feen. And, fince you confine me not to Time or Place, perhaps, I fhall be three or four Years in completing it, becaufe I fhall referve fome Subjects to my further Experience in Childrens Ways and Tempers, and in order to benefit myfelf by thofe good Inftructions, which I fhall receive from your delightful Converfation, in that Compafs of Time, if God fpare us to one another : And then it will, moreover, be ftill worthier, than it can otherwife be, of the Perufal of the moft honour'd and beft beloved of all my Correfpondents, much honour'd and beloved, as they all are.

I muft needs fay, my dear Mr B. that this is a Subject to which I was always particularly attentive, and among the Charities your bountiful Heart permits me to difpenfe to the Poor and Indigent, I have had always a watchful Eye upon the Children of fuch, and endeavour'd, by Queftions put to them, as well as to their Parents, to inform myfelf of their little Ways and Tempers, and how Nature delights to work in different Minds, and how it might be pointed to their Good, according to their refpective Capacities, and I have for this Purpofe erected, with your Approbation, a little School of Seven or Eight Children, among which are four in the earlieft Stages, when they can but juft fpeak, and call for what they want, or love: And I am not a little pleas'd to obferve, when I vifit them in their School-time, that

Principles

Principles of Goodness and Virtue may be inftilled into their little Hearts much earlier than is ufually imagin'd  And why fhould it not be fo ? For may not the Child, that can tell its Wants, and make known its Inclination, be eafily made fenfible of *yours*, and what you expect from it, provided you take a proper Method ? For, fometimes, Signs and Tokens, (and even Looks) uniformly practis'd, will do as well as Words, as we fee in fuch of the Young of the Brute Creation, as we are difpos'd to domefticate, and to teach to practife thofe little Tricks, of which the Aptnefs or Docility of their Natures makes them capable.

But yet, deareft Sir, I know not enough of the next Stage, the *maturer* Part of Life, to touch upon that, as I wifh to do, and yet there is a natural Connection and Progreffion from the one to the other  And I would not be thought a vain Creature, who believes herfelf equal to *every* Subject, becaufe fhe is indulg'd with the good Opinions of her Friends, in a *few*, which are fuppofed to be within her own Capacity

For, I humbly conceive, that it is no fmall Point of Wifdom to know, and not to miftake, one's own Talents, and for this Reafon, permit me, dear Sir, to fufpend, till I am better qualify'd for it, even my own Propofal of beginning my little Book, and, in the mean time, to touch upon a few Places of the admirable Author you have put into my Hand, that feem to me to warrant another way of Thinking, than that which he prefcribes.

But, dear Sir, let me premife, that all that your dear Babies can demand of my Attention for fome time to come, is their Health ; and it has pleas'd God to blefs them with fuch found Limbs, and, to all Appearance, good Conftitutions, that I have very little to do, but to pray for them every time I pray for their dear Papa, and that is hourly , and yet not

fo

ſo often as you confer upon me Benefits, and Favours, and new Obligations, even to the Prevention of all my Wiſhes, were I to ſit down to ſtudy for what muſt be the next.

As to this Point of *Health*, Mr. *Locke* gives theſe plain and eaſy to be obſerved Rules

He preſcribes, Firſt, *Plenty of open Air* That this is right, the Infant will inform one, who, tho' it cannot ſpeak, will make Signs to be carry'd abroad, and is never ſo well pleas'd, as when it is enjoying the open and free Air, for which Reaſon I conclude, that this is one of thoſe natural Pointings, as one may call them, that are implanted in every Creature, teaching it to chuſe its Good, and to avoid its Evil

*Sleep* is the next, which he injoins to be indulg'd to its utmoſt Extent: An admirable Rule, as I humbly conceive, ſince ſound Sleep is one of the greateſt Nouriſhers in Nature, both to the *once* Young, and to the *twice* Young, if I may be allow'd the Phraſe, And I the rather approve of this Rule, becauſe it keeps the Nurſe unimploy'd, who otherwiſe, perhaps, would be doing it the greateſt Miſchief, by cramming and ſtuffing its little Bowels, till they were ready to burſt And, if I am right, what an inconſiderate, and fooliſh, as well as pernicious Practice is it, for a Nurſe to *waken* the Child from its nouriſhing Sleep, for fear it ſhould ſuffer by Hunger, and inſtantly pop the Breaſt into its pretty Mouth, or provoke it to feed, when it has no Inclination to either; and, for want of Digeſtion, muſt have its Nutriment turn to Repletion, and bad Humours!

Excuſe me, dear Sir, theſe leſſer Particulars. Mr *Locke* begins with them, and ſurely they may be allowed in a young *Mamma*, writing (however it be to a Gentleman of Genius and Learning) to a *Papa*, on a Subject, that in its loweſt Beginnings ought not to be unattended to by either. I will therefore purſue my excellent Author without further Apology,

Apology, since you have put his Work into my Hands.

The next Thing then, which he prescribes, is *plain Diet*. This speaks for itself, for the Baby can have no corrupt Taste to gratify. All is pure, as out of the Hand of Nature; and what is not plain and natural, must vitiate and offend.

Then, *no Wine*, or *strong Drink*. Equally just, and for the same Reasons.

*Little* or *no Physick* Undoubtedly right. For the *Use* of Physick, without Necessity, or by way of *Precaution*, as some call it, begets the *Necessity* of Physick, and the very *Word* supposes *Distemper* or *Disorder*, and where there is none, would a Parent beget one, or, by frequent *Use*, render the salutary Force of Medicine ineffectual, when it was wanted?

Next, he forbids *too warm* and *too streight Cloathing*. Dear Sir, this is just as I wish it. How has my Heart ached, many and many a time, when I have seen poor Babies roll'd and swath'd, ten or a dozen times round; then Blanket upon Blanket, Mantle upon that, its little Neck pinn'd down to one Posture; its Head, more than it frequently needs, triple-crown'd like a young Pope, with Covering upon Covering, its Legs and Arms, as if to prevent that kindly Stretching, which we rather ought to promote, when it is in Health, and which is only aiming at Growth and Inlargement, the former bundled up, the latter pinn'd down; and how the poor Thing lies on the Nurse's Lap, a miserable little pinion'd Captive, goggling and staring with its Eyes, the only Organs it has at Liberty, as if it was supplicating for Freedom to its fetter'd Limbs! Nor has it any Comfort at all, till, with a Sigh or two, like a dying Deer, it drops asleep; and happy then will it be, till the officious Nurse's Care shall awaken it for its undesired Food, just as if the good Woman were
resolv'd

I

resolv'd to try its Constitution, and were willing to see how many Difficulties it could overcome.

Then this Gentleman advises, that the Head and Feet should be kept cold; and the latter often us'd to cold Water, and expos'd to Wet, in order to lay the Foundation, as he says, of an healthy and hardy Constitution.

Now, Sir, what a Pleasure is it to your *Pamela,* that her Notions, and her Practice too, fall in so exactly with this learned Gentleman's Advice, that, excepting one Article, which is, that your *Billy* has not yet been accustom'd to be *wet-shod,* every other Particular has been observ'd !——And don't you see what a charming, charming Baby he is ?——Nay, and so is your little *Davers,* for his Age—— pretty Soul !

Perhaps some, were they to see this, would not be so ready, as I know *you* will be, to excuse me ; and would be apt to say, What Nursery Impertinencies are these, to trouble a Man with !——But, with all their Wisdom, they would be mistaken ; for if a Child has not good Health, (and are not these Rules, the moral Foundation, as I may say, of that Blessing ?) its animal Organs will play but poorly in a weak or crazy Case   These, therefore, are necessary Rules to be observed for the first two or three Years ; for then the little Buds of their Minds will begin to open, and their watchful Mamma will be imploy'd, like a skilful Gardener, in assisting and encouraging the charming Flower thro' its several hopeful Stages to Perfection, when it shall become one of the principal Ornaments of that delicate Garden, your honour'd Family.   Pardon me, Sir, if in the above Paragraph I am too figurative.   I begin to be afraid I am out of my Sphere, writing to your dear Self, on these important Subjects.

But be that as it may, I will here put an End to this my first Letter, (on the earliest Part of my Subject) rejoicing in the Opportunity you have given me of

producing

producing a fresh Instance of that Duty and Affection, wherewith I am, and shall ever be, my dearest Mr B

*Your gratefully happy*    P B

---

## LETTER XLIX.

I WILL now, my dearest, my best beloved Correspondent of all, begin, since the tender Age of my dear Babies will not permit me to have an Eye yet to their *better* Part, to tell you what are the little Matters, to which I am not quite so well reconcil'd in Mr. *Locke* And this I shall be better enabled to do, by my Observations upon the Temper and natural Bent of my dear Miss *Goodwin*, as well as by those, which my Visits to the bigger Children of my little School, and those at the Cottages adjacent, have enabled me to make· For human Nature, Sir, you are not to be told, is human Nature, whether in the High-born, or in the Low.

This excellent Author, in his Fifty-second Section, having justly disallow'd of slavish and corporal Punishments in the Education of those we would have to be wise, good, and ingenious Men, adds .----' On
' the other Side, to flatter Children by Rewards of
' Things, that are pleasant to them, is as carefully
' to be avoided He that will give his Son Apples,
' or Sugar-plums, or what else of this kind he is
' most delighted with, to make him learn his Book,
' does but authorize his Love of Pleasure, and
' cockers up that dangerous Propensity, which he
' ought, by all means, to subdue and stifle in him
' You can never hope to teach him to master it,
' whilst you compound for the Check you give his
' Inclination in one Place, by the Satisfaction you
' propose to it in another· To make a good, a
' wise, and a virtuous Man, 'tis fit he should learn
                                                    ' to

4

' to crofs his Appetite, and deny his Inclination to
' Riches, Finery, or pleafing his Palate, &c'

This, Sir, is excellently faid ; but is it not a little
too philofophical and abftracted, not only for the
Generality of Children, but for the Age he fuppofes
them to be of, if one may guefs by the Apples and
the Sugar-plums propofed for the Rewards of their
Well-doing ? Would not this, Sir, require that Memory or Reflection in Children, which the fame
Author, in another Place, calls the Concomitant of
Prudence and Age, and not of Childhood ?

It is undoubtedly very right, to check an unreafonable Appetite, and that at its firft Appearance But
if fo fmall and fo reafonable an Inducement will prevail,
furely, Sir, it might be comply'd with  A generous
Mind takes Delight to win over others by good Ufage
and Mildnefs, rather than by Severity, and it muft be
a great Pain to fuch an one, to be always inculcating,
on his Children or Pupils, the Doctrine of Self-denial,
by Methods quite grievous to his own Nature.

What I would then humbly propofe, is, That the
Encouragements offer'd to Youth, fhould, indeed, be
innocent ones, as the Gentleman injoins, and not fuch
as would lead to Luxury, either of Food or Apparel. But I humbly think it neceffary, that Rewards,
*proper* Rewards, fhould be propos'd as Incentives to
laudable Actions  For is it not by this Method, that
the whole World is influenc'd and govern'd ? Does
not GOD himfelf, by Rewards and Punifhments make
it our *Intereft*, as well as our *Duty*, to obey HIM ?
And can we propofe to ourfelves, for the Government of our Children, a better Example than that
of the Creator ?

This fine Author feems, dear Sir, to think he had
been a little of the ftricteft, and liable to fome Exception  ' I fay not this, *proceeds he*, (§ 53) that I
' would have Children kept from the Conveniencies
' or Pleafures of Life, that are not injurious to their

' Health or Virtue  On the contrary, I would have
' their Lives made as pleasant and as agreeable to
' them as may be, in a plentiful Enjoyment ot what-
' soever might innocently delight them'  And yet,
dear Sir, he immediately subjoins a very hard and difficult Proviso to the Indulgence he has now granted.
----' Provided, *says he*, it be with this Caution,
' That they have those Enjoyments only as the Con-
' sequences of the State of Esteem and Acceptation
' they are in with their Parents and Governors'

I doubt, my dear Mr *B.* this is expecting such a
Distinction and Discretion in Children, as they are
seldom capable of in their tender Years, and requiring
such Capacities as are not commonly to be met with
So that it is not prescribing to the *Generality*, as this
excellent Author intended.   'Tis, I humbly conceive,
next to impossible, that their tender Minds should
distinguish beyond Facts : They covet this or that
Plaything, and the Parent, or Governor, takes Advantage of its Desires, and annexes to the Indulgence
which the Child hopes for, such or such a Task or
Duty, as a Condition , and shews himself pleas'd
with its Compliance with it  So the Child wins its
Plaything, and receives the Praise and Commendation so necessary to lead on young Minds to laudable Pursuits.   But, dear Sir, shall it not be suffered
to enjoy the innocent Reward of its Compliance,
unless it can give Satisfaction, that its greatest Delight
is not in having the Thing coveted, but in performing the Task, or obeying the Injunctions, impos'd
upon it as a Condition of its being oblig'd ? I doubt,
Sir, this is a little too strict, and not to be expected
from Children  A Servant, full grown, would not
be able to shew, that, on Condition he comply'd
with such and such Terms, (which, it is to be sup-
pos'd by the *Offer*, he would not have comply'd with,
but for that Inducement) he should have such and
such a Reward, I say, he would hardly be able
to

to fhew, that he preferr'd the Pleafure of performing the requifite Conditions to the ftipulated Reward. Nor is it neceffary he fhould, for he is not the lefs a good Servant, or a virtuous Man, if he own the Conditions painful, and the Reward neceffary to his low State in the World, and that o herwife he would not undergo any Service at all — Why then fhould this be exacted from a Child?

Let therefore, if I may prefume to fay fo, innocent Rewards be propos'd, and let us be contented to lead on the ductile Minds of Children to a Love of their Duty, by obliging them with fuch: We may tell them what we *expect* in this Cafe, but we ought not, I humbly conceive, to be too rigorous in *exacting* it, for, after all, the Inducement will certainly be the uppermoft Confideration with the Child 'Tis out of Nature to fuppofe it otherwife, nor, as I hinted, had it been offer'd to it, if the Parent himfelf had not thought fo And therefore we can only let the Child know his Duty in this refpect, and that he *ought* to give a Preference to that, and then reft ourfelves contented, altho' we fhould difcern, that the Reward is the chief Incentive, if it do but oblige to the Performance of it For this, from whatever Motive inculcated, may beget a Habit in the Child of doing it, and then, as it improves in Years, one may hope, that Reafon will take place, and enable him, from the moft folid and durable Motives, to give a Preference to the Duty

Upon the Whole, then, may I, Sir, venture to fay, That we fhould not infift upon it, that the Child fhould fo nicely diftinguifh away its little *innate* Paffions, as if we expected it to be born a Philofopher? Self-denial is indeed a moft excellent Doctrine, to be inculcated into Children, and it muft be done *early* too But we muft not be too fevere in our exacting it, for a Duty too rigidly infifted upon, will make it odious. This Mr *Locke* himfelf excel-

lently

lently obferves in another Place, on the Head of too
great Severity; which he illuftrates by a familiar
Comparifon ' Offenfive Circumftances, *fays he,*
' ordinarily infect innocent Things, which they are
' joined with   And the very Sight of a Cup, where-
' in any one ufes to take naufeous Phyfick, turns his
' Stomach, fo that nothing will relifh well out of
' it, tho' the Cup be never fo clean and well-fhap'd,
' and of the richeft Materials'

Permit me, dear Sir, to add, That Mr *Lock*
proceeds to explain himfelf ftill more rigoroufly on
the Subject of Rewards; which I quote, to fhew I
have not mifunderftood him · ' But thefe Enjoy-
' ments, *fays he,* fhould *never* be offer'd or beftow'd
' on Children, as the Rewards of this or that par-
' ticular Performance, that they fhew an Averfion to,
' or to which they would not have apply'd them
' felves without that Temptation'   If, my dear
Mr. *B* the Minds of Children *can* be led on by
innocent Inducements to the Performance of a
Duty, of which they are capable, what I have humbly offer'd, is enough, I prefume, to convince one,
that it *may* be done.  But if ever a particular Study be
propos'd to be mafter'd, or a Byas to be overcome,
(that is not an *indifpenfable* Requifite to his future
Life or Morals) to which the Child fhews an Averfion, I would not, methinks, have him be too much
tempted or compell'd to conquer or fubdue it, efpecially if it appear to be a *natural* or rivetted Averfion.

For, Sir, permit me to obferve, that the Education and Studies of Children ought, as much as
poffible, to be fuited to their Capacities and Inclinations   And, by this means, we may expect to have
always *ufeful*, and often *great* Men, in different Profeffions   For, that Genius, which does not prompt
to the Profecution of one Study, may fhine in another no lefs neceffary Part of Science   But, if the
Promif-

Promise of innocent Rewards *would* conquer this Aversion, yet they should not be applied with this View, for the best Consequence that can be hop'd-for, will be tolerable Skill in one thing, instead of most excellent, in another.

Nevertheless, I must repeat, that if, as the Child grows up, and is capable of so much Reason, that, from the Love of the *Inducement,* one can raise his Mind to the Love of the *Duty,* it should be done by all means. But, my dear Mr *B* I am afraid, that *that* Parent or Tutor will meet but with little Success, who, in a Child's *tender* Years, shall refuse to comply with its Foibles, till he sees it values its Duty, and the Pleasure of obeying its Commands, beyond the little Enjoyment on which its Heart is fixed. For, as I humbly conceive, that Mind, which can be brought to prefer its Duty to its Appetites, will want little of the Perfection of the wisest Philosophers.

Besides, Sir, permit me to say, That I am afraid, this perpetual Opposition between the Passions of the Child, and the Duty to be inforced, especially when it sees how other Children are indulg'd, (for if this Regimen could be obferv'd by *any,* it would be impossible it should become *general,* while the fond and the inconsiderate Parents are so large a Part of Mankind) will cow and dispirit a Child, and will, perhaps, produce a Necessity of making use of Severity to subdue him to this Temper of Self-denial, for if the Child refuses, the Parent *must* insist, and what will be the Consequence? --- Must it not introduce a harsher Discipline than this Gentleman allows of? --- And which, I presume to say, did never yet do Good to any but to slavish and base Spirits, it to them · A Discipline which Mr. *Locke* every-where justly condemns.

See here, dear Sir, a Specimen of the Presumption of your Girl: What will she come to in time?

you will perhaps fay---Her next Step will be to arraign myfelf---No, no, dear Sir, don't think fo For my Duty, my Love, and my Reverence, fhall be your Guards, and defend you from every thing faucy in me, but the bold Approaches of my Gratitude, which fhall always teftify for me, how much I am

*Your obliged and dutiful*

P B

## LETTER L.

*My deareft Mr.* B

I WILL continue my Subject, altho' I have not had an Opportunity to know whether you approve of my Notions or not, by reafon of the Excurfions you have been pleas'd to allow me to make in your beloved Company, to the Sea-ports of this Kingdom, and to the more noted inland Towns of *Effex*, *Kent*, *Suffex*, *Hampfhire*, and *Dorfetfhire*, which have given me infinite Delight and Pleafure, and inlarged my Notions of the Wealth and Power of the Kingdom, in which God's Goodnefs has given you fo confiderable a Stake

My next Topick will be upon a *Home* Education, which Mr *Locke* prefers, for feveral weighty Reafons, to a *School* one, provided fuch a Tutor can be procur'd, as he makes next to an Impoffibility to procure  The Gentleman has fet forth the Inconveniencies of both, and was himfelf fo difcourag'd on a Review of them, that he was ready, as he fays, to throw up his Pen  My chief Cares, dear Sir, on this Head, are Three·  1*ft*, The Difficulty, which, as I faid, Mr *Locke* makes almoft infuperable, to find a qualify'd Tutor  2*dly*, The Neceffity there is, according to Mr *Locke*, of keeping the Youth out of the Company of the meaner Servants, who

may

may set him bad Examples  And, 3*dly,* Those still greater Difficulties, which will arise from the Examples of his Parents, if they are not very discreet and circumspect

As to the Qualifications of the Tutor, Mr *Locke* supposes, that he is to be so learned, so discreet, so wise, in short, so *perfect* a Man, that, I doubt, and so does Mr. *Locke,* such a one is hardly possible to be met with for this *humble* and *slavish* Imployment. I presume, Sir, to call it so, because of the too little Regard that is generally paid to these useful Men in the Families of the Great, where they are frequently put upon a Foot with the uppermost Servants, and the rather, if they happen to be Men of Modesty

' I would, *says this Gentleman,* from Childrens ' first beginning to talk, have some discreet, sober, ' nay, *wise* Person about them, whose Care it should ' be to fashion them right, and to keep them from ' all Ill, especially the Infection of bad Company. ' I think, *continues he,* this Province requires great ' Sobriety, Temperance, Tenderness, Diligence, and ' Discretion; Qualities hardly to be found united in ' Persons that are to be had for ordinary Salaries, ' nor easily to be found any-where '

If this, Sir, be the Case, does not this excellent Author recommend a Scheme, that is render'd in a manner impracticable from this Difficulty?

As to these Qualities being more rarely to be met with in Persons that are to be had for *ordinary Salaries,* I cannot help being of Opinion, (altho' with Mr *Locke,* I think, no Expence should be spared, if that *would* do) that there is as good a Chance for finding a proper Person among the needy Scholars, (if not of a low and sordid Turn of Mind) as among the more Affluent· Because the narrow Circumstances of the former, (which probably became a Spur to his own Improvement) will, it is likely, at

O 4

firft

firſt ſetting out in the World, make him be glad to embrace an Offer of this kind in a Family, which has Intereſt enough to prefer him, and will quicken his Diligence to make him *deſerve* Preferment · And if ſuch a one wanted any thing of that requiſite Politeneſs, which ſome would naturally expect from Scholers of better Fortune, might not that be ſupply'd to the Youth by the Converſation of Parents, Relations, and Viſitors, in Conjunction with thoſe other Helps which young Gentlemen of Family and large Expectations conſtantly have, and which few learned Tutors can give him

I ſay not this, dear Sir, to countenance the wretched Niggardlineſs (which this Gentleman juſtly cenſures) of thoſe who grudge a handſome Conſideration to ſo neceſſary and painful a Labour as that of a Tutor, which, where a deſerving Man can be met with, cannot be too genteelly rewarded, nor himſelf too reſpectfully treated    I only take the Liberty to deliver my Opinion, that a low Condition is as likely, as any other, with a Mind not ungenerous, as I ſaid, to produce a Gentleman who has theſe good Qualities, as well for the Reaſons I have hinted at, as for others, which might be mentioned    To which, to name no more, the Merit of Mr. *Williams* and Mr *Adams* will bear Witneſs.

But Mr. *Locke* proceeds with his Difficulties in this Particular. ‘ To form a young Gentleman as he
‘ ſhould be, *ſays he*, 'tis fit his Governor ſhould be
‘ well-bred, underſtand the Ways of Carriage, and
‘ Meaſures of Civility, in all the Variety of *Perſons, Times,* and *Places*; and keep his Pupil, as far
‘ as his Age requires, conſtantly to the Obſervation
‘ of them.    This is an Art, *continues he*, not to be
‘ learnt or taught by Books    Nothing can give it,
‘ but good Company, and Obſervation, join'd to-
‘ gether.’

And

And in another Place, ‘ Befides being well-bred,
‘ the Tutor fhould know the World well, the Ways,
‘ the Humours, the Follies, the Cheats, the Faults
‘ of the Age he is fallen into, and particularly of
‘ the Country he lives in : Thefe he fhould be able
‘ to fhew to his Pupil, as he finds him capable ;
‘ teach him Skill in Men and their Manners, pull
‘ off the Mask, which their feveral Callings and
‘ Pretences cover them with; and make his Pupil
‘ difcern what lies at the Bottom, under fuch Ap-
‘ pearances, that he may not, as unexperienc’d
‘ young Men are apt to do, if they are unwarn’d,
‘ take one thing for another, judge by the Outfides,
‘ and give himfelf up to Shew, and the Infinuation
‘ of a fair Carriage, or an obliging Application ·
‘ Teach him to guefs at, and beware of, the De-
‘ figns of Men he hath to do with, neither with too
‘ much Sufpicion, nor too much Confidence’

This, dear Sir, is excellently faid: ’Tis noble
*Theory.* And if the Tutor be a Man void of Refentment and Caprice, and will not be govern’d by
partial Confiderations in his own Judgment of Perfons and Things, all will be well But if otherwife,
may he not take Advantage of the Confidence placed
in him, to the Injury of fome worthy Perfon, and
by Degrees monopolize the young Gentleman to
himfelf, and govern his Paffions as abfolutely, as I
have heard fome Firft Minifters have done thofe of
their Prince, equally to his own perfonal Difreputa-
tion, and to the Difadvantage of his People? But,

All this, and much more, according to Mr *Locke,*
is the Duty of a Tutor; and on the finding out fuch
a one, depends his Scheme of a Home Education. No Wonder then, that he himfelf fays, ‘ When
‘ I confider the Scruples and Cautions I here lay
‘ in your Way, methinks it looks as if I advifed you
‘ to fomething, which I would have offer’d at, but
‘ in Effect not done,’ *&c* Permit me, dear Sir, in

this Place, to exprefs my Fear, that it is hardly poffible for any one, of Talents inferior to thofe of
Mr *Locke* himfelf, to come up to the Rules he has
laid down upon this Subject, and 'tis to be queftion'd,
whether even *he*, with all that vaft Stock of natural
Reafon, and folid Senfe, for which, as you tell me,
Sir, he was fo famous, had attain'd to thefe Perfections, at his firft fetting out into Life

Now, therefore, dear Sir, you can't imagine, how
thefe Difficulties perplex me, as to my knowing
how to judge which is beft, a *Home* or a *School*
Education ---- For hear what this excellent Author
juftly obferves on the latter, among other things no
lefs to the Purpofe · ' I am fure, he who is able to
' be at the Charge of a Tutor at Home, may there
' give his Son a more genteel Carriage, more manly
' Thoughts, and a Senfe of what is worthy and be-
' coming, with a greater Proficiency in Learning
' into the Bargain, and ripen him up fooner into a
' Man, than any at School can do  Not that I blame
' the School-mafter, in this, *fays he*, or think it to
' be laid to his Charge  The Difference is great
' between two or three Pupils in the fame Houfe,
' and three or fourfcore Boys lodg'd up and down·
' For, let the Mafter's Induftry and Skill be never
' fo great, it is impoffible he fhould have 50 or 100
' Scholars under his Eye, any longer than they are
' in the School together ' But then, Sir, if there be
fuch a Difficulty, as Mr *Locke* fays, to meet with
a proper Tutor, for the Home Education which he
thus prefers, what a perplexing thing is this?

But ftill, according to this Gentleman, another
Difficulty attends a Home Education; and that is,
what I hinted at before, in my fecond Article, The
Neceffity of keeping the Youth out of the Company
of the meaner Servants, who may fet him bad Examples  For thus he fays: ' Here is another great
' Inconvenience, which Children receive from the

' ill Examples, which they meet with from the
' meaner *Servants.* They are *wholly*, if possible, to
' be kept from such Conversation. For the Conta-
' gion of these ill Precedents, both in Civility and
' Virtue, horribly infects Children, as often as they
' come within Reach of it  They frequently learn
' from unbred or debauched Servants, such Lan-
' guage, untowardly Tricks, and Vices, as otherwise
' they would be ignorant of, all their Lives  'Tis a
' hard Matter wholly to prevent this Mischief, *con-*
' *tinues he* ; you will have very good Luck, if you
' never have a clownish or vicious Servant, and if
' from them your Children never get any Infection.'

Then, Sir, my third Point (which I mention'd in
the Beginning of this Letter) makes a still stronger
Objection, as it may happen, against a Home Education, to wit, The Example of the Parents themselves, if they be not very circumspect and discreet.

All these Difficulties being put together, let me,
dear Sir, humbly propose it, as a Matter for your
Consideration and Determination, Whether there
be not a middle Way to be found out in a School
Education, that may remedy some of these Inconveniencies? For suppose you cannot get a Tutor
so qualified, as Mr *Locke* thinks he ought to be,
for your *Billy*, as he grows up  Suppose there is
Danger from your meaner *Servants;* and suppose
we his Parents should not be able to lay ourselves
under the requisite Restraints, in order to form his
Mind by our own Examples, which, I hope, by
God's Grace, however, will not be the Case -----
Cannot some Master be found out, who shall be
so well rewarded for his Care of a *few* young
Gentlemen, as shall make it worth his while to be
contented with those *few* ? suppose Five, Six, Seven,
or Eight at most, whose Morals and Breeding
he may attend to, as well as to their Learning ? The
farther this Master lives from the young Gentlemens

Friends,

Friends, the better it may be. We will hope, that he is a Man of a mild Difposition, but ftrict in his Difcipline, and who fhall make it a Rule not to give Correction for fmall Faults, or till every other Method has been try'd; who carries fuch a juft Dignity in his Manner, without the Appearance of Tyranny, that his Looks may be of greater Force, than the Words of fome, and his Words than the Blows of others; and who will rather endeavour to fhame, than terrify, a Youth out of his Faults. Then, Sir, fuppofe this Gentleman was to allot a particular Portion of Time for the *more learned* Studies; and before the Youth was tir'd with *them*, fuppofe another Portion was allotted for the *Writing* and *Arithmetick* Parts, and then, to relieve his Mind from both, fuppofe the *Dancing-mafter* fhould take his Part, and innocent Exercifes of mere Diverfion, to fill up the reft, at his own Choice; in which, diverted by fuch a Rotation of Imployments, (all thus render'd delightful by their fucceffive Variety) he would hardly wifh to pafs much Time   For the Dancing of itfelf will anfwer both Parts, that of good Breeding, and that of Exercife   And thus different Studies, at one time, may be mafter'd.

Moreover the Emulation, which will be infpir'd, where there are feveral young Gentlemen, will be of inconceivable Ufe both to Tutor and Pupil, in leffening the Trouble of the one, and advancing the Learning of the other, which cannot be expected, where there is but a fingle Youth to be taken care of.

Such a Mafter will know it to be his Intereft, as well as his Duty, to have a watchful Eye over the Conduct and Behaviour of his Servants   His Affiftants, in the different Branches of Science and Education, will be Perfons of approved Prudence, for whom he will think himfelf anfwerable, fince his own *Reputation*, as well as his *Livelihood*, will depend upon their Behaviour. The young Gentlemen

men will have young Gentlemen for their Companions, all under the Influence of the fame Precepts and Directions; and if fome chofen Period were fixed, once a Week, as a Reward for fome Excellence, where, at a little Desk, rais'd a Step or two above the other Seats, the excelling Youth fhould be fet to read, under the Mafter's Direction, a little Portion from the beft Tranflations of the *Greek* and *Roman* Hiftorians, and even from the beft *Eng'ifh* Authors, this might, in a very engaging manner, initiate them into the Knowlege of the Hiftory of paft Times, and of their own Country, and give them a Curiofity to pafs fome of their vacant Hours in the fame laudable Purfuit: For, dear Sir, I muft ftill infift, that Rewards, and innocent Gratifications, as alfo little Honours and Diftinctions, muft needs be very attractive to the Minds of Youth

For, don't you think, dear Sir, that the pretty Ride, and Dairy-houfe Breakfafting *, by which Mifs *Goodwin*'s Governefs diftinguifhes the little Ladies, who excel in their allotted Tasks, is a fine Encouragement to their ductile Minds? --- Yes, it is, to be fure! --- And I have often thought of it with Pleafure, and have, in a manner, partaken of the Delight, with which I have fuppofed their pretty Hearts muft be fill'd, on that Occafion And why may not fuch little Triumphs be, in Proportion, as incentive to Children, to make them endeavour to mafter laudable Tasks, as the *Roman* Triumphs, of different Kinds, and their Mural and Civick Crowns, all which I have heard you fpeak of, were to their Heroes and Warriors of old? For Mr. *Dryden* well obferves, That

* *See* Vol. II. *p* 630.

Mc n

*Men are but Children of a larger Growth.*
*Our Appetites are apt to change, as theirs,*
*And full as craving too, and full as vain*

Permit me, Sir, to tranfcribe four or five Lines more, for the Beauty of the Thought·

*And yet the Soul, fhut up in her dark Room,*
*Viewing fo clear abroad, at home fees nothing·*
*But like a Mole in Earth, bufy and blind,*
*Works all her Folly up, and cafts it outward*
*To the World's open View ---*

Improving the Thought, methinks, I can fee the dear little Mifs, who has, in fome eminent Task, borne away the Palm, make her publick Entry, as I may call it, after her Dairy Breakfaft, and pretty Airing, into her Governefs's Court-yard, through a Row of her School-fellows, drawn out on each Side, to admire her, her Governefs and Affiftants receiving her at the Porch, their little Capitol, and lifting her out with Applaufes and Encomiums, with a *Thus fhall it be done to the Mifs, whom her Governefs delighteth to honour!* I fee not, my Mr. *B.* why the dear Mifs, in this Cafe, as fhe moves thro' her admiring School-fellows, may not have her little Heart beat with as much Delight, be as glorioufly elated, proportionably, as that of the greateft Hero in his Triumphal Car, who has return'd from Exploits, perhaps, much lefs laudable

But how I ramble!---Yet, furely, Sir, you don't expect Method or Connexion from your Girl The Education of our Sex will not permit that, where it is beft We are forced to ftruggle for Knowlege, like the poor feeble Infant in the Month, who, as I defcrib'd in my firft Letter on this Subject, is pinn'd and fetter'd down upon the Nurfe's Lap, and who if its little Aims happen, by Chance, to efcape its Nurfe's Obfervation, and offer but to expand

them-

themfelves, are immediately taken into Cuftody, and pinion'd down to their paffive Behaviour So, when a poor Girl, in fpite of her narrow Education, breaks out into Notice, her Genius is immediately tamed by trifling Imployments, left, perhaps, fhe fhould become the Envy of one Sex, and the Equal of the other. But you, Sir, act more nobly with your *Pamela*, for you throw in her Way all the Opportunities of Improvement that can offer; and fhe has only to regret, that fhe cannot make a better Ufe of them, and, of confequence, render herfelf more worthy of your generous Indulgence.

I know not how, Sir, to recover my Thread; and fo muft break off with that Delight, which I always take, when I come near the Bottom of my Letters to your dear Self, becaufe then I can boaft of the Honour which I have in being

*Your ever dutiful*

P B.

---

## LETTER LI.

WELL, but, my dear Mr *B* you will, perhaps, think from my laft rambling Letter, that I am moft inclin'd to a *School* Education for your *Billy*, fome Years hence, if it fhall pleafe GOD to fpare him to us But indeed I cannot fay, that I am · I only lay feveral things together in my ufual indigefted and roving way, to take your Opinion upon, which, as it ought, will be always decifive with me And indeed I am fo throughly convinc'd by Mr *Locke's* Reafons, where the Behaviour of Servants can be fo well anfwer'd for, as that of yours can be, and where the Example of the Parents will be, as I hope, rather edifying than otherwife, that, without being fway'd, as I think, by maternal

Fondnefs,

Fondnefs, in this Cafe, I muft needs give a Preference to the Home Education; and the little Scheme
I prefum'd to form in my laft, was only, as you will
be pleas'd to remember, on a Suppofition, that thofe
neceffary Points could not be fo well fecur'd

In my Obfervations on this Head, I fhall take
the Liberty, in one or two Particulars, a little to
differ from an Author, that I admire exceedingly,
and that is the prefent Defign of my writing thefe
Letters; for I fhall hereafter, if GOD fpare my Life,
in my little Book, (when you have kindly decided
upon the Points in which I prefume to differ from
that Gentleman) fhew you, Sir, my great Reverence
and Efteem for him, and fhall then be able to let
you know all my Sentiments on this important Subject, and that more undoubtingly, as I fhall be more
improv'd by Years, and your Converfation, efpecially, Sir, if I have the Honour and Happinefs of a
foreign Tour with you, of which you give me Hope,
fo much are you pleas'd with the Delight I take in
thefe improving Excurfions, which you have now
favour'd me with, at times, thro' more than half
the Kingdom.

Well then, Sir, I will proceed to confider a little
more particularly the Subject of a Home Education, with an Eye to thofe Difficulties, of which
Mr *Locke* takes notice, as I mention'd in my laft

As to the firft, that of finding a quality'd Tutor;
we muft not expect fo much Perfection, I doubt, as
Mr *Locke* lays down as neceffary What, therefore, I humbly conceive is beft to be done, will be
to avoid chufing a Man of bigotted and narrow Principles, who yet fhall not be tainted with fceptical or
heterodox Notions; who fhall not be a mere Scholar or Pedant, who has travell'd, and yet preferv'd
his moral Character untainted, and whofe Behaviour
and Carriage is eafy, unaffected, unformal, and genteel, as well acquiredly as naturally fo, if poffible;
who

who fhall not be dogmatical, pofitive, overbearing, on one hand, nor too yielding, fuppliant, fawning, on the other; who fhall ftudy the Child's natural Bent, in order to direct his Studies to the Point, in which he is moft likely to excel In order to preferve the Refpect due to his own Character from every one, he muft not be a Bufy-body in the Family, a Whifperer, a Tale-bearer, but be a Perfon of a benevolent Turn of Mind, ready to compofe Differences · who fhall avoid, of all things, that Foppifhnefs of Drefs and Appearance, which diftinguifhes the Petits-maîtres, and *French* Ufhers, (that I have feen at fome Boarding-fchools) for Coxcombs, rather than Guides of Education For, as I have heard you, my beft Tutor, often obferve, the Peculiarities of Habit, where a Perfon aims at fomething fantaftick, or out of Character, are an undoubted Sign of a wrong Head. For fuch a one is fo kind, as always to hang out on his Sign, what fort of Furniture he has in his Shop, to fave you the Trouble of asking Queftions about him, fo that one may as eafily know by his outward Appearance what he is, as one can know a Widow by her Weeds

Such a Perfon as I have thus negatively defcrib'd, may be found without very much Difficulty perhaps, becaufe fome of thefe Requifites are perfonal, and others are fuch as are obvious, at firft Sight, to a common Penetration; or, where not fo, may be found out, by Inquiry into his general Character and Behaviour: And to the Care of fuch a one, dear Sir, let me for the prefent fuppofe your *Billy* is committed: And fo we acquit ourfelves of the firft Difficulty, as well as we can, that of the Tutor; who, to make himfelf more perfect, may form himfelf, as to what he wants, by Mr *Locke's* excellent Rules on that Head.

But before I quit this Subject, will you give me Leave, Sir, to remind you of your own Opinion upon

upon it, in a Conversation that pass'd between you
and Sir *George Stuart*, and his Nephew, in *London*;
in which you seem'd to prefer a *Scottish* Gentleman
for a Tutor, to those of your own Nation, and still
more than to those of *France*? Don't you remember it, dear Sir? And how much those Gentlemen
were pleas'd with your facetious Freedom with their
Country, and said, You made them Amends for
that, in the Preference you gave to their learn'd and
travell'd Youth? If you have forgot it, I will here
transcribe it from my *Records*, as I call my Book
of Memorandums, for every time I am pleas'd with
a Conversation, and have Leisure, before it goes out
of my Memory, I enter it down as near the very
Words as I can, and now you have made me your
Correspondent, I shall sometimes perhaps give you
back some Valuables from your own Treasure.

Miss *Darnford*, and Mr. *Turner*, and Mr *Fanshaw*, were present, I well remember  These are
your Words, as I have written them down

‘Since the Union of the Two Kingdoms, we have
‘ many Persons of Condition, who have taken Tutors
‘ for their Sons from *Scotland*, which Practice, to
‘ speak impartially, has been attended with some ad-
‘ vantageous Circumstances, that should not be over-
‘ look'd  For, Sir *George*, it must be confess'd, that
‘ notwithstanding your narrow and stiff manner of
‘ Education in *Scotland*, a Spirit of manly Learning,
‘ a kind of poetick Liberty, as I may call it, has
‘ begun to exert itself in that Part of the Island  The
‘ blustering North, forgive me Gentlemen, seems
‘ to have harden'd the Foreheads of her hungry Sons;
‘ and the Keenness with which they set out for Pre-
‘ ferment in the kindlier South, has taught them to
‘ know a good deal of the World betimes  Thro'
‘ the easy Terms on which Learning is generally
‘ attain'd there, as it is earlier inculcated, so it may,
‘ probably, take deeper Root: And since 'tis hardly
         ‘ possible,

'possible, forgive me, dear Sir *George*, and Mr. *Stu-*
'*art*, they can go to a worse Country on this Side
'*Greenland*, than some of the Northern Parts of
'*Scotland*, so their Education, with a View to travel,
'and to better themselves by Settlements in other
'Countries, may perhaps be so many Reasons for
'them to take greater Pains to qualify themselves
'for this Imployment, and may make them succeed
'better in it, especially when they have been able
'to shake off the Fetters which are rivetted upon
'them under the narrow Influences of a too tyran-
'nical Kirk-discipline, which you, Sir *George*, have
'just now so freely censur'd.

'To these Considerations, when we add the Ne-
'cessity, which these remote Tutors lie under, of
'behaving well, because, in the first place, they sel-
'dom wish to return to their own Country; and
'in the next, because *that* cannot prefer them, if
'it would, and, thirdly, because it would not, if
'it could, if the Gentleman be of an inlarged Ge-
'nius, and generous way of Thinking; I say, when
'we add to the Premises these Considerations, they
'all make a kind of Security for their good Behavi-
'our: While those of our own Country have often
'Friends or Acquaintance, on whose Favour they
'are apt to depend, and for that Reason give less
'Attention to the Duties requisite for this important
'Office

'Besides, as their kind Friend *Æolus*, who is
'accustom'd to spread and strengthen the bold
'Muscles of the strong-featur'd *Scot*, has generally
'blown away that inauspicious Bashfulness, which
'hangs a much longer time, commonly, on the
'Faces of the Southern Students, such a one (if
'he falls not too egregiously into the contrary Ex-
'treme, so as to become insufferable) may still be
'the more eligible Person for a Tutor, as he may
'teach a young Gentleman, betimes, that necessary
'Presence

‘ Prefence of Mind, which thofe who are confin’d
‘ to a private Education, fometimes want.

‘ But, after all, if a Gentleman of this Nation be
‘ chofen for this Imployment, it may be neceffary,
‘ that he fhould be one who has had as genteel and
‘ free an Education himfelf, as his Country and Op-
‘ portunities will afford ; and has had, moreover,
‘ the native Roughnefs of his Climate filed off and
‘ polifhed by Travel and Converfation, who has.
‘ made, at leaft, the Tour of *France* and *Italy*, and
‘ has a Tafte for the Politenefs of the former Na-
‘ tion, for, from the natural Boifteroufnefs of a
‘ *North Briton*, and the fantaftick Politenefs of a
‘ *Frenchman*, if happily blended, fuch a Mixture
‘ may refult, as may furnifh out a more complete
‘ Tutor, than either of the Two Nations, fingly,
‘ may be able to produce. But it ought to be re-
‘ member’d, that this Perfon fhould, by all means,
‘ have conquer’d his native Brogue, as I may call it,
‘ and be a Mafter of the *Englifh* Pronunciation,
‘ otherwife his Converfation will be very difagree-
‘ able to an *Englifh* Ear.

‘ And permit me, Gentlemen, to add, That as
‘ an Acquaintance with the *Mufes* contributes not
‘ a little to foften the Manners, and to give a grace-
‘ ful and delicate Turn to the Imagination, and a
‘ kind of Polifh to feverer Studies, I believe it
‘ would not be amifs, that he fhould have a Tafte of
‘ Poetry, altho’ perhaps it were not to be wifh’d he
‘ had fuch ftrong Inclinations that way, as to make
‘ that lively and delectable Amufement his predomi-
‘ nant Paffion For we fee very few Poets, whofe
‘ warm Imaginations do not run away with their
‘ Judgments. And yet, in order to learn the dead
‘ Languages in their Purity, it will be neceffary, as
‘ I apprehend, to inculcate both the Love and the
‘ Study of the antient Poets, which cannot fail of
‘ giving the Youth a Tafte for Poetry in general ’

Permit

Permit me, dear Sir, to ask you, Whether you advanc'd this for Argument-sake, as sometimes you love to amuse and entertain your Friends in an uncommon way? For I should imagine, that our Two Universities, which you have been so good as to shew me, and for which I have ever since had even a greater Reverence, than I had before, are capable of furnishing as good Tutors as any Nation in the World: For here the young Gentlemen seem to me to live both in the *World*, and in the *University*, and we saw several Gentlemen who had not only fine Parts, but polite Behaviour, and deep Learning, as you assur'd me; some of whom you entertain'd, and were entertained by, in so elegant a manner, that no travell'd Gentleman, if I may be allow'd to judge, could excel them: And besides, my dear Mr *B* I know who is reckon'd one of the politest and best-bred Gentlemen in *England* by every body, and learned, as well as polite, and yet had his Education in one of those celebrated Seats of Learning. I wish your *Billy* never may fall short of the Gentleman I mean, in all these Acquirements, and he will be a dear happy Creature, I am sure!

But how I wander again from my Subject!---I have no other way to recover myself, when I thus ramble, but by bringing back myself to that one delightful Point of Reflection, that I have the Honour to be, dearest Sir,

*Your ever-dutiful and obliged*

P. B.

---

# LETTER LII.

*Dearest Sir,*

I Now resume my Subject. I had gone thro' the Article of the Tutor, as well as I could; and now let me trouble you with a few Lines upon what

Mr.

Mr *Locke* fays, That Children are wholly, if poſſible, to be kept from the Converſation of the meaner Servants, whom he ſuppoſes to be, as too frequently they are, *unbred and debauch'd*, to uſe his own Words.

Now, Sir, let me obſerve, on this Head, that I think it is very difficult to keep Children from the Converſation of Servants at all times.  The Care of perſonal Attendance, eſpecially in the Child's early Age, muſt fall upon Servants of one Denomination or other, who, little or much, muſt be converſant with the inferior Servants, and ſo be liable to be tainted by their Converſation, and it will be difficult in this Caſe to prevent the Taint being communicated to the Child   Wherefore it will be a *ſurer*, as well as a more *laudable* Method, to inſiſt upon the regular Behaviour of the whole Family, than to expect the Child, and its immediate Attendant or Tutor, ſhould be the only good ones in it

Nor is this ſo difficult a thing to bring about, as may be imagin'd   Your Family, dear Sir, affords an eminent Inſtance of it ·  The Good have been confirm'd, the Remiſs have been reform'd, the Paſſionate have been tam'd, and there is not a Family in the Kingdom, I will venture to ſay, to the Honour of every Individual of it, more uniform, more regular, and freer from Evil, and more regardful of what they ſay and do, than yours   And, I believe, Sir, you will allow, that tho' they were always honeſt, yet they were not always ſo laudably, ſo exemplarily virtuous, as of late   Which I mention only to ſhew the Practicableneſs of a Reformation, even where bad Habits have taken place---- For your *Pamela*, Sir, arrogates not to herſelf the Honour of this Change   'Tis owing to the Divine Grace ſhining upon Hearts naturally good, for elſe an Example ſo eaſy, ſo plain, ſo ſimple, from ſo young a Miſtreſs, who, moreover, had been exalted from
their

I

their own Station, could not have been attended with such happy Effects.

You see, dear Sir, what a Master and Mistress's Example could do, with a poor Soul so far gone as Mrs *Jewkes.* And I dare be confident, that if, on the Hiring of a new Servant, Sobriety of Manners, and a virtuous Conversation, were insisted upon; and they were told, that a general Inoffensiveness in Words, as well as Actions, was expected from them, as indispensable Conditions of their Service, and that a Breach of that kind would be no more pass'd over, than a wilful Fraud, or Act of Dishonesty, and if, added to these Requisites, their Principals take care to support these Injunctions by their own Example; I say, in this Case, I dare be confident, that if such a Service did not *find* them good, it would *make* them so.

And why, indeed, should we not think this a very practicable Scheme, when it is consider'd, that the Servants we take, are at Years of Discretion, and have the strong Tie of *Interest* superadded to the Obligations we require of them; and which, they must needs know, (let 'em have what bad Habits they will) are right for *themselves* to discharge, as well as for *us* to exact?

We all know of how much Force the Example of Superiors is to Inferiors. It is generally and too justly said, That the Courts of Princes abound with the most profligate of Men, insomuch that you cannot well give a Man a more significantly bad Title, than by calling him a COURTIER: Yet even among these, one shall see the Force of *Example*, as I have heard you, Sir, frequently observe · For, let but the Land be blest with a pious and religious Prince, who makes it a Rule with him to countenance and promote Men of Virtue and Probity, and, to put the Case still stronger, let such a one even succeed to the most libertine Reign, wherein the Manners

of

of the People have feem'd to be wholly deprav'd, yet a wonderful Change will be immediately effected. The flagitious Livers will be chas'd away, or reform'd, or at leaft will think it their Duty, or their *Intereft*, which is a ftronger Tie with fuch, to *appear* reform'd, and not a Man will feek for the Favour or Countenance of his Prince, but by laudable Pretences, or by worthy Actions

There was a Time, the Reign of King *Richard* III. when, as I have read, Deformity of Body was the Fafhion, and the Nobility and Gentry of the Court thought it an indifpenfable Requifite of a graceful Form to pad for themfelves a round Shoulder, becaufe the King was crooked. And can we think human Nature fo abfurdly wicked, that it would not much rather have try'd to imitate a perfonal Perfection, than a Deformity fo fhocking in its Appearance, in People who were naturally ftrait ?

'Tis a melancholy thing to reflect, that of all Profeffions of Men, the Mariners, who moft behold the Wonders of Almighty Power difplay'd in the great Deep, (a Sight that has ftruck me with Awe and Reverence only from a Coaft Profpect) and who every Moment of their Lives, while at Sea, have but one frail Plank betwixt themfelves and inevitable Deftruction, are yet, generally fpeaking, as I have often heard it obferv'd, the moft abandon'd Invokers and Blafphemers of the Name of that GOD, whofe Mercies they every Moment unthankfully, altho' fo vifibly, experience Yet, as I heard it once remark'd at your Table, Sir, on a particular Occafion, we have now living one Commander in the *Britifh* Navy, who, to his Honour, has fhewn the Force of an excellent Example fupporting the beft Precepts: For on board of his Ship not an Oath or Curfe was to be heard ; while Vollies of both (iffued from impious Mouths in the fame Squadron out of his Knowlege) feem'd to fill the Sails of other Ships with guilty Breath,

Breath, calling aloud for that Perdition to overtake them, which perhaps his worthy Injunctions and Example, in his own, might be of Weight to suspend

If such then, dear Sir, be the Force of a good Example, what have Parents to do, who are difpos'd to bring up a Child at home under their own Eye, according to Mr *Locke's* Advice, but, first, to have a strict Regard to *their own* Conduct? This will not want its due Influence on the Servants, efpecially if a proper Inquiry be made in o the r Cha, acters, before they are entertain'd, and a watchful Eye be had over them, to keep them up to thofe Characters afterwards And when they know they muft forfeit the Favour of a worthy Mafter, and their Places too, (which may be thought to be the reft of Places, becaufe an *uniform* Character muft make all around it eafy and happy) they will readily obferve fuch Rules and Directions as fhall be prefcribed to them. ---Rules and Directions, which their own Confciences will tell them are *right* to be prefcrib'd, and even *right* for them to follow, were they *not* infifted upon by their Superiors And this Conviction muft go a great way towards their *thorough* Reformation. For a Perfon wholly convinc'd, is half reform'd And thus the Hazard a Child will run of being corrupted by converfing with the Servants, will be remov'd, and all Mr *Locke's* other Rules be better inforc'd

I have the Boldnefs, Sir, to make another Objection, and that is, to the Diftance which Mr *Locke* prefcribes to be kept between Children and Servants: For may not this be a Means to fill the Minds of the former with a Contempt of thofe below them, and an Arrogance that is not warranted by any Rank or Condition, to their Inferiors of the fame Species?

I have

I have tranfcrib'd * what Mr *Locke* has injoined
in relation to this Diftance, where he fays, That the
Children are by all means to be kept *wholly* from
the Converfation of the meaner Servants ----But
how much better Advice does the fame Author
give for the Behaviour of Children to Servants in
the following Words? Which, I humbly prefume to
think, are not fo intirely confiftent with the former,
as might be expected from fo admirable an Author

'Another way, *fays he*, (§ 111 ) to inftil Senti-
'ments of Humanity, and to keep them lively in
'young Folks, will be, to accuftom them to Civi-
'lity in their Language and Deportment towards
'their Inferiors, and the meaner fort of People, par-
'ticularly Servants  It is not unufual to obferve the
'Children in Gentlemens Families treat the Servants
'of the Houfe with domineering Words, Names of
'Contempt, and an imperious Carriage, as if they
'were of another Race and Species beneath them.
'Whether ill Example, the Advantage of Fortune,
'or their natural Vanity, infpire this Haughtinefs, it
'fhould be prevented or weeded out, and a gentle,
'courteous, affable Carriage towards the lower Ranks
'of Men, placed in the Room of it  No Part of
'their Superiority, *continues this excellent Author,*
'will be hereby loft, but the Diftinction increa;'d,
'and their Authority ftrengthen'd, when Love in
'Inferiors is join'd to outward Refpect, and an
'Efteem of the Perfon has a Share in their Sub
'miffion  And Domefticks will pay a more ready
'and chearful Service, when they find themfelves
'not fpurn'd, becaufe Fortune has laid them below
'the Level of others at their Mafter's Feet'

Thefe, dear Sir, are certainly the Sentiments of
a generous and inlarg'd Spirit  But I hope I fhall

---

* *See p* 298, 299

be forgiven, if I obferve, that the great Diftance
Mr. *Locke* before injoins to be kept between Children and Servants, is not very confiftent with the
above-cited Paragraph: For if we would prevent
this undue Contempt of Inferiors in the Temper of
Children, the beft way, as I humbly prefume to
think, is not to make it fo unpardonable a Fault for
them, efpecially in their early Years, to be in their
Company. For can one make the Children fhun
the Servants, without rendering them odious or contemptible to them, and reprefenting them to the
Child in fuch difadvantageous Lights, as muft needs
make the Servants vile in their Eyes, and themfelves
lofty and exalted in their own? and thereby caufe
them to treat them with ' domineering Words, and
' an imperious Carriage, as if they were of another
' Race or Species beneath them, and fo, *as Mr.*
' *Locke fays,* nurfe up their natural Pride into an
' habitual Contempt of thofe beneath them And
' then, *as he adds,* where will that probably end, but
' in Oppreffion and Cruelty?'---But this Matter,
dear Sir, I prefume to think, will all be happily
accommodated and reconcil'd, when the Servants
good Behaviour is fecured by the Example and Injunctions of the Principals.

Upon the Whole, then, of what Mr. *Locke* has
injoin'd, and what I have taken the Liberty to fug-
geft on this Head, it fhall be my Endeavour, in that
early Part of your dear *Billy's* Education, which your
Goodnefs will intruft to me, to inculcate betimes in
his Mind the Principles of univerfal Benevolence and
Kindnefs to others, efpecially to Inferiors.

Nor, dear Sir, fhall I fear, that the little Dear will
be wanting to himfelf in affuming, as he grows up,
an Air of Superiority and Diftance of Behaviour equal
to his Condition, or that he will defcend too low
for his Station For, Sir, there is a Pride and Self-
Love natural to human Minds, that will feldom be

kept ſo low, as to make them humbler than they
ought to be

I have obſerv'd, before now, Inſtances of this,
in ſome of the Families we viſit, between the young
Maſters or Miſſes, and thoſe Children of lower De
gree, who have been brought to play with them, or
divert them. On the Maſters and Miſſes Side, I
have always ſeen, they lead the Play, and preſcribe
the Laws of it, be the Diverſion what it will,
while, on the other hand, their lower-rank Play
fellows have generally given into their little Humours,
tho' ever ſo contrary to their own, and the Difference of Dreſs and Appearance, and the Notion they
have of the more eminent Condition of their Play-
fellows Parents, have begot in them a kind of Awe
and Reſpect, that perhaps more than ſufficiently
ſecures the Superiority of the one, and the Subordi
nation of the other.

The Advantage of this univerſal Benevolence to
a young Gentleman, as he grows up, will be, as I
humbly conceive, that it will ſo diffuſe itſelf over
his Mind, as to influence all his Actions, and give a
Grace to every thing he does or ſays, and make him
admir'd and reſpected from the beſt and moſt du
rable Motives, and will be of greater Advantage to
him for his attaining a handſome Addreſs and Be
haviour, (for it will make him conſcious, that he
*merits* the Diſtinction he will meet with, and encourage him ſtill *more* to merit it) than the beſt Rule
that can be given him for that Purpoſe

I will therefore teach the little Dear Courteouſ
neſs and Affability, from the propereſt Motives I
am able to think of, and will inſtruct him in only
one Piece of Pride, That of being above doing a
mean or low Action. I will caution him not to
behave in a lordly or inſolent manner, even to the
loweſt Servants I will tell him, as I do my dear
Miſs *Goodwin*, That that Superiority is the moſt com
n.endable

mendable, and will be beſt maintained, that is owing to Humanity and Kindneſs, and which is grounded on the Perfections of the *Mind*, rather than on the *accidental* Advantages of *Fortune* and *Condition*. That it his Conduct be ſuch as it ought to be, there will be no Occaſion to tell a Servant, that he *will* be obſerv'd and reſpected. That *Humility*, as I once told my Miſs *Goodwin* \*, is a charming Grace, and moſt conſpicuouſly charming in Perſons of Diſtinction; for that the Poor, who are humbled by their Condition, cannot glory in it, as the Rich may; and that it makes the lower Ranks of People love and admire the High-born, who can ſo condeſcend. Whereas *Pride*, in ſuch, is Meanneſs and Inſult, as it owes its Boaſt and its Being to accidental Advantages, which, at the ſame time, are ſeldom of h.s procuring, who can be ſo mean as to be proud That even I would ſooner forgive Pride in a low Degree, than in an high, for it may be a Security in the firſt, againſt doing a baſe thing. But in the Rich, it is a baſe thing itſelf, and an impolitick one too, for the more Diſtinction a proud Mind graſps at, the leſs it will have, and every poor deſpiſed Perſon can whiſper ſuch an one in the Ear, when ſurrounded with, and adorned by, all his glittering Splendors, that he *was* born, and *muſt* die, in the *ſame manner* with thoſe whom he deſpiſes

Thus will the Doctrine of Benevolence and Affability, implanted early in the Mind of a young Gentleman, and duly cultivated as he grows up, inſpire him with the requiſite Conduct to command Reſpect from *proper* Motives, and at the ſame time that it will make the Servants obſerve a Decorum towards him, it will oblige them to have a Guard upon their Words and Actions in the Preſence of one, whoſe manner of Education and Training-up would be ſo great a

---

\* *See p* 264 *l* 10

Reproach

Reproach to them, if they were grofly faulty. So that hereby, as I conceive, a mutual Benefit will flow to the Manners of each, and *his* good Behaviour will render him, in fome meafure, an inftructive Monitor to the whole Family

But permit me, Sir, to inlarge on the Hint I have already given, in relation to the Example of Parents, in cafe a Preference be given to the Home Education   For if this Point cannot be fe-cur'd, I fhould always imagine it were beft to put the Child to fuch a School, as I have taken the Li-berty to mention *   But yet the Subject might be fpar'd by me in the prefent Cafe, as I write with a View only to your Family; though you will re-member, that while I follow Mr. *Locke*, whofe Work is publick, I muft be confider'd as if I was directing myfelf to the Generality of the World. For, Sir, I have the Pleafure to fay, That your Conduct in your Family is unexceptionable, and the Pride to think, that mine is no Difgrace to it.   No one hears a Word from your Mou h unbecoming the Character of a polite Gentleman, and I fhall always endeavour to be very regardful of what falls from mine   Your Temper, Sir, is equal and kind to all your Servants, and they love you, as well as awfully refpect you: And well does your Generofity, and bountiful and confiderate Mind, deferve it of them all · And they, feeing I am watchful over my own Conduct, fo as not to behave unworthy of your kind Example, re-gard me as much as I could wifh they fhould, for well do they know, that their beloved Mafter will have it fo, and greatly honours and efteems me him felf ---- Your Table-talk is fuch as Perfons of the ftricteft Principles may hear, and join in: Your Guefts, and your Friends, are, generally fpeaking, Perfons of the genteeleft Life, and of the beft Man-

* See p 299

ners

ners ---- So that Mr. *Locke* would have advis'd *you*, of all Gentlemen, had he been living, and known you, to give your Children a Home Education, and assign'd thefe, and still stronger, Reasons for it

But, dear Sir, were we to speak to the Generality of Parents, it is to be fear'd, this would be an almost insuperable Objection to a Home Education For (I am sorry to say it) when one turns one's Eyes to the bad Precedents given by the Heads of some Families, it is hardly to be wonder'd at, that there is so little Virtue and Religion among Men. For can those Parents be surpris'd at the Ungraciousness of their *Children*, who hardly ever shew them, that their *own* Actions are govern'd by reasonable or moral Motives? Can the gluttonous Father expect a self-denying Son? With how ill a Grace must a Man who will often be disguis'd in Liquor, preach Sobriety? A passionate Man, Patience? An irreligious Man Piety? How will a Parent, whose Hands are seldom without Cards or Dice in them, be observ'd in Leffons against the pernicious Vice of Gaming? Can the profuse Father, who is squandering away the Fortunes of his Children, expect to be regarded in a Leffon of Frugality? 'Tis impossible he should, except it were, that the Youth, seeing how pernicious his Father's Example is, should have the Grace to make a proper Use of it and look upon it as a Sea-mark, as it were, to enable him to shun the dangerous Rocks, on which he sees his Father splitting. And even in this *best* Case, let it be consider'd, how much Shame and Disgrace this thoughtless Parent ought to take to himself, who can admonish his Child by nothing but the *Odiousness* of his own Vice, and how little it is owing to him, that his Guilt is not *doubled*, by his Son's treading in his Steps! Let such an unhappy Parent duly weigh this, and think how likely he may be, by his bad Example, to be

the

the Caufe of his Child's Perdition, as well as his own, and ftand unfhock'd and unamended, if he can!

Give me Leave to add, That it is then of no Avail to wifh for difcreet Servants, if the Conduct of the Parens is faulty. If the Fountain head be polluted, how fhall the Under-currents run clear? That Mafter and Miftrefs, who would exact from their Servants a Behaviour which they themfelves don't practife, will be but ill obferv'd. And that Child, who difcovers great Exceffes and Errors in his Parents, will be found to be lefs profited by their good Precepts, than prejudic'd by their bad Examples. Exceffive Fondnefs this Hour, violent Paffions, and perhaps Execrations, the next, unguarded Jefts, an Admiration of fafhionable Vanities, rafh Cenfures, are perhaps the beft, that the Child fees in, or hears from, thofe who are moft concern'd to inculcate good Precepts into his Mind. And where it is fo, a Home Education is not by any means, furely, to be chofen.

Having thus, as well as my flender Abilities will permit, prefum'd to deliver my Opinion upon Three great Points, *viz.* The Qualifications of a Tutor, The Neceffity of having an Eye to the Morals of Servants, and, The Example of Parents (all which, being taken care of, will give a Preference, as I imagine, to a Home Education), permit me, dear Sir, to fpeak a little further to a Point, that I have already touched upon.

It is that of *Emulation*, which I humbly conceive to be of great Efficacy to lead Children on in their Duties and Studies. And how, dear Sir, fhall this Advantage be procur'd for a young Mafter, who has no Schoolfellows, and who has no Example to follow, but that of his Tutor, whom he cannot, from the Difparity of Years, and other Circumftances, without Pain, (becaufe of this Difparity) think of emulating?

emulating ? And this, I conceive, is a very great Advantage to fuch a School Education, as I mentioned in my former Letter \*, where there are no more Scholars taken in, than the Mafter can with Eafe and Pleafure inftruct.

But one way, in my humble Opinion, is left to anfwer this Objection, and ftill preferve the Reafon for the Preference which Mr. *Locke* gives to a Home Education, and that is, what I formerly hinted to you, dear Sir †, to take into your Family the Child of fome honeft Neighbour of but middling Circumftances, and like Age with your own, but who fhould give apparent Indications of his natural Promptitude, ingenuous Temper, obliging Behaviour, and good Manners; and to let him go hand-in hand with yours in his feveral Studies and Leffons under the fame Tutor.

This Child would be fenfible of the Benefit, as well as of the Diftinction he receiv'd, and confequently of what was expected from him, and would double his Diligence, and exert all his good Qualities, which would infpire the young Gentleman with the wifh'd-for Emulation, and, as I imagine, would be fo promotive of his Learning, that it would greatly compenfate the Tutor for his Pains with the additional Scholar, for the young Gentleman would be afham'd to be out-done by one of like Years and Stature with himfelf  And little Rewards might be propos'd to the greateft Proficient, in order to heighten the Emulation.

Then, Sir, permit me to add, That the *Generofity* of fuch a Method, to a Gentleman of your Fortune, and beneficent Mind, would be its own Reward, were there no other Benefit to be received from it

\* See p. 300      † See p. 127.

P 5                              More-

Moreover, fuch an ingenious Youth might, by his good Morals and Induftry, hereafter, be of Service in fome Place of Truft in the Family; or it would be eafy for a Gentleman of your Intereft in the World, if fuch a thing offer'd not, to provide for the Youth in the Navy, in fome of the publick Offices, or among your private Friends —— If he prov'd faulty in his Morals, his Difmiffion would be in your own Power, and would be Punifhment enough

But if, on the other hand, he prov'd a fober and hopeful Youth, fuch a one would make an excellent Companion for your *Billy* in riper Years; as he would be, in a manner, a Corroborator of his Morals; for, as his Circumftances would not fupport him in any Extravagance, fo thofe Circumftances would be a Check upon his Inclinations; and this being feconded by the Hopes of future Preferment from your Favour and Intereft, which he could not expect but upon the Terms of his Perfeverance in Virtue, he would find himfelf under a Neceffity of fetting fuch an Example, as might be of great Benefit to his Companion · Who fhould be watch'd as he grew up, that he did not (if his ample Fortune became dangerous to his Virtue) contribute out of his Affluence to draw the other after him into Extravagance And to this End, as I humbly conceive, the noble Doctrine of *Independence* fhould be early inftill'd into both their Minds, and, upon all Occafions, inculcated and inforc'd, which would be an Inducement for the one to endeavour to *improve* his Fortune by his honeft Induftry, left he fhould never be inabled to rife out of a State of Dependence; and to the other, to *keep*, if not to *improve*, his own, left he fhould ever fall into fuch a fervile State, and thereby lofe the glorious Power of conferring Obligations on the Deferving, which furely is one of the higheft Pleafures that a generous Mind can know.

A Plea-

A Pleasure, Sir, which you have oftener experienc'd than Thousands of Gentlemen. And which may you still-continue to experience for a long, long, and happy Succession of Years to come, is the Prayer of one, the most oblig'd of all others in her own Person, as well as in the Persons of her dearest Relations, and who owes to this glorious Beneficence the Honour she boasts, of being

*Your ever dutiful and grateful*

P B:

## LETTER LIII.

BUT now, my dear Mr. *B* if you will indulge me in a Letter or two more, preparative to my little Book, that I mention'd, I will take the Liberty to touch upon one or two other Places, wherein I differ from this learned Gentleman. But, first, permit me to observe, that if Parents are, above all things, to avoid giving bad Examples to their Children, they will be no less careful to shun the Practice of such fond Fathers and Mothers, as are wont to indulge their Children in bad Habits, and give them their Head, at a time when, like Wax, their tender Minds may be moulded into what Shape they please This is a Point, that, if it please G O D, I will carefully attend to, because it is the Foundation, on which the Superstructure of the whole future Man is to be erected For, according as he is indulg'd or check'd in his childish Follies, a Ground is laid for his future Happiness or Misery, and if once they are suffer'd to become habitual to him, it cannot but be expected, that they will grow up with him, and that they will hardly ever be eradicated. ' Try it, *says Mr.* Locke, *speaking to this very Point,* ' in a Dog, or a Horse, or any other Creature;

P 6 ' and

'and fee whether the ill and refty Tricks they have
'learn'd when young, are eafily to be mended, when
'they are knit  And yet none of thefe Creatures
'are half fo wilful and proud, or half fo defirous to
'be Mafters of themfelves, as Men.'

And this brings me, dear Sir, to the Head of
*Punifhments*, in which, as well as in the Article of
*Rewards*, which I have touch'd upon, I have a little
Objection to what Mr *Locke* advances

But permit me, however, to premife, that I am
exceedingly pleafed with the Method laid down by
this excellent Writer, rather to fhame the Child out
of his Fault, than beat him; which latter ferves generally for nothing but to harden his Mind

*Obftinacy*, and telling a *Lye*, and committing a
*wilful* Fault, and then *perfifting* in it, are, I agree
with this Gentleman, the only Caufes for which the
Child fhould be punifh'd with Stripes  And I admire
the Reafons he gives againft a too rigorous and fevere
Treatment of Children

But I will give Mr *Locke's* Words, to which I
have fome Objection

'It may be doubted, *fays he*, concerning Whip-
'ping, when, as the *laft* Remedy, it comes to be
'neceffary, at *what time*, and by *whom*, it fhould
'be done, whether prefently, upon the committing
'the Fault, whilft it is yet frefh and hot----I think it
'fhould not be done prefently, *adds he*, left Paffion
'mingle with it, and fo, tho' it exceed the juft Pro-
'portion, yet it lofe of its due Weight  For even
'Children difcern whenever we do things in a
'Paffion'

I muft beg Leave, dear Sir, to differ from Mr
*Locke* in this Point, for I think it ought rather to
be a Rule with Parents, who fhall chaftife their
Children, to conquer what would be extreme in
*their own* Paffion on this Occafion, (for thofe Pa
rents, who cannot do it, are very unfit to be Pu-
nifhers

nifhers of the wayward Paffions of their Children) than to *defer* the Punifhment, efpecially if the Child knows its Fault has reach'd its Parents Ear. It is otherwife, methinks, giving the Child, if of an obftinate Difpofition, fo much more Time to harden its Mind, and bid Defiance to its Punifhment

Juft now, dear Sir, your *Billy* is brought into my Prefence, all fmiling, crowing to come to me, and full of heart-chearing Promifes , and the Subject I am upon goes to my Heart   Surely, furely, I can never beat your *Billy* ! --- Dear little Life of my Life ! how can I think that thou canft ever deferve it, or that I can ever inflict it ? --- No, my Baby, that fhall be thy Papa's Task, if ever thou art fo heinoufly naughty , and whatever *he* does, muft be right ---- Pardon my foolifh Fondnefs, dear Sir ! --- I will proceed.

If then, the Fault be fo atrocious as to deferve Whipping, and the Parent be refolv'd on this exemplary Punifhment, the Child ought not, as I imagine, to come into one's Prefence without meeting with it : For elfe, a Fondnefs too natural to be refifted, will probably get the Upper-hand of one's Refentment, and how fhall one be able to whip the dear Creature one hath ceafed to be angry with ? Then after he has once feen one without meeting his Punifhment, will he not be inclin'd to hope for Connivance at his Fault, unlefs it fhould be repeated? And may he not be apt (for Childrens Refentments are ftrong) to impute to Cruelty, a Correction, (when he thought the Fault had been forgotten) that fhould always appear to be inflicted with Reluctance, and thro' Motives of Love ?

If, from Anger at his Fault, one fhould go *above the due Proportion,* (I am fure I might be trufted for this !) let it take its Courfe ! --- How barbaroufly, methinks, I fpeak ! --- He ought to *feel* the Lafh, firft, Becaufe he *deferves* it, poor little Soul ! Next, Becaufe

caufe it is *propos'd* to be exemplary  And laftly, Becaufe it is not intended to be *often* us'd : And the
very Paffion or Difpleafure one expreffes, (if it be
not enormous) will fhew one is in Earneft, and
create in him a neceffary Awe, and make him be
afraid to offend again  The *End* of the Correction
is to fhew him the Difference betwixt Right and
Wrong  And as it is proper to take him at his firft
Offer of a full Submiffion and Repentance, (and not
before) and inftantly difpaffionate one's felf, and fhew
him the Difference by Acts of Pardon and Kindnefs, (which will let him fee, that one punifhes him
out of Neceffity rather than Choice) fo one would
not be afraid to make him fmart fo fufficiently, that
he fhould not foon forget the Severity of the Difcipline, nor the Difgrace of it.  There's a cruel Mamma
for you, Mr *B* ! What my *Practice* may be, I can't
tell, but this *Theory*, I prefume to think, is right

As to the *Act* itfelf, I much approve Mr *Locke's*
Advice, to do it by Paufes, mingling Stripes and
Expoftulations together, to fhame and terrify the
more ; and the rather, as the Parent, by this flow
manner of inflicting the Punifhment, will lefs need
to be afraid of giving too violent a Correction ; for
thofe Paufes will afford *him*, as well as the *Child*,
Opportunities for Confideration and Reflection

But as to the *Perfon*, by whom the Difcipline
fhould be perform'd, I humbly conceive, that this
excellent Author is here alfo to be objected to

‘ If you have a difcreet Servant, *fays he*, capable
‘ of it, and has the Place of governing your Child,
‘ (for if you have a Tutor, there is no Doubt) I think
‘ it is beft the Smart fhould come immediately from
‘ another's Hand, tho' by the Parent's Order, who
‘ fhould fee it done, whereby the Parent's Autho-
‘ rity will be preferv'd, and the Child's Averfion for
‘ the Pain it fuffers, rather be turned on the Perfon
‘ that immediately inflicts it.  For I would have a
‘ Father

‘ Father feldom ftrike the Child, but upon very
‘ urgent Neceffity, and as the laft Remedy’

’Tis in fuch an urgent Cafe, dear Sir, that we are
fuppofing it fhould be done at all  If there be not
a Reafon ftrong enough for the Father’s whipping the
Child himfelf, there cannot be any fufficient for his
ordering any other to do it, and ftanding by to fee
it done : But, I humbly prefume to think, that if
there be a Neceffity for it, no one can be fo fit as
the Father himfelf to do it   The Child cannot difpute *his* Authority to punifh, from whom he receives
and expects all the good Things of this Life . He
cannot queftion *his* Love to him, and, after the
Smart is over, and his Obedience fecur’d, muft believe
that fo tender, fo indulgent a Father, could have no
other End in whipping him, but his Good   Againft
*him*, he knows, he has no Remedy, but muft paf-
fively fubmit ; and when he is convinc’d he *muft*,
he will in time conclude, that he *ought.*

But to have this fevere Office perform’d by a
Servant, tho’ at the Father’s Command , and that
profeffedly, that the Averfion of the Child for the
Pain it fuffers, fhould be turn’d on the Perfon who
immediately inflicts it, is, I am humbly of Opinion,
the *Reverfe* of what ought to be done   And *more*
fo, if this Servant has any Direction of the Child’s
Education ; and ftill *much* more fo, if it be his Tutor,
notwithftanding Mr. *Locke* fays, there is no Doubt,
if there be a Tutor, that it fhould be done by him.

For, dear Sir, is there no Doubt, that the Tutor
fhould lay himfelf open to the Averfion of the Child,
whofe Manners he is to form ? Is it not the beft
Method a Tutor can take, in order to inforce the
Leffons he would inculcate, to endeavour to attract
the Love and Attention of his Pupil by the moft
winning, mild, and inviting Ways that he can poffibly think of ? And yet is *he*, this very Tutor, *out*
*of all Doubt*, to be the Inftrument of doing an harfh
and.

and difgraceful thing, and that in the laft Reforc,
when all other Methods are found ineffectual, and
that too, becaufe he ought to incur the Child's Refentment and Averfion, rather than the Father? No,
furely, Sir, it is not reafonable it fhould be fo. Quite
contrary, in my humble Notion, there can be no
Doubt, but that it fhould be *otherwife*

It fhould, methinks, be enough for a Tutor, in
cafe of a Fault in the Child, to threaten to complain
to his Father, but yet not to make fuch Complaint,
without the Child obftinately perfifts in his Error,
which, too, fhould be of a Nature to merit fuch an
Appeal · And this, methinks, would highly contribute to preferve the Parent's Authority, who, on
this Occafion, fhould never fail of extorting a Promife of Amendment, or of inftantly punifhing him
with his own Hands. And, to foften the Diftafte
he might conceive in Refentment of too rigid Complainings, it might not, poffibly, be amifs, that his
Interpofition in the Child's Favour, if the Fault were
not too flagrant, fhould be permitted to five him
once or twice from the impending Difcipline

'Tis certain, that the Paffions, if I may fo call
them, of Affection and Averfion are very early dif-
coverable in Children, infomuch that they will,
even before they can fpeak, afford us Marks for the
Detection of an hypocritical Appearance of Love
to it before the Parents Faces  For the Fondnefs
or Averfenefs of the Child to fome Servants, as I
have obferved in other Families, will at any time let
one know, whether their Love to the Baby is uniform
and the fame, when one is abfent, as prefent  In
one Cafe the Child will reject with Sullennefs all the
little Sycophancies, that are made to it in one's Sight,
while, on the other, its Fondnefs of the Perfon, who
generally obliges it, is an infallible Rule to judge of
fuch a one's Sincerity behind one's Back  This
little Obfervation fhews the Strength of a Child's
　　　　　　　　　　　　　　　　　　　Refent

Resentments, and its Sagacity, at the earliest Age, in discovering who obliges, and who disobliges it. And hence one may infer, how improper a Person *he is*, whom we would have a Child to love and respect, or by whose Precepts we would have it directed, to be the Punisher of its Faults, or to do any harsh or disagreeable Office to it

For my own Part, dear Sir, I must take the Liberty to declare, that if the Parent were not to inflict the Punishment himself, I think it much better it should be given him, in the Parent's Presence, by the Servant of the lowest Consideration in the Family, and whose Manners and Example one would be the least willing of any other he should follow Just as the common Executioner, who is the lowest and most flagitious Officer of the Commonwealth, and who frequently deserves, as much as the Criminal, the Punishment he is chosen to inflict, is pitch'd upon to perform, as a Mark of greater Ignominy, those Sentences which are intended as Examples to deter others from the Commission of heinous Crimes. And this was the Method the Almighty took, when he was dispos'd to correct severely his chosen People. For in that Case He generally did it by the Hands of the most profligate Nations around them, as we read in many Places of the Old Testament.

But the following Rule, among a thousand others, equally excellent, I admire in Mr. *Locke* ' When, ' *says he,* (for any Misdemeanour) the Father or ' Mother looks sour on the Child, every one else ' should put on the same Coldness to him, and no- ' body give him Countenance till Forgiveness ask'd, ' and a Reformation of his Fault has set him right ' again, and restor'd him to his former Credit If ' this were constantly observ'd, *adds he,* I guess there ' would be little Need of Blows or Chiding Their ' own Ease or Satisfaction would quickly teach Chil- ' dren to court Commendation, and avoid doing
' that

' that which they found every body condemn'd, and
' they were sure to suffer for, without being chid
' or beaten  This would teach them Modesty and
' Shame, and they would quickly come to have a
' natural Abhorrence for that which they found made
' them slighted and neglected by every body '

This affords me, dear Sir, a pretty Hint  For if
ever your charming *Billy* shall be naughty, what
will I do, but proclaim throughout your worthy Family, that the little Dear is in Disgrace ! And one
shall shun him, another shall decline answering him,
a third shall say, No, Master, I cannot obey you,
till your Mamma is pleas'd with you . A fourth,
Who should mind what little Masters bid them do,
when little Masters won't mind what their Mamma's
say to them ? And when the dear little Soul finds
this, he will come in my Way, (and I see, pardon
me, my dear Mr. *B* he has some of his Papa's Spirit
already, indeed he has !) and I will direct myself with
double Kindness to your beloved *Davers*, and to my
Miss *Goodwin*, and take no Notice at all of the
dear Creature, if I can help it, till I see his *Papa*
(forgive my Boldness) banished from his little sullen
Brow, and all his *Mamma* rise to his Eyes. And
when his musical Tongue shall be unlock'd to own
his Fault, and promise Amendment---O then ' how
shall I clasp him to my Bosom ' and Tears of Joy,
I know, will meet his Tears of Penitence'

How these Flights, dear Sir, please a body '---
What Delights have those Mamma's, (which some
fashionable Ladies are quite unacquainted with) who
can make their dear Babies, and their first Educa-
tions, their Entertainment and Diversion ! To watch
the Dawnings of Reason in them, to direct their
little Passions, as they shew themselves, to this or
that particular Point of Benefit and Use, and to
prepare the sweet Virgin Soil of their Minds to receive
the Seeds of Virtue and Goodness so early, that as
they

they grow up, one need only now a little Pruning, and now a little Watering, to make them the Ornaments and Delights of the Garden of this Life! And then their pretty Ways, their fond and grateful Endearments, some new Beauty every Day rising to Observation——O my dearest Mr *B* whose Enjoyments and Pleasures are so great, as those of such Mamma's as can bend their Minds, two or three Hours every Day, to the Duties of the Nursery?

I have a few other Things to observe upon Mr. *Locke's* Treatise, which when I have done, I shall read, admire, and improve by the rest, as my Years and Experiences advance, of which, in my propos'd little Book, I shall give you better Proofs than I am able to do at present, raw, crude, and indigested as the Notions of so young a Mamma must needs be.

But these shall be the Subjects of another Letter, for now I am come to the Pride and the Pleasure I always have, when I subscribe myself, dearest Sir,

*Your ever dutiful and grateful*

P. B.

## LETTER LIV.

*Dear Sir,*

MR. *Locke* gives a great many very pretty Instructions relating to the Play-games of Children, but I humbly presume to object to what he says, in one or two Places.

He would not indulge them in any Playthings, but what they make themselves, or endeavour to make 'A smooth Pebble, a Piece of Paper, the 'Mother's Bunch of Keys, or any thing they cannot 'hurt themselves with, *he rightly says,* serves as 'much to divert little Children, as those more
'chargeable

' chargeable and curious Toys from the Shops,
' which are presently put out of Order, and broken '

These Playthings may certainly do well enough, as he observes, for little ones But, methinks, to a Person of easy Circumstances, since the making these Toys imploys the industrious Poor, the buying them for the Child might be dispens'd with, tho' they *were* easily broken, and especially as they are of all Prices, and some less costly, and more durable, than others

' Tops, Gigs, Battledors, *Mr* Locke *observes,*
' which are to be used with Labour, should indeed
' be procur'd them --- not for Variety, but Exercise
' But if they had a Top, the Scourge-stick and Lea-
' ther-strap should be left to their own making and
' fitting.'

But may I presume to say, That whatever be the Good Mr *Locke* proposes by this, it cannot be equal to the Mischief Children may do themselves in making these Playthings ? For must they not have Implements to work with ? And is not a Knife, or other edg'd Tool, without which it is impossible they can make or shape a Scourge-stick, or *any* of their Playthings, a fine Instrument in a Child's Hands ? This Advice is the Reverse of the Caution warranted from all Antiquity, *That it is dangerous to meddle with edg'd Tools* · And I am afraid, the Tutor must often act the Surgeon, and follow the Indulgence with a Styp- tick and a Plaister, and the young Gentleman's Hands might be so often bound up, that it might indeed perhaps be one way to cure him of his earnest Desire to play, but I can hardly imagine any other Good that it can do him For, I doubt, the excellent Con- sequences propos'd by our Author from this Doctrine, such as to teach the Child Moderation in his Desires, Application, Industry, Thought, Contrivance, and good Husbandry, Qualities that, as he observes, will be useful to him when he is a Man, are too remote to be ingrafted upon such Beginnings · Altho' it must be confessed, that, as Mr *Locke* wisely observes, good Habits and Industry cannot be too early inculcated

But then, Sir, may I ask, Are not the very Plays and Sports, to which Children accustom themselves, whether they make their own Playthings or not, equivalent to the Work or Labour of grown Persons ? Yes, Sir, I will venture to say, they are, and more than equivalent to the Exercises and Labour of many

Mr. *Locke* advises, that the Child's Playthings should be as few as possible, in which I intirely agree with him : That they should be in his Tutor's Power, who is to give him but one at once  But since it is the Nature of the human Mind to court most what is prohibited, and to set light by what is in its own Power ; I am half doubtful, (only that Mr *Locke* says it, and the Matter may not be so very important, as other Points, in which I have taken the Liberty to differ from that Gentleman) Whether the Child's absolute Possession of his own Playthings in some little Repository, of which he may be permitted to keep the Key, especially if he make no bad Use of the Privilege, would not make him more indifferent to them , while the contrary Conduct might possibly inhance his Value of them   And if, when he had done with any Plaything, he were oblig'd to put it into its allotted Place, and were accustom'd to keep Account of the Number and Places of them severally, this would teach him Order, and at the same time instruct him to keep a proper Account of them, and to avoid being a Squanderer or Waster  And if he should omit to put his Playthings in their Places, or be careless of them, the taking them away for a time, or threatening to give them to others, would make him be more heedful

Mr

Mr. *Locke* fays, ' That he has known a Child fo
' diftracted with the Number and Variety of his
' Playthings, that he tired his Maid every Day to
' look them over · And was fo accuftom'd to Abun-
' dance, that he never thought he had Enough, but
' was always asking, What more? What new thing
' fhall I have? A good Introduction, *adds he, iron-*
' *cally*, to moderate Defires, and the ready way to
' make a contented happy Man!'

All that I fhall offer to this, is, that there are few
*Men* fo philofophical as one would wifh them to
be; much lefs *Children*. But no Doubt, that this
Variety engag'd the Child's Activity, which, of the
two, might be turn'd to better Purpofes, than Sloth
or Indolence, and if the Maid was tired, it might
be, becaufe fhe was not fo much *alive*, as the Child,
and perhaps this Part of the Grievance might not be
fo great, becaufe, if fhe was his Attendant, 'tis probable fhe had nothing elfe to do.

However, in the main, as Mr *Locke* fays, it is
no matter how few Playthings the Child is indulg'd
with · But yet I can hardly perfuade myfelf, that
Plenty of them can have fuch bad Confequences, as
the Gentleman apprehends, and the rather, becaufe
they will excite his Attention, and promote his Induftry and Activity His Inquiry after new Things,
let him have few or many, is to be expected as a
Confequence of thofe natural Defires, which are implanted in him, and will every Day increafe · But
this may be obferv'd, That as he grows in Years, he
will be above fome Playthings, and fo the Number
of the old ones will be always reducible, perhaps, in
a greater Proportion, than the new ones will increafe

Mr *Locke* obferves, on the Head of good Breeding, That ' There are two Sorts of ill Breeding, the
' one a fheepifh Bafhfulnefs, and the other a mif-
' becoming Negligence and Difrefpect in our Car-
' riage,

' riage, both which, *says he,* are avoided by duly
' obferving this one Rule, Not to think meanly of
' ourfelves, and not to think meanly of others.' I
think, as Mr. *Locke* explains this Rule, it is an excellent one. But on this Head I would beg Leave to
obferve, that however difcommendable a bafhful
Temper is, in fome Inftances, where it muft be
deem'd a Weaknefs of the Mind, yet, in my humble
Opinion, it is generally the Mark of an ingenious
one, and is always to be preferr'd to an undiftin-
guifhing and hardy Confidence, which, as it feems
to me, is the genuine Production of invincible Ignorance

What is faulty in it, which Mr. *Locke* calls *Sheep-
ifhnefs,* fhould indeed be fhaken off as foon as poffible, becaufe it is an Enemy to Merit in its Advance-
ment in the World But, Sir, were I to chufe a
Companion for your *Billy,* as he grows up, I fhould
not think the worfe of the Youth, who, not having
had the Opportunities of knowing Men, or feeing
the World, had this Defect. On the contrary, I
fhould be apt to look upon it as an outward Fence
or Inclofure, as I may fay, to his Virtue, which might
keep off the lighter Attacks of Immorality, the *Huffars*
of Vice, as I may fay, who are not able to carry on
a formal Siege againft his Morals, and I fhould expect
fuch an one to be docile, humane, good-humour'd,
diffident of himfelf, and therefore moft likely to improve as well in Mind as Behaviour · While a harden'd Mind, that never doubts itfelf, muft be a
Stranger to its own Infirmities, and, fufpecting none,
is impetuous, over-bearing, incorrigible, and if rich,
a Tyrant, if not, poffibly an Invader of other Mens
Properties, or at leaft, fuch a one, as allows itfelf
to walk fo near the Borders of Injuftice, that,
where *Self* is concern'd, it hardly ever does right
things.

Mr

Mr *Locke* proposes (§ 148) a very pretty Method to chear Children, as it were, into Learning But then, he adds, ' There may be Dice and Playthings ' with the Letters on them to teach Children the ' Alphabet by playing' And in another Place, (§ 151) ' I know a Person of great Quality --- who ' by pasting on the six Vowels (for in our Language ' *y* is one) on the six Sides of a Die, and the re- ' maining eighteen Consonants on the Sides of three ' other Dice, has made this a Play for his Children, ' that *he* shall win, who at one Cast throws most ' Words on these four Dice, whereby his eldest Son, ' yet in Coats, has *play'd* himself *into Spelling* with ' great Eagerness, and without once having been ' chid for it, or forc'd to it'

I must needs say, my dear Mr *B* that I had rather your *Billy* should be a Twelvemonth backwarder for want of this Method, than forwarded by it For what may not be apprehended from so early allow- ing, or rather inculcating the Use of Dice and Ga- ming upon the Minds of Children? Let Mr *Locke* himself speak to this in his § 208 and I should be glad to be able to reconcile the two Passages in this excellent Author - - ' As to Cards and Dice, *says he*, ' I think the safest and best way, is, never to learn ' any Play upon them, and so to be incapacitated ' for these dangerous Temptations, and incroaching ' Wasters of useful Time' --- and, he might have added, of the noblest Estates and Fortunes, while Sharpers and Scoundrels have been lifted into Di- stinction upon their Ruins Yet, in § 153 Mr *Locke* proceeds to give particular Directions in rela tion to the Dice he recommends

But, after all, if some innocent Plays were fix'd upon to cheat Children into Reading, that, as he says, should look as little like a Task as possible, it must needs be of Use for that Purpose But let every Gentleman, who has a Fortune to lose, and who, as he the games, is on a Foot with the vileſt Company, who generally have nothing at all to riſque, tremble at the Thoughts of teaching his Son, tho' for the moſt laudable Purpoſes, the early Uſe of Dice and Gaming.

But, dear Sir, permit me to ſay, how much I am charm'd with a Hint in Mr *Locke,* which makes your *Pamela* hope, ſhe may be of greater Uſe to your Children, even as they *grow up,* than ſhe could ever have flatter'd herſelf to be. - - 'Tis a charming Paragraph; I muſt not skip one Word of it Thus it begins, and I will obſerve upon it as I go along. ' §177 But under whoſe Care ſoever a Child is ' put to be taught, *ſays* Mr Locke, during the ' tender and flexible Years of his Life, this is certain, ' it ſhould be one, who thinks *Latin* and Language ' the leaſt Part of Education '

How agreeable is this to my Notions, which I durſt not have avow'd, but after ſo excellent a Scholar ! For I have long had the Thought, that a great deal of precious Time is waſted to little Purpoſe in the Attaining of *Latin.* Mr *H.* I think, ſays, he was Ten Years in endeavouring to learn it, and, as far as I can find, knows nothing at all of the Matter neither¹ ---- Indeed he lays that to the wicked Picture in his Grammar, which he took for granted, (as he has ſaid ſeveral times, as well as once written) was put there to teach Boys to rob Orchards, inſtead of improving their Minds in Learning, or common Honeſty

But (for this is too light an Inſtance for the Subject) Mr *Locke* proceeds---- ' One who, knowing ' how much Virtue and a well-temper'd Soul is to ' be preferr'd to any ſort of *Learning* or *Language,* ' [*What a noble Writer is this* ¹] makes it his chief ' Buſineſs to form the Mind of his Scholars, and ' give that a right Diſpoſition . [*Ay there, dear Sir,*

' *is the Thing* '] Which if once got, tho' all the reft
' fhould be neglected, [*charmingly obferv'd* !] would
' in *due time*, [*without wicked Dice*, *I hope* '] pro
' duce all the reft, and which if it be not got and
' fettled, fo as to keep out ill and vicious Habits,
' *Languages* and *Sciences*, and all the other Accom-
' plifhments of Education, will be to no Purpofe, but
' to make the worfe or more dangerous Man
' [*Now comes the Place I am fo much delighted with* !]
' And indeed, whatever Stir there is made about
' getting of *Latin*, as the great and difficult Bufinefs,
' his Mother [*O thank you, thank you, dear Sir,*
' *for putting this excellent Author into my Hands* ']
' may teach it him herfelf, if fhe will but fpend
' two or three Hours in a Day with him, [---*If fhe*
' *will*? *Never fear, dear Sir, but I will, with the*
' *higheft Pleafure in the World* '] and make him read
' the Evangelifts in *Latin* to her [*How I long to be*
' *five or fix Years older, as well as my deareft Babies,*
' *that I may enter upon this charming Scheme!*] For
' fhe need but buy a *Latin* Teftament, and having
' got fomebody to mark the laft Syllable but one,
' where it is long, in Words above two Syllables,
' (which is enough to regulate her Pronunciation
' and Accenting the Words) read daily in the Gofpels,
' and then let her avoid underftanding them in
' *Latin*, if fhe can.'

Why, deareft, dear Sir, you have taught me
almoft all this already, and you, my beft and moft
beloved Tutor, have told me often, I read and pronounce *Latin* more than tolerably, tho' I don't underftand it But this Method will teach *me*, as well
as your dear *Children*. But thus the good Gentleman proceeds ' And when fhe underftands the
' Evangelifts in *Latin*, let her in the fame manner
' read *Æfop*'s Fables, and fo proceed on to *Eutro-*
' *pius*, *Juftin*, and fuch other Books. I do not mention
' this,

'this, *adds Mr Locke*, as an Imagination of what I
'fanfy *may* do, but as of a thing I have *known* done,
'and the *Latin* Tongue got with Eafe this way'

Mr *Locke* proceeds to mention other Advantages,
which the Child may receive from his Mother's Inftruction, which I will endeavour more and more to
qualify myfelf for· Particularly, after he has intimated, That 'At the fame time that the Child is
'learning *French* and *Latin*, he may be enter'd alfo in
'Arithmetick, Geography, Chronology, Hiftory, and
'Geometry too, for if, *fays he*, thefe be taught him
'in *French* or *Latin*, when he begins once to un-
'derftand either of thefe Tongues, he will get a
'Knowlege in thefe Sciences, and the Language to
'boot' After he has intimated this, I fay, he pro-
ceeds· 'Geography, I think, fhould be begun with:
'For the learning of the Figure of the Globe, the
'Situation and Boundaries of the Four Parts of the
'World, and that of particular Kingdoms and Coun-
'tries, being only an Exercife of the Eyes and Memo-
'ry, a Child with Pleafure will learn and retain them.
'And this is fo certain, that I now live in a Houfe
'with a Child, whom his MOTHER has fo well
'inftructed this way in Geography, [*But had fhe*
'*not, do you think, dear Sir, fome of this good Gen-*
'*tleman's kind Affiftance* ?] that he knew the Limits
'of the Four Parts of the World, would readily
'point, being ask'd, to any Country upon the Globe,
'or any County in the Map of *England*, knew all
'the great Rivers, Promontories, Streights, and Bays
'in the World, and could find the Longitude and
'Latitude of any Place, before he was Six Years old'

There's for you, dear Sir!--- See what a Mother
can do, if fhe pleafes '

I remember, Sir, formerly, in that fweet * Chariot Conference, at the Dawning of my Hopes,

* *See* Vol. II *p.* 61—65.

when

when all my Dangers were happily over, (a Conference I shall always think of with Pleasure) that you ask'd me, How I would bestow my Time, supposing the neighbouring Ladies would be above being seen in my Company; when I should have no Visits to receive or return; no Parties of Pleasure to join in; no Card-tables to imploy my Winter Evenings?

I then, Sir, transported with my opening Prospects, prattled to you, how well I would endeavour to pass my Time in the Family Management and Accounts, in Visits now-and-then to the indigent and worthy Poor, in Musick sometimes, in Reading, in Writing, in my superior Duties --- And I hope I have not behaved quite unworthily of my Promises

But I also remember, dear Sir, what once you said on a certain Occasion, which *now*, since the fair Prospect is no longer distant, and that I have been so long your happy, thrice happy Wife, I may repeat without those Blushes which then cover'd my Face. Thus then, with a *modest* Grace, and with that *virtuous* Endearment, that is so *beautiful* in *your* Sex, as well as in *ours*, whether in the Character of Lover or Husband, Maiden or Wife, you were pleased to say, ' And I hope, my *Pamela*, to ' have superadded to all these, such an Imployment' ---- as --- in short, Sir, I am now bless'd with, and writing of, no less than the useful Part I may be able to take in the first Education of your beloved Babes!

And now I must add, That this pleasing Hope sets me above all other Diversions I wish for no Parties or Pleasure but with you, my dearest Mr *B* and these are Parties that will improve me, and make me more capable of the other, and more worthy of your Conversation, and of the Time you pass (beyond what I could ever have promised to my utmost Wishes) in such poor Company as mine, to no other Reaſon but becauſe I love to be inſtructed, and take my Leſſons well, as you are pleas'd to ſay And indeed I muſt be a ſad Dunce, if I did not, from ſo skilful and ſo beloved a Maſter

I want no Card-table Amuſements   For I hope, in a few Years, (and a proud Hope it is) to be able to teach your dear Little-ones the firſt Rudiments, as Mr *Locke* points the Way, of *Latin,* of *French,* and of Geography, and Arithmetick

O my dear Mr. *B* by your Help and Countenance, what may I not be able to teach them! and how may I prepare the Way for a Tutor's Inſtructions, and give him up Minds half cultivated to his Hands! --- And all this time improve myſelf too, not only in Science, but in Nature, by tracing in the little Babes what all Mankind are, and have been, from Infancy to riper Years, and watching the ſweet Dawnings of Reaſon, and delighting in every bright Emanation of that Ray of Divinity lent to the human Mind, for great and happy Purpoſes, when rightly pointed and directed!

There is going no further in this Letter, after theſe charming Recollections and Hopes. For they bring me to that grateful Remembrance, to whom, under GOD, I owe them all, and alſo what I have been for ſo happy a Period, and what I am, which is, what will be ever my Pride and my Glory, and well it may, when I look back to my Beginning, which I ever ſhall, with humble Acknowlegement, and can call myſelf, deareſt Mr. *B.*

*Your honoured and honouring,*

*and, I hope I may ſay,*

*in time, uſeful Wife,*

P. B.

## LETTER LV.

*My dearest Mr B*

HAving in my former Letters said as much as is
necessary to let you into my Notion of the
excellent Book you put into my Hands, and having
touch'd those Points in which the Children of both
Sexes may be concern'd, (with some *Art* in my In
tention, I own) in Hopes that they would not be so
much out of the way, as to make you repent of the
Honour and Pleasure you have done me in committing the dear Miss *Goodwin* to my Care, I shall
now very quickly set myself about the little Book
which I have done myself the Honour to mention
to you.

   You have been so good as to tell me, (at the same
time that you have not disapprov'd these my Specimen Letters, as I may call them) that you will
kindly accept of my intended Present, and you encourage me to proceed in it; and as I shall leave
one Side of the Leaf blank for your Corrections and
Alterations, those Corrections will be a fine Help
and Instruction to me in the pleasing Task, which I
propose to myself, of assisting in the early Education
of the dear Children, which it has pleased GOD to
give you    And as, possibly, I may be Years in write-
ing it, as the dear Babies improve, and as I myself improve, by the Opportunities which their Ad
vances in Years will give me, and the Experience I
shall gain, I shall then, perhaps, venture to give my
Notions and Observations on the more material and
nobler Parts of Education, as well as the inferior
For (but that I think the Subjects above my present
Abilities) Mr *Locke*'s Book would lead me into several Remarks, that might not be 'unuseful, and which
appear to me intirely new, tho' that may be owing
to my slender Reading and Opportunities, perhaps
                                                      But

But what, my deareft Mr *B* I would now touch upon, is a Word or two ftill more particularly upon the Education of my own Sex, a Topick which naturally rifes to me from the Subject of my laft Letter For there, dear Sir, we faw, that the Mothers might teach the Child *this* Part of Science, and *that* Part of Inftruction, and who, I pray, as our Sex is generally educated, fhall teach the *Mothers?* How, in a Word, fhall *they* come by their Knowlege?

I know you'll be apt to fay, That Mifs *Goodwin* gives all the Promifes of becoming a fine young Lady, and takes her Learning, and loves Reading, and makes very pretty Reflections upon all fhe reads, and asks very pertinent Queftions, and is as knowing, at her Years, as moft young Ladies This is very true, Sir; but it is not every one that can boaft Mifs *Goodwin's* Capacity, and Goodnefs of Temper, which have enabled her to get up a good deal of *loft* Time, as I muft call it, for the firft Four Years in the dear Child were a perfect Blank, as far as I can find, juft as if the pretty Dear was born the Day fhe was Four Years old · For what fhe had to *unlearn* as to Temper, and Will, and fuch things, fet againft what little Improvements fhe had made, might very fairly be compounded for, as a Blank

I would indeed have a Mifs brought up to her Needle, but I would not have *all* her Time imploy'd in Samplers, and learning to mark, and to do thofe unneceffary things, which fhe will never, probably, be call'd upon to practife.

And why, pray, my dear Mr *B.* are not Girls intitled to the fame *firft* Education, tho' not to the fame Plays and Diverfions, as Boys, fo far at leaft, as it is fuppofed by Mr. *Locke* a Mother can inftruct them?

Would not this lay a Foundation for their future Improvement, and direct their Inclinations to ufeful

Subjects,

Subjects, such as would make them above the Imputations of some unkind Gentlemen, who allot to their Parts common Tea-table Prattle, while they do all they can to make them fit for nothing else, and then upbraid them for it? And would not the Men find us better and more suitable Companions and Assistants to them in every useful Purpose of Life?---O that your lordly Sex were all like my dear Mr *B* --- I don't mean, that they should all take raw uncouth, unbred, lowly Girls, as I was, from the Cottage, and, destroying all Distinction, make such their Wives I cannot mean this Because there is a far greater Likelihood, that such a one, when she comes to be lifted up into so dazling a Sphere, would have her Head made giddy with her Exaltation, than that she would balance herself well in it And then to what a Blot, over all the fair Page of a long Life, would this little Drop of dirty Ink spread itself! What a standing Disreputation to the Choice of a Gentleman!

But *this* I mean, That after a Gentleman had enter'd into the Marriage State with a young Creature (saying nothing at all of Birth or Descent) far inferior to him in Learning, in Parts, in Knowlege of the World, and in all the Graces which make Conversation agreeable and improving, he would, as you do, endeavour to make her fit Company for himself, as he shall find she is *willing* to improve, and *capable* of Improvement That he would direct her Taste, point out to her proper Subjects for her Amusement and Instruction, travel with her now-and-then, a Month in a Year perhaps, and shew her the World, after he has encourag'd her to put herself forward at his own Table, and at the Houses of his Friends, and has seen, that she will not do him great Discredit any-where What Obligations, and Opportunities too, will this give her to love and honour such a Husband, every Hour, more and more!

more! as fhe will fee his Wifdom in a thoufand
Inftances, and experience his Indulgence to her in
ten thoufand, (for which otherwife no Opportunity
could have fo fitly offer'd) to the Praife of his Politenefs, and the Honour of them both!——And
then, when felect Parties of Pleafure or Bufinefs
engag'd him not abroad, in his home Converfation,
to have him, as my dear Mr. *B* does, delight to
inftruct, and open her Views, and infpire her with
an Ambition to inlarge her Mind, and more and
more to excel! What an intellectual Kind of marry'd Life, as I may call it, would fuch Perfons find
theirs! And how fuitable to the Rules of Policy
and Self-love in the Gentleman! For is not the
Wife, and are not her Improvements, all *his own?*---
*Abfolutely,* as I may fay, *his own?* And does not
every Excellence fhe can be adorned by, redound
to her Husband's Honour, becaufe fhe is *his,* even
more than *to her own?*---- In like manner as no
Difhonour affects a Man fo much, as that which he
receives from a bad Wife.

But where, would fome fay, were they to fee
what I write, is fuch a Gentleman as Mr *B* to be
met with? Look around, and fee where, with all
the Advantages of Sex, of Education, of Travel, of
Converfation in the open World, a Gentleman of
his Abilities to inftruct and inform, is to be found?
And there are others, who, perhaps, will queftion
the Capacities or Inclinations of our Sex in general,
to improve in ufeful Knowlege, were they to meet
with fuch kind Inftructors, either in the Characters
of Parents or Husbands

As to the firft, I grant, that it is not eafy to find
fuch a Gentleman· But for the fecond; (if it would
be excus'd in me, who am one of the Sex, and fo
may be thought partial to it) I could, by Compari-
fons drawn from the Gentlemen and Ladies within
the Circle of my own Acquaintance, produce In-

ftances,

stances, which are so flagrantly in their Favour, as might make it suspected, that it is Policy more than Justice, in those who would keep our Sex unacquainted with that more eligible Turn of Education, which gives the Gentlemen so many Advantages over us in *that*, and which will shew, they have none at all in *Nature* or *Genius*

I know you'll pardon me, dear Sir, for you are so exalted above your *Pamela*, by Nature and Education too, that you cannot apprehend any Inconvenience from bold Comparisons  I will take the Liberty therefore to mention a few Instances among our Friends, where the Ladies, notwithstanding their more cramp'd and confin'd Education, make *more* than an equal Figure with the Gentlemen in all the graceful Parts of Conversation, in Spite of the Contempts pour'd out upon our Sex by some witty Gentlemen, whose Writings I have in my Eye.

To begin then with Mr *Murray*, and Miss *Darnford* that was  Mr *Murray* has the Reputation of Scholarship, and has travell'd too; but how infinitely is he surpass'd in every noble and useful Quality, and in Greatness of Mind, and Judgment, as well as Wit, by the young Lady I have nam'd? This we saw, when last at the Hall, in Fifty Instances, where the Gentleman was, you know, Sir, on a Visit to Sir *Simon* and his Lady

Next, dear Sir, permit me to observe, that my good Lord *Davers*, with all his Advantages, born a Counsellor of the Realm, and educated accordingly, does not surpass his Lady, your noble Sister.

*My* Countess, as I delight to call her, and Lady *Betty*, her eldest Daughter, greatly surpass the Earl, and my Lord, her eldest Brother, in every Point of Knowlege, and even Learning, as I may say, altho' both Ladies owe that Advantage principally to their own Cultivation and Acquirement

Let

Let me prefume, Sir, to name Mr *H*; and when I *have* nam'd him, fhall we not be puzzled to find any-where in our Sex, one Remove from vulgar Life, a Woman that will not out-do Mr *H*?

Lady *Darnford*, upon all ufeful Subjects, makes a much brighter Figure than Sir *Simon*, whofe Knowlege of the World has not yet made him acquainted with himfelf.——Mr. *Arthur* excels not his Lady

Mrs. *Towers*, a Maiden Lady, is an Over-match for half a dozen of the neighbouring Gentlemen I could name, in what is call'd Wit and Politenefs, and not inferior to any of them in Judgment.

I could multiply Inftances of this Nature, were it needful, to the Confutation of that low, and I had almoft faid *unmanly* Contempt, with which a certain celebrated Genius treats our Sex in general, in moft of his Pieces that I have *feen*, particularly in his *Letter of Advice to a new-marry'd Lady* · A Letter written in fuch a manner, as muft difguft, inftead of inftructing; and looks more like the Advice of an Enemy to the *Sex*, and a bitter one too, than a Friend to the *particular Lady.* But I ought to beg Pardon for this my Prefumption, for two Reafons, firft, Becaufe of the truly admirable Talents of this Writer, and next, Becaufe we know not what Ladies the ingenious Gentleman may have fallen among in his younger Days

Upon the Whole, therefore, I conclude, That Mr *B* is almoft the only Gentleman, who excels *every* Lady that I have *feen*; fo *greatly* excels, that even the Emanations of his Excellence irradiate a low Cottage-born Girl, and make her pafs among Ladies of Birth and Education for Somebody

Forgive my Pride, dear Sir, but it would be almoft a Crime in your *Pamela* not to exult in the mild Benignity of thofe Rays, by which her beloved Mr. *B* endeavours to make her look up to his own funny Sphere, while fhe, by the Advantage only of·

Q 6                                                          his

his reflected Glory, in *his* Absence, which makes a dark Night to her, glides along with her paler and fainter Beaminess, and makes a distinguishing Figure among such lesser Planets, as can only poorly twinkle and glimmer, for want of the Aid she boasts of

I dare not, dear Sir, conjecture, whence arises this more than Parity in the Genius of the Sexes, among the Persons I have mention'd, notwithstanding the Disparity of Education, and the Difference in the Opportunities of each This might lead one into too proud a Thought in Favour of a Sex too contemptuously treated by some *other* Wits I could name, who, indeed, are the less to be regarded, as they love to jest upon all God Almighty's Works Yet might I better do it, too, than any body, since, as I have intimated above, I am so infinitely transcended by my dear Gentleman, that no Competition, Pride or Vanity, could be apprehended from me

But, however, I would only beg of the Gentlemen, who are so free in their Contempts of us, that they would, for *their own* sakes, (and that, with such, generally goes a great way) rather try to *improve* than *depreciate* us . We should then make better Daughters, better Wives, better Mothers, and better Mistresses And who (permit me, Sir, to ask these People) would be so much the better for these Opportunities and Amendments, as our Upbraiders themselves ?

On re-perusing what I have written, I must repeatedly beg your Excuse, dear Sir, for these proud Notions in behalf of my Sex I can truly say, That they are not, if I know myself, owing to Partiality, because I have the Honour to be one of it, but to a better Motive by far For what does this contemptuous Treatment of one Half, if not the better Half, of the human Species, naturally produce, but Libertinism, and abandon'd Wickedness ? For does it not tend to make the Daughters, the Sisters, the Wives

or

of Gentlemen, the Subjects of profligate Attempts?
--Does it not render the Sex vile in the Eyes of the
moſt Vile? And when a Lady is no longer beheld
by ſuch Perſons with that Dignity and Reverence,
with which perhaps, the Graces of her Perſon, and
the Innocence of her Mind, ſhould ſacredly; as it
were, encompaſs her, do not her very Excellencies
become ſo many Incentives for baſe Wretches to
attempt her Virtue, and bring about her Ruin?

What then may not wicked Wit have to anſwer
for, when its Poſſeſſors proſtitute it to ſuch unmanly Purpoſes? And, as if they had never had a
Mother, a Siſter, a Daughter of their own, throw
down, as much as in them lies, thoſe ſacred Fences,
which may lay the fair Incloſure open to the In-
vaſions of every clumſier and viler Beaſt of Prey,
who, tho' deſtitute of *their* Wit, yet corrupted by
it, ſhall fill their Mouths, as well as their Hearts,
with the borrow'd Miſchief, and propagate it, from
one to another, to the End of Time, and who,
otherwiſe, would have paſs'd by the uninvaded Fence,
and only ſhew'd their Teeth, and ſnarl'd at the well-
ſecured Fold within it!

You cannot, my deareſt Mr. *B.* I know you cannot, be angry at this Romantick Painting, ſince you
are not affected by it For when you were at worſt,
you acted (more dangerouſly, 'tis true, for the poor
Innocents) a *principal* Part, and were as a Lion
among Beaſts----- Do, dear Sir, let me ſay *among,*
this one time--- You ſcorn'd to borrow any Man's
Wit *, and if nobody had follow'd your Example,
till they had had your Qualities, the Number of
Rakes would have been but ſmall Yet, deareſt Sir,
don't miſtake me neither, I am not ſo mean as to
beſpeak your Favour by extenuating your Failings:
If I *were,* you would deſervedly deſpiſe me For,
undoubtedly, (I *muſt* ſay it, Sir) your Faults were the

* *See* Vol. II *p.* 70.                    greater

greater for your Perfections, and such Talents mis-
apply'd, as they made you more capable of Mischief,
so did they increase the Evil of your Practices All
then that I mean by saying you are not affected by
this Painting, is, that you are not affected by the
Description I have given of clumsy and sordid Rakes,
whose *Wit* is *borrow'd*, and their *Wickedness* only
what they may call *their own*

Then, dear Sir, since that noble Conversation,
which you held with me at *Tunbridge*, in relation
to the Consequences, that might, had it not been
for GOD's Grace intervening, have follow'd the
Masquerade Affair, I have the Pleasure, the inexpressible Pleasure, to find a thorough Reformation,
from the *best* Motives, taking Place, and your joining with me in my Closet, (as Opportunity permits)
in my Evening Duties, is the charming Confirmation of your kind, and voluntary, and, I am proud
to say, your *pious* Assurances! So that this makes me
fearless of your Displeasure, while I rather triumph
in my Joy, for your precious Soul's sake, than presume to think of recriminating, and when (only this
one time for all, and for ever) I take the Liberty of
looking back from the delightful *Now*, to the painful *Formerly* !

But, what a Rambler am I again! You command
me, Sir, to write to you all I think, without Fear.
I obey, and, as the Phrase is, do it without either
*Fear* or *Wit*

If you are *not* displeas'd, it is a Mark of the true
Nobleness of your Nature, and the Sincerity of your
late pious Declarations

If you *are*, I shall be sure I have done wrong in
having apply'd a Corrosive to eat away the *Proud
Flesh* of a *Wound*, that is not yet so throughly *digested*,
as to bear a painful Application, and requires Bal-
sam, and a gentler Treatment But when we were
at *Bath*, I remember what you said once of the
Benefit

Benefit of Retrofpection, and you charg'd me, whenever a *proper* Opportunity offer'd, to remind you, by that one Word, *Retrofpection,* of the charming Converfation we had there, on our Return from the Rooms.

If this be not one of thofe *proper* Opportunities, forgive, deareft Sir, the Unfeafonablenefs of your very impertinent, but, in Intention, and Refolution,

*Ever dutiful,*

P. B.

## LETTER LVI.

*From Mrs. B. to her Father and Mother.*

*Ever dear, and Ever honoured,*

I Muft write this one Letter to you, altho' I have had the Happinefs to fee you fo lately; becaufe Mr B is now about to honour me with the Tour he fo kindly promifed to me, when with you, and it may therefore be feveral Months, perhaps, before I have again the Pleafure of paying you the like dutiful Refpects

You know his kind Promife, That he would, for every dear Baby I prefent him with, take an Excurfion with me afterwards, in order to eftablifh and confirm my Health.

The Task I have undertaken of dedicating all my Writing Amufements to the deareft of Gentlemen; the full Imployment I have, when at home, the frequent Rambles he has been fo often pleas'd to indulge me in, with my dear Mifs *Goodwin,* to *Kent,* to *London,* to *Bedfordfhire,* to *Lincolnfhire,* and to my Lady *Davers's,* take from me the Neceffity of writing to your honoured Selves, to my Mifs *Darnford* that was, and to Lady *Davers,* fo often as I formerly thought

thought myfelf obliged to do, when I faw all my worthy Friends fo feldom , the fame things, moreover, with little Variation, occurring this Year, as to our Converfations, Vifits, Friends, Imployments, and Amufements, that fell out the laft, as muft be the Cafe, in a Family fo uniform and methodical as ours

I have, for thefe Reafons, more Leifure to purfue my domeftick Duties, which are increas'd upon me, and when I have faid, That I am every Day more and more happy in my beloved Mr *B* in Mifs *Goodwin*, my *Billy*, and my *Davers*, and now, newly, in my fweet little *Pamela*, (for fo, you know, Lady *Davers* would have her called, rather than by her own Name) what can I fay more ?

As to the Tour I fpoke of, you know, the firft Part of Mr *B*'s obliging Scheme is to carry me to *France*; for he has already travell'd with me over the greateft Part of *England*, and I am fure, by my Paffage laft Year, to the *Ifle of Wight*, I fhall not be afraid of croffing the Water from *Dover* thither; and he will, when we are at *Paris*, he fays, take *my* further Directions (that was his kind Expreffion) whither to go next.

My Lord and Lady *Davers* are fo good as to promife to accompany us to *Paris*, provided Mr. B. will give them his and my Company to *Aix la Chapelle*, for a Month or fix Weeks, whither my Lord is advifed to go  And Mr *H* if he can get over his Fear of croffing the falt Water, is to be of the Party

Lady *G*  Mifs *Darnford* that was, (who likewife has lately lain-in of a fine Daughter) and I, are to correfpond, as Opportunity offers, and fhe is fo good as to promife to fend to you what I write, as formerly  But I have refufed to fay one Word in my Letters of the Manners, Cuftoms, Curiofities, &c of the Places we fee, becaufe, firft, I fhall not have Leifure , and, next, becaufe thofe things are fo much

beter

better defcribed in Books already printed, written by Perfons who made ftricter and better Obfervations than I can pretend to make: So that what I fhall write will relate only to our private Selves, and fhall be as brief as poffible.

If we are to do as Mr. *B* has it in his Thought, he intends to be out of *England* Two Years : --- But how can I bear that, if for your fakes only, and for thofe of my dear Babies ! ----- But this muft be my Time, my *only* Time, Mr. *B* tells me, to ramble and fee diftant Places and Countries, for he is pleas'd to fay, That as foon as his Little-ones are capable of my Inftructions, and begin to underftand my Looks and Signs, he will not fpare me from them a Week together, and he is fo kind as to propofe, that my dear bold Boy (for every one fees how greatly he refembles his Papa in his dear forward Spirit) fhall go with us; and this pleafes Mifs *Goodwin* highly, who is very fond of *him*, and my little *Davers*, but vows fhe will never love fo well my pretty black-ey'd *Pamela*

You fee what a fweet Girl Mifs is, and you admir'd her much. Did I tell you, what fhe faid to me, when firft fhe faw you both, with your filver Hairs, and reverend Countenances? --- Madam, faid fhe, I dare fay, your Papa and Mamma *honoured their Father and Mother*. They did, my Dear, but what is your Reafon for faying fo ? ------- Becaufe, reply'd fhe, *they have lived fo long in the Land which the Lord their GOD has given them* I took the Charmer in my Arms, and kifs'd her three or four times, as fhe deferv'd, for was not this very pretty in the Child ?

I muft, with inexpreffible Pleafure, write you word, how happily GOD's Providence has now, at laft, turn'd that Affair, which once made me fo uneafy, in relation to the fine Countefs, (who has been fome time abroad) of of whom you had heard, as you told me, some Reports, which had you known at the Time, would have made you very apprehensive for Mr *B*'s Morals, as well as for my Repose.

I will now (because I can do it with the highest Pleasure, by reason of the Event which it has produced) give you the Particulars of that dark Affair, so far as shall make you Judges of my present Joy. altho' I had hitherto avoided entring into that Subject to you. For now I think myself, by God's Grace, secure of the Affection and Fidelity of the best of Husbands, and that from the worthiest Motives, as you shall hear.

There was but one thing wanting, my dear Parents, to complete all the Happiness I wish'd for in this Life, and that was, The remote Hope I had entertain'd, that one Day, my dear Mr *B.* who from a licentious Gentleman, became a Moralist, would be so touch'd by the Divine Grace, as to become, in time, more than a Moral, a *Religious* Gentleman, and that he would, at last, join in the Duties which he had the Goodness to countenance.

For this Reason I began with mere *Indispensables.* I crouded not his Gate with Objects of Charity. I visited them at their Homes, and reliev'd them; distinguishing the worthy Indigent (made so by unavoidable Accidents and Casualties) from the wilfully, or perversly, or sottishly such, by *greater* Marks of my Favour.

I confin'd my Morning and Evening Devotions to my own Closet, as privately as possible, left I should give Offence and Discouragement to so gay a Temper, so unaccustom'd (poor Gentleman!) to Acts of Devotion and Piety; while I met his Houshold together, only on Mornings and Evenings of the Sabbath-day, to prepare them for their publick Duties in the one, and in hopes to confirm them in what they had heard at Church in the other, leaving them to their own Reflections for the reft of the Week, after I had fuggefted to them a Method I wifh'd to be follow'd by themfelves, and in which they conftantly oblig'd me.

This good Order had its defired Effect, and our Sabbath-day Affemblies were held with fo little Parade, that we were hardly any of us mifs'd. All, in fhort, was done with chearful Eafe and Compofure, and every one of us was better difpos'd to our dome-ftick Duties by this Method. I, to attend the good Pleafure of my beft Friend, and they, to attend that of us both

In this manner, we went on, very happily, my neighbourly Vifits of Charity taking up no more Time than common Airings, and paffing, many of them, for fuch, my *private Duties* being only be-tween my FIRST, my HEAVENLY BENEFACTOR, and myfelf, and my Family-ones (perfonally) con-fin'd to the Day, feparated for thefe beft of Services, And Mr B. pleas'd with my Manner, beheld the good Effects, and countenanc'd me by his Praifes and his Endearments, *as* acting difcreetly, *as* not falling into Enthufiafm, and (as he ufed to fay) *as* not aiming at being *righteous over-much*

But ftill I wanted, and I waited for, with humble Impatience, and I made it part of my conftant Prayers, that the Divine Grace would at laft touch his Heart, and make him *more* than a Countenancer, *more* than an Applauder, of my Duties· That he might, for his own dear fake, become a Partaker, a Partner in them, and then, thought I, when we can Hand in Hand, Heart in Heart, one Spirit, as well as one Flefh, join in the fame Clofet, in the fame Prayers and Thankfgivings, what a happy Creature fhall I be!

I fay, *Clofet*; for, I durft not afpire fo high, as to hope he would favour me with his Company among his Servants, in our *Sunday* Devotions ---- I
knew

knew it would be going too far, in *his* Opinion, to expect it from him. In *me* their Miftrefs, had I been ever fo high-born, it was not amifs, becaufe I, and they, *every one* of us, were *his*; I in one Degree, Mr *Longman* in another, Mrs *Jervis* in another--- But from a Gentleman of his high Temper, and manner of Education, I knew I could never hope for it, fo would not lofe *every* thing, by grafping at *too much*.

But in the midft of all thefe comfortable Proceedings, and my further charming Hopes, a nafty Mafquerade threw into the dear Gentleman's Way a Temptation, which for a time, blafted all my Profpects, and indeed made me doubt my own Head almoft. For, judge what my Difappointment muft be, when I found all my Wifhes fruftrated, all my Prayers render'd ineffectual. His very Morality, which I had flatter'd myfelf, in time, I fhould be an humble Inftrument to exalt into Religion, fhock'd, and in Danger; and all the good Work to begin again, if offended Grace fhould ever again offer itfelf to the dear wilful Trefpaffer!

But who fhall pretend to fcrutinize the Councils of the Almighty?--- For out of all this *evil Appearance* was to proceed the *real Good*, I had been fo long, and fo often, fupplicating for!

The dear Gentleman *was* to be on the Brink of relapfing. It was proper, that I fhould be fo very uneafy, as to affume a Conduct not natural to my Temper, and to raife his generous Concern for me. And, in the very Crifis, Divine Grace interpofed, made him fenfible of his Danger, made him refolve againft his Error, before it was yet too late, and his fliding Feet, quitting the flippery Path he was in, collected new Strength, and he ftood the firmer, and more fecure, for his Peril.

For, my dear Parents, having happily put an End to that Affair, and, by his uniform Conduct, for a
con-

confiderable Length of Time, fhew'd me that I had
nothing to apprehend from it, he was pleas'd, when
we were laft at *Tunbridge* together, and in very ferious Difcourfe upon Divine Subjects, to fay to this
Effect. Is there not, my *Pamela*, a Text, *That the
unbelieving Husband fhall be faved by the believing
Wife, while he beholds her chafte Converfation coupled
with Fear?*

I need not tell you, my dear Mr. *B.* that there
is, nor where it is

Then, my Dear, I begin to hope, *that* will be
my Cafe. For, from a former Affair, of which this
Spot of Ground puts me more in mind, I fee fo
much Reafon to doubt my own Strength, which I
had built, and, as I thought, fecurely, on *moral*
Foundations, that I muft look out for a *better*
Guide to conduct me, than the proud Word *Honour*
can be, in the general Acceptation of it among us
lively young Gentlemen

How often, my deareft Love, continu'd he, have
I promifed, (and I never promifed, but I intended
to perform) that I would be faithfully and only
yours! How often have I declar'd, that I did not
think I could poffibly deferve my *Pamela*, till I
could fhew her, in my own Mind, a Purity as
nearly equal to hers, as my paft Conduct would
admit of!

But I depended too much upon my own Strength:
And I am now convinc'd, that nothing but

## RELIGIOUS CONSIDERATIONS,

and a Refolution to watch over the very *firft* Appear-
arces of Evil, and to chcck them, as they arife, can
be of fufficient Weight to keep fteady to his good
Purpo es, a vain young Man, too little accuftom'd
to Reftraint, and oo much us'd to play upon the Brink
of Dangers, from a Temerity, and Love of Intrigue,
natural to enterprifing Minds.

I would

I would not, my beſt Love, make this Declaration of my Convictions to you, till I had throughly examin'd myſelf, and had Reaſon to hope, that I ſhould be enabled to make it good  And now, my *Pamela*, from this Inſtant, you ſhall be my Guide; and, only taking care, that you do not, all at once, by Injunctions too rigorous, damp and diſcourage the riſing Flame, I will leave it to You to direct it as you pleaſe, till, by degrees, it may be deem'd worthy to mingle with your own.

Judge, my dear Parents, how rapturous my Joy was upon this Occaſion, and how ready I was to bleſs GOD for a Danger (ſo narrowly eſcap'd) which was attended with the *very* Conſequences, that I had ſo long pray'd for, and which I little thought the Divine Providence was bringing about by the very Means, that, I apprehended, would put an End to all my pleaſing Hopes and Proſpects of that Nature

It is in vain for me to think of finding Words to expreſs what I felt, and how I acted, on this Occaſion  I heard him out with twenty different and impatient Emotions, and then threw myſelf at his Feet, embracing his Knees, with Arms the moſt ardently claſping! My Face lifted up to Heaven, and to his Face, by Turns; my Eyes overflowing with Tears of Joy, which half choak'd up the Paſſage of my Words --- At laſt, his kind Arms claſping my Neck, and kiſſing my tearful Cheek, I could only ſay --- My Prayers, my ardent Prayers, are at laſt --- at laſt --- heard --- May GOD Almighty, dear Sir, confirm your pious Purpoſes! --- And, Oh! what a happy *Pamela* have you at your Feet!

I wept for Joy, till I ſobb'd again --- and he raiſing me to his kind Arms, when I could ſpeak, I ſaid, To have this *heavenly* Proſpect, O beſt Beloved of my Heart! added to all my *earthly* Bleſſings! ------ how ſhall I contain my Joy! --- For, Oh! to think that my dear Mr. *B.* is, and will be, mine, and I

his,

his, thro' the Mercies of GOD, when this tranfitory Life is paft and gone, to all Eternity; what a rich Thought is this!---- Methinks, I am already, dear Sir, ceafing to be mortal, and beginning to tafte the Perfection of thofe Joys, which this thrice welcome Declaration gives me Hope of, hereafter!--- But, what fhall I fay, oblig'd as I was beyond Expreffion before, and now doubly oblig'd in the rapturous View you have open'd to me, into a happy Futurity!

He was pleas'd to fay, He was delighted with me beyond Expreffion, that I was his ecftatick Charmer! --- That the Love I fhew'd for his future Good was the moving Proof of the Purity of my Heart, and my Affection for him. And that very Evening he was pleas'd to join with me in my retired Duties; and, at all proper Opportunities, favours me with his Company in the fame manner; liftening attentively to all my Leffons, as he calls my chearful Difcourfes on ferious Subjects

And now, my dear Parents, do you not rejoice with me, in this charming, charming Appearance? For, *before,* I had the moft generous, the moft beneficent, the moft noble, the moft affectionate, but, *now,* I am likely to have the moft *pious,* of Husbands! What a happy Wife, what a happy Daughter, is *his* and *your Pamela!* ----- GOD, of his infinite Mercy, continue and improve the ravifhing Profpect!

I was forced to leave off here, to enjoy the charming Reflections, which this lovely Subject, and my bleffed Profpects, filled me with. And now proceed to write a few Lines more.

I am under fome Concern on account of our going to travel into *Roman-catholick* Countries, for fear we fhould want the publick Opportunities of Divine Service. For, I prefume, the Embaffador's Chapel will be the only Proteftant Place of Worfhip allow'd allow'd of, and *Paris* the only City in *France* where there is one. But we muſt endeavour to make it up in our private and domeſtick Duties. For, as the Phraſe is, when we are at *Rome*, we muſt do as they do at *Rome*; that is to ſay, ſo far, as not to give Offence, on one hand, to the People we are among; nor Scandal, on the other, by Compliances hurtful to one's Conſcience. But my Protector knows all theſe things ſo well, (no Place in what is call'd the Grand Tour, being New to him) that I have no Reaſon to be very uneaſy on theſe Accounts.

And now, my deareſt dear honour'd Parents, let me, by Letter, as I did on my Knees at Parting, beg the Continuance of your Prayers and Bleſſings, and that GOD will preſerve us to one another, and give us, and all our worthy Friends, a happy Meeting again.

*Kent*, you may be ſure, will be our firſt Viſit, on our Return, for Your ſakes, for my dear *Davers's* ſake, and for my little *Pamela's* ſake, who will be both ſent down, and put into your Protection, while my *Billy*, and Miſs *Goodwin*, (for, ſince I began this Letter, it is ſo determin'd) are to be my delightful Companions, for Mr. *B* declar'd, His Boy ſhall not be one Day out of my Preſence, if he can help it, becauſe, he is pleas'd to ſay, his Temper wants looking after, and his Notices of every thing are ſtrong and ſignificant.

Poor little Dear! he has indeed a little ſort of Perverſeneſs and Headſtrongneſs, as one may ſay, in his Will. But he is but a Baby, and I ſhall, I hope, manage him pretty well, for he takes great Notice of all I ſay, and of every Look of mine, already --- He is, beſides, very good-humour'd, and willing to part with any thing for a kind Word, and this gives me Hope of a docile and benevolent Diſpoſition, as he grows up.

I thought,

I thought, when I began the laſt Paragraph but one, that I was within a Line of concluding, but it is *to* You, and *of* my Babies, I am writing, ſo ſhall go on to the Bottom of this new Sheet, if I do not directly put an End to my Scribbling: Which I do, with aſſuring you both, my dear good Parents, that where-ever I am, I ſhall always be thoughtful of you, and remember you in my Prayers, as becomes

*Your ever dutiful Daughter,*

P. B.

My Reſpects to all your good Neighbours in general. Mr. *Longman* will viſit you now-and-then Mrs *Jervis* will take one Journey to *Kent,* ſhe ſays, and it ſhall be to accompany my Babies, when they are carried down to you. Poor *Jonathan,* and ſhe, good Folks! ſeem declining in their Health, which much grieves me. --- Once more, GOD ſend us all a happy Meeting, if it be his bleſſed Will! Adieu, Adieu, my dear Parents!

*Your ever dutiful,* &c.

---

## LETTER LVII.

*My dear Lady* G.

I Received your laſt Letter at *Paris,* as we were diſpoſing every thing for our Return to *England,* after an Abſence of near Two Years, in which, as I have inform'd you, from time to time, I have been a great Traveller, into *Holland,* the *Netherlands,* through the moſt conſiderable Provinces of *France,* into *Italy,* and, in our Return to *Paris* again, (the principal Place of our Reſidence) through ſeveral Parts of *Germany.*

I told

I told you of the Favours and Civilities we receiv'd at *Florence*, from the then Countess Dowager of— who, with her Humble Servant Lord *C*.----(that had so assiduously attended her for so many Months in *Italy*) accompany'd us from *Florence* to *Infpruck*.

Her Ladyship made that worthy Lord happy in about a Month after she parted from us; and the noble Pair gave us an Opportunity at *Paris*, in their Way to *England*, to return some of the Civilities, which we receiv'd from them in *Italy* And they are now arriv'd at her Ladyship's Seat on the Forest

Her Lord is exceedingly fond of her, as he well may, for she is one of the most charming Ladies in *England*, and behaves to him with so much Prudence and Respect, that they are as happy in each other, as can be wish'd And let me just add, That both in *Italy* and at *Paris*, Mr *B*'s Demeanour and her Ladyship's to one another, was so nobly open, and unaffectedly polite, as well as highly difcreet, that neither Lord *C* who had once been jealous of Mr. *B* nor the *other Party*, who had had a Tincture of the same Yellow Evil, as you know, because of the Countess, had so much as a Shadow of Uneafiness remaining on that Occafion

Lord *Davers* has had his Health (which had begun to decline in *England*) so well, that there was no persuading Lady *Davers* to return before now; altho' I begg'd and pray'd I might not have another little *Frenchman*, for fear they should, as they grew up, forget, as I pleasantly used to say, the Obligations which their Parentage lays them under to dearer *England*

And now, my dearest Friend, I have shut up my Rambles for my whole Life; for Three little *Englifh* Folks, and One little *Frenchman*, (but a charming Baby, as well as the rest, *Charley* by Name) and a near Prospect of a further Increafe, you will say, are Famny enough to imploy all my Cares at home

I have

I have told you, from time to time, altho' I could
not write to you so often as I would, because of our
being constantly in Motion, what was most worthy
of your Knowlege relating to our Particular, and
how happy we have all been in one another    And
I have the Pleasure to confirm to you what I have
several times written, that Mr *B* and my Lord and
Lady *Davers* are all that I could wish and hope
for, with regard to their first Duties    Indeed, indeed, we are a happy Family, united by the best and
most solid Ties !

Miss *Goodwin* is a charming young Lady !---I cannot express how much I love her.  She is a perfect Mistress of the *French* Language, and speaks
*Italian* very prettily ·  And, as to myself, I have improved so well under my dear Tutor's Lessons, together with the Opportunity of conversing with the
politest and most learned Gentry of different Nations, that I will hold a Conversation with you in
two or three Languages, if you please, when I have
the Happiness to see you.    There's a learned Boaster
for you, my dear Friend ! (if the Knowlege of different Languages makes one learned)    But I shall
bring you an Heart as intirely *English* as ever, for
all that !

We landed on *Thursday* last at *Dover*, and directed
our Course to the dear Farm house , and you can
better imagine, than I express, what a Meeting we
had with my dear Father and Mother, and my beloved *Davers* and *Pamela*, who are charming Babies---
But is not this the Language of every fond Mamma ?

Miss *Goodwin* is highly delighted now with my sweet
little *Pamela*, and says, She shall be her Sister indeed !
For, Madam, said she, Miss is a Beauty !---And we
see no *French* Beauties like Master *Davers* and Miss

Beauty ! my dear Miss *Goodwin*, said I, what is
Beauty, if she be not a good Girl ?---Beauty is but
a specious, and, as it may happen, a dangerous Re-

com-

Commendation, a mere skin-deep Perfection; and if, as she grows up, she is not as good as my Miss *Goodwin*, she shall be none of my Girl

What adds to my Pleasure, my dear Friend, is to see them both so well got over the Small-pox. It has been as happy for them, as it was for their Mamma and her *Billy*, that they had it under so skilful and kind a Manager in that Distemper, as my dear Mother. I wish, if it please GOD, it was as happily over with my little pretty *Frenchman*

Every body is surpris'd to see what the past two Years have done for Miss *Goodwin*, and my *Billy* -- O my dear Friend, they are both of them almost---nay, quite, I think, for their Years, all that I wish them to be

In order to make them keep their *French*, which Miss so well speaks, and *Billy* so prettily prattles, I oblige them, when they talk to one another, and are in the Nursery, to speak nothing else But at Table, except on particular Occasions, when *French may* be spoken, they are to speak in *English*; that is to say, when they *do* speak . For I tell them, that little Masters must do nothing but ask Questions for Information, and say Yes, or No, till their Papa's or Mamma's give them Leave to speak , nor little Ladies neither, till they are Sixteen , for, my dear Loves, cry I, You would not speak before you know *how* And Knowlege is obtained by *Hearing*, and not by *Speaking* And setting my *Billy* on my Lap, in Miss's Presence, Here, said I, taking an Ear in the Fingers of each Hand, are two Ears, my *Billy*; and, then pointing to his Mouth, but one Tongue, my Love So you must be sure to mind, that you *hear* twice as much as you *speak*, even when you grow a bigger Master than you are now.

You have so many pretty Ways to learn one, Madam, says Miss, now-and-then, that it is impos-sible we should not regard what you say to us

Several

Several *French* Tutors, when we were abroad, were recommended to Mr *B*. But there is one *English* Gentleman, now on his Travels with young Mr *R* with whom Mr. *B* has agreed ; and in the mean time, my beſt Friend is pleas'd to compliment me, that the Children will not ſuffer for want of a Tutor, while I can take the Pains I do · Which he will have to be too much for me ; eſpecially, that now, on our Return, my *Davers* and my *Pamela* are added to my Cares But what Mother can take too much Pains to cultivate the Minds of her Children ?--- If, my dear Lady *G*. it were not for theſe *frequent* Lyings-in !--- But this is the Time of Life--- Tho' little did I think, ſo early, I ſhould have ſo many careful Bleſſings !

I have as great Credit as Pleaſure from my little Family All our Neighbours here in *Bedfordſhire* admire us more and more. You'll excuſe my ſeeming (for it is but ſeeming) Vanity, I hope I know better than to have it real---Never, ſays Mrs *Towers*, who is ſtill a ſingle Lady, did I ſee, before, a Lady ſo much advantag'd by her Reſidence in that fantaſtick Nation, (for ſhe loves not the *French*) and who brought home with her nothing of their Affectations !--- She will have it, that the *French* Politeneſs, and the *Engliſh* Frankneſs and Plainneſs of Heart, appear happily blended in all we ſay and do And ſhe makes me a thouſand Compliments upon Lord and Lady *Davers*'s Account, who, ſhe would fain perſuade me, owe a great deal of Improvement (my Lord in his Converſation, and my Lady in her Temper) to living in the ſame Houſe with us.

Indeed my Lady *Davers* is exceeding kind and good to me, is always magnifying me to every body, and ſays, ſhe knows not how to live from me, and that I have been a Means of ſaving half an hundred Souls, as well as her dear Brother's On an Indiſpoſition of my Lord's at *Montpelier*, which made

R 3 her

her Ladyſhip very apprehenſive, ſhe declar'd, that were ſhe to be depriv'd of his Lordſhip, ſhe would not let us reſt, till we had conſented to her living with us; ſaying, that we had Room enough in *Lincolnſhire*, and ſhe would inlarge the *Bedfordſhire* Seat at her own Expence.

Mr *H* is Mr. *H.* ſtill, and that's the beſt I can ſay of him. For, I verily think, he is more an Ape than ever. His *whole* Head is now *French* 'Twas *half* ſo before. We had great Difficulties with him abroad. His Aunt and I endeavouring to give him a ſerious and religious Turn, we had like to have turn'd him into a *Roman* Catholick. For he was pleaſed much with the ſhewy Part of that Religion, and the fine Pictures and Decorations in the Churches of *Italy*, and having got into Company with a *Dominican* at *Padua*, a *Franciſcan* at *Milan*, and a *Jeſuit* at *Paris*, they lay ſo hard at him, in their Turns, that we had like to have loſt him to each Aſſailant, ſo were forced to let him take his own Courſe, for, his Aunt would have it, that he had no other Defence from the Attacks of Perſons to make him embrace a faulty Religion, than to permit him to continue as he was, that is to ſay, to have none at all. So ſhe ſuſpended attempting to proſelyte the thoughtleſs Creature, till he came to *England*. I wiſh her Ladyſhip Succeſs here, but, I doubt, he will not be a Credit to any Religion, for a great while. And as he is very deſirous to go to *London*, as he has always been, it will be found, when there, that any fluttering Coxcomb will do more to make him one of that Claſs, in an Hour, than his Aunt's Leſſons, to make him a good Man, in a Twelvemonth. *Where much is given, much is required.* The contrary of this, I doubt, is all poor Mr *H.* has to truſt to.

Juſt now we have a Meſſenger to tell us, that his Father, who has been long ill, is dead. So, now, he is a Lord indeed! He flutters and ſtruts about moſt
ſtrangely,

ſtrangely, I warrant, and is wholly imploy'd in giving
Directions relating to his Mourning Equipage---And
now there will be no holding of him in, I doubt ; except
his new Title has ſo much Virtue in it, as to make
him a wiſer and a better Man

He will now have a Seat in the Houſe of Peers
of *Great Britain* ; but I hope, for the Nation's ſake,
he will not meet with many more like himſelf there !
---For, to me, that is one of the moſt venerable
Aſſemblies in the World, and it appears the more
ſo, ſince I have been abroad, for an *Engliſh* Gentleman is reſpected, if he be any thing of a Man,
above a foreign Nobleman, and an *Engliſh* Nobleman, above ſome petty Sovereigns

If our travelling Gentry duly conſider'd this Diſtinction in their Favour, they would, for the Honour of their Country, as well as for their own Credit,
behave in a better manner, in their foreign Tours,
than, I am ſorry to ſay it, ſome of them do  But
what can one expect, from the unlick'd Cubs, pardon the Term, ſent abroad with only Stature, to
make them look like Men, and Equipage to attract
Reſpect, without one other Qualification to inforce it ?

Here let me cloſe this, with a few Tears, to the
Memory of my dear Mrs *Jervis*, my other Mother,
my Friend, my Adviſer, my Protectreſs, in my
ſingle State, and my faithful Second and Partaker in
the Comforts of my higher Life, and better Fortunes !

What would I have given to have been preſent,
as, it ſeems, ſhe ſo earneſtly wiſhed, to cloſe her
dying Eyes ! I ſhould have done it, with the Piety
and the Concern of a truly affectionate Daughter
But that melancholy Happineſs was deny'd to us
both ; for, as I told you in the Letter on the Occaſion, the dear good Woman (who now is in the Poſſeſſion of her bleſſed Reward, and rejoicing in God's
Mercies) was no more, when the News reached me,

so far off, as at *Heidelburgh*, of her last Illness and Wishes.

I cannot forbear, every time I enter her Parlour, (where I used to see, with so much Delight, the good Woman sitting, always imploy'd in some useful or pious Work) shedding a Tear to her Memory· And in my Sabbath Duties, missing *her*, I miss half a dozen Friends, methinks, and I sigh in Remembrance of her, and can only recover that chearful Frame, which the Performance of those Duties always gave me, by reflecting, that she now is reaping the Reward of that sincere Piety, which used to edify and encourage us all

The Servants we brought home with us, and those we left behind us, met in Tears at the Name of Mrs *Jervis* Mr *Longman* too, lamented the Loss of her, in the most moving Strain. And all I can do now, in Honour of her Memory and her Merit, is to be a Friend to those she loved most, as I have already begun to be; and none of them shall suffer in those Concerns that can be answer'd, now she is gone. For the Loss of so excellent a Friend and Relation, is Loss enough to all who knew her, and claim'd Kindred with her

Poor worthy *Jonathan* too, ('tis almost a Misery to have so soft, so susceptible an Heart as I have, or to have such good Servants and Friends as one cannot lose without such Emotions as I feel for the Loss of them!) his Silver Hairs, which I have beheld with so much Delight, and thought I had a Father in Presence, when I saw them adorning so honest and comely a Face, how are they now laid low!--- Forgive me, my dear Lady G *Jonathan* was not a common Servant, neither are *any* of ours so But *Jonathan* excell'd all that excell'd in his Class!---I am told, That these two worthy Folks dy'd within two Days of one another; a Circumstance you mention'd not in your Letter to me, on which Occasion

cafion I could not help faying to myfelf, in the
Words of *David* over *Saul* and his Son *Jonathan,*
the Namefake of our worthy Butler, *They were lovely
and pleafant in their Lives, and in their Deaths they
were not divided.*

I might have continu'd on in the Words of the
Royal Lamenter, for, furely, never did one Fellow-
fervant love another in my Maiden State, nor Servant love a Mift efs in my exalted Condition, better
than *Jonathan* lov'd me ! I could fee in his Eyes a
gliftening Pleafure, whenever I pafs'd by him . If at
fuch times I fpoke to him, as I feldom failed to do,
with a *God blefs you, too* ! in Anfwer to his repeated
Bleffings, he had a kind of Re-juvenefcence (may I
fay?) vifibly running thro' his whole Frame. And,
now-and-then, if I laid my Hand upon his folded
ones, as I pafs'd him on a *Sunday* Morning or Evening, praying for me, with a *How do you, my worthy
old Acquaintance?* his Heart would fpring to his
Lips in a kind of Rapture, and his Eyes would run
over.

O my beloved Friend! how the Lofs of thefe
two Worthies of my Family oppreffes me at times !

Mr *B.* likewife fhew'd a generous Concern on
the Occafion And when all the Servants welcom'd
us in a Body, on our Return, Methinks, my Dear,
faid the good Gentleman, I mifs your Mrs *Jervis,*
and honeft *Jonathan* A ftarting Tear, and, They
are happy, dear honeft Souls ! and a Sigh, were the
Tribute I paid to their Memories, on their beloved
Mafter's fo kindly repeating their Names.

Who knows, had I been here --- But, away, too
painful Reflection! They lived to a good old Age,
and fell like Fruit fully ripe: They *died the Death
of the Righteous,* I muft follow them in time, GOD
knows how foon: And, *Oh! that my latter End may
be like theirs !*

R 5

Once

Once more, forgive me, my dear Friend, this
small Tribute to their Memories: And believe, that
I am not so ungrateful for God's Mercies, as to let
the Loss of these dear good Folks lessen with me
the Joy, and the Delight, I have still (more than any
other happy Creature) left me, in the Health, and
the Love, of the best of good Husbands, and good
Men, in the Children, charming as ever Mother
could boast of! charming, I mean principally, in
the dawning Beauties of their Minds, and in the
Pleasure their Towardliness of Nature gives me; including, as I always do, my dear Miss *Goodwin*, and
have Reason to do, from her dutiful Love, as I may
call it, for me, and Observation of all I say to her;
in the Preservation to me of the best and worthiest
of Parents, hearty, tho' aged, as they are; in the
Love and Friendship of good Lord and Lady *Davers*,
and my excellent Friend Lady *G*; not forgetting
even worthy Mr *Longman*. God preserve all these
to me, as I am truly thankful for His Mercies[1]----
And then, notwithstanding my affecting Losses, as
above, who will be so happy as I?

That you, my dear Lady *G*. may long continue
so, likewise, in the Love of a worthy Husband, and
the Delights of an increasing hopeful Family, which
will make you some Amends for the heavy Losses
you also have sustain'd, in the two last Years, of an
affectionate Father, and a most worthy Mother, and,
in Mrs *Jones*, of a good Neighbour, prays

*Your ever affectionate Friend and Servant,*

P. B.

LETTER

# LETTER LVIII.

*My beloved Lady* G.

YOU will excufe my long Silence, when I fhall tell you the Occafions of it

In the firft Place, I was oblig'd to pay a dutiful and concerning Vifit to *Kent,* where my good Father was taken ill of a Fever, and my Mother of an Ague. And think, Madam, how this muft affect me, at their Time of Life!---O Death! Death! thou mayft knock at the Doors of Tenements fo frail, and fo beloved: We cannot help ourfelves: But we will not let thee in, if we can poffibly avoid it, for the Lives of fuch dear Parents are a Part of my own Life: And, if GOD fee fit, I cannot fpare them! Indeed I cannot!

Mr. *B* kindly accompany'd me, apprehending, that his beloved Prefence would be neceffary, if the Recovery of them both, in which I thankfully re-joice, had not happen'd, efpecially, as a Circum-ftance I am, I think, *always* in, added more Weight to his Apprehenfions.

I had hardly return'd from *Kent* to *Bedfordfhire,* and look'd around, when I was oblig'd to fet out to attend Lady *Davers,* who fent me word, that fhe fhould *die,* that was her ftrong Term, if fhe faw me not, to comfort and recover, by my Counfel and Prefence, fo fhe was pleas'd to exprefs herfelf, her fick Lord, who was juft got out of an intermittent Fever, which left him without any Spirits, and was occafion'd by fretting at the Conduct of her *ftupid Nephew,* thofe alfo were her Words

For you muft have heard, (Every-body hears when a Man of Quality does a foolifh Thing!) and it has been in all the News-papers, That---' On *Wednefday* ' laft the Right Honourable *John* (*Jackey,* they ' fhould have faid) Lord *H* Nephew to the Right

R 6 ' Honour-

' Honourable *William* Lord *Davers*, was marry'd to
' the Honourable Mrs. P. Relict of *J* P. of *Twick-*
' *enham*, Efq, a Lady of celebrated Beauty, and
' ample Fortune

Now, my dear Friend, you muft know, that this
celebrated Lady is, 'tis true, of the——Family,
whence her Title of *Honourable*; but is indeed fo
*celebrated*, that every fluttering Coxcomb in Town
can give fome Account of her, even before fhe was
in Keeping of the Duke of——, who had caft her
off to the Town he had robb'd of her.

In fhort, my Dear, fhe is quite a common Woman;
has no Fortune at all, as one may fay, only a fmall
Jointure incumber'd, and is much in Debt. —— She
is a Shrew into the Bargain, and the poor Wretch is
a Father already; for he has had a Girl of Three
Years old (her Husband has been dead Seven) brought
him home, which he knew nothing of, nor ever in-
quir'd, Whether his Widow had a Child! —— And he
is now imploy'd in paying the Mother's Debts, and
trying to make the beft of his Bargain

This is the Fruit of a *London* Journey, fo long
defir'd by him, and his fluttering about there with
his new Title

He was drawn in-by a Brother of his Lady, and
a Friend of that Brother's, two Town Sharpers, Game-
fters, and Bullies ——Poor Sir *Joseph Wittol*! That
was his Cafe, and his Character, it feems, in *London*

Shall I prefent you with a Curiofity? 'Tis a Copy
of his Letter to his Uncle, who had, as you may well
think, loft all Patience with him, on occafion of this
abominable Folly

*My Lord* D AVE RS,

' FOR iff you will nott call mee Neffew, I have
' no Reafon to call you Unkell, Shurely you for-
' gett who it was you held up youre Kane to I
' have as little Reafon to valew your Difpleaffure, as
             ' you

' you have mee, for I am, God be thanked, a Lord,
' and a Peere of the Realme, as well as you : And as
' to youre nott owneing me, nor youre Brother *B.*
' nott looking upon me, I care nott a Fardinge ;
' and, bad as you thinke I have done, I have mar-
' ry'd a Woman of Familly --- Take thatt among
' you !

' As to youre perfonall Abufes of her, take care
' whatt you fay.  You know the Stattute will defende
' us as well as you ---- And, befides, fhe has a Bro-
' ther, that won't lett her good Name be call'd in
' Queftion --- Mind thatt !

' Some Thinges I wifh had been otherwife --- Per-
' happs I do --- What then ? --- Muft you, my Lord,
' make more Mifchieff, and adde to my Plagues,
' iff I have any ? --- Is this your Unkelfhip ?

' Butt I fhan't want your Advife   I have as good
' an Eftate as you have, and am as much a Lord as
' yourfelfe.   Why the Devill then, am I to be treated
' as I am ? --- Why the Plague --- But I won't fware
' neither --- I defire not to fee you, any more then
' you doe me, I can tell you thatt.   And iff we ever
' meet under one Roofe with my Likeing, it muft
' be att the Houfe of Peeres, where I fhall be upon
' a Parr with you in every thing, that's my Cum-
' furte.

' As to my Lady *Davers,* I defire not to fee her
' Ladyfhipp, for fhee was always plaguy nimbel with
' her Fingers, but, lett my falfe Stepp be whât itt
' will, I have, in other refpectes, marry'd a Lady,
' who is as well defcended as herfelfe, and no Difpa-
' ragement neither, fo have nott thatt to anfwer for
' to her Pride ; and who has as good a Spiritt too,
' if they were to come Face too Face, or I am
' miftaken  Nor will fhee take Affruntes from any
' one  So, my Lord, leave mee to make the beft
' of my Matters, as I will you of youres.   So no
' more, but thatt I am

' Youre Servante,   H.

' *P. S* I meane no Affrunte to Mrs. *B.* She is the
beſt of yee all --- by G---.

I will not take up your Time with further Obſervations upon this poor Creature's bad Conduct His
Reflection muſt proceed from *Feeling* , and will,
that's the worſt of it, come too late, come *when* or
*how* it will I will only ſay, I am ſorry for it on his
own Account, but more for that of Lord and Lady
*Davers,* who take the Matter very heavily, and wiſh
he had marry'd the loweſt-born Creature in *England,*
(ſo ſhe had been honeſt and virtuous) rather than
done as he has done.

But, I ſuppoſe, the poor Gentleman was reſolv'd
to ſhun, at all Adventures, Mr. *B* 's Fault, and keep
up to the Pride of Deſcent and Family , --- and ſo
marry'd the *only* Creature, as I hope, (ſince it cannot be help'd) that is ſo great a Diſgrace to both.
For I preſume to flatter myſelf, for the ſake of my
Sex, that, among the poor Wretches, who are ſunk
ſo low as the Town-Women are, there are very few
of Birth or Education; but ſuch, principally, as have
had their Neceſſities or their Ignorance taken Advantage of by baſe Men, ſince Birth and Education
muſt needs ſet the moſt unhappy of the Sex above ſo
ſordid and ſo abandon'd a Guilt, as the hourly Wicked-
neſs of ſuch a Courſe of Life ſubjects them to

But let me purſue my Purpoſe of excuſing my
long Silence I had hardly return'd from Lord and
Lady *Davers's,* and recovered my Family Management, and reſum'd my Nurſery Duties, when my
Fourth dear Boy, my *Jemmy* --- (for, I think, I am
going on to make out the Number Lady *Davers*
allotted * me) preſs'd upon me in ſuch a manner,
as not to be refus'd, for one Month or Six Weeks

* *See this* Vol p 29, 30.

close

clofe Attention And then a Journey to Lord *Davers's*,
and that noble Pair accompanying us to *Kent*, and
daily and hourly Pleafures crouding upon us, narrow
and confin'd as our Room there was, (tho' we went
with as few Attendants as poffible) engroffed *more* of
my Time. So that I hope you will forgive me, on
all thefe Accounts, becaufe, as foon as I return'd, I
fet about writing this, as an Excufe for myfelf, in the
firft place, to promife you the Subject you infift upon,
in the next, and to tell you, that I am incapable of
Forgetfulnefs or Negligence to fuch a Friend as
Lady G. For I muft always be, dear Madam,

*Your faithful and affectionate humble Servant,*

P. B.

---

# LETTER LIX.

*My dear Lady* G

THE Remarks which, your Coufin *Fielding* tells
you, I have made on the Subject of young
Gentlemens Travelling, and which you requeft me
to communicate to you, are Part of a little Book
upon Education, which I wrote for Mr B's Correction and Amendment, on occafion of his putting
Mr. *Locke*'s Treatife on that Subject into my Hands,
and requiring my Obfervations upon it.

I cannot flatter myfelf, that they will anfwer your
Expectation; for I am fenfible they muft be unworthy even of the Opportunities I have had in the Excurfions, in which I have been indulged by the beft
of Gentlemen

But your Requefts are fo many Laws to me, and
I will give you a fhort Abftract of what I read to
Mifs *Fielding*, who has fo greatly over-rated it to
you.

That

That Gentleman's Book contains many excellent Rules on the Subject of Education: But this of Travel I will only refer you to at present  You will there fee his Objections against the Age at which young Gentlemen are fent abroad, from Sixteen to Twenty-one, the Time in all their Lives, he fays, in which young Men are the leaft fuited to thefe Improvements, and in which they have the leaft Fence and Guard againft their Paffions.

The Age he propofes is from Seven to Fourteen, becaufe of the Advantage they will then have to mafter Foreign Languages, and to form their Tongue to the true Pronunciation, as well as that then they will be more eafily directed by their Tutors or Governors  Or elfe he propofes that more fedate Time of Life, when the Gentleman is able to travel without a Tutor, and to make his own Obfervations; and when he is thoroughly acquainted with the Laws and Fafhions, the natural and moral Advantages and Defects of his own Country, by which means, as Mr. *Locke* wifely obferves, the Traveller will have fomething to exchange with thofe abroad, from whofe Converfation he hopes to reap any Knowlege  This Gentleman fupports his Opinion by excellent Reafons, to which I refer you

What I have written in my little Book, which I have not yet quite finifh'd, on *this* Head, relates principally to *Home Travelling*, which Mr *B* was always refolv'd his Sons fhould undertake, before they enter'd upon a Foreign Tour  I have there obferv'd, That *England* abounds with Curiofities, both of Art and Nature, worth the Notice of a diligent Inquirer, and equal with fome of thofe we admire in Foreign Parts, and that if the Youth be not fent abroad at Mr *Locke*'s earlieft Time, from Seven to Fourteen, (which I can hardly think will be worth while, merely for the fake of attaining a Perfection in the Languages) he may with good Advantage

tage begin, at Fourteen or Fifteen, the Tour of *Great
Britain*, now-and-then by Excurſions in the Summer
Months, between his other Studies, and as a Diver-
ſion to him.

This I ſhould wiſh might be enter'd upon in his
Papa's Company, as well as his Tutor's, if it could
conveniently be done, who thus initiating both the
Governed and the Governor in the Methods he
would have obſerv'd by both, will obtain no ſmall
Satisfaction and Amuſement to himſelf.

For the Father would by this means be an Eye-
witneſs of the Behaviour of the one and the other,
and have a Specimen, how fit the young Man was
to be truſted, or the Tutor to be depended upon,
when they went abroad, and were out of his Sight ;
as *they* would of what was expected from them by
the Father    And hence a thouſand Benefits, as I
humbly conceive, would ariſe to the young Gentleman from the Obſervations and Reflections he would
receive from his Father, as Occaſion offer'd, with
regard to Expence, Company, Converſation, Hours,
and ſuch-like

If the Father could not himſelf accompany his
Son, he might appoint the Stages the young Gentleman ſhould take, and injoin both Tutor and Son to
give, at every Stage, an Account of whatever they
obſerved curious and remarkable, not omitting the
minuteſt Occurrences    By this means, and the Probability, that he might hear of them, and their Proceedings, from his Friends, Acquaintance, and Relations, who might fall in with them, or at whoſe
Seats they might ſometimes be entertained, they would
have a greater Regard to their Conduct , and ſo much
the more, if the young Gentleman were to keep an
Account of his Expences, which upon his Return,
he might lay before his Father

By ſeeing thus the different Cuſtoms, Manners,
and Oeconomy of different Perſons and Families,
(for

(for in fo mix'd a Nation as ours is, there is as great a Variety of that fort to be met with, as in moft) and from their different Treatment at their feveral Stages, a great deal of the World may be learn'd by the young Gentleman   He would be prepar'd to go abroad with more Delight to himfelf, as well as more Experience, and greater Reputation to his Family and Country.   In fuch Excurfions as thefe, the Tutor would fee the Temper and Inclination of the young Gentleman, and might give proper Notices to the Father, if any thing was amifs, that it might be fet right, while the Youth was yet in his Reach, and more under his Infpection, than he would be in a foreign Country   And the Obfervations the young Gentleman would make at his Return, as well as in his Letters, would fhew how fit he was to be trufted, and how likely to improve, when at a greater Diftance.

After *England* and *Wales*, as well the inland Parts, as the Sea-coafts, let them, if they behave according to Expectation, take a Journey into *Scotland* and *Ireland*, and vifit the principal Iflands, as *Guernfey*, *Jerfey*, &c the young Gentleman continuing to write down his Obfervations all the way, and keeping a Journal of Occurrences· And let him imploy the little Time he will be on board of Ship in thefe fmall Trips from Ifland to Ifland, or Coaftwife, in obferving upon the noble Art of Navigation ; of the Theory of which, it will not be amifs, that he has fome Notion, as well as of the curious Structure of a Ship, its Tackle, and Furniture   A Knowlege very far from being infignificant to a Gentleman who is an Iflander, and has a Stake in the greateft maritime Kingdom in the World, and hence he will be taught to love and value that moft ufeful and brave Set of Men, the *Britifh* Sailors, who are the natural Defence and Glory of the Realm

Hereby he will confirm his Theory of the Geography of the *Britifh* Dominions in *Europe*. He
will

will be appris'd of the Situation, Conveniencies, Interests and Constitution of his own Country ; and will be able to lay a Ground-work for the future Government of his Thoughts and Actions, if the Interest he bears in his native Country should call him to the publick Service in either House of Parliament

With this Foundation, how excellently would he be qualify'd to go abroad ? and how properly then would he add to the Knowlege he had attain'd of his own Country, that of the different Customs, Manners, and Forms of Government of others ? How would he be able to form Comparisons, and to make all his Inquiries appear pertinent and manly ? All the Occasions of that ignorant Wonder, which renders a Novice the Jest of all about him, would be taken away   He would be able to ask Questions, and to judge without Leading-strings   Nor would he think he has seen a Country, and answer'd the Ends of his Father's Expence, and his own Improvement, by running thro' a Kingdom, and knowing nothing of it, but the Inns and Stages, at which he stopp'd to eat and drink   For, on the contrary, he would make the best Acquaintance, and contract worthy Friendships with such as would court and reverence him as one of the rising Genius's of his Country

Whereas most of the young Gentlemen, who are sent abroad raw and unprepar'd, as if to wonder at every thing they see, and to be laugh'd at by all that see them, do but expose themselves, and their Country   And if at their Return, by Interest of Friends, by Alliances or Marriages, they should happen to be promoted to Places of Honour or Profit, their unmerited Preferment will only serve to make those Foreigners, who were Eye-witnesses of their Weakness and Follies, when among them, conclude greatly in Disfavour of the whole Nation, or, at
leaft,

leaft, of the Prince, and his Adminiftration, who could find no fitter Subjects to diftinguifh

This, my dear Friend, is a brief Extract from my Obfervations on the Head of qualifying young Gentlemen to travel with Honour and Improvement I doubt you'll be apt to think me not a little out of my Element, but fince you *would* have it, I claim the Allowances of a Friend, to which my ready Compliance with your Commands the rather intitles me

I am very forry Mr. and Mrs *Murray* are fo unhappy in each other Were he a generous Man, the heavy Lofs the poor Lady has fuftained, as well as her Sifter, my beloved Friend, in fo excellent a Mo.her, and fo kind a Father, would make him bear with her Infirmities a little

But, really, I have feen on Twenty Occafions, that, notwithftanding all the fine Things Gentlemen fay to Ladies before Marriage, if the latter do not *improve* upon their Husbands Hands, their imputed Graces, when fingle, will not protect them from Indifference, and, probably, from worfe, while the Gentleman, perhaps, thinks *he* only, of the Two, is intitled to go backward in Acts of Kindnefs and Complaifance A ftrange and a fhocking Difference, which too many Ladies experience, who, from fond Lovers, proftrate at their Feet, find furly Husbands, trampling upon their Necks!

You, my dear Friend, were happy in your Days of Courtfhip, and are no lefs fo in your State of Wedlock And may you continue to be fo to a good old Age, prays

*Your affectionate and faithful Friend,*

P B.

LETTER

# LETTER LX.

*My dear Lady* G.

I WILL chearfully caufe to be tranfcribed for you the Converfation you defire, between myfelf, Mrs *Towers,* and Mrs. *Arthur,* and the Three young Ladies their Relations, in Prefence of the Dean and 'his Daughter, and Mrs *Brooks,* and glad I fhall be, if it may be of Ufe to the two thoughtlefs Miffes your Neighbours; who, you are pleafed to tell me, are great Admirers of my Story, and my Example; and will therefore, as you fay, pay greater Attention to what I write, than to the more paffionate and interefted Leffons of their Mamma.

I am only forry, that you fhould have been under any Concern about the fuppofed Trouble you give me, by having miflaid my former Relation of it. For, befides obliging my dear Lady G. the Hope, that I may be able to do Service by it to a Family fo worthy, in a Cafe fo nearly affecting its Honour, as to make two headftrong young Ladies recollect what belongs to their Sex and their Characters, and what their filial Duties require of them, affords me high Pleafure, and if it fhall be attended with the wifh'd Effects, it will be an Addition to my Happinefs

I faid, *caufe* to be tranfcribed; becaufe I hope to anfwer a double End by it, for, after I had re-confider'd it, I let Mifs *Goodwin* to tranfcribe it, who writes a very pretty Hand, and is not a little fond of the Task, nor, indeed, of any Task I fet her; and will be more affected, as fhe *performs* it, than fhe could be by *reading* it only, altho' fhe is a very good Girl at prefent, and gives me Hopes, that fhe will continue to be fo

As foon as it is done, I will inclofe it, that it may be read to the Parties without this Introduction, if
you

you think fit   And you will forgive me for having
added a few Obfervations to this Tranfcription, with
a View to the Cafes of your inconfiderate young
Ladies, and for having corrected the former Narrative in feveral Places

*My dear Lady* G

THE Papers you have miflaid, relating to the
Converfation between me and the young Ladies,
Relations of Lady *Towers*, and Lady *Arthur*, in
Prefence of thefe two laft-named Ladies, Mrs *Brooks*,
and the worthy Dean, and Mifs *L* (of which, in
order to perfect your kind Collection of my Com-
munications, you requeft another Copy) contained
as follows

I firft began with apprifing you, that I had feen thefe
three Ladies twice or thrice before, as Vifitors, at
their Kinfwomens Houfes, fo that they and I were
not altogether Strangers to one another   And my
two Neighbours acquainted me with their refpective
Taftes and Difpofitions, and gave me their Hiftories,
preparatory to this Vifit, to the following Effect

‘ That Mifs STAPYLTON is over-run with the
‘ Love of Poetry and Romance, and delights much
‘ in flowery Language, and metaphorical Flourifhes
‘ Is about Eighteen, wants not either Senfe or Po-
‘ litenefs , and has read herfelf into a Vein, that is
‘ more amorous ( that was Lady *Towers*'s Word)
‘ than difcreet   Has extraordinary Notions of a
‘ *Firft-fight* Love , and gives herfelf greater Liber-
‘ ties, with a Pair of fine Eyes, (in hopes to make
‘ fudden Conquefts in purfuance of that Notion )
‘ than is pretty in her Sex and Age , which makes
‘ thofe who know her not, conclude her bold and
‘ forward ; and is more than fufpected, with a Mind
‘ thus prepared for inftantaneous Impreffions, to have
‘ experienced the Argument to her own Difadvan-
‘ tage, and to be *ftruck* by (before fhe has *ftricken*)
‘ a Gen-

' a Gentleman, whom her Friends think not at all
' worthy of her, and to whom she was making some
' indiscreet Advances, under the Name of PHILO-
' CLEA to PHILOXENUS, in a Letter which she in-
' trusted to a Servant of the Family, who, disco-
' vering her Design, prevented her Indiscretion for
' that Time

' That, in other respects, she has no mean Ac-
' complishments, will have a fine Fortune, is gen-
' teel in her Person, though with some visible Affecta-
' tion, dances well, sings well, and plays prettily on
' several Instruments; is fond of reading, but affects
' the Action, and Air, and Attitude, of a Tragedian;
' and is too apt to give an Emphasis in the wrong
' Place, in order to make an Author mean more
' significantly than it is necessary he should, even
' where the Occasion is common, and in a mere
' historical Fact, that requires as much Simplicity
' in the Reader's Accent, as in the Writer's Style.
' No Wonder then, that when she reads a Play, she
' will put herself into a Sweat, as Lady *Towers* says;
' distorting very agreeable Features, and making a
' *Multitude* of wry Mouths, with *one* very pretty
' one, in order to convince her Hearers, what a
' near Neighbour her Heart is to her Lips.

' Miss COPE is a young Lady of Nineteen, lovely
' in her Person, with a handsome Fortune in Pos-
' session, and great Prospects  Has a soft and gen-
' tle Turn of Mind, which disposes her to be easily
' imposed upon  Is address'd by a Libertine of
' Quality, whose Courtship, while permitted, was
' Imperiousness, and whose Tenderness, Insult, have-
' ing found the young Lady too susceptible of Im-
' pression, open and unreserv'd, and even valuing
' him the more, as it seem'd, for treating her with
' ungenerous Contempt, for that she was always
' making Excuses for Slights, Ill-manners, and even
' Rudeness, which no other young Lady would forgive.
                                        ' That

' That this Facility on her Side, and this Infolence
' on his, and an over-free, and even indecent De-
' gree of Ramping, as it is called, with Mifs, which
' once her Mamma furpris'd them in, made her Papa
' forbid *his* Vifits, and *her* receiving them

' That this, however, was fo much to Mifs's
' Regret, that fhe was detected in a Defign to elope
' to him out of the private Garden-door, which,
' had fhe effected, in all Probability, the indelicate
' and difhonourable Peer would have triumphed over
' her Innocence; having given out fince, that he
' intended to revenge himfelf on the Daughter, for
' the Difgrace he had receiv'd from the Parents

' That tho' fhe was convinc'd of this, 'twas fear'd
' fhe ftill lov'd him, and would throw herfelf in his
' way the firft convenient Opportunity; urging, that
' his rafh Expreffions were the Effect only of his
' Paffion, for that fhe knows he loves her too well,
' to be difhonourable to her : And, by the fame
' Degree of favourable Prepoffeffion, fhe will have
' it, That his brutal Roughnefs, is the Manlinefs of his
' Nature, That his moft fhocking Expreffions, are
' Sincerity of Heart; That his Boafts of his former
' Lewdnefs, are but Inftances that he knows the
' World, That his Freedoms with her Perfon, are
' but Excefs of Love, and innocent Gaiety of
' Temper, That his refenting the Prohibition he
' has met with, and his Threats, are other Inftances
' of his Love and his Courage: And Peers of the
' Realm ought not to be bound down by little narrow
' Rules, like the Vulgar; for, truly, their *Honour*,
' which is regarded in the greateft Cafes, as equal
' with the *Oath* of a common Gentleman, is a Se-
' curity that a Lady may truft to, if he is not a Pro-
' fligate indeed; and that Lord **P** *cannot* be.

' That excepting thefe Weakneffes, Mifs has many
' good Qualities, is charitable, pious, humane, hum-
' ble, fings fweetly, plays on the Spinnet charmingly,
' is

' is meek, fearful, and never was refolute or cou-
' rageous enough to ftep out of the regular Path,
' till her too flexible Heart became touched with a
' Paffion, that is faid to polifh the moft brutal Temper,
' and therefore her rough Peer has none of it, and
' to animate the Dove, of which Mifs *Cope* has too
' much

' That Mifs SUTTON, a young Lady of the like
' Age with the two former, has too lively and airy
' a Turn of Mind; affects to be thought well read
' in the Hiftories of Kingdoms, as well as in polite
' Literature Speaks *French* fluently, talks upon all
' Subjects much, and has a great deal of that flip-
' pant Wit, which makes more Enemies than Friends.
' However is innocent, and unfufpectedly virtuous
' hitherto, but makes herfelf cheap and acceffible
' to Fops and Rakes, and has not the worfe Opinion
' of a Man for being fuch. Liftens eagerly to Sto-
' ries told to the Difadvantage of Individuals of her
' own Sex, tho' affecting to be a great Stickler for
' the Honour of the Sex in general Will unpityingly
' propagate fuch Stories: Thinks (without confider-
' ing to what the Imprudence of her own Conduct
' may fubject her) the Woman, that flips, inexcu-
' fable, and the Man who feduces her, much lefs
' faulty ·'And by this means, encourages the one
' Sex in their Vilenefs, and gives up the other for
' their Weaknefs, in a kind of filly Affectation, to
' fhew her Security in her own Virtue, at the very
' time, that fhe is dancing upon the Edge of a Pre-
' cipice, prefumptuoufly inattentive to her own
' Danger.'

The worthy Dean, knowing the Ladies Intention
in this Vifit to me, brought his Daughter with him,
as if by Accident: For Mifs L with many good
Qualities, is of a remaikably foft Temper, tho' not
fo inconfiderately foft as Mifs *Cope* But is too cre-

dulous; and, as her Papa fufpects, entertains more than a Liking to a wild young Gentleman, the Heir to a noble Fortune, who makes Vifits to her, full of Tendernefs and Refpect, but without declaring himfelf This gives the Dean a good deal of Uneafinefs, and he is very defirous, that Mifs fhould be in my Company on all Occafions, as fhe is fo kind to profefs a great Regard to my Opinion and Judgment

'Tis eafy to fee the poor young Lady is in Love; and fhe makes no doubt, that the young Gentleman loves *her* : But, alas ! why then (for he is not a bafhful Man, as you fhall hear) does he not fay fo? ---- He has deceived already two young Creatures. His Father has cautioned the Dean againft his Son Has told him, that he is fly, fubtle, full of Stratagem, yet has fo much Command of himfelf, (which makes him more dangerous) as not to precipitate his Defigns, but can wait with Patience, till he thinks himfelf fecure of his Prey, and then pulls off the Mask at once, and, if he fucceeds, glories in his Villainy.

Yet does the Father beg of the Dean to permit his Vifits, for he would be glad he would marry Mifs *L* tho' greatly unequal in Fortune to his Son; wifhing for nothing fo much, as that he *would* marry. And the Dean, owing his principal Preferment to the old Gentleman, cares not to difoblige him, or affront his Son without fome apparent Reafon for it, efpecially, as the Father is wrapt up in him, having no other Child, and being himfelf half afraid of him, left, if too much thwarted, he fhould fly out intirely

So here, Madam, are Four young Ladies of like Years, and different Inclinations and Tempers, all of whom may be faid to have Dangers to encounter, refulting from their refpective Difpofitions And who, profeffing to admire my Character, and the Example I had fet, were brought to me, to be benefited,

nefited, as Lady *Towers* was pleafed to fay, by my Converfation· And all was to be as if accidental, none of them knowing how well I was acquainted with their feveral Characters.

How proud, my dear Lady *G* would this Compliment have made me, from fuch a Lady as Mrs. *Towers*, had I not been as proud as proud could be before, of the good Opinion of Four beloved Perfons, Mr. *B* Lady *Davers*, the Countefs of *C* and your dear Self!

We were attended only by *Polly Barlow*, who was as much concern'd as any body in fome of the Points that came before us.   And as you know this was in the Time of the Vifit paid us by Lord and Lady *Davers*, and that noble Countefs, 'tis proper to fay, they were abroad together upon a Vifit, from which, knowing how I was to be engag'd, they excus'd me

The Dean was well known to, and valu'd by, all the Ladies ; and therefore was no manner of Reftraint upon the Freedom of our Converfation.

I was above in my Clofet when they came, and Lady *Towers*, having prefented each young Lady to me when I came down, faid, being all feated, I can guefs at your Imployment, Mrs *B* --- Writing, I dare fay ? I have often wifh'd to have you for a Correfpondent, for every one who can boaft of that Favour, exalts you to the Skies, and fays, Your Letters exceed your Converfation, but I always infifted upon it, that *that* was impoffible

Lady *Towers*, faid I, is always faying the moft obliging Things in the World of her Neighbours : But may not one fuffer, dear Madam, for thefe kind Prepoffeffions, in the Opinion of greater Strangers, who will judge more impartially than your Favour will permit you to do ?

That, faid Lady *Arthur*, will be fo foon put out of Doubt, when Mrs. *B*. begins to fpeak, that we

will

will refer to that, and so put an End to every thing that looks like Compliment

But, Mis *B* said Lady *Towers*, may one ask, What particular Subject was at this Time your Imployment?

I had been writing, (you must know, Lady *G*) for the sake of suiting Miss *Stapylton*'s flighty Vein, a little Sketch of the Style she is so fond of, and hoped for some such Opportunity as this Question gave me, to bring it on the Carpet; for my only Fear, with her, and Miss *Cope*, and Miss *Sutton*, was, that they would deem me too grave, and so what should fall in the Course of Conversation, would make the less Impression upon them For even the best Instructions in the World, you know, will be ineffectual, if the Method of conveying them is not adapted to the Taste and Temper of the Person you would wish to influence And, moreover, I had a View in it, to make this little Sketch the Introduction to a future Occasion for some Observations on the stiff and affected Style of Romances, which might put Miss out of Conceit with them, and make her turn the Course of her Studies another Way, as I shall mention in its Place

I answer'd, That I had been meditating upon the Misfortune of a fine young Lady, who had been seduced and betrayed by a Gentleman she loved, and who, notwithstanding, had the Grace to stop short, (indeed, later than were to be wished) and to abandon Friends, Country, Lover, in order to avoid any farther Intercourse with him, and that God had blessed her Penitence and Resolution, and she was now very happy in a neighbouring Dominion

A fine Subject, said Miss *Stapylton* !---- Was the Gentleman a Man of Wit, Madam? Was the Lady a Woman of Taste?

The Gentleman, Mifs, was all that was defirable in Man, had he been virtuous . The Lady, all that was excellent in Woman, had fhe been more circumfpect. But it was a firft Love on both Sides ; and little did fhe think he could have taken Advantage of her Innocence and her Affection for him

A fad, fad Story! faid Mifs *Cope* But, pray, Madam, did their Friends approve of their Vifits ? For Danger fometimes, as I have heard, arifes from the Cruelty of Friends, who force Lovers upon private and clandeftine Meetings, when, perhaps, there can be no material Objection, why the Gentleman and Lady may not come together

Well obferv'd, Mifs *Cope*, thought I! How we are for making every Cafe applicable to our own, when our Hearts are fix'd upon a Point ?

It cannot be called *Cruelty* in Friends, Mifs, faid I, when their Cautions, or even *Prohibitions*, are fo well juftify'd by the Event, as in *this* Cafe —— and, *generally*, by the wicked Arts and Practices of Seducers. And how happy is it for a Lady, when fhe fuffers herfelf to be convinc'd, that thofe who have lived *Forty* Years in the World, may know twice as much, at leaft, of that World, as fhe can poffibly know at *Twenty*, Ten of which moreover are almoft a Blank! If they do *not*, the one muft be fuppofed very ignorant ; the other, very knowing

But, Mifs, the Lady, whofe hard Cafe I was confidering, *hop'd* too much, and *fear'd* too little; that was her Fault ; which made her give Opportunities to the Gentleman, which neither *Liberty* nor *Reftraint* could juftify in her She had not the Difcretion, poor Lady! in this one great Point of all, that the Ladies I have in my Eye, I dare fay, would have had in her Cafe

I beg Pardon, faid Mifs, and blufh'd I know not the Cafe, and ought to have been filent.

Ay, Miſs, thought I, ſo you would, had not you thought yourſelf more affected by it, than it were to be wiſh'd you were

I think, ſaid Miſs *Sutton*, the Lady was the leſs to be pity'd, as ſhe muſt know what her Character re-quir'd of her; and that Men will generally deceive, when they are truſted. There are very few of them, who *pretend* to be virtuous, and it is allow'd to be *their* Privilege to ask, as it is the *Lady's* to deny

So, Miſs, reply'd I, you are ſuppoſing a continual State of War between the Two Sexes; one offenſive, the other defenſive: And, indeed, I think the Notion not altogether amiſs, for a Lady will aſſuredly be leſs in Danger, where ſhe rather *fears* an *Enemy* in the Acquaintance ſhe has of that Sex, than *hopes* a *Friend*, eſpecially as ſo much depends upon the Iſſue, either of her Doubt, or of her Confidence.

I don't know *neither*, Madam, return'd Miſs, very briskly, whether the Men ſhould be ſet out to us as ſuch Bugbears, as our Mamma's generally repreſent them It is making them too conſiderable, and is a kind of Reflection upon the Diſcretion and Virtue of our Sex, and ſuppoſes us weak indeed.

The late Czar, I have read, continued Miſs, took a better Method with the *Swedes*, who had often beat him, when, after a great Victory, he made his Cap tives march in Proceſſion, thro' the Streets of his principal City, to familiarize them to the *Ruſſes*; and ſhew them they were *but* Men

Very well obſerv'd, Miſs, reply'd I · But then, did you not ſay, that this was thought neceſſary to be done, becauſe the *Ruſſes* had been often *defeated* by theſe *Swedes*, and thought *too highly* of them, and when the *Swedes*, taking Advantage of that Pre-poſſeſſion, had the *greater Contempt* of the *Ruſſes*?

Miſs looked a little diſconcerted, and being ſilent, I proceeded.

I am

I am very far, Miſs, from thinking the Generality of Men very formidable, if our Sex do Juſtice to themſelves, and to what their Characters require of them. Nevertheleſs, give me Leave to ſay, that the Men I thought contemptible, I would not think worthy of my Company, nor give it to them, when I could avoid it    And as for thoſe, who are more to be regarded, I am afraid, that when they can be aſſured, that a Lady allows it to be their Privilege to ſue for Favours, it will certainly imbolden them to ſolicit, and to think themſelves acting in Character when they put the Lady upon hers, to refuſe them    And yet I am humbly of Opinion with the Poet:

> He *comes* too near, *who comes to be* deny'd.

For theſe Reaſons, Miſs, I was pleaſed with your Notion, that it would be beſt to look upon that Sex, eſpecially if we allow them the Privilege you ſpeak of, in an *hoſtile* Light

But permit me to obſerve, with regard to the moſt contemptible of the Species, Fops, Coxcombs, and Pretty Fellows, that many a *good* General has been defeated, when, truſting to his great Strength and Skill, he has deſpis'd a *truly weak* Enemy

I believe, Madam, return'd Miſs, your Obſervation is very juſt    I have read of ſuch Inſtances  But, dear Madam, permit me to aſk, Whether we ſpeak not too generally, when we condemn every Man who dreſſes well, and is not a Sloven, as a Fop or a Coxcomb?

No doubt, we do, when this is the Caſe    But permit me to obſerve, that you haidly ever in your Life, Miſs, ſaw a Gentleman who was *very* nice about his Perſon and Dreſs, that had any thing he thought of *greater* Conſequence to himſelf, to regard. 'Tis natural it ſhould be ſo, for ſhould not the Man of *Body* take the greateſt Care to ſet out and adorn

S 4    the

the Part for which he thinks himfelf moft valuable?
And will not the Man of *Mind* beftow his principal
Care in improving that Mind? Perhaps, to the Neglect of Drefs, and outward Appearance, which is
a Fault. But furely, Mifs, there is a Middle-way to
be obferved, in thefe, as in moft other Cafes, for
a Man need not be a Sloven, any more than a Fop.
He need not fhew an utter Difregard to Drefs, nor
yet think it his firft and chief Concern, be ready to
quarrel with the Wind for difcompofing his Peruque,
or fear to put on his Hat, left he fhould deprefs his
Fore-top, more diflike a Spot upon his Cloaths, then
in his Reputation. Be a Self-admirer, and always at
the Glafs, which he would perhaps never look into,
cou'd it fhew him the Deformity of his Mind, as well
as the Finery of his Perfon.---Who has a Tailor for
his Tutor, and a Milaner for his School-miftrefs,
who laughs at Men of Senfe (excufably enough, perhaps in Revenge becaufe they laugh at him) Who
calls Learning Pedantry; and looks upon the Knowlege of the Fafhions, as the only ufeful Science to a
fine Gentleman.

Pardon me, Ladies. I could proceed with the
Character of this Species of Men, but I need not,
becaufe every Lady prefent, I am fure, would defpife
fuch a one, as much as I do, were he to fall in her
way. And the rather, becaufe it is certain, that he
who admires himfelf, will never admire his Lady as
he ought, and if he maintains his Nicenefs after
Marriage, it will be with a Preference to his own
Perfon. If not, will fink, very probably into the
worft of Slovens. For whoever is capable of one
Extreme, (take almoft all the Cafes in human Life
through) when he recedes from that, if he be not a
Man of Prudence, will go over into the other.

But to return to the former Subject, (for the
general Attention encourag'd me to proceed) permit me, Mifs *Sutton*, to add, That a Lady muft run
great

great Rifques to her Reputation, if not to her Virtue, who will admit into her Company, *any* Gentleman, who fhall be of Opinion, and *know* it to be *hers,* that it is *his* Province to afk a Favour, that it will be her Duty to deny

I believe, Madam, faid Mifs, I fpoke thefe Words a little too carelefly But I meant *honourable* Queftions, to be fure

There can be but *one* honourable Queftion, Mifs, reply'd I, and that is feldom afk'd, but when the Affair is brought near a Conclufion, and there is a Probability of its being granted, and which a Single Lady, while fhe has Parents or Guardians, fhould never think of permitting to be put to herfelf, much lefs of approving, nor, perhaps, as the Cafe may be, of denying But I make no doubt, Mifs, that you meant honourable Queftions A young Lady of Mifs *Sutton's* good Senfe, and worthy Character, could not mean otherwife And I have faid, perhaps, more than I needed to fay, upon this Subject, becaufe we all know how ready the Prefuming of the other Sex are, right or wrong, to conftrue the moft innocent Meanings in favour of their own Views

Very true, faid Mifs, but appear'd to be under an agreeable Confufion, every Lady, by her Eye, feeming to think fhe had met with a deferv'd Rebuke, and which not feeming to expect, it abated her Livelinefs all the Time after

Lady *Towers* feafonably reliev'd us both from a Subject too *applicable*, if I may fo exprefs it, faying, But, dear Mrs B will you favour us with the Refult of your Meditation, if you have committed it to Writing, on the unhappy Cafe you mention'd?

I was rather, Madam, exercifing my Fancy than my Judgment, fuch as it is, upon the Occafion I was aiming at a kind of allegorical or metaphorical

Style,

Style, I know not which to call it, and it is not fit to be read before such Judges, I doubt

O pray, dear Madam, said Miss *Stapylton*, favour us with it *to chuse*, for I am a great Admirer of that Style

I have a great Curiosity, said Lady *Arthur*, both from the *Subject* and the *Style*, to hear what you have written: And I beg you will oblige us all

It is short and unfinish'd  It was written for the sake of a Friend, who is fond of such a Style, and what I shall add to it, will be principally some slight Observations upon this Way of Writing  But, let it be ever so censurable, I should be *more* so, if I made any Difficulties after such an unanimous Request.  So taking it out of my Letter-case, I read as follows:

" While the *Banks* of *Discretion* keep the *proud*
" *Waves* of *Passion* within their natural Chanel, all calm
" and serene, glides along the silver Current, enlivening
" the adjacent Meadows, as it passes, with a brighter
" and more flow'ry Verdure.  But if the *Torrents*
" of *sensual Love* are permitted to descend from
" the *Hills* of *credulous Hope*, they may so swell the
" gentle Stream, as to make it difficult, if not im-
" possible, to be retain'd within its usual Bounds.
" What then will be the Consequence? --- Why,
" the *Trees of Resolution*, and the *Shrubs of cautious*
" *Fear*, which grew upon the frail Mound, and
" whose intertwining Roots had contributed to sup-
" port it, being loosen'd from their Hold, *they*, and
" all that would swim of the *Bank* itself, will be seen
" floating on the Surface of the triumphant Waters.
" But here, a dear Lady, having unhappily failed,
" is enabled to set her *Foot* in the *new-made* Breach,
" while yet it is *possible* to stop it, and to say, with
" little Variation, in the Language of that Power,
" which

" which only could enable her to fay it, *Hither, ye*
" *proud Waves of diffolute Love, altho' you* HAVE
" *come, yet no farther* SHALL *ye come* ; is fuch an
" Inftance of magnanimous Refolution and Self-
" conqueft, as is very rarely to be met with "

Mifs *Stapylton* feem'd pleas'd (as I expected) with
what I read, and told me, That fhe fhould take it
for a high Favour, if I would permit her, if it were
not improper, to fee the whole Letter, when I had
finifh'd it.

I faid, I would oblige her with all my Heart.
But you muft not expect, Mifs, that altho' I have
written what I have read to you, I fhall approve of it
in my Obfervations upon it ; for I am convinc'd,
that no Style can be proper, which is not plain,
fimple, eafy, natural, and unaffected

She was fure, fhe was pleas'd to fay, That whatever my Obfervations were, they would be equally
juft and inftructive.

I too, faid the Dean, will anfwer for that ; for
I dare fay, by what I have already heard, That
Mrs *B.* will diftinguifh properly between the Style,
and the Matter too, which captivates the Imagination, and that which informs the Judgment.

Our Converfation, after this, took a more general
Turn, as to the Air of it, if I may fay fo , which I
thought right, left the young Ladies fhould imagine
it was a defigned Thing againft them : But yet it
was fuch, that every one of them found her Character and Tafte, little or much, concerned in it ;
and all feem'd, as Lady *Towers* afterwards obferv'd
to me, by their Silence and Attention, to be bufy'd
in private Applications

The Dean began it, with a high Compliment to me,
having a View, no doubt, by his kind Praifes, to make
my Obfervations have the greater Weight upon the
young Ladies. He was pleas'd to fay, That it was

Matter

Matter of great Surprize to him, that, my tender Years confider'd, I fhould be capable of making thofe Reflections, by which Perfons of twice my Age and Experience might be inftructed. You fee, Madam, faid he, how attentive we all are, when your Lips begin to open, and I beg we may have nothing to do, but to *be* attentive

I have had fuch Advantages, Sir, reply'd I, from the Obfervations and Cautions of my late excellent Lady, that did you but know half of them, you would rather wonder I had made *no greater* Improvement, than that I have made *fo much* She ufed to think me pretty, and not ill-temper'd, and, *of courfe*, not incredulous, where I conceiv'd a good Opinion, and was always arming me on that Side, as believing I might be the Object of wicked Attempts, and the rather, as my low Fortunes fubjected me to Danger For, had I been born to Rank and Condition, as thefe young Ladies here, I fhould have had Reafon to think of *myfelf*, as juftly, as, no doubt, *they* do, and, of confequence, beyond the Reach of any vile Intriguer, as I fhould have been above the greateft Part of that Species of Mankind, who, for want of Underftanding or Honour, or thro' pernicious Habits, give themfelves up to Libertinifm

Thefe were great Advantages, no doubt, faid Mifs *Sutton*, but in *you*, they met with a furprifing Genius, 'tis very plain, Madam, and there is not, in my Opinion, a Lady in *England* of your Years, who would have improv'd by them, as you have done

I anfwer'd, That I was much oblig'd to her for her good Opinion And that I had always obferv'd, that the Perfon who admir'd any good Qualities in another, gave a kind of *natural*-Demonftration, that fhe had the fame in an eminent Degree herfelf, altho', perhaps, her modeft Diffidence would not permit her to trace the generous Principle to its Source.

The

The Dean, in order to bring us back again to the Subject of *Credulity*, repeated my Remark, that it was safer, in Cases where so much depended upon the Issue, as a Lady's Honour and Reputation, to *fear* an *Enemy*, than to *hope* a *Friend*, and praised my Observation, that even a *weak* Enemy is not to be too much despised

I said, I had very high Notions of the Honour and Value of my own Sex, and very mean ones of the gay and frothy Part of the other, insomuch that I thought they could have no Strength, but what was founded in our Weakness· That, indeed, the Difference of Education must give Men Advantages, even where the Genius is naturally equal; That, besides, they have generally more Hardness of Heart, which makes Ladies, where they meet not with Men of Honour, to engage with that Sex upon very unequal Terms; for that it is so customary with them to make Vows and Promises, and to set light by them, *when made*, that an innocent Lady cannot guard too watchfully against them, and, in my Opinion, should believe nothing they said, or even *vow'd*, but what carry'd Demonstration with it.

I remember, continu'd I, my Lady used often to observe, That there is a Time of Life in all young Persons, which may properly be called, *The Romantick,* which is a very dangerous Period, and requires therefore a great Guard of Prudence· That the Risque is not a little augmented by reading Novels and Romances; and that the Poetical Tribe have much to answer for on this Head, by reason of their heighten'd and inflaming Descriptions, which do much Hurt to thoughtless Minds, and lively Imaginations  For to those, she would have it, are principally owing, the Rashness and Indiscretion of *soft* and *tender* Dispositions, which, in Breach of their Duty, and even to the Disgrace of their Sex, too frequently set them upon Enterprizes; like those

they

they have read In thofe pernicious Writings, which not feldom make them fall a Sacrifice to the bafe Defigns of fome vile Intriguer, and even in Cafes where their Precipitation ends the beft, that is to fay, in *Marriage*, they too frequently (in direct Oppofi ion to the Cautions and Commands of their *try'd*, their *experienc'd*, and *unqueftionable* Friends) throw themfelves upon an *almoft Stranger*, who, had he been worthy of them, would not, nor *needed* to have taken indirect Methods to obtain their Favour

And the Misfortune is, continu'd I, the moft innocent are generally the moft credulous. Such a Lady would do no Harm to others herfelf, and cannot think others would do her any And with regard to the particular Perfon who has obtain'd, perhaps, a Share in her Confidence, *he* cannot, furely, fhe thinks, be fo *ingrateful*, as to return irreparable Mifchief for her Good-will to him. Were all the Men in the World, befides, to prove falfe, the *beloved* Perfon cannot. 'Twould be unjuft to *her own Merit*, as well as to *his Vows*, to fuppofe it And fo *Defign* on his Side, and *Credulity* and *Self-opinion* on the Lady's, at laft inroll the unhappy Believer in the Lift of the too-late Repenters

And what, Madam, faid the Dean, has not that Wretch to anfwer for, who makes Sport of deftroying a virtuous Character, and in being the wicked Means of throwing, perhaps, upon the Town, and into the Dregs of Proftitution, a poor Creature, whofe Love for him, and Confidence in him, was all her Crime? And who otherwife might have made a worthy Figure at the Head of fome reputable Family, and fo have been an ufeful Member of the Commonwealth, propagating good Examples, inftead of Ruin and Infamy, to Mankind? To fay nothing of, what is ftill worfe, the dreadful Crime of occafioning the Lofs of a Soul, fince final Impenitence too generally
follows

follows the firſt Sacrifice which the poor Wretch is ſeduced to make of her Honour?

There are ſeveral Gentlemen in our Neighbour-hood, ſaid Mrs *Brooks,* who might be benefited by this touching Reflection, if it was repreſented in the ſame ſtrong Lights from the Pulpit  And permit me to ſay, Mr. Dean, that, I think, you ſhould give us a Sermon upon this Subject, for the ſake of both Sexes; one for Caution, the other for Conviction.

I will think of it, reply'd he  But I am ſorry to ſay, that we have too many among our younger Gentry, who would think themſelves pointed at, were I to touch this Subject ever ſo cautiouſly

I am ſure, ſaid Lady *Towers,* there cannot well be a more uſeful one; and the very Reaſon the Dean gives, is a convincing Proof of it to me.

When I have had the Pleaſure of hearing the further Sentiments of ſuch an Aſſembly as this, upon the delicate Subject, reply'd this polite Divine, I ſhall be better enabled to treat it.  And, pray, Ladies, proceed; for it is from your Converſation, that I muſt take my Hints.

You have nothing to do then, ſaid Lady *Towers,* but to engage Mrs *B.* to ſpeak; and you may be ſure, we will all be as attentive to *her,* as we ſhall be to *you,* when we ſhall have the Pleaſure to hear ſo fine a Genius improving upon her Hints, from the Pulpit.

I bow'd (as the Dean did) to Lady *Towers;* and knowing, that ſhe praiſed me, with the Dean's View, in order to induce the young Ladies to give the greater Attention to what ſhe wiſhed I ſhould ſpeak, I ſaid, It would be a great Preſumption in me, after ſo high a Compliment, to open my Lips · Neverthe-leſs, as I was ſure, by ſpeaking, I ſhould have the Benefit of Inſtruction, whenever it made *them* ſpeak, I would not be backward to enter upon any Sub-ject; for that I ſhould conſider myſelf as a young

Counſel,

Counfel, in fome great Caufe, who ferved but to open it, and prepare the Way for thofe of greater Skill and Abilities

I beg then, Madam, faid Mifs *Stapylton*, you will *open the Caufe*, be the Subject what it will And I could almoft wifh, that we had as many Gentlemen here as Ladies, who would have Reafon to be afham'd of the Liberties they take in cenfuring the Conver-fations of the Tea-table; fince the Pulpit, as the worthy Dean gives us Reafon to hope, may be beholden to that of Mrs *B*

Nor is it much Wonder, reply'd I, when the Dean himfelf is with us, and it is graced by fo charming and diftinguifh'd a Circle

If many of our young Gentlemen were here, faid Lady *Towers*, they might improve themfelves in all the Graces of polite and fincere Complaifance But, compar'd to this, I have generally heard fuch true and coarfe Stuff from our Race of Wou'd-be-wits, that what they fay, may be compar'd to the Fawn-ings and Salutations of the Afs in the Fable, who emulating the Lap-dog, merited a Cudgel rather than Encouragement

But, Mrs *B* continu'd fhe, begin, I pray you, to *open* and *proceed* in the Caufe, for there will be no Counfel imploy'd but you, I can tell you

Then give me a Subject, that will fuit me, Ladies, and you fhall fee how my Obedience to your Com-mands will make me run on

Will you, Madam, faid Mifs *Stapylton*, give us a few Cautions and Inftructions on a Theme of your own, That a young Lady fhould rather *fear* too much, than *hope* too much? A neceffary Doctrine perhaps, but a difficult one to be practifed by a Lady, who has begun to love, and fuppofes all Truth and Honour in the Object of her Favour

*Hope*, Mifs, faid I, in my Opinion, fhould never be unaccompany'd by *Fear*, and the more Reafon will
a La...

a Lady ever have to fear, and to fufpect herfelf, and doubt her Lover, when fhe once begins to find in her own Breaft an Inclination to him. For then her Danger is doubled, fince fhe has *herfelf* (perhaps, the more dangerous Enemy of the two) to guard againft, as well as *him*

She may fecretly wifh the beft indeed, but what *has been* the Fate of others, *may be* her own, and tho' fhe thinks it not *probable* from fuch a faithful Profeter, as he appears to her to be, yet while it is *poffible*, fhe fhould never be off her Guard: Nor will a prudent Woman truft to his Mercy or Honour, but to her own Difcretion, and the rather, becaufe, if he mean well, he *himfelf* will value her the more for her Caution, fince every Man defires to have a virtuous and prudent Wife; if not well, fhe will detect him the fooner; and fo, by her Prudence, fruftrate all his bafe Defigns.

The Ladies feeming, by their Silence, to approve what I faid, I proceeded:

But let me, my dear Ladies, ask, What that Paffion is, which generally we dignify by the Name of *Love*, and which, when *fo* dignify'd, puts us upon a thoufand Extravagancies? I believe, if it were to be examin'd into, it would be found too generally to owe its Original to *ungovern'd Fancy*, and were we to judge of it by the Confequences that ufually attend it, it ought rather to be called *Rafhnefs, Inconfideration, Weaknefs*, any thing but *Love*, for, very feldom, I doubt, is the *folid Judgment* fo much concern'd in it, as the *airy Fancy* But when once we dignify the wild Mifleader with the Name of *Love*, all the Abfurdities, which we read in Novels and Romances, take Place, and we are induc'd to follow Examples that feldom end happily but in *them*

But, permit me further to obferve, that Love, as we call it, operates differently in the Two Sexes, as to its Effects. For in Woman it is a *creeping* Thing,

in

in Man an *Incroacher*; and this ought, in my humble Opinion, to be very feriously attended to Mifs *Sutton* intimated thus much, when fhe obferv'd, that it was the Man's Province to ask, the Lady's to deny: —— Excufe me, Mifs, the Obfervation was juft, as to the Mens Notions, altho', methinks, I wou'd not have a Lady allow of it, except in Cafes of Caution to themfelves.

The Doubt, therefore, proceeded I, which a Lady has of her *Lover*'s Honour, is needful to preferve *her own*, and *his* too And if fhe does him Wrong, and he fhould be too juft to deceive her, fhe can make him Amends, by Inftances of greater Confidence, when fhe pleafes But if fhe has been accuftom'd to grant him little Favours, can fhe eafily recal them? and will not the *Incroacher* grow upon her Indulgence, pleading for a Favour To-day, which was not refufed him Yefterday, and reproaching her want of Confidence, as a want of Efteem, till the poor Lady, who, perhaps, has given way to this *creeping, infinuating* Paffion, and has avow'd her Efteem for him, puts herfelf too much in his Power; in order to manifeft, as fhe thinks, the *Generofity* of her Affection, and fo, by Degrees, is carry'd farther than fhe intended, or nice Honour ought to have permitted, and all becaufe, to keep up to my Theme, fhe *hopes* too much, and *doubts* too little? And, permit me, Ladies, to add, That there have been Cafes, where a Gentleman himfelf, purfuing the Dictates of his *incroaching* Paffion, and finding a Lady *too conceding*, has taken Advantages, that, probably, at firft, he did not prefume to think of

Mifs *Stapylton* faid, That *Virtue* itfelf fpoke when I fpoke; and fhe was refolv'd, when fhe came home, to recollect as much of this Converfation as fhe could, and write it down in her Common-place Book, where it would make a better Figure than any thing fhe had there

I fuppofe,

I fuppofe, Mifs, faid Lady *Towers,* your chief Collections are Flowers of Rhetorick, pick'd up from the *French* and *Englifh* Poets, and Novel-writers. I would give fomething for the Pleafure of having it two Hours in my Poffeffion.

Fie, Madam, reply'd Mifs, a little abafh'd, How can you expofe your Kinfwoman thus, before the Dean and Mrs *B*?

Lady *Towers,* Mifs, faid I, only fays this to provoke you to fhew your Collections I wifh I had the Pleafure of feeing them. I doubt not but your Common-place Book is a Store-houfe of Wifdom

There is nothing bad in it, I hope, reply'd Mifs; but I would not, that Mrs *B.* fhould fee it, for the World But, let me tell you, Madam, (to Lady *Towers*) there are many beautiful Things, and good Inftructions, to be collected from Novels, and Plays, and Romances, and from the poetical Writers particularly, light as you are pleafed to make of them. Pray, Madam, (to me) have you ever been at all converfant in fuch Writers?

Not a great deal in the former, Mifs; there were very few Novels and Romances, that my Lady would permit me to read; and thofe I did, gave me no great Pleafure, for either they dealt fo much in the *Marvellous* and *Improbable,* or were fo unnaturally *inflaming* to the *Paffions,* and fo full of *Love* and *Intrigue,* that hardly any of them but feem'd calculated to *fire* the *Imagination,* rather than to *inform* the *Judgment* Tilts and Tournaments, breaking of Spears in Honour of a Miftrefs, fwimming over Rivers, engaging with Monfters, rambling in Search of Adventures, making unnatural Difficulties, in order to fhew the Knight-Errant's Prowefs in overcoming them, is all that is requir'd to conftitute the *Hero* in fuch Pieces And what principally diftinguifhes the Character of the *Heroine,* is, when fhe is taught to confider her Father's Houfe as an inchanted Caftle,

Caftle, and her Lover as the Hero who is to diffolve the Charm, and to fet her at Liberty from one Confinement, in order to put her into another, and, too probably, a worfe. To inftruct her how to climb Walls, drop from Windows, leap Precipices, and do twenty other extravagant Things, in order to fhew the mad Strength of a Paffion fhe ought to be afham'd of. To make Parents and Guardians pafs for Tyrants, and the Voice of Reafon to be drown'd in that of indifcreet Love, which exalts the other Sex, and debafes her own. And what is the Inftruction, that can be gather'd from fuch Pieces, for the Conduct of common Life?

Then have I been ready to quarrel with thefe Writers for another Reafon, and that is, The dangerous Notion which they hardly ever fail to propagate, of a *Firft fight Love*. For there is fuch a Sufceptibility fuppofed on both Sides, (which, however it may pafs in a Man, very little becomes a Lady's Delicacy) that they are fmitten with a Glance; the fictitious blind God is made a *real* Divinity: and too often Prudence and Difcretion are the firft Offerings at his Shrine.

I believe, Madam, faid Mifs *Stapylton*, blufhing, and playing with her Fan, there have been many Inftances of Peoples Loving at firft Sight, which have ended very happily.

No doubt of it, Mifs, reply'd I. But there are three Chances to one, that fo precipitate a Liking does not. For where can be the Room for Caution, for Inquiry, for the Difplay of Merit, and Sincerity, and even the Affurance of a *grateful Return*, to a Lady, who thus fuffers herfelf to be prepoffefs'd? Is it not a Random Shot? Is is not a Proof of Weaknefs? Is it not giving up the Negative Voice, which belongs to the Sex, even while fhe doubts to meet the Affirmative one from him fhe wifhes for?

Indeed,

Indeed, Ladies, continued I, I cannot help concluding, (and I am the lefs afraid of fpeaking my Mind, becaufe of the Opinion I have of the Prudence of every Lady that hears me) that where this Weaknefs is found, it is no way favourable to a Lady's Character, nor to that Difcretion which ought to diftinguifh it. It looks to me, as if a Lady's *Heart* were too much in the Power of her *Eye*, and that fhe had permitted her *Fancy* to be much more bufy than her *Judgment*

Mifs *Stapylton* blufh'd, and look'd atound her

But I have generally obferv'd, Mrs B faid Lady *Towers*, that whenever you cenfure any Indifcretion, you feldom fail to give Cautions how to avoid it: And pray let us know what is to be done in this Cafe? That is to fay, How a young Lady ought to guard againft and overcome the firft favourable Impreffions?

What I imagine, reply'd I, a young Lady ought to do, on any the *leaft* favourable Impreffions of this kind, is immediately to *withdraw into herfelf*, as one may fay; to reflect upon what fhe owes to her Parents, to her Family, to her Character, and to her Sex, and to refolve to check fuch a random Prepoffeffion, which may much more probably, as I hinted, make her a Prey to the Undeferving than otherwife, as there are fo many of that Character to one Man of real Merit.

The moft that I apprehend a *Firft-fight* Approbation can do, is to infpire a *Liking*, and a Liking is conquerable, if the Perfon will not brood over it, til fhe hatches it into *Love* Then every Man and Woman has a black and a white Side, and it is eafy to fet the Imperfections of the Perfon againft the fuppofed Perfections, while it is only a *Liking* But if the bufy Fancy be permitted to work as it pleafes, uncheck'd, uncontroul'd, then, 'tis very likely, were the Lady but to keep herfelf in Countenance for re-

ceiving

ceiving firſt Impreſſions, ſhe will ſee Perfections in the Object, which no living Soul can ſee but herſelf And it will hardly be expected, but that, as a Conſequence of her firſt Indiſcretion, ſhe will confirm, as an Act of her Judgment, what her wild and ungovern'd Fancy had miſled her to think of with ſo much partial Favour And too late, as it may probably happen, ſhe will ſee and lament her fatal, and, perhaps, undutiful Error.

We are talking of the Ladies only, added I (for I ſaw Miſs *Stapylton* was become very grave): But I believe Firſt-ſight Love often operates too powerfully in both Sexes. And where it does ſo, it will be very lucky, if either Gentleman or Lady find Reaſon, on cool Reflection, to approve a Choice, which they were ſo ready to make without Thought.

'Tis allow'd, my dear Mrs. *B.* ſaid Lady *Towers*, that raſh and precipitate Love may operate pretty much alike in the Raſh and Precipitate of both Sexes; and which-ſoever loves, generally exalts the Perſon beloved, above his or her Merits · But I am deſirous, for the ſake of us Maiden Ladies, ſince 'tis a Science in which you are ſo great an Adept, to have your Advice, how we ſhould watch and guard againſt its firſt Incroachments, and that you will tell us what you apprehend gives the Men moſt Advantage over us

Nay, now, Lady *Towers*, you railly my Preſumption indeed!

I admire you, Madam, reply'd ſhe, and every thing you ſay and do, and I won't forgive you to call what I ſo ſeriouſly *ſay* and *think*, Raillery For my own Part, continued ſhe, I never was in Love yet, nor, I believe, were any of theſe young Ladies --- (Miſs *Cope* looked a little ſilly upon this ---) And who can better inſtruct us to guard *our Hearts*, than a Lady who has ſo well defended *her own*?

Why

Why then, Madam, if I muſt ſpeak, I think, what gives the other Sex the greateſt Advantage, over even many of the moſt Deſerving of ours, is, that dangerous Foible, The *Love of Praiſe*, and the Deſire to be *flatter'd* and *admir'd*: A Paſſion that I have obſerv'd to predominate, more or leſs, from Sixteen to Sixty, in moſt of our Sex. We are too generally delighted with the Company of thoſe who extol our Graces of Perſon or Mind; for, will not a *grateful* Lady ſtudy hard to return a *few* Compliments to a Gentleman, who makes her ſo *many*? She is concern'd to *prove* him a Man of diſtinguiſhing Senſe, or a polite Man, at leaſt, in regard to what ſhe *thinks* of herſelf, and ſo the Flatterer ſhall be preferr'd to ſuch of the Sincere and Worthy, as cannot ſay what they do not think. And by this means many an excellent Lady has fallen a Prey to ſome ſordid Deſigner.

Then, I think, nothing gives Gentlemen ſo much Advantage over our Sex, as to ſee how readily a virtuous Lady can forgive the capital Faults of the moſt abandon'd of the other, and that ſad, ſad Notion, *That a Reform'd Rake makes the beſt Huſband*, a Notion that has done more Hurt, and Diſcredit too, to our Sex, (as it has given more Encouragement to the profligate, and more Diſcouragement to the ſober Gentlemen) than can be eaſily imagin'd A fine thing indeed! as if the Wretch, who had run thro' a Courſe of Iniquity to the endangering of Soul and Body, was to be deem'd the beſt Companion for Life, to an innocent and virtuous young Lady, who is to owe the Kindneſs of his Treatment of her, to his having never before accompany'd with a modeſt Woman, nor, till his Intereſt on one hand, (to which his Extravagance, perhaps, compels him to attend) and his impair'd Conſtitution on the other, oblige him to it, ſo much as *wiſh'd* to accompany with one, and who always

made

made a Jeſt of the marry'd State, and, perhaps, of every thing either ſerious or ſacred !

You obſerve very well, my dear Mrs *B* ſaid Lady *Towers*; but People will be apt to think, that you have leſs Reaſon than any of our Sex, to be ſevere againſt the Notion you ſpeak of  For who was a greater Rake than a certain Gentleman, and who a better Husband ?

Madam, reply'd I, the Gentleman you mean, never was a common Town-Rake  He is a Gentleman of Senſe, and fine Underſtanding, and his Reform-ation, *ſecondarily*, as I may ſay, has been the natural Effect of thoſe extraordinary Qualities  But beſides, Madam, I will preſume to ſay, That that Gentle-man, as he has not many Equals in the Nobleneſs of his Nature, ſo is not likely, I doubt, to have many Followers, in a Reformation begun in the Bloom of Youth, upon *Self-conviction*, and altoge-ther, humanly ſpeaking, *ſpontaneous* --- Thoſe young Ladies, who would plead his Example, in Support of this pernicious Notion, ſhould find out the ſame generous Qualities in the Gentleman, before they truſt to it, and it will then do leſs Harm: tho' even then, I could not wiſh it to be generally enter-tained.

It is really unaccountable, ſaid Lady *Towers*, af er all, as Mrs *B* I remember, ſaid, on another Occaſion, That our Sex ſhould not as much inſiſt upon Virtue and Sobriety, in the Character of a Gentleman, as the Gentleman, be he ever ſuch a Rake, does in that of a Lady  And 'tis certainly a great Encou-ragement to Libertiniſm, that a worn-out Debauchee ſh a l think himſelf at any time good enough for a Husband, and have the Confidence to imagine, that a modeſt Lady will accept of his Addreſs with a *Pre-ference* of h.m to any other

I can account for it but one way, ſaid the Dean. And that .s, that a modeſt Lady is apt to be *diffident*

of

of her own Merit and Underſtanding, and ſhe thinks this Diffidence an Imperfection  A Rake *never is :* So he has in Perfection a Quality ſhe thinks ſhe wants, and, knowing *too little* of the World, imagines ſhe mends the Matter by accepting of one who knows *too much*

That's well obſerv'd, Mr Dean, ſaid Lady *Towers·* But there is another Fault in our Sex, which Mrs *B* has not touch'd upon, and that is, The fooliſh Vanity ſome Ladies have in the Hopes of reforming a wild Fellow, and that they ſhall be able to do more than any of their Sex before them could do: A Vanity that often coſts them dear, as I know in more than one Inſtance.

Another Weakneſs, ſaid I, might be produced againſt ſome of our Sex, who join too readily to droll upon, and ſneer at, the Misfortune of any poor young Creature, who has ſhewn too little Regard for her Honour  And who (inſtead of ſpeaking of it with Concern, and inveighing againſt the Seducer) too lightly ſport with the unhappy Perſon's Fall; induſtriouſly ſpread the Knowlege of it --- (I would not look upon Miſs *Sutton*, while I ſpoke this) --- and avoid her, as one infected, and yet ſcruple not to admit into their Company the vile Aggreſſor, and even to ſmile with him, at his barbarous Jeſts upon the poor Sufferer of their own Sex

I have known three or four Inſtances of this in my Time, ſaid Lady *Towers*, that Miſs *Sutton* might not take it to herſelf, for ſhe look'd down, and was a little ſerious

This, reply'd I, puts me in mind of a little humourous Copy of Verſes, written, as I believe, by Mr *B* And which, to the very Purpoſe we are ſpeaking of, he calls`

Benefit of making others Misfortunes our own

*Thou'ft heard it, or read it, a Million of Times,*
*That Men are made up of Falshoods and Crimes·*
*Search all the old Authors, and ranfack the new,*
*Thou'lt find in Love-Stories, fcarce one Mortal true*
*Then why this complaining ? And why this wry Face ?*
*Is it 'caufe thou'rt affected most, with thy own Cafe ?*
*Hadf thou fooner made* OTHERS *Misfortunes thy own,*
*T'ou never,* THYSELF, *this Difafter hadft known;*
*Th, compaffionate Caution had kept thee from Evil,*
*And thou mightft have defy'd Mankind and the Devil*

The Ladies were pleas'd with the Lines, but Lady
*Towers* wanted to know, fhe faid, at what Time of
Mr *B*.'s Life they could be written. Becaufe, added
fhe, I never fufpected before, that the good Gentleman ever took Pains to write Cautions or Exhorta-
tions to our Sex, to avoid the Delufions of his own

Thefe Verfes, and this facetious, but fevere Remark of Lady *Towers*, made every young Lady look
up with a chearful Countenance, becaufe it pufhed
the Ball from *Self* And the Dean faid to his Daughter, So, my Dear, You, that have been fo attentive, muft let us know, what ufeful Inferences you
can draw from what Mrs *B* and the other Ladies
have fo excellently faid ?

I obferve, Sir, faid Mifs, from the Faults the
Ladies have fo juftly imputed to fome of our Sex,
that are Advantage the Gentlemen *chiefly* have over
us, is from our own Weaknefs, and that it behoves
a prudent Lady to guard againft *firft Impreffions* of
Favour, fince fhe will think herfelf oblig'd, in Compliment to *her own* Judgment, to find Reafons, if
poffible, to confirm them

But I would be glad to know, Ladies, added Mifs,
Is there be any way, that a Lady can judge, whether
a Gen-

a Gentleman means honourably or not, in his Addreſs to her ?

Mrs *B.* can beſt inform you of that, Miſs *L.* ſaid Lady *Towers* · What ſay you, Mrs *B* ?

There are a few Signs, anſwer'd I, eaſy to be known, and, I think, almoſt infallible

Pray let's have 'em, ſaid Lady *Arthur*, and they all were very attentive.

Theſe are they, reply'd I. I lay it down as an undoubted Truth, That true Love is one of the moſt *reſpectful* Things in the World It ſtrikes with Awe and Reverence the Mind of the Gentleman, who boaſts its Impreſſion. It is chaſte and pure in Word and Deed, and cannot bear to have the leaſt Indecency mingle with it.

If therefore a Gentleman, be his Birth or Quality what it will, the higher the worſe, preſume to wound a Lady's Ears with indecent Words If he endeavour, in his Expreſſions or Sentiments, to convey groſs or impure Ideas to her Mind . If he is continually preſſing for *her Confidence* in *his* Honour: If he requeſts Favours, which a Lady ought to refuſe . If he can be regardleſs of his Conduct or Behaviour to her If he can uſe *boiſterous* or *rude* Freedoms, either to her *Perſon* or *Dreſs* ---- (Here poor Miſs *Cope*, by her Bluſhes, bore Witneſs to her Caſe ----) If he avoids *ſpeaking* of *Marriage*, when he has a *fair Opportunity* of doing it (---Here Miſs *L* look'd down, and bluſh'd ---) or leaves it *once* to a Lady to wonder that he does not

In any, or in all of theſe Caſes, he is to be ſuſpected, and a Lady can have little Hope of ſuch a Perſon, nor, as I humbly apprehend, conſiſtent with Honour and Diſcretion, encourage his Addreſs

The Ladies were ſo kind, as to applaud all I ſaid, and ſo did the Dean. Miſs *Stapylton*, and Miſs *Cope*, and Miſs *L.* were to try to recollect it when they came home, and to write down what they could

T 2 remem-

remember of the Conversation. And our noble Guests coming in soon after, with Mr *B* the Ladies would have departed, but he prevailed upon them, with some Difficulty, to pass the Evening, and Miss *L* who has an admirable Finger on the Harpsichord, as I have heretofore told you, obliged us with two or three Lessons Each of the Ladies did the like, and prevailed upon me to play a Tune or two But Miss *Cope*, as well as Miss *L* surpass'd me much We all sung too in Turns, and Mr *B* took the Violin, in which he excels Lord *Davers* oblig'd us on the Violincello Mr *H* play'd on the *German* Flute, and sung us a Fop's Song, and perform'd it in Character So that we had an exceeding gay Evening, and parted with great Satisfaction on *all* Sides, particularly on the young Ladies, for this put them all into good Humour, and good Spirits, enlivening the former Scene, which otherwise might have closed, perhaps, more gravely than efficaciously

The Distance of Time since this Conversation passed, enables me to add what I could not do, when I wrote the Account of it, which you have mislaid And which take briefly, as follows

Miss *Stapylton*, upon her Return home, was as good as her Word, and wrote down all she could recollect of the Conversation, and I having already sent her the Letter she had desir'd, containing my Observations upon the flighty Style she so much admir'd, she suffered it to have such an Effect upon her, as to turn the Course of her Reading and Studies, to weightier and more solid Subjects, and, avoiding the Gentleman she had begun to favour, gave way to her Parents Recommendation, and is happily marry'd to Sir *Jonathan Barnes*

Miss *Cope* came to me a Week after this, with the Leave of both her Parents, and tarry'd with me Three Days, in which time she open'd all her worthy Heart to me, and return'd in such a Disposition,

poſition, and with ſuch Reſolutions, that ſhe never would ſee her Peer again ; nor receive Letters from him, which ſhe own'd to me ſhe had done clandeſtinely before · And ſhe is now the happy Lady of Sir *Michael Beaumont*, who makes her the beſt of Husbands, and permits her to follow her charitable Inclinations, according to a Scheme, which ſhe prevail'd upon me to give her

Miſs *L* by the Dean's indulgent Prudence and Diſcretion, has eſcaped her Rake, and, upon the Diſcovery of an Intrigue he was carrying on with another, conceived a juſt Abhorrence of him , and is ſince marry'd to Dr *Jenkins*, as you know, with whom ſhe lives very happily

Miſs *Sutton* is not quite ſo well off, as the Three former, tho' not altogether unhappy neither, in her Way She could not indeed conquer her Love of Dreſs and Tinſel, and ſo became the Lady of Col. *Wilſon* And they are thus far eaſy in the Marriage State, that, being ſeldom together, in all Probability they ſave a Multitude of Miſunderſtandings, for, the Colonel loves Gaming, in which he is generally a Winner, and ſo paſſes his Time moſtly in Town. His Lady has her Pleaſures, neither laudable nor criminal ones, which ſhe purſues in the Country And now-and-then a Letter paſſes on both Sides, by the Inſcription and Subſcription of which, they remind one another, that they have been *once* in their Lives at *one* Church together

And what now, my dear Lady *G* have I to add to this tedious Account (for Letter I can hardly call it) but that I am, with great Affection,

*Your true Friend and Servant,*

P B.

LET-

## LETTER LXI.

*My dear Lady* G.

YOU defire me to fend you a little Specimen of my *Nurfery Tales* and *Stories*, with which, as Mifs *Fenwick* told you, on her Return to *Lincoln-ſhire*, I entertain my Mifs *Goodwin*, and my little Boys But you make me too high a Compliment, when you tell me, it is for *your own* Inftruction and Example Yet you know, my dear Lady G be your Motives what they will, I muſt obey you, al-ho', were others to fee it, I m ght expofe myfelf to the Smiles and Contempt of Judges lefs prejudic'd in my Favour. So I will begin without any further Apology ; and, as near as I can, give you thofe very Stories with which Mifs *Fenwick* was fo pleafed, and of which fhe has made fo favourable a Report

Let me acquaint you then, that my Method is, To give Characters of Perfons I have known in one Part or other of my Life, in feigned Names, whofe Conduct may ferve for Imitation or Warning to my dear attentive Mifs ; and fometimes I give Inftances of good Boys and naughty Boys, for the fake of my *Billy*, and my *Davers*, and they are continually coming about me, Dear Madam, a pretty Story now, cries Mifs And, Dear Mamma, tell me of good Boys, and of naughty Boys, cries *Billy*

Mifs is a furprifing Child, for her Age, and is very familiar with many of the beft Characters in the *Spectators* , and having a Smattering of *Latin*, and more than a Smattering of *Italian*, and being a perfect Miftrefs of *French*, is feldom at a Lofs for the Derivation of fuch Words, as are not of *Englifh* Original And fo I fhall give you a Story in feigned Names, with which fhe is fo delighted, that fhe has

written

written it down  But I will first trespass on your Patience with one of my childish Tales

Every Day once or twice, if I am not hinder'd, I cause Miss *Goodwin*, who plays and sings very prettily, to give a Tune or two to me and my *Billy* and *Davers*, who, as well as my *Pamela*, love and learn to touch the Keys, young as the latter is, and she will have a sweet Finger, I can see that, and a charming Ear ; and her Voice is Musick itself! ---- O the fond, fond Mother! I know you will say, on reading this.

Then, Madam, we all proceed hand in hand together to the Nursery, to my *Charley* and *Jemmy* : And in this happy Retirement, so much my Delight in the Absence of my best Beloved, imagine you see me seated, surrounded with the Joy and the Hope of my future Prospects, as well as my present Comforts

Miss *Goodwin* imagine you see, on my Right Hand, sitting on a Velvet Stool, because she is eldest, and a Miss · *Billy* on my Left, in a little Cane Elbow Chair, because he is eldest, and a good Boy · My *Davers*, and my sparkling ey'd *Pamela*, with my *Charley* between them, on little silken Cushions at my Feet, hand in hand, their pleased Eyes looking up to my more delighted ones, and my sweet-natur'd promising *Jemmy* in my Lap, the Nurses and the Cradle just behind us, and the Nursery Maids delightedly pursuing some useful Needlework, for the dear Charmers of my Heart --- All as hush and as still, as Silence itself, as the pretty Creatures generally are, when their little watchful Eyes see my Lips beginning to open  For they take great notice already, of my Rule of Two Ears to * One Tongue, insomuch that if *Billy* or *Davers* are either of them for breaking the Mum, as they call it, they

---

* *See this Vol. p.* 364

T 4

are

are immediately hush, at any time, if I put my Finger to my Lip, or if Miss points hers to her Ears, even to the breaking of a Word in two, as it were And yet all my Boys are as lively as so many Birds, while my *Pamela* is chearful, easy, soft, gentle, always smiling, but modest and harmless as a Dove

I began with a Story of Two little Boys, and Two little Girls, the Children of a fine Gentleman and a fine Lady, who lov'd them dearly · That they were all so good, and loved one another so well, that every body who saw them, admired them, and talked of them far and near That they would part with any thing to one another · Loved the Poor Spoke kindly to the Servants Did every thing they were bid to do; were not proud, and knew no Strife, but who should learn their Books best, and be the prettiest Scholar That the Servants loved them, and would do any thing they desired, that they were not proud of fine Cloaths, let not their Heads run upon their Playthings, when they should mind their Books, said Grace before they eat, their Prayers before they went to-bed, and as soon as they rose, were always clean and neat; would not tell a Fib for the World, and were above doing any thing that requir'd one That GOD blessed them more and more, and blessed their Papa and Mamma, and their Uncles and Aunts, and Cousins, for their sakes. And there was a happy Family, my dear Loves! --- No one idle, all prettily imploy'd, the Masters at their Books, the Misses at their Books too, or their Needles, except at their Play hours, when they were never rude, nor noisy, nor mischievous, nor quarrelsome. And no such Word was ever heard from their Mouths, as, Why mayn't I have this or that, as well as *Billy* or *Bobby* ? --- Or, Why should *Sally* have this or that, any more than I ? --- But it was, As my Mamma pleases; My Mamma knows
best;

beſt; and a Bow and a Smile, and no Surlineſs, or ſcouling Brow to be ſeen, if they were deny'd any thing; for well did they know, that their Papa and Mamma loved them ſo dearly, that they would re-fuſe them nothing that was for their Good, and they were ſure, when they *were* refuſed, they asked for ſomething that would have done them hurt, had it been granted  Never were ſuch good Boys and Girls as theſe! And they grew up, and the Maſters became fine Scholars, and fine Gentlemen, and every body honour'd them, and the Miſſes became fine Ladies, and fine Houſewives, and this Gentle-man, when they grew to be Women, ſought to marry one of the Miſſes, and that Gentleman the other; and happy was he that could be admitted into their Companies! So that they had nothing to do but to pick and chuſe out of the beſt Gentlemen in the County: While the greateſt Ladies for Birth, and the moſt remaikable for Virtue, (which, my Dears, is better than either Birth or Fortune) thought themſelves honour'd by the Addreſſes of the Two Brothers. And they marry'd, and made good Papas and Mammas, and were ſo many Bleſſings to the Age in which they lived  There, my dear Loves, were happy Sons and Daughters! For good Maſters ſeldom fail to make good Gentlemen, and good Miſſes, good Ladies, and God bleſſes them with as good Chil-dren as they were to *their* Parents, and ſo the Bleſſ-ing goes round! --- Who would not but be good?

Well, but, Mamma, we will all be good· Won't we, Maſter *Davers,* cries my *Billy*? Yes, Brother *Billy*  Then they kiſs one another, and if they have Playthings, or any thing they like, exchange with each other, to ſhew the Effect my Leſſons have upon them  But what will become of the naughty Boys? Tell us, Mamma, about the naughty Boys!

Why, there was a poor, poor Widow Woman, who had Three naughty Sons, and One naughty

Daughter;

Daughter; and they would do nothing that their Mamma bid them do, were always quarrelling, fcratching, and fighting; would not fay their Prayers; would not learn their Book, fo that the little Boys ufed to laugh at them, and point at them, as they went along, for Blockheads; and nobody loved them, or took notice of them, except to beat and thump them about, for their naughty Ways, and their Undutifulnefs to their poor Mother, who worked hard to maintain them As they grew up, they grew worfe and worfe, and more and more ftupid and ignorant, fo that they impoverifhed their poor Mother, and at laft broke her Heart, poor, poor Widow Woman !--- And her Neighbours join'd together to bury the poor Widow Woman, for thefe fad ungracious Children made away with what little fhe had left, while fhe was ill, before her Heart was quite broken· And this helped to break it the fooner, for had fhe lived, fhe faw fhe muft have wanted Bread, and had no Comfort from fuch wicked Children.

Poor, poor Widow Woman ! faid my *Billy*, with Tears, and my little Dove fhed Tears too, and *Davers* was moved, and Mifs wiped her fine Eyes

But what became of the naughty Boys, and the naughty Girl, Mamma !--- Became of them ! Why one Son was forced to go to Sea, and there he was drowned Another turned Thief, (for he would not work) and he came to an untimely End: The third was idle, and ignorant, and nobody, who knew how he had ufed his poor Mother, would imploy him, and fo he was forced to go into a far Country, and beg his Bread And the naughty Girl, having never loved Work, pined away in Sloth and Filthinefs, and at laft broke her Arm, and died of a Fever, lamenting too late, that fhe had been fo wicked a Daughter to fo good a Mother !--- And fo there was a fad End of all the Four ungracious Children, who never
would

would mind what their poor Mother faid to them; and GOD punifhed their Naughtinefs, as you fee! --- While the good Children I mentioned before, were the Glory of their Family, and the Delight of every body that knew them.

Who would not be good! was the Inference· And the Repetition from *Billy*, with his Hands clapt together, Poor, poor Widow Woman!---gave me much Pleafure

So my childifh Story ended, with a Kifs of each pretty Dear, and their Thanks for my Story. And then came on Mifs's Requeft for a *Woman*'s Story, as fhe called it I difmifs'd my Babies to their Play in the Apartment allotted for that Purpofe, and taking Mifs's Hand, fhe ftanding before me, all Attention, began in a more womanly Strain to *her*; for fhe is very fond of being thought a Woman. and indeed is a prudent, fenfible Dear, comprehends any thing inftantly, and makes very pretty Reflections upon what fhe hears or reads, as you will obferve in what follows·

There is nothing, my dear Mifs `Goodwin*, that young Ladies fhould be fo watchful over, as their Reputation 'Tis a tender Flower, that the leaft Froft will nip, the leaft cold Wind will blaft, and when once blafted, it will never flourifh again, but wither to the very Root. But this I have told you fo often, that I am fure I need not repeat what I have faid. So to my Story.

There were Four pretty Ladies lived in one genteel Neighbourhood, the Daughters of Four feveral Families, but all Companions, and Vifitors, and yet all of very different Inclinations COQUETILLA we will call one, PRUDIANA another, PROFUSIANA the third, and PRUDENTIA the fourth, their feveral Names denoting their refpective Qualities.

COQUETILLA was the only Daughter of a worthy Baronet, by a Lady very gay, but rather indifcreet

T 6

creet than unvirtuous, who took not the requifite
Care of her Daughter's Education, but let her be
over-run with the Love of Fashions, Drefs, and
Equipage, and when in *London*, Balls, Operas, Plays,
the Park, the Ring, the Withdrawing-Room, took
up her whole Attention. She admir'd nobody but
herfelf, flutter'd about, laughing at, and defpifing a
Croud of Men-Followers, whom fhe attracted by
gay, thoughtlefs Freedoms of Behaviour, too nearly
treading on the Skirts of Immodefty. Yet made fhe
not one worthy Conqueft, exciting, on the contrary,
in all fober Minds, that Contempt to herfelf, which
fhe fo profufely would be thought to pour down upon
the reit of the World. After fhe had feveral Years
flutter'd about the dangerous Light, like fome filly
Fly, fhe at laft findged the Wings of her Reputation,
for, being defpifed by every worthy Heart, fhe became too eafy and cheap a Prey to a Man the moft
unworthy of all her Followers, who had Refolution
and Confidence enough to break thro' thofe few
cobweb Referves, in which fhe had incircled her
precarious Virtue, and which were no longer of
Force to preferve her Honour, when fhe met with a
Man more bold and more enterprifing than herfelf,
and who was as defigning as fhe was thoughtlefs.
And what then became of *Coquetilla* ?--- Why, fhe
was forced to pafs over Sea, to *Ireland*, where nobody
knew her, and to bury herfelf in a dull Obfcurity,
to go by another Name, and at laft, unable to fupport a Life fo unfuitable to the natural Gaiety of her
Temper, fhe pin'd herfelf into a Confumption, and
dy'd unpity'd and unlamented, among Strangers,
having not one Friend but whom fhe bought with
her Money.

Poor Lady *Coquetilla* ! faid Mifs; what a fad thing
it is, to have a wrong Education ! And how happy
am I, who have fo good a Lady to fupply the Place
of

of a dear diftant Mamma!---But be pleafed, Madam, to proceed to the next.

PRUDIANA, my Dear, was the Daughter of a Gentleman who was a Widower, and had, while the young Lady was an Infant, bury'd her Mamma. He was a good fort of Man, but had but one Leffon to teach to *Prudiana*, and that was, To avoid all manner of Converfation with the Men, but never gave her the right Turn of Mind, nor inftilled into it that Senfe of her religious Duties, which would have been her beft Guard in all Temptations For, provided fhe kept out of the Sight and Converfation of the Gentlemen, and avoided the Company of thofe Ladies, who more freely converfed with the other Sex, it was all her Papa defired of her This gave her a haughty, fullen, and referved Turn; made her ftiff, formal, and affected She had Senfe enough to difcover early the Faults of *Coquetilla*, and, in Diflike of them, fell the more eafily into that contrary Extreme which her recluse Education, and her Papa's Cautions, naturally led her So that Pride, Referve, Affectation, and Cenforioufnefs, made up the Effentials of her Character, and fhe became more unamiable even than *Coquetilla*, and as the other was too acceffible, *Prudiana* was quite unapproachable by Gentlemen, and unfit for any Converfation, but that of her Servants, being alfo deferted by thofe of her own Sex, by whom fhe might have improv'd, on account of her cenforious Difpofition And what was the Confequence? Why this Every worthy Perfon of both Sexes defpifing her, and fhe being ufed to fee nobody but Servants, at laft throws herfelf upon one of that Clafs. In an evil Hour, fhe finds fomething that is taking to her low Tafte in the Perfon of her Papa's Valet, a Wretch fo infinitely beneath her, (but a gay Coxcomb of a Servant) that every body attributed to her the Scandal of making the firft Advances; for, otherwife, it was prefumed,

he

he durft not have looked up to his Mafter's Daughter.
So here ended all her Pride  All her Referves
came to this ' Her Cenforioufnefs of others, re-
doubled Peoples Contempts upon herfelf, and made
nobody pity her  She was, finally, turned out of
Doors, without a Peny of Fortune · The Fellow
was forced to fet up a Barber's Shop in a Country
Town, for all he knew, was to fhave, and drefs a
Peruque, and her Papa would never look upon her
more  So that *Prudiana* became the Outcaft of her
Family, and the Scorn of all that knew her, and was
forced to mingle in Converfation and Company,
with the Wretches of her Husband's Degree '

Poor, miferable *Prudiana* ' faid Mifs --- What a
fad, fad Fall was hers'--- And all owing to the Want
of a proper Education too '---- And to the Lofs of
fuch a Mamma, as I have an 'Aunt, and fo wife a
Papa, as I have an Uncle '---How could her Papa,
I wonder, reftrain her Perfon as he did, like a poor
Nun, and make her unacquainted with the generous
Reftraints of the Mind ?

I am fure, my dear good Aunt, it will be owing
to you, that I fhall never be a *Coquetilla*, nor a *Prudiana* neither  Your Table is always furrounded
with the beft of Company, with worthy Gentlemen,
as well as Ladies, and you inftruct me to judge of
both, and of every new Gueft, in fuch a manner,
as makes me efteem them all, and cenfure nobody,
but yet to fee Faults in fome to avoid, and Graces
in others to imitate, but in nobody but Yourfelf and
my Uncle, any thing fo like Perfection, as fhall attract one's Admiration to one's own Ruin

You are young yet, my Love, and muft always
doubt your own Strength ; and pray to GOD, more
and more, as your Years advance, to give you more
and more Prudence, and Watchfulnefs over your
Conduct

But

But yet, my Dear, you muſt think juſtly of your-ſelf too, for let the young Gentlemen be ever ſo learned, and diſcreet, your Education intitles you to think as well of yourſelf, as of them: For, don't you ſee, the Ladies who are ſo kind to viſit us, that have not been abroad, as you have been, when they were young, yet make as good Figures in Conver-ſation, ſay as good things, as any of the Gentlemen? For, my Dear, all that the Gentlemen know more than the Ladies, except here and there ſuch a one as your dear Uncle, with all their learned Education, is only, that they have been *diſciplin'd* perhaps, into an Obſervation of a few Accuracies in Speech, which, if they know no more, rather diſtinguiſh the *Pedant*, than the *Gentleman* Such as the avoiding of a falſe Concord, as they call it, and which you know how to do, as well as the beſt, not to put a *was* for a *were*, an *are* for an *is*, and to be able to ſpeak in Mood and Tenſe, and ſuch-like valuable Parts of Education · So that, my Dear, you can have no Reaſon to look upon that Sex in ſo high a Light, as to depreciate your own · And yet you muſt not be proud nor conceited neither, but make this one Rule your Guide.

In your *maiden State*, think yourſelf *above* the Gentlemen, and they'll think you ſo too, and ad'dreſs you with Reverence and Reſpect, if they ſee there be neither Pride nor Arrogance in your Behaviour, but a Conſciouſneſs of Merit, a true Dignity, ſuch as becomes Virgin Modeſty, and untainted Purity of Mind and Manners, like that of an Angel among Men, for ſo young Ladies ſhould look upon them-ſelves to be, and will then be treated as ſuch by the other Sex

In your *marry'd State*, which is a kind of State of Humiliation for a Lady, you muſt think yourſelf ſubordinate to your Husband, for ſo it has pleaſed God to make the Wife. You muſt have no Will
of

of your own, in *petty* Things . And if you marry a
Gentleman of Senfe and Honour, fuch a one as
your Uncle, he will look upon you as his Equal,
and will exalt you the more, for your abafing yourfelf —In fhort, my Dear, he will act by you, juft
as your dear Uncle does by me : And then, what a
happy Creature will you be '

So I fhall, Madam ' To be fure I fhall ' —But I
know I fhall be happy whenever I marry, becaufe
I have fuch wife Directors, and fuch an Example
before me : And if it pleafe GOD, I will never think
of any Man, (in purfuance of your conftant Advice
to young Ladies at the Tea-table) who is not a Man
of Senfe and a virtuous Gentleman   But now, dear
Madam, for your next Character   There are Two
more yet to come, that's my Pleafure ! I wifh there
were Ten '

Why the next was PROFUSIANA, you remember,
my dear Love   *Profufiana* took another Courfe to
*her* Ruin   She fell into fome of *Coquetilla's* Foibles,
but purfued them for another End, and in another
Manner   Struck with the Grandeur and Magnifi-
cence of what weak Peop'e call the *Upper Life*, fhe
gives herfelf up to the Circus, to Balls, to Operas,
to Mafquerades, and Affemblées , affects to fhine at
the Head of all Company, at *Tunbridge*, at *Bath*,
and every Place of publick Refort , plays high, is
always receiving and paying Vifits, giving Balls, and
making Treats and Entertainments , and is fo much
*above* the Conduct which moftly recommends a young
Lady to the Efteem of the Deferving of the other
Sex, that no Gentleman, who prefers folid Happinefs, can think of addreffing her, tho' fhe is a fine
Perfon, and has many outward Graces of Behaviour
She becomes the favourite Toaft of the Places fhe
frequents, is proud of that Diftinction , gives the
Fafhion, and delights in the Pride, that fhe can make
Apes in Imitation, whenever fhe pleafes   But yet,

endeavourerdeavouring to avoid being thought proud, makes herself cheap, and is the Subject of the Attempts of every Coxcomb of Eminence, and with much ado, preferves her Virtue, tho' not her Character

What, all this while, is poor *Profufiana* doing? She would be glad, perhaps, of a fuitable Propofal, and would, it may be, give up fome of her Gaieties and Extravagancies, for *Profufiana* has Wit, and is not totally deftitute of Reafon, when fhe fuffers herfelf to think But her Conduct procures her not one fond Friendfhip, and fhe has not in a Twelvemonth, among a thoufand Profeffions of Service, one Devoir that fhe can attend to, or a Friend that fhe can depend upon All the Women fhe fees, if fhe excels them, hate her; the gay Part of the Men, with whom fhe accompanies moft, are all in a Plot againft her Honour Even the Gentlemen, whofe Conduct in the general is govern'd by Principles of Virtue, come down to thefe publick Places to partake of the innocent Freedoms allowed there, and oftentimes give themfelves Airs of Gallantry, and never have it in their Thoughts to commence a Treaty of Marriage, with an Acquaintance begun upon that gay Spot What folid Friendfhips and Satisfactions then is *Profufiana* excluded from?

Her Name indeed is written in every publick Window, and proftituted, as I may call it, at the Pleafure of every Profligate, or Sot, who wears a Diamond to ingrave it · And that, it may be, with moft vile and barbarous Imputations and Freedoms of Words, added by Rakes, who very probably never exchanged a Syllable with her The wounded Trees are perhaps taught alfo to wear the Initials of her Name, linked, not unlikely, and widening as they grow, with thofe of a Scoundrel But all this while, fhe makes not the leaft Impreffion upon one noble Heart : And at laft, perhaps, having run on to the End of an uninterrupted Race of Follies, fhe is

cheated

cheated into the Arms of some vile Fortune-hunter, who quickly lavishes away the Remains of that Fortune which her Extravagance had left, and then, after the worst Usage, abandoning her with Contempt, she sinks into an Obscurity, that cuts short the Thread of her Life, and leaves no Remembrance, but on the brittle Glass, and more faithful Bark, that ever she had a Being.

Alas, alas! what a Butterfly of a Day, said Miss, (an Expression she remember'd of Lady *Towers's*) was poor *Profusiana!*—What a sad thing to be so dazled by worldly Grandeur, and to have so many Admirers, and not one real Friend!

Very true, my Dear, and how carefully ought a Person of a gay and lively Temper to watch over it! And what a Rock may publick Places be to a Lady's Reputation, if she be not doubly vigilant in her Conduct, when she is exposed to the Censures and Observations of malignant Crouds of People, many of the worst of whom spare the least, those who are most unlike themselves!

But then, Madam, said Miss, would *Profusiana* venture to play at publick Places? Will Ladies game, Madam? I have heard you say, that Lords, and Sharpers but just out of Liveries, in Gaming, are upon a Foot in every thing, save that one has nothing to lose, and the other much, besides his Reputation? And will Ladies so disgrace their Characters, and their Sex, as to pursue this pernicious Diversion in publick?

Yes, my Dear, they will, too often, the more's the Pity! And don't you remember, when we were at *Bath*, in what a Hurry I once passed by some Knots of genteel People, and you asked, What those were doing? I told you, whisperingly, They were Gaming, and loth I was, that my Miss *Goodwin* should stop to see some Sights, to which, till she arrived at Years of Discretion, it was not proper to

familiarize

familiarize her Eye; in fome fort acting like the
antient *Romans*, who would not affign Punifhments
to certain atrocious Crimes, becaufe they had fuch
an high Idea of human Nature, as to fuppofe it incapable of committing them : So I was not for having
you, while a little Girl, fee thofe things, which I
knew would give no Credit to our Sex, and which
I thought, when you grew older, fhould be new and
fhocking to you  But now you are fo much a Woman in Difcretion, I may tell you any thing

She kifs'd my Hand, and made me a fine Cour-
tefy––And told me, That now fhe long'd to hear of
*Prudentia's* Conduct  *Her* Name, Madam, faid
fhe, promifes better things, than thofe of her Three
Companions , and fo it had need · For how fad is it
to think, that out of Four Ladies of Diftinction,
Three of them fhould be naughty, and, *of courfe,*
unhappy ––Thefe two Words, *of courfe,* my Dear,
faid I, were very prettily put in  Let me kifs you
for them  Since every one that is naughty, firft or
laft, muft be *certainly* unhappy.

Far otherwife than what I have related, was it
with the amiable PRUDENTIA  Like the induftri-
ous Bee, fhe makes up her Honey-hoard from every
Flower, bitter as well as fweet ; for every Character
is of Ufe to her, by which fhe can improve her own.
She had the Happinefs of an Aunt, who loved her,
as I do you, and of an Uncle, who doted on her, as
yours does. For, alas ! poor *Prudentia* loft her Papa
and Mamma almoft in her Infancy, in one Week :
But was fo happy in her Uncle and Aunt's Care, as
not to mifs them in her Education, and but juft to
remember their Perfons  By Reading, by Obfervation, and by Attention, fhe daily added new Advantages to thofe which her Education gave her.
She faw, and pitied, the fluttering Freedoms, and dangerous Flights, of COQUETILLA  The fullen Pride,
the Affectation, and ftiff Referves, which PRUDIANA
assum'd,

aſſum'd, ſhe penetrated, and made it her Study to avoid And the gay, hazardous Conduct, extravagant Temper, and Love of tinſell'd Grandeur, which were the Blemiſhes of PROFUSIANA's Character, ſhe dreaded and ſhunn'd She fortifies herſelf with the excellent Examples of the paſt and preſent Ages, and knows how to avoid the Faults of the Faulty, and to imitate the Graces of the moſt Perfect. She takes into her Scheme of that future Happineſs, which ſhe hopes to make her own, what are the *true* Excellencies of her Sex, and endeavours to appropriate to herſelf the domeſtick Virtues, which ſhall one Day make her the Crown of ſome worthy Gentleman's earthly Happineſs, and which, *of courſe*, as you prettily ſaid, my Dear, will ſecure and heighten her own

That noble Frankneſs of Diſpoſition, that ſweet and unaffected Openneſs and Simplicity, which ſhine in all her Actions and Behaviour, commend her to the Eſteem and Reverence of all Mankind, as her Humility and Affability, and a Temper uncenſorious, and ever making the beſt of what is ſaid of the abſent Perſon, of either Sex, do to the Love of every Lady. Her Name indeed is not proſtituted on Windows, nor carved on the Barks of Trees in publick Places But it ſmells ſweet to every Noſtril, dwells on every Tongue, and is ingraved on every Heart She meets with no Addreſs but from Men of Honour and Probity · The fluttering Coxcomb, the inveigling Paraſite, the inſidious Deceiver, the mercenary Fortune-hunter, ſpread no Snares for a Heart guarded by Diſcretion and Prudence, as hers is. They ſee, that all her amiable Virtues are the happy Reſult of an uniform Judgment, and the Effects of her own Wiſdom, founded in an Education to which ſhe does the higheſt Credit. And at laſt, after ſeveral worthy Offers, enough to perplex any Lady's Choice, ſhe bleſſes ſome one happy Gentleman,

man, more diftinguifh'd than the reft, for Learning, good Senfe, and *true Politenefs*, which is but another Word for *Virtue* and *Honour*, and fhines, to her laft Hour, in all the Duties of domeftick Life, as an excellent Wife, Mother, Miftrefs, Friend, and Chriftian, and fo confirms all the Expectations of which her Maiden Life had given fuch ftrong and fuch edifying Prefages

Then folding my dear Mifs in my Arms, and kiffing her, Tears of Pleafure ftanding in her pretty Eyes, Who would not, faid I, fhun the Examples of the COQUETILLA's, the PRUDIANA's, and the PROFUSIANA's of this World, and chufe to imitate the Character of PRUDENTIA!—the Happy, and the Happy-making PRUDENTIA!

O Madam! Madam! faid the dear Creature, fmothering me with her rapturous Kiffes, PRUDENTIA is YOU!----Is YOU indeed!---It *can* be nobody elfe!---O teach me, good GOD! to follow *your* Example, and I fhall be a SECOND PRUDENTIA—Indeed I fhall!

GOD fend you may, my beloved Mifs! And may He blefs you more, if poffible, than *Prudentia* was bleffed!

And fo, my dear Lady G you have fome of my Nurfery Tales, with which, relying on your kind Allowance and Friendfhip, I conclude myfelf,

*Your affectionate and faithful*

P B

---

# CONCLUSION.

THE Editor thinks proper to conclude in this Place, that he may not be thought to deferve a Sufpicion, that the Extent of the Work was to be meafured but by

the

the Patience of its Readers. But he thinks it neceſſary, in order to elucidate the Whole, to ſubjoin a brief Note of the following Facts.

That Mr. *B* (after the Affair which took Date at the Maſquerade, and ſo happily concluded) continued to be one of the beſt and moſt exemplary of Men, an Honour to his Country, both in his publick and private Capacity, having, at the Inſtances of ſome of his Friends, in very elevated Stations, accepted of an honourable Imployment abroad in the Service of the State, which he diſcharged in ſuch a manner, as might be expected from his Qualifications, and Knowlege of the World  And on his Reutrn, after an Abſence of Three Years, reſiſting all the Temptations of Ambition, devoted himſelf to his privater Duties, and joined with his excellent Lady in every pious Wiſh of her Heart. Adorning the married Life with all the Warmth of an elegant Tenderneſs  Beloved by his Tenants, reſpected by his Neighbours, rever'd by his Children, and almoſt ador'd by the Poor, in every County where his Eſtates gave him Intereſt, as well for his own bountiful Temper, as for the Charities which he permitted to be diſpenſed, with ſo liberal a Hand, by his Lady

That ſhe made him the Father of Seven fine Children, Five Sons, and Two Daughters, all adorned and accompliſhed by Nature, to be the Joy and Delight of ſuch Parents, being educated, in every reſpect, by the Rules of their inimitable Mother, laid down in that Book which ſhe mentions to have been written by her for the Reviſal and Correction of her Conſort, the Contents of which may be gather'd from her Remarks upon Mr. *Locke*'s Treatiſe of Education, in her Letters to Mr *B* and in thoſe to Lady *G*.

That Miſs Goodwin, at the Age of Eighteen, was married to a young Gentleman of fine Parts, and great Sobriety and Virtue · And that both ſhe and her Spouſe, in every material Part of their Conduct, and in their Behaviour to one another, emulated the great and good Examples ſet them by Mr. and Mrs. *B*.

That Lord Davers dying Two Years before this Marriage, his Lady went to reſide at the Hall in *Lincolnſhire*,

the

the Place of her Birth, that she might enjoy the Company and Conversation of her excellent Sister, who, for Conveniency of the Chapel, and Advantage of Room and Situation, had prevailed upon Mr *B* to make That the chief Place of his Residence, and there the noble Lady lived long (in the strictest Friendship with the happy Pair) an honourable Relict of her affectionate Lord

That the worthy Mr ANDREWS, and his Wife, lived together in the sweet Tranquillity, set forth in their Letters, for the Space of Twelve Years, at the *Kentish* Farm, where the good old Gentlewoman then died first, full of Years and Comfort, her dutiful Daughter performing the last pious Offices to so beloved and so loving a Parent Her Husband surviving her about a Year only.

That Lady *G.* Miss DARNFORD that was, after a happy Marriage of several Years, died in Childbed of her Fourth Child, to the inexpressible Concern of her affectionate Consort, and of her dear Friend Mrs. *B*

That Lord *H* after having suffer'd great Dishonour by the ill Courses of his Wife, and great Devastations in his Estate, thro' her former Debts, and continued Extravagance, (intimidated and dispirited by her perpetual Insults, and those of her gaming Brother, who with his bullying Friends terrify'd him into all their Measures) threw himself upon the Protection of Mr *B.* who, by his Spirit and Prudence, saved him from utter Ruin, punish'd his Wife's Accomplices, and obliged her to accept of a separate Maintenance, and then taking his Affairs into his own Management, in due Course of Time intirely re-establish'd them And after some Years, his Wife dying, he became wiser by his past Sufferings, and married a second, of Lady *Davers's* Recommendation; who, by her Prudence and Virtue, made him happy for the Remainder of his Days

That Mr LONGMAN lived to a great Age in the worthy Family, much esteemed by every one, having trained up a diligent Youth, whom he had recommended, to ease him in his Business, and who, answering Expectation, succeeded him in it, after his Death.

That, dying rich, out of his great Love and Gratitude to the honourable Family, in whose Service he had acquired
most

moſt of his Fortune, and in D.ſ.uſt to his neareſt Relations, who had perverſely diſobliged him, he bequeathed
to Three of them One hundred Pounds apiece, and left
all the reſt to his honoured Principal Mr *B* Who, as
ſoon as he came to know it, being at that Time abroad,
directed his Lady to call together the Relations of the
o'd Gentleman, ana, after touching them to the Heart
with a juſt and effectual Reproof, and finding them fill'd
with due Senſe of their Demerit, which had been the
Cauſe of their ſuffering, then to divide the Whole, which
had been left him among them, in greater Proportions,
as they were more nearly related An Action worthy of
ſo generous and ennobled a Spirit, and which procured
him the Prayers and Bleſſings, not only of the Benefited,
but of all who heard of it. For it is eaſy to imagine,
how chearfully, and how gracefully, his benevolent Lady
diſcharged a Command ſo well ſuited to her natural
Generoſity

---

## ADVERTISEMENT.

THERE being Reaſon to apprehend, from the former Attempts
of ſome Imitators, who ſuppoſing the Story of PAMELA a
Fiction, have murder'd that excellent Lady, and miſtaken ai
miſrepreſented other (ſuppos'd imaginary) CHARACTERS, that Per
ſons may not be wanting, who will impoſe new Continuations upon
the Publick

It is with a View to ſome Deſigns of this Nature, that the Edito
gives this publick Aſſurance, by way of Prevention, That all the
Copies of Mrs *B* 's Obſervations and Writings, upon every Subject
hinted at in the preceding Four Volumes, and in particular thoſe
relating to *Devotion*, *Education*, *Plays*, &c are now in One Hand
Only. And that, if ever they ſhall be publiſhed, (which at preſent
is a Point undetermined) it muſt not be, till after a certain Event,
as unwiſhed, as deplorable And then, ſolely, at the Aſſignment of
SAMUEL RICHARDSON, of *Salisbury-Court*, *Fleetſtreet*, the Editor
of theſe Four Volumes of *PAMELA*, or, VIRTUE RE
WARDED.

Lightning Source UK Ltd.
Milton Keynes UK
UKHW021353160219
337363UK00006B/1097/P

9 781385 541401